## Praise for Justin Marozzi's *The Way of Herodotus*

"A delightful scrawl. . . .Marozzi's book is an excellent introduction to [Herodotus] and is great fun in its own right."
—*National Geographic Adventure*

"An excellent new book . . . [Marozzi is] excellent at evoking character and scene. . . .His descriptions sparkle."
—*Washington Post*

"An enjoyable, highly readable book, and its digressive, loose structure and high entertainment quotient make it a pleasant descendant of Herodotus' writings."
—*Richmond Times-Dispatch*

"Open-hearted and deft, Marozzi does for us what Herodotus does for him: provides an introduction to places new to us."
—*Raleigh News and Observer*

"This isn't just a dusty look at history."         —*New York Press*

"Marozzi has penned something of a classic, taking on the ancient world through modern eyes and bringing fresh impressions to such familiar, even cliché, places."         —*Washington Times*

"[A] vivid travelog . . . a lively and accessible narrative that's often as eclectic as its spiritual predecessor."         —*Library Journal*

"Never less than entertaining . . . a tour de force of travel writing."
—*Literary Review*

"A remarkable travel history."         —*Booklist*

"[A] scintillating, thought-provoking and entertaining homage."
—Paul Cartledge, Professor of Greek History,
Cambridge University

# The Way of Herodotus

# The Way of Herodotus

*Travels with the Man
Who Invented History*

## JUSTIN MAROZZI

**DA CAPO PRESS**
A Member of the Perseus Books Group

Cataloging-in-Publication data for this book is available from the Library of
Congress.

First Da Capo Press edition 2008
First Da Capo Press paperback edition 2010
Reprinted by arrangement with John Murray (Publishers)
An Hachette Livre UK Company
HC ISBN: 978-0-306-81621-5
PB ISBN: 978-0-306-81857-8
Library of Congress Control Number: 2008938709

Published by Da Capo Press
A Member of the Perseus Books Group
www.dacapopress.com

Da Capo Press books are available at special discounts for bulk purchases in the
U.S. by corporations, institutions, and other organizations. For more information,
please contact the Special Markets Department at the Perseus Books Group, 2300
Chestnut Street, Suite 200, Philadelphia, PA 19103, or call (800) 810-4145,
extension 5000, or e-mail special.markets@perseusbooks.com.

*Once again to Julia*

The appeal of history to us all is in the last analysis poetic. But the poetry of history does not consist of imagination roaming at large, but of imagination pursuing the fact and fastening upon it. That which compels the historian to 'scorn delights and live laborious days' is the ardour of his own curiosity to know what really happened long ago in that land of mystery which we call the past. To peer into that magic mirror and see fresh figures there every day is a burning desire that consumes and satisfies him all his life, that carries him each morning, eager as a lover, to the library and muniment room. It haunts him like a passion of terrible potency, because it is poetic. The dead were and are not. Their place knows them no more, and is ours today. Yet they were once as real as we, and we shall tomorrow be shadows like them . . .

G. M. Trevelyan, *Autobiography and Other Essays*

I need not apologise for the digression. It has been my habit throughout this work.

Herodotus, *Histories*

Reader, I think proper, before we proceed any farther together, to acquaint thee, that I intend to digress, through this whole History, as often as I see Occasion.

Henry Fielding, *Tom Jones*

# Contents

Acknowledgements     xi

Maps     xvi

Introduction: Dog-Headed Men, Gold-Digging
Ants and Flying Snakes, or Why We Should
All Read Herodotus     1

PART I   TURKEY     29
1. Priestesses with Beards     31
2. Underwater Herodotus     46

PART II   IRAQ     67
3. Fools and Wars     69
4. Baghdad, Evangelicals and Mocking Madmen     87
5. Babylon     111

PART III   EGYPT     135
6. Memphis and Thebes: Tall Stories and
Self-Immolating Cats, or No Sex in Temples,
Please, We're Egyptian     137
7. Herodotus in Hollywood (and the Sahara)     164
8. Cairo, Mother of the World     179

PART IV   GREECE     195
9. Athens, City Hall of Wisdom     197
10. Herodotus Meets Aristotle     224
11. Thessaloniki: History on the Front Line     247

ix

12. An Exorcism 258
13. Lunch (and a Good Deal of Retsina) with
    Patrick Leigh Fermor 262
14. 'Fill High the Bowl with Samian Wine!' 274
15. Wassailing Gods, Pious Priests and Tearful
    Monks 299

   *Bibliography* 327

# Acknowledgements

A JOURNEY WITH HERODOTUS is the work – and pleasure – of a lifetime. I have had the great fortune to be accompanied every step of the way by Paul Cartledge, Professor of Greek History at Cambridge University, to whom I offer my greatest thanks. Although Herodotus died almost 2,500 years ago, he remains capable of inspiring lasting friendships, a wonderful posthumous tribute to his breadth of vision and generosity of spirit. I count myself lucky to have met Paul and so to have benefited undeservedly from his font of Herodotean wisdom.

Thank you to my friend Tom Sutherland, who first put me on the trail of Herodotus, and to Dr Angus Bowie, Lobel Praelector in Classics at Oxford University, for providing an initial steer in the dense and often impenetrable world of Herodotean studies.

Travels with Herodotus can take you anywhere. He is as relevant to ancient Egypt as to contemporary Washington. I concentrated on Turkey, Iraq, Egypt and Greece, an ambitious itinerary made possible in large part thanks to the enlightened support of Rahul Jacob, the incomparable travel editor of the *Financial Times*, who consistently said yes when others would have said no.

The Herodotus who kept me company during my journeys, and from whom I quote most often, can be found in the highly access-ible – and portable – Penguin Classics edition of the *Histories*.

In Turkey, I enjoyed the water-borne hospitality of Gurkan Kinaci in Bodrum, onetime Halicarnassus, Herodotus' hometown. Thanks to Meltem Ozer, Mazlum Ağan, the town's mayor, Oğuz Alpözen, direc-tor of the Bodrum Museum of Underwater Archaeology, Tufan Turanli and Dr George Bass of the Institute of Nautical Archaeology, and Çanan Küçükeren, historian and irrepressible Herodotus devotee.

In Iraq, I am grateful first of all to Lieutenant-Colonel Tim Spicer OBE for giving me the opportunity to live and work in Baghdad for more than a year and take Herodotus to war. Thank you to His Excellency Samir Sumaida'ie, Iraq's ambassador to Washington, National Security Adviser Mowaffak Rubaie, Defence Minister Saadoun Dulaimi, Brigadier James Ellery CBE, Dr Thair Ali and Catriona Laing for their friendship, support and humour in challenging times and to Dr Donny George, director of the National Museum in Baghdad, for a private tour of one of the world's greatest collections of antiquities. Dr Abdul Aziz Hamid, chairman of the State Board of Antiquities, enabled us to make a small donation to preserving the house in Baghdad that houses the museum's archives. The Polish archaeologist Agnieszka Dolatowska gave a memorable guided tour of Babylon during its catastrophic occupation by Coalition forces. Joan Porter MacIver and Dr Lamia al Gailani of the British School of Archaeology in Iraq and Professor Amélie Kuhrt FBA of University College, London, kindly assisted with later research. Thank you to all those unnamed colleagues who kept me out of harm's way.

In Egypt, my thanks to Philip Hamilton-Grierson and Mark Stacey of Cox & Kings for arranging a long Herodotean itinerary so masterfully. My friend Mandi Mourad was an inspired and indefatigable guide to getting hold of all the right people in Cairo. Herodotus has a good deal to teach the modern world about interfaith relations. In this regard, I enjoyed revealing conversations with Ali Gomaa, the Grand Mufti of Egypt, Mouneer Anis, the Anglican Bishop of Egypt, and Dr Ali al Semman of the Supreme Council for Islamic Affairs. Thanks also to Gamila Ismail, wife of the jailed opposition leader Ayman Nur, the human rights lawyer Amir Salem, Leila Soueif, Professor Assem Deif, for sharing his understanding of pyramidal mathematics, Heba Saleh of the BBC, the novelists Alaa al Aswany and Bahaa Taher, Max Rodenbeck, Salima Ikram, professor of Egyptology at the American University in Cairo, the Luxor Museum of Mummification for helping me test Herodotus' reliability in the crusty world of embalming, Ehab Gaddis, Dr Nasry Iskander, director general of Conservation and Preservation in the Egyptian Antiquities Organisation, generally regarded as the Daddy of Mummies at the

Egyptian Museum, Abd al Monem Abu al Futuh of the Muslim Brotherhood, Hani Shukrallah, director of the Heikal Foundation, the democracy activist Saad Eddin Ibrahim, chairman of the Ibn Khaldun Centre for Democracy Studies, the prolific blogger Issandr al Amrani, the activist Bothaina Kamel, the actor Khaled Abul Naga and Rabab Abdelaziz Othman, who can dance with a blazing candelabrum on her head. Herodotus would have been thrilled, as I was, to listen to the controversial film director Inas al Deghedy and Hind al Hinnawy, the country's most famous and infamous single mother, breaking taboos and lifting the lid on Egypt's sexual mores. In the oasis of Siwa my research into illicit homosexuality, among other things, was assisted by the anthropologist Fathi Malim and the tribal leaders Sheikhs Fathi Kilane and Omar Rageh and Mohammed Abd al Wahab Tayeb Mosallim. In Aswan, thanks to Esmat Abd al Malak, director of the Elephantine Museum, and Mohammed Talat Abdul Aziz, chairman of the High Dam and Aswan Dams Authority, for explaining the mysterious workings of the Nile. Good guides in Egypt were as indispensable to me as they were to Herodotus. Thank you to Abd al Sattar in Aswan, Refaat al Hakim in Luxor, Atef in Siwa and Galal Moawad in Cairo.

In Greece, thank you to Rachel Howard for setting the ball rolling and pointing me towards so many helpfully Herodotean people in Athens, beginning with Cleopatra van de Winkel, Vassilis Papadimitriou, his wife Sofka Zinovieff and colleague Anna Bakola, who all displayed humbling hospitality and kindness. Thank you to former prime minister Tzannis Tzannetakis, to Irene Noel-Baker and Garth Fowden for providing the perfect start to a journey in Greece in the form of a classically Herodotean conference in Athens, at which I had the good fortune to meet Professor Vassos Karageorghis of the University of Cyprus and Dr Miltiades Hatzopoulos, director of the Institute of Greek and Roman Antiquity at the National Hellenic Research Foundation. Thank you to Amalia Zepou for pointing the way to groundbreaking history in Thessaloniki, where I am indebted to Nenad Sebek of the Centre for Democracy and Reconciliation in South-east Europe. On the open seas to Samos Captain Vassilis Theodore was a generous guide to Greek seafaring.

Herodotus sought out priests wherever he went, hitting them for information. I would like to thank the writer Takis Michas, Haralambos Konidaris and Father Timotheos of the late Archbishop Christodoulos' office, and Father Sotirios in Samos, for sharing their thoughts on the Greek Orthodox Church.

Michael Cullen led me to Jonathan Tite and his wife Eleni Halkias, who treated me to Persian Wars battlefield tours at Salamis and Plataea. The visit to Thermopylae was a truly suspension-challenging retracing of the treacherous Ephialtes route across the mountains that led to the glorious defeat of the Spartans under their brave king Leonidas in 480 BC. Jonathan's car was no less brave. Kerin Hope, the *FT*'s correspondent in Athens, and Catherina Mytilineou paved the way for more discoveries (and boundless hospitality) in Samos, where Apostolos Sikelianos was my guide and mentor. On the same island thanks also to the archaeologist Nikolaos Tsoulos, the historian Christos Landros, the philologist Professor Giorgos Angelinaras and my *souma*-fuelled companion Dimos. I am indebted to Marianna Koromila, great-great-granddaughter of the man who published the first edition of the *Histories* in modern Greek, for showing me his monumental 1836 edition. Thank you to Iannis Trephilis, Maria Papaconstantinou at the British School at Athens, Anna Missirian for the decidedly unSpartan accommodation of the Imaret in Kavala, and to Maria Strati at the King George II Palace in Athens, to Stavros Karkaletsis, and the Greek and Turkish diplomats at Xanthi and Komotini respectively. Michael Lychounas, Thodoros Mouriadis and Theodoros Spanellis were all generous with their time and historical expertise in Kavala. In the Peloponnese village of Kardamyli, I spent the afternoon of my life with the great Sir Patrick Leigh Fermor, the first sight of whom mugging up on Herodotus before our lunch meeting will live with me for ever. Thank you to Giorgos Giannakeas for helping me find him.

Particular thanks to Mairi Yossi, shining beacon of Greek *philoxenia* and wisdom, and Alexandra Melista, who took me under her Herodotean wing during my travels in Greece and continued answering all sorts of questions great and small when she must have hoped I had disappeared for good.

Thank you to Andrew Roberts, John Adamson at Peterhouse, Cambridge, and Richard Evans, Professor of Modern History at Cambridge, for their historical encouragement, the staff of the much loved Rare Books and Music room of the British Library, my London home, and to Michael Prodger at the *Sunday Telegraph*, David Sexton at the *Evening Standard*, Nancy Sladek at the *Literary Review* and Gail Pirkis at *Slightly Foxed* for providing a constant flow of literary diversions. In Norfolk, I pay tribute to the excessive hospitality of my uncle and aunt, Nick and Susan Ward, who kept the wine flowing in the darkest days of winter.

Sincere thanks to my agent Georgina Capel for maintaining stoic optimism in the face of a lack of progress that would have led others to despair. At John Murray I am unspeakably grateful to my editor Roland Philipps for exhibiting patience that can only be described as epic and for his acute comments on the manuscript. Thank you also to Rowan Yapp, Peter James and Nikki Barrow for all their help.

Finally, my thanks as ever to my stepdaughter and budding Herodotean Clemmie, for putting up with my many disappearances, and to my darling Julia, to whom this book is dedicated. Having been married to Tamerlane for four years, she found herself through no fault of her own saddled with Herodotus for another four. I like to think he has proved better company, but that may have been little consolation when her husband was holed up in Baghdad and the mortars and rockets were coming in.

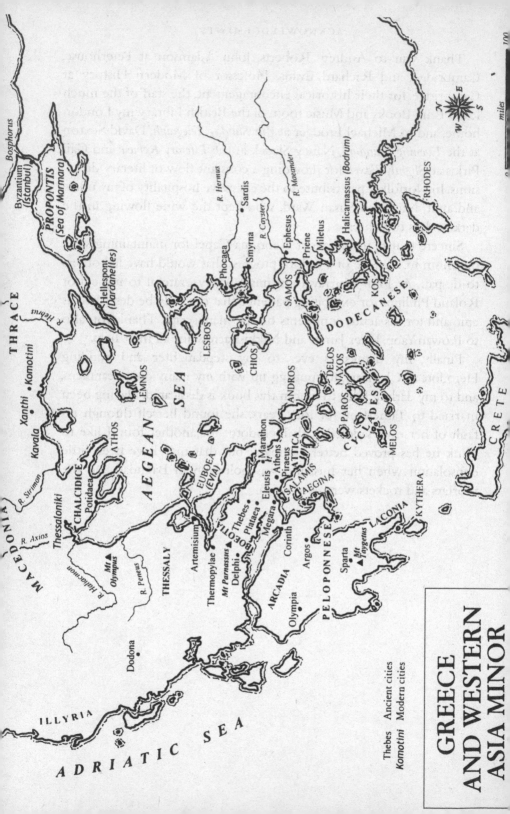

# GREECE
# AND WESTERN
# ASIA MINOR

Thebes    Ancient cities
Komotini   Modern cities

ADRIATIC SEA

ILLYRIA

MACEDONIA
R. Axios
Thessaloniki
R. Haliacmon
R. Peneus
Mt Olympus
THESSALY

Dodona

CHALCIDICE
Potidaea
ATHOS
Mt Athos

THRACE
R. Strimon
Kavala
Xanthi • Komotini
R. Hebrus

AEGEAN SEA

LEMNOS

LESBOS

Artemisium
Thermopylae
Mt Parnassus
Delphi
BOEOTIA
Thebes
Plataea
Megara
Corinth
ARCADIA
Argos
Olympia
PELOPONNESE
Sparta
Mt Taygetus
LACONIA

EUBOEA
(EVIA)
Marathon
Athens
Eleusis
Piraeus
ATTICA
SALAMIS
AEGINA

KYTHERA

ANDROS
DELOS
NAXOS
PAROS
CYCLADES
MELOS

CHIOS

SAMOS

Phocaea
Smyrna
Sardis
R. Hermus
R. Cayster
Ephesus
Priene
Miletus
R. Maeander
KOS
Halicarnassus (Bodrum)
DODECANESE
RHODES

THRACE

Byzantium
(Istanbul)
Bosphorus
PROPONTIS
(Sea of Marmara)
Hellespont
(Dardanelles)

CRETE

N
W  E
S

0        miles        100

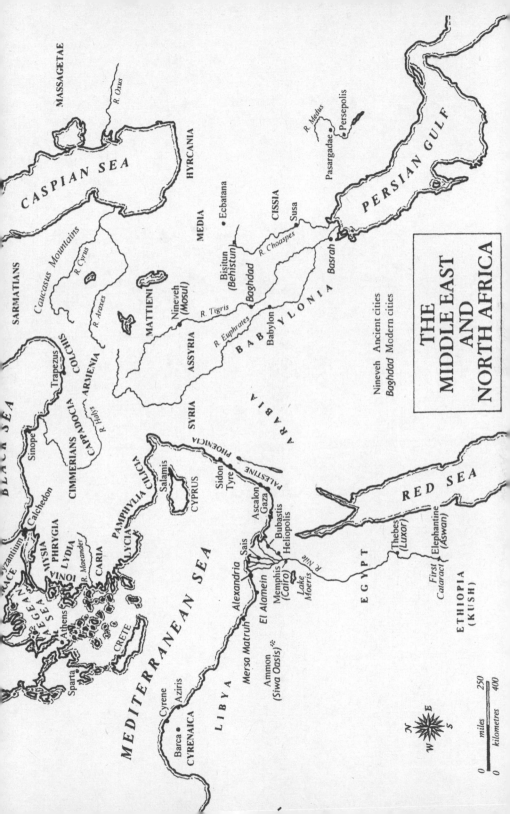

MASSAGETAE

R. Oxus

CASPIAN SEA

HYRCANIA

SARMATIANS

Caucasus Mountains

R. Cyrus

R. Araxes

MATTIENI

COLCHIS

ARMENIA

Trapezus

R. Halys

CAPPADOCIA

CIMMERIANS

Sinope

Calchedon

Byzantium

PHRYGIA

MYSIA

LYDIA

R. Maeander

IONIA

CARIA

Athens

Sparta

CRETE

R. Medus

Persepolis

Pasargadae

PERSIAN GULF

Ecbatana

MEDIA

CISSIA

Susa

Bisitun
(Behistun)

R. Choaspes

Baghdad

Basrah

Nineveh
(Mosul)

R. Tigris

R. Euphrates

Babylon

BABYLONIA

ASSYRIA

SYRIA

ARABIA

PHOENICIA

Salamis

CYPRUS

Sidon
Tyre

PALESTINE

Ascalon
Gaza

PAMPHYLIA   CILICIA

LYCIA

BLACK SEA

AEGEAN SEA

MEDITERRANEAN SEA

RED SEA

Bubastis
Heliopolis

Sais

Alexandria

Memphis
(Cairo)

El Alamein

Lake
Moeris

R. Nile

EGYPT

Thebes
(Luxor)

First
Cataract

Elephantine
(Aswan)

ETHIOPIA
(KUSH)

Mersa Matruh

Ammon
(Siwa Oasis)

LIBYA

Cyrene

Barca

Aziris

CYRENAICA

## THE
## MIDDLE EAST
## AND
## NORTH AFRICA

Nineveh   Ancient cities
Baghdad   Modern cities

N
E
S
W

miles        250
0
kilometres        400
0

# Introduction
## Dog-Headed Men, Gold-Digging Ants and Flying Snakes, or Why We Should All Read Herodotus

*Anybody can make history. Only a great man can write it.*
Oscar Wilde, 'The Critic as Artist', *Intentions* (1891)

THIS IS HOW it begins:

Herodotus of Halicarnassus here displays his inquiry, so that human achievements may not become forgotten in time, and great and marvellous deeds – some displayed by Greeks, some by barbarians – may not be without their glory; and especially to show why the two peoples fought each other.

There it is. The birth of history in a paragraph. With these few words, written in the fifth century BC, Herodotus first formulates humankind's burning interest in the past, an obsession that has remained with us ever since. His mission, as noble as it is ambitious, is to record and explain what has been before, to ensure that glorious achievements and remarkable events are preserved in memory and not forgotten, to make sense of the cataclysm of the Persian Wars and try to understand why the weaker side won and the more powerful lost, to examine, through his travels and on-the-road researches, the clash of cultures and customs between the Greek and barbarian worlds. Technically history will come later, but it will come from the Greek word Herodotus uses here: ἱστορίη or *historie*, inquiry or investigation.

Although I never came across Herodotus at university, I wish I had. Quite by accident I found myself reading history at Cambridge in the early Nineties. I went up to read Arabic and French but quickly revolted, dillied with English, dallied with social and political science and worked

1

my way methodically if unsuccessfully around the entire corpus of the humanities until, after a brief flirtation with philosophy, a sceptical look at archaeology and anthropology and dire warnings of immediate expulsion, eventually there was nothing else left to study. Not having a history A Level didn't seem to matter. By sheer chance, Gonville and Caius College was at that time the closest thing the country had to a history factory. Year after year its conveyor belt churned out historians ready to don tweed and do battle with the past. Some of them became extremely distinguished, if unknown beyond the world of dreaming spires and ivory towers. Others, like Norman Stone, Quentin Skinner, Orlando Figes, Andrew Roberts, Simon Sebag Montefiore and Alain de Botton, became familiar to a wider public (to the inevitable chagrin, and occasionally green-tinged disgust, of the academics).

I didn't give it a second thought at the time, but over the next three years Herodotus, the Father of History, was nowhere to be seen among the Renaissance-with-a-dash-of-Gothic-splendour of Caius. Had I been more attentive, I might have picked up on references to him in E. H. Carr's vituperative classic *What is History?* and Geoffrey Elton's elegantly vitriolic *The Practice of History* and understood why.

Hovering nervously between subjects one bleak weekend in December, steeling myself for a stab at theology, on the brink of being sent down in humiliation, I went to see Neil McKendrick, the legendary head of the Caius history factory, a latter-day Bismarck (history was his empire) with an astonishing record of producing first-class degrees. Perhaps it was worth having a crack at history.

'You're in danger of becoming a laughing-stock,' he said, slowly crushing a piece of paper in his perfectly manicured hands.

He handed me Carr and Elton, those feuding giants of English history, as an encouragement to make up my mind. Failure to do so, he reminded me, would end my university career before it had started.

'History's your last chance,' he said.

I made up my mind there and then. History was the future.

Carr, my first brush with history since long-forgotten O Levels, gave Herodotus a couple of mentions, neither of which inspired great confidence. 'He found few disciples in the ancient world' was his first comment. 'Herodotus as the father of history had few children' was the second. And beyond that Carr did not go. In his own book, Elton observed, in a strikingly similar phrase, that 'Herodotus may have been the father of history, but for a good many centuries the child he begot was to enjoy but a restricted and intermittent life.' He continued: 'History had barely begun when Thucydides attacked the methods and purposes of Herodotus.' And that was the only look-in Herodotus got.

The thing about Herodotus, and it was years before I discovered this, is he doesn't really feature on historians' radars any more. It has been a long time since he did. He has been cast off, jettisoned, thrown to the dogs, forgotten. History, grown-up, self-confident and professional, has committed patricide, rubbing out the man who gave birth to it. With few exceptions, historians have become, in their own minds at least, far too sophisticated for simple old Herodotus, who is but an entertaining amateur. Nowadays he belongs to the classicists.

And yet, although a few ancients put the boot in, it had all started out more promisingly. Lucian, the second-century AD satirist and rhetorician, said he wished he could match Herodotus' ineffable style, captivated by 'the beauty of his diction, the careful arrangement of his words, the aptness of his native Ionic, his extraordinary power of thought, the countless jewels which he has wrought into a unity beyond hope of imitation'. Cicero called his prose 'copious and polished', Quintilian, 'sweet, pure and flowing'. Longinus thought him 'the most Homeric of historians'. His fellow Greek and fellow-Halicarnassian Dionysius, won over by the marrying of sublime beauty with rigorous historical method, sensibly preferred him to that earnest windbag Thucydides.

But it was an uncharacteristically mean-spirited Plutarch who really did the damage in what has been called literature's first 'slashing review', devoting a whole book to trashing the poor man. Turning Cicero's more affectionate 'Father of History' moniker on its head, he christened Herodotus the 'Father of Lies' in *The Malice of Herodotus*, a malicious title of a book if ever there was one. As with the best stinking reviews, it's a wonderfully readable put-down.

'I'm reminded of Hippocleides, who danced with his legs on the table,' he writes of one of Herodotus' many stories about the Persian Great King Xerxes. 'Herodotus seems to be dancing away the truth, and saying, "I could hardly care less." ' Plutarch doesn't pull his punches. Herodotus is a smooth-talking deceiver. ' "Persuasion's face", as Sophocles says, "is fearsome to behold," especially when it is part of a style so charming and effective as to conceal not just an author's historical but especially his personal flaws.' Ouch. 'Herodotus outdoes the tragic poets in all . . . sorts of nonsense.' He's a dangerous 'barbarian-lover' (than which no greater heresy can be imagined) who praises foreigners and denigrates 'the most solemn and holy truths of Greek religion with Egyptian humbug and fairytale'.

With every page of this fantastically unpleasant little volume, Plutarch plunges the dagger further in. 'The malice in Herodotus is certainly less chafing and gentler than that in Theopompus, but it takes better hold and bites deeper, like winds that come as draughts through cracks compared with those that blow in the open.' With an entertaining if unintentional irony, Plutarch launches repeated broadsides against a dead man he accuses of 'mean and partisan attacks'.

The lasting effect was devastating. Ever since Plutarch, Herodotus has never quite escaped the slur that he was a bit of a fibber, a fantasist, an elegant charlatan, a classical-world Walter Mitty who told whoppers, a peerless stylist who simply made a lot of it up. Not that I knew any of this when I was studying history. I only picked up the *Histories* years later, curious to read a man whose name had a forbidding ring to it, a distant voice from an impenetrable, ancient world that my history education had drawn a curtain smartly across. As soon as I did, I was instantly hooked.

The *Histories* is a masterpiece on the grandest scale, a chronological history of the Persian Wars – a sweeping survey from the invasions of empire-building Cyrus in the middle of the sixth century BC through the stories of ill-fated Cambyses and the opportunist regicide Darius to the depredations of arch-megalomaniac Xerxes in the early fifth.

Writing with a novelist's flair for pace and suspense, Herodotus builds up to this spectacular confrontation over the course of almost 400 pages. The fearful tumult of the Persian Wars wells up like a wave and only comes crashing down upon his narrative in the final third of the book.

4

Before he gets there he takes us back into the world of myth and legend to try to understand the quarrel between Greeks and barbarians. He explores the reign of the Lydian king Croesus and his fateful encounter with world-conquering Cyrus and his wondrous campaigns; the rise of Sparta and the accession of Cyrus' son Cambyses to the Persian throne in 530 BC; the new Great King's rage-fuelled invasion of Egypt and Ethiopia; Sparta's war against Samos, the first time the military regime flexed its naval muscles. Then it's back to Persia for the revolt of the Magi, the death of Cambyses in 522 and the rise of Darius, setting about his conquests in the Aegean, Scythia, North Africa and Thrace. With the seeds of democracy planted in Athens in around 508 and the outbreak of the Ionian revolt against the Persian empire in 499, the drumbeat of war becomes ever louder. Darius leads the way with his invasion of Greece and the debacle at Marathon, and now it's the clash of civilisations and war all the way, on into the reign of Xerxes and the glorious battles of Thermopylae, Salamis and Plataea that echo – only because Herodotus has preserved them – across the millennia.

Yet the *Histories* is much, much more than that. This is no conventional history as we understand the word today. It is an epic about war and empire, the frailty of the human condition, fortune's ebb and flow, freedom versus tyranny, history with a piercing moral message. Herodotus tells us he'll look at cities great and small because those which were once great have now declined and those which were once modest have since risen to greatness. It is about the immutability of fate, the vanity of power, religion, love, the importance of custom and the capriciousness of the gods. 'Often enough God gives man a glimpse of happiness then utterly ruins him,' Herodotus' wise man Solon warns the prodigiously rich Croesus shortly before his catastrophic fall. Through the stories of recklessly powerful men, above all the Persian kings, it offers sobering lessons about hubris and its tragically inevitable consequences of nemesis, an eloquent caution against going beyond one's natural limits. It explores the human motives of greed and lust and overweening pride without ever sounding dull or worthy. Tolerance rings out clearly on every page.

It may be that as Herodotus watched feuding Athens and Sparta drift towards the ruinous Peloponnesian War (431–404 BC), the

*Histories* also stood as a prophetic warning. He gives one of the most memorable lines in the book to the conquered Croesus, who has just lost his empire to Cyrus in 546 BC. Brought before the Persian King of Kings, he tries to explain why he decided to fight him. 'No one is fool enough to choose war instead of peace – in peace sons bury fathers, but in war fathers bury sons,' he says ruefully. Perhaps, Herodotus may be thinking, if Greeks can understand the past, they will be able to avoid making the same mistakes twice. It is one of history's most enduring illusions.

Herodotus deliberately awards himself the widest possible remit in his history. Announcing his interest in 'great and marvellous deeds' provides him with the stepping-stones from which to spring the most elaborate digressions, from a penetrating study of the Nile to a survey of the strange sexual practices of the Scythians. He celebrates the wonders of the world with a life-grabbing energy that is never less than infectious. The weird and wonderful roam like wild animals through his pages. He introduces us to dog-headed men that live in mountains, the gold-digging ants of India, bigger than a fox, smaller than a dog, and the fabulous flying snakes of Arabia.\* The anecdotes jostle for space in a lively narrative full of verve, blithely zigzagging through time and place yet without ever losing track of his over-arching themes which are set within a clearly discernible moral universe.

Interwoven within the central political narrative are discrete sections on foreign nations that give Herodotus the opportunity to rove exuberantly from one subject to the next. The 600 pages teem with illicit eroticism, sex, love, violence, crime, strange customs of foreign peoples, imagined scenes in royal bedrooms, flashbacks, dream sequences, political theory, philosophical debate, encounters with oracles, geographical speculation, natural history, short stories and Greek myths. If this is the world's first history book, it is also – without

---

\* Some scholars believe the gold-digging ants may have been marmots. As for the flying snakes, 'a fiery flying serpent' is also mentioned in Isaiah 14:29. Once considered to be locusts, these curious animals are now thought to have been inspired by the pictures of snakes with wings that Herodotus would have seen on Egyptian monuments during his travels in the country.

6

question – the world's first page-turner. Even more astonishing, the *Histories* is its first prose epic.

Herodotus celebrates the glory of human diversity with a vigour that infuriated parochial Plutarch. Like a nineteenth-century explorer kicking off African dust from his boots as he lectures in the hallowed halls of the Royal Geographical Society on some far-off tribe unknown to his audience, Herodotus takes us into the mysterious world of the Libyans and Lydians, Egyptians and Ethiopians, the Massagetae and the Scythians, Thracians, Persians, Babylonians and Indians . . . Who are these people, he asks, what are they like, where did they come from, what makes them tick? How do their customs and traditions – political, social, sexual, architectural, religious, commercial – differ from our own?

So Herodotus is the world's first historian, but he is also its first foreign correspondent, investigative journalist, anthropologist and travel writer. He is an aspiring geographer, a budding moralist, a skilful dramatist, a high-spirited explorer and an inveterate storyteller. He is part learned scholar, part tabloid hack, but always broad-minded, humorous and generous-hearted, which is why he's so much fun. He examines the world around him with the benevolence of a Micawber, with an unerring eye for thrilling material to inform and amuse, to horrify and entertain. As Edward Gibbon noted, 'Herodotus sometimes writes for children, and sometimes for philosophers.'

He also writes for the normal man and woman. Like any tabloid newspaper editor who knows that sex sells, Herodotus understands his audiences' desire for titillation. The *Histories* was written to be read aloud, probably in symposia around the Greek world, the fifth-century BC equivalent of a high-toned series of Reith Lectures or a talk and book-signing at a literary festival. Herodotus knows he's got to hold the attention of the people sitting cross-legged in front of him with aching backs and pins and needles in their legs. He's got to keep them interested for hours at a time.

So sex figures prominently. He describes how every Babylonian woman is forced to sit outside the temple of Aphrodite until a man throws a coin into her lap for the right to have sex with her. Only after that is she set free. He describes the prostitute tomb-builders of

Lydia and their phallic pillars of stone, shows us an ancient India where tribes 'copulate in the open like cattle' ejaculating semen as black as their skins. Some of the tribes eat anyone who is sick, he reports, killing them before the disease worsens to avoid wasting the meat. 'The invalid, in these circumstances, protests that there is nothing wrong with him – but to no purpose. His friends refuse to accept his protestations, kill him and hold a banquet.' Into the pot he goes. Then there are the Massagetae of the Caspian Sea region where 'all wives are used promiscuously'. This is very much a male world. 'If a man wants a woman, all he does is to hang up his quiver in front of her wagon and then enjoy her without misgiving.' Herodotus does not shrink from delicate subjects. Anal sex even gets a look-in. He writes of Pisistratus, son of Hippocrates and tyrant of Athens, who 'did not want children from his new wife, and to prevent her from having any refused normal intercourse and lay with her in an unnatural way' to the great fury of the woman's father, who considered this a terrible dishonour to his daughter and ran Pisistratus out of town. (It is amusing to discover that Herodotus was less repressed than his Victorian translators. George Rawlinson, the most celebrated among them, was one of the most squeamish. Pisistratus, he wrote in the late 1850s, 'determined that there should be no issue from the marriage', and left it at that). He tells us of the peculiar post-coital habits of the Babylonians, who fumigate their genitals with incense after a bout of love-making, and the 'most curious incident' in Egypt of a goat having sex with a woman in public.

The *Histories* overflows with the room-filling personality of its creator. Discussing the Scythians of the Black Sea region, who delight in getting high by inhaling the smoke of burning cannabis plants (it makes them 'howl with pleasure'), Herodotus suddenly feels impelled to discuss the difficulties of breeding mules. 'I need not apologise for the digression,' he says. 'It has been my habit throughout this work.' These authorial interventions come thick and fast, no fewer than 1,086 times, as one academic has had the patience to count. The frequency of the first-person gives the book its distinctive personality and flavour, a refreshing riposte to the more impersonal history writing of today where the word 'I' is virtually unacceptable. What was Orwell thinking

of when he argued, in *Why I Write*, that 'one can write nothing readable unless one constantly struggles to efface one's own personality'?
Herodotus' first-person comments and asides reveal an educated,
enlightened, adventurous, endlessly curious man with a dancing intellect and a felicitous turn of phrase, someone with a powerful sense of
wonder and an all-encompassing humanity, brimming with relentless
wanderlust and an irrepressible storytelling zeal, revelling in his fizzing
sexual curiosity and fierce tolerance of other cultures, buoyed along
on the currents of historical inquiry by his continent-spanning
humour, ranging wit and questing wisdom. His intrusion into the text
gives us the chance, again and again, to see how the mind of a man
who lived twenty-six centuries ago works as he seeks to understand
the world about him. Everything about it. To give just one example,
rubbishing the tales of feathers falling from the Scythian sky so thickly
that people can neither see nor travel, Herodotus puts forward his own
eminently sensible explanation. 'My own opinion is that to the north
of this country it snows continually, though less in summer than
winter, as you would expect; anyone, for example, who has seen a blizzard of snow at close quarters knows what I mean: the snow is very
like feathers.'

Sometimes, especially to a contemporary audience, the stories
appear tall, to say the least, a feature of the *Histories* which was seized
upon by Plutarch among others to ridicule its author. Take, for instance,
the endearing account of the celebrated lyre-player and singer Arion
narrowly avoiding death at the hands of a crew of murderous sailors.
Jumping into the sea to escape, he was rescued by a helpful dolphin
which brought him safely back to the Laconian peninsula, from where
he made his way back to the court of the tyrant ruler Periander at
Corinth. Questioned by the king, the crew said they had delivered
Arion safely to his port. When he glided into the royal audience
chamber in his finest singing costume, their lies were revealed.

Sometimes, as a man, you hope he *is* having you on. How about
the leg-crossingly awful story of an embittered eunuch called
Hermotimus, favourite servant of Xerxes, who in later life ran into
Panionius, the very man who had castrated him as a boy? Telling his
tormentor how happy he now was, how greatly he had prospered,

Hermotimus promised to do as much for his former master and family if they came to settle in his home town of Sardis. No sooner had Panionius arrived with his four sons than Hermotimus turned on him, vowing vengeance for the 'beastly practice' that had turned him into 'a nothing instead of a man'. At which point he forced Panionius to castrate all four sons, one by one, with his own hands. And then, as if that wasn't horrendously painful – or messy – enough, his sons were made to castrate him. Herodotus is always fascinated by the concept of *tisis* or divine retribution. In this case, revenge is a dish best served with a sharp knife.

Life-saving dolphins, multiple testicle slicers, otherworldly animals, beard-growing priestesses . . . it's hardly surprising Herodotus has taken such a knocking from the critics, or that he is no longer required reading for today's historians. In fact, more often than not he is scrupulous about sourcing his stories. He knows a good deal of the information he has gleaned on his travels is hearsay, rumour and legend, some of it nonsense. He's quite clear about this. 'I am obliged to record the things I am told, but I am certainly not required to believe them – this remark may be taken to apply to the whole of my account,' he writes.

It is easy to mock Herodotus, but his achievement was nothing short of phenomenal. In an era when poetry was the ultimate form of literary expression, overnight he became a pioneer of prose and author of what was then the world's longest volume by far. The *Histories* is twice the length of Homer's *Iliad*, a work as distant from Herodotus' time as Milton from our own. Prose was the new kid on the block, literally in its infancy, a second-class citizen dismissively referred to as *pedzos logos*, language that walks on foot, rather than soaring aloft in poetry's winged chariot. Herodotus changed all that. Little wonder that the *Histories* was likened by one critic to a voyage of discovery on a par with Columbus' crossing of the Atlantic. On the ground, across seas, over deserts, Herodotus was a fearless, indefatigable traveller. He was also a literary explorer without equal.

The first historian, travel writer, anthropologist, political theorist, foreign correspondent, prose stylist . . . So many firsts. There seems no end to the man's accolades, but astonishingly we can still find room for another.

Herodotus invented the West. It is a big claim and it might appear presumptuous (Aeschylus, the father of tragedy, and the lyric poet Simonides both wrote about the Persian Wars, too), but to see how he did it and why this is no idle boast we must first travel back to ancient Greece to take a look at one of history's most decisive, world-changing encounters. Herodotus was in the thick of it.

If you want to put a finger on it and say, that's when the West was born, you could make a decent case for 490 BC. Battle of Marathon. Perhaps that sounds a little arbitrary, as is often the case when plucking dates from history. We might rephrase it and say the West was conceived at Marathon, went through a difficult pregnancy that lasted a decade, was almost aborted, survived the scare and was then delivered, kicking and screaming in its own blood, and that of the East, on the battlefield of Plataea and the foam-flecked seas of Mycale in 479 BC. And the Greek historian Herodotus, born around 490 himself, was its retrospective literary midwife.

We'll begin in September 490, when a Persian fleet loyal to the Great King Darius I, hell-bent on destroying Athens, sailed across the Aegean from Asia and landed on Greek soil at Marathon. The bristling expeditionary force was commanded by the generals Datis and Artaphernes. We don't know what the weather was like that day, but as it was late summer we can guess that it would have been delightful: playful breezes, powder-blue skies and seas seared into a pointillist blaze in this archipelago of light. It was a glorious day on which to kill or be killed.

The Persian plan was straightforward. One half of the expeditionary force, led by Artaphernes, would sail around Attica to begin the attack on Athens, the other would remain at Marathon under Datis to pin down the Greek defenders. Athens, in their absence, would be sacked and burned, raped and pillaged in revenge for its support of the Ionian revolt against the Persian empire a decade earlier. That much was certain. The Persian fleet had already inflicted carnage upon Naxos and Eretria. Athens was next. Darius had been planning this expedition for years. 'Remember Athens,' a specially tasked servant had been whispering in his ear daily, stoking the fires of imperial fury.

Facing the Persians across the mountain-rimmed coastal plain was a flimsy-looking Athenian and Platoean army numbering around 10,000 hoplites, or heavily armed infantrymen, tucked away on higher ground in the foothills of the Vrana valley with a small detachment of reinforcements from Plataea. The Greeks were under the military commander, or War Archon, Callimachus. One of his subordinate generals, Miltiades, was to play the decisive role on the battlefield. The swarming ranks of Persians, who outnumbered them considerably, sharpened their swords and prepared for a rout.

Success seemed to have been scorched into their DNA. They were part of a formidable war machine that was accustomed to winning victory after blood-soaked victory. From the time of Cyrus the Great, slayer of Medes, Lydians and Babylonians, scourge of Central Asia, founder of the earth-shaking Persian empire from the middle of the sixth-century BC, Persians had terrorised the world.

The Athenians had never scared anyone. As they stared across the mile or so of empty ground that separated the two forces, treading time in those dreadful slow moments before battle, some of the younger men probably discovered a warm trickle of fear running down their legs. The sharp stench of urine mingled with sweat, stale onion, garlic and wine.

And then, unexpectedly, came the call to charge, a desperate ruse by Miltiades to close on the enemy before the Persian archers were able to unleash more than a few volleys of arrows. Miltiades, who had anticipated the Persian plan to sail against Athens, wanted to force the issue as quickly as possible.

Down rushed the Greeks to do battle with the mighty Persians, screaming their war-cry of *eleleu!* The Persians, wrote Herodotus, could scarcely believe their eyes, 'thinking it suicidal madness for the Athenians to risk an assault with so small a force – rushing in with no support from either cavalry or archers'. Lunacy or no, the smaller army had stolen the initiative. The Athenians, Herodotus continued, 'fought in a way not to be forgotten; they were the first Greeks, so far as we know, to charge at a run, and the first who dared to look without flinching at Persian dress and the men who wore it ...'

The Greek line, stretched to the limit to prevent the greater Persian numbers outflanking it, immediately buckled in the centre under the onslaught of Datis' cavalry charges. Miltiades, who was familiar with Persian military strategy, had deliberately reinforced his wings, leaving the centre a good deal weaker than the twelve-man depth favoured for the phalanx. The centre was broken, but both wings now surged forward with their heavy shields, driving back the lightly armed Persian flanks and wheeling inward so that the Greek army soon encircled the larger force. As the Athenians drove on in a hedgehog of spears, the Persians, led by their wings, turned tail and beat a turbulent retreat towards the shore and the safety of their ships, harried every step of the way. Many were cut down on the beach, where the Athenian general Callimachus fell in frenzied hand-to-hand fighting. Seven Persian ships were seized. The rest of the fleet got away, pulling away in stinging disbelief from a shore curdled with the flowing entrails and hacked corpses of their defeat. The final casualties, according to Herodotus, were astounding. The Persians lost 6,400 men, the Athenians just 192.

It was now a race for Athens. The Persian fleet had to sail south around Cape Sunium to Phalerum, on the fringes of Athens, a distance of seventy miles. The Athenians were left with a march of around twenty-six miles. Miltiades is said to have despatched the famously fleet-footed runner Pheidippides to announce the victory and bolster morale among the city's defenders. Legend has it that his headlong dash to Athens was the world's first marathon. By the time the Persian fleet was approaching the shores, its leaders saw the Greek army had beaten them to it. Artaphernes was too late. The order to withdraw, to sail back to Asia, was given. Athens breathed again.

Marathon changed everything. It shattered the long-held dread of Persian invincibility, Herodotus wrote, 'for until that day came, no Greek could hear even the word Persian without terror'. For Aristotle, writing more than a century later, the battle was a defining moment for Greek confidence, the birth-pangs of democracy. Aeschylus was so proud of his participation in the battle that he mentioned it – to the complete exclusion of his literary triumphs – in the epitaph he wrote for himself:

This tomb the dust of Aeschylus doth hide,
Euphorion's son and fruitful Gela's pride.
How tried his valour, Marathon may tell
And long-haired Medes, who knew it all too well.

In the words of John Stuart Mill, 'the battle of Marathon, even as an event in English history, is more important than the battle of Hastings'.

Fast-forward a decade. It is 480 BC. Darius is dead. Persia is ruled by his world-conquering son and heir Great King Xerxes, King of Kings, worshipper of Ahura Mazda, Lord of Light. Revolts in Babylon and Egypt have delayed his plans to invade Greece and make it pay for the humiliation of Marathon, but Xerxes is now ready. He addresses his nobles. An expedition against Greece, he says in Herodotus' account, is in accordance with the Persian tradition of action and expansion.

Of our past history you need no reminder; for you know well enough the famous deeds of Cyrus, Cambyses and my father Darius, and their additions to our empire. Now I myself, ever since my accession, have been thinking how not to fall short of the kings who have sat upon this throne before me.

The invasion of Greece, a large and rich country, is the fitting course of action. With Athens and her neighbours crushed, 'we shall so extend the empire of Persia that its boundaries will be God's own sky, so that the sun will not look down upon any land beyond the boundaries of what is ours'. (His words were an early harbinger of much later imperial boasts. The Spanish king Charles V in the sixteenth century, and the British in the nineteenth, used to crow that the sun never set on their empires either.)

And so in May 480 BC the largest army the world had ever witnessed thundered west over two specially constructed pontoon bridges across the Hellespont (Dardanelles). The force was so large, Herodotus tells us, that it took seven days and nights to make the crossing from Asia into Europe. Not until the Second World War would a larger invasion force be put into the field. Victory, once again, was assured. It was the birthright of the Persians. They would march and ride and sail to glory just as they had stormed across the plains and mountains and deserts of Asia, amassing an empire that stretched from India to the Aegean, subduing everything in their path. The embarrassment at Marathon was a freak hiccup. Xerxes would have the dreadful revenge that his father had not lived long enough to exact.

In the stifling heat of late August, Xerxes' all-powerful army found its route south out of Thessaly blocked at the narrow pass of Thermopylae by a ragtag rump of Greek defenders commanded by the Spartan king Leonidas. Precipitous cliffs and mountains to the south, to the north the frothing sea. And threading its way between them for three miles a sliver of land the width of a stone's throw, in places only wide enough for a wagon. To the east, the steaming sulphur springs that gave the Hot Gates their name.

For several days, Xerxes waited patiently at the entrance to the pass, concentrating the minds of the 7,000 or so Greeks with the terrifying sight of his vast host approaching under rolling storm-clouds of dust. According to Greek spies, it numbered a horizon-filling 1,700,000. Modern historians prefer something closer to 250,000, a size that would still have made the heart beat quicker and the adrenaline surge.

A message was sent to Leonidas, ordering him to surrender his arms. Back came the defiantly laconic reply: '*Molon labe!*'; 'Come and get them!' Every hour the pass was held was an hour gained for Athens to prepare for a naval battle, every day Xerxes lost was a day won for the Greeks to organise their defences against this monstrous invading army.

Outnumbered by the massed lines of the Persian soldiers, Leonidas' men carefully combed their hair, stripped naked for a spot of exercise, polished their shields and sharpened their weapons, resolved to do and die. Such fatalism was incomprehensible to Xerxes who was offering the Greeks an honoured place in his god-given empire in return for their surrender. Opposition was pointless. Yet the Spartans were gloriously unperturbed by all this pomp and menace. Herodotus describes a local Greek warning the Spartan warrior Dieneces before the battle that Xerxes had so many archers in his army that when they shot their arrows, they eclipsed the sun. 'This is pleasant news that the stranger from Trachis brings us,' the magnificently unruffled Dieneces replied. 'If the Persians hide the sun, we shall have our battle in the shade.'

Xerxes stationed his throne where he could watch the battle, sat back and prepared to watch the inevitable victory unfold. First into the Hot Gates went the Medes, able soldiers but with their shorter spears and wicker shields no match for the Spartan hoplites in bronze armour. Revelling in the patriotic glory of spilling enemy blood in hand-to-hand combat, Leonidas' men, trained to be the most ferocious and disciplined soldiers the world had ever seen, saw them off contemptuously. The pass filled with blood. Beneath the cliffs, the stink of putrefying fly-ridden corpses hung heavy in the air.

With the Medes despatched, Xerxes sent in an elite detachment of the Immortals, feared across a continent as the finest of the Great King's soldiers. The Spartans found they had a tougher adversary. They fought, says Herodotus, 'in a manner never to be forgotten', and still the pass was defended, the Persians held back. A third force of men handpicked from the subject countries of the empire fared no better. For two days the fighting raged as Spartan heroics inflicted untold damage on the invaders. The Great King's blood boiled. Three times Xerxes leapt to his feet as some of his best men fell before his eyes. The resistance was intolerable. Then, on the second day, a traitor called Ephialtes, 'in hope of a rich reward', says Herodotus, gave the Persians a crucial piece of intelligence. He told them of the Anopaea Path, a tiny trail that climbed Mount Callidromus through thick oak forests, ran along its ridge and descended sharply to the east. If taken, this route would outflank the Greeks and bring their defence of the Hot Gates to a swift end. Xerxes ordered immediate action. It was time for one of history's earliest special-forces operations. During a moonlit night, a corps of Persians selected from the royal guard of Immortals, guided by Ephialtes (whose name, appropriately, means 'nightmare' in modern Greek), marched into the mountains, overcame the defenders of the forest track and emerged largely unscathed into the Hot Gates below. Leonidas was undone.

On the morning of the third day, by which time most of his army had either been dismissed or fled, the rest of his 300 Spartans, together with a body of hostage Thebans and valiant Thespians, made their last stand. The Persians advanced relentlessly. The front lines were driven forward with the whip, says Herodotus, and their sheer numbers started to tell. Leonidas, encircled by his enemy, withdrew his men on to a small hill in the pass, fighting with reckless bravery. After their spears and swords were shattered, they fought on with hands and teeth until not a single man breathed. Leonidas fell with his men in a hail of sun-darkening arrows, his corpse seized by the Persians, decapitated and crucified. Xerxes had lost 20,000 men in an unimaginable – and unforgettable – encounter.

Thermopylae was the turning point. As the French essayist Michel de Montaigne wrote in 1580, 'there are triumphant defeats that rival victories. Nor did those four sister victories, the fairest that the sun ever set eyes on – Salamis, Plataea, Mycale, and Sicily – ever dare match all their combined glory against the glory of the annihilation of King Leonidas and his men at the pass of Thermopylae.' In defeat, victory. In victory for Xerxes, the seeds of his ultimate defeat.

The suicidal last stand galvanised the ever-feuding band of Greek city-states into a united, impassioned and heroic defence of their freedom. Without victory in the Persian Wars, the West would not have been born (it is difficult to imagine the Aristotles, Platos and, Socrates of the world emerging from a Greece subject to the Persian empire). And without the magnificent defeat at Thermopylae, that victory might never have come.

But we are getting a little ahead of ourselves. Other battles awaited. At Artemisium, fought within a few days of Leonidas' heroics, Greek and Persian fleets engaged in the naval counterpart to Thermopylae. Persian losses, multiplied by a violent storm that destroyed 200 ships, were heavy, but so were those suffered by the Greeks under the brilliant Athenian ruffian Themistocles, who withdrew his battered fleet to Salamis across the water from Athens.

With Thermopylae forced open, the Persian army poured through and flooded south. Athens fell. The Acropolis and her defenders were put to the sword then burnt to the ground. As Tom Holland writes in his history of the Persian Wars, 'The great storehouse of Athenian memories, accumulated over centuries – the city's very past – was wiped out in a couple of hours.'

At Salamis later that summer, once again the grandstanding Xerxes selected higher ground from which to watch his hordes romp to victory, this time by sea. The imperial throne was set down on the base of Mount Aegaleos across the strait. According to Herodotus, 'whenever he saw one of his officers behaving with distinction, he would find out his name, and his secretaries wrote it down, together with his city and parentage'. But as the hours passed, Xerxes' secretaries had less and less good news to record. Themistocles' stroke of genius in luring the Persian fleet into the narrow straits, where their numerical advantage no longer worked in their favour but positively counted against them, wreaked havoc. Half of the Persian fleet of some 700 fighting vessels were sunk or captured. Greek losses were just forty ships. When the remarkable Artemisia, his only female commander, was pointed out to him fighting with conspicuous gallantry and success, Herodotus reports a furious Xerxes remarking, 'My men have turned into women, my women into men.' And with that the Great King bowed out of the wars and returned to Sardis, unable to stomach the sight of further Greek resistance. Buoyed by events at Thermopylae, the Greeks had dealt a mortal blow to the greatest ever invasion.

Xerxes left behind his general Mardonius to prosecute the rest of the campaign. In the high summer of 479 BC, Greeks and Persians faced each other one last time on the battlefield at Plataea. Rallying to the defence of a nation that had yet to be founded, the Greeks mustered the largest ever army of hoplites, a force of 40,000 men hunkered down on the slopes of Mount Cithaeron. Mardonius' Persians, swelled with the ranks of turncoat Thebans, probably outnumbered them two to one, but his men were lightly armed and armoured. It was a desperately hard-fought battle, the advantage swinging like a pendulum between the sides. One of the decisive moments came with the very public killing of the Persian commander Masistius, brought to the ground after a well-aimed shot had felled his horse. Then followed a far more damaging loss, when Mardonius himself, astride his white charger, was killed by a Spartan missile. His death hastened the rout. The hybrid army of squabbling Spartans, Athenians, Tegeans and Corinthians, boosted by smaller contingents from a host of other Greek cities, had prevailed. Tradition has it that on the same day as the Persians stumbled to a calamitous defeat at Plataea, Greek forces smashed the Persian fleet at the battle of Mycale, off the Ionian island of Samos in the Aegean, putting an ignominious end to Xerxes' invasion in a crescendo of violence. The Great King and his empire never recovered. He was assassinated in 465.

The few had defeated the many in the most momentous clash of civilisations. The odds had counted heavily against the Greeks. Victory had appeared inconceivable, the consequences of defeat incalculable. As Hegel wrote with the benefit of twenty-four centuries of hindsight, the history of the world 'hung trembling in the balance' as the two sides did their worst. The fractious Greek mainland and archipelago had united to repel a far more powerful enemy. Invaders from the east had met defenders in the west and the encounter proved decisive. So decisive, in fact, that east became East and west became West. It was Herodotus, in his unrivalled account of the Persian Wars, who supplied the capital letters. Never again would Persia attempt a conquest of Greece.

Something truly extraordinary had happened.

Something equally extraordinary followed. To give it its familiar shorthand, it was the golden age of Greece. From the vantage point of the twenty-first century, fabled fifth-century BC Greece looks like a small and sunlit world of limitless possibility, excellence and invention. Human civilisation seemed to soar to the heights. The glorious military triumphs were just one aspect of this sudden supremacy.

Off the battlefield the achievements were even more remarkable. With Athens as its centre, there was an efflorescence of Greek culture. Drama took root and tragedy was born. Sculpture discovered lines whose easy beauty came close to perfection. Architecture evolved into models of grace still aspired to – and slavishly copied – in the modern world. The investigation of the human condition began in philosophical earnest. Painting developed into a fine art. The concentration of genius within such a short space of time in such a small city is difficult to fathom. Athens was the beacon which attracted the most brilliant minds of the Greek world.

J. C. Stobart encapsulated it in *The Glory that was Greece* (1911): 'One Athenian family', he wrote, 'might have known Miltiades, Themistocles, Aeschylus, Sophocles, Euripides, Socrates, Phidias, Pericles, Anaxagoras, Aristophanes, Herodotus, Thucydides, Polygnotus, and Ictinus.' To that list might be added the orator Antiphon, the musician Damon, philosophers Protagoras and Democritus, the paradoxical Zeno, the prizewinning comic poets Cratinus and Crates, Cimon the statesman and admiral, Hippocrates of medical fame ... When you think that some of these great men also had day jobs, that Socrates served in the army, that Sophocles was a senior military official, that Thucydides was a general and Antiphon briefly at the head of the state, you start to appreciate that the gods had blessed this modest little corner of Attica with staggering talent.

Only one of those men from the fifth-century Greek *Who's Who* concerns us here. It is tempting to argue that rather than being outshone by these brilliant contemporaries – a more daunting list of which it is virtually impossible to contrive – he blazed across the stage with his own inimitable sparkle and chutzpah. His invention, though he may not have known it at the time, was one of the greatest of all: history. And his lifetime's preoccupation was to explain the most incomprehensible drama of his lifetime. How had the Greeks managed to overcome the might of Persia?

Herodotus and his fellow Greeks knew that something astonishing had taken place on the mainland and in the waters of the Aegean. You can hear in those opening lines – in the desire to ensure that 'human achievements may not become forgotten in time, and great and marvellous deeds ... may not be without their glory; and especially to show why the two peoples fought each other' – the insistent question, some forty years or so after Xerxes' invasion had been sent packing: *What the hell happened?* The Persian Wars had changed the world as Greeks – and Persians – knew it. Turned it upside down.

Herodotus chose his moment to invent history and the West brilliantly. The Persian Wars were still within living memory, allowing him to talk to survivors, veterans and witnesses to help him understand how they happened and why.

History has come a long way since Herodotus. Our innately human fascination with the past has guaranteed that. Ask people why they thronged to Pall Mall to celebrate Queen Elizabeth II's golden jubilee, for example, and chances are you'll hear they wanted 'to be a part of history'. As a species, we are inordinately vain. History is our mirror.

Yet the puzzling irony about the history Herodotus invented is this. Although he demonstrated an extraordinary breadth of vision, the historians he sired for the best part of 2,500 years proved acutely short-sighted. At almost any point during that time, the answer to the age-old question (and title of Carr's classic monograph), *What is History?*, was straightforward. History was the exclusive pageant of kings, battles, empires, statesmen and laws, what was later called political and constitutional history. The rest of the human race, the seething mass of men and women who weren't monarchs, statesmen or generals, simply weren't invited. When Carr wrote that Herodotus found 'few disciples in the ancient world' he neglected to say there weren't very many for the next two millennia either. It was the uniquely political model of Thucydides, emphatically not that of Herodotus, which historians followed, right into the twentieth century.

Only with the birth of social history – presented as the 'new history' by the American historian James Harvey Robinson in 1912 – did the freewheeling spirit of Herodotean inquiry return. History, ever since, has rolled back the barriers. The historian's proper field of inquiry has expanded dizzyingly across miles and miles of uncharted terrain. It is perhaps the greatest posthumous tribute Herodotus could have hoped for. There is economic history, women's history, demographic history, intellectual history, feminist history, gender history, sexual history, black history, attitudinal history, microhistory, oral history, cultural history, environmental history, psychohistory, history of history, and so it goes on. Historians no longer blush when they say they study the history of slaves, witches, criminals, deviants, capitalists, farmers, virgins.

Later we will come across brand-new history textbooks in which the echoes of Herodotus sound like thunder. We will hear them in the stories of famines, earthquakes and plagues, sexual assignations, battlefield reporting, sporting achievements, religious rites and regulations, personal letters between husbands and wives, atrocities, drinking songs and madcap journeys.

History rumbles on like an insatiable omnivore, devouring everything before it. Science, economics, business, agriculture, anthropology, exploration, art, literature, law, sex, love, sport, the full spectrum of human life feeds its relentless hunger. In the 1980s, postmodernism mounted a fierce attack on the very discipline of history, challenging its assumptions and methods and arguing that history was merely one discourse among many. Many historians wondered whether Herodotus' creation would survive the onslaught. What happened? History simply swallowed up postmodernist theory, keeping what was useful (a little) and spitting out the rest (a lot).

Outside the world of academe, storytelling is prized again, literary talent is admired and thrilling historical narratives are eagerly consumed by record numbers. (Inside academe is another matter. Carr rightly dismissed the 'vast and growing mass of dry-as-dust factual histories, of minutely specialised monographs of would-be historians knowing more and more about less and less, sunk without trace in an ocean of facts'. That mass is still growing.)

We have come a long way but we have also come full circle. Historians may not realise it, but Herodotus is back.

———————

When you read Herodotus, you discover a wonderful companion. He kept the globe-trotting Polish war correspondent and writer Ryszard Kapuściński company for most of his life, a voice of sanity, restraint and humanity amid the barbarism of the many conflicts he covered. He never left the side of another wartime devotee, Count László de Almásy, the enigmatic Hungarian soldier, spy and explorer whose real-life exploits in North Africa were fictionalised in Michael Ondaatje's novel *The English Patient*. The Oscar-winning film was such a hit that sales of the *Histories* went stratospheric.

One of the joys of Herodotus, and there are many, is that you can dip in and out at whim, pick him up for a foray among the Scythians or a blood-curdling battle in Greece, join him on his architectural survey of Egypt or on a grand tour of ancient-world geography, take him on holiday, read him on the loo, there's no end to it.

Over the years I have come back again and again to Herodotus. People do that with books all the time, of course; there's nothing unusual about it. But with Herodotus it's different. You return not to the *Histories* so much as to its author. It's not the book, in other words, it's the man: his voice and his thoughts, his hopes, jokes and asides, a personality so obviously effervescent, startlingly modern in outlook, highly amusing, freedom-loving, broad-minded and humane. In time I started to think of him as the ideal travel companion, though we never went much further than the beach together.

I remember reading him one afternoon beneath a slate-grey Norfolk sky unravelling across a wilderness of sand. Skeins of pink-footed geese arrowed across the gloaming in their thousands, honking away like pigs possessed as they dropped out of the cloud, gently spiralling down to form a tufty grey carpet across the reclaimed saltmarshes. The wintering birds were a reminder of the dark months ahead and I found myself longing for Herodotus' turquoise world, a light so piercing you had to squint to see anything, the warmth of a topaz sun that wasn't a wan white disc besieged by cloud, a limpid sea you wanted to swim in rather than one so gaspingly cold it was a childish dare just to plunge in for a few seconds. I wanted olives and oranges, feta cheese and falafel, bobbing fishing boats and battlefields, pyramids, tombs and temples, marble columns hurled across sylvan groves in Ozymandian disarray. I wanted grand civilisation and the birth of history, not darkness at three o'clock and cold wet patches on my moleskins.

Idly, I started wondering where the two of us – because we were a team now – could go. Willed into life as the Norfolk chill took hold, a Herodotean expedition started to emerge from the frost-wrapped fields. It made more sense the longer I considered it, as anything sun-kissed and exotic will in the draughty ooze of a British winter. Rather than just returning to Herodotus and the *Histories*, I would go one better and take Herodotus with me and together we would return to his (much warmer) world. I would travel with the world's first travel writer. A journey in history with the Father of History.

At a time when the confrontation between East and West was, once again, at the centre of international affairs, who better to take than the man who described their first clash? When the Western world was fretting about the spread of freedom and democracy to benighted parts, who could be a more engaging mind than the man who recorded the birth of democracy in Athens, who wondered aloud about tyranny and freedom 2,500 years ago? Cultural awareness, insults against religion, the dangers of offending foreign civilisations, it was all straight from Herodotus, the world's first multiculturalist. 'Everyone without exception believes his own native customs, and the religion he was brought up in, to be the best,' he writes in a telling remark whose truth has reverberated throughout history.

Unlike so many of the other ancients, there was nothing formal or fusty about him. To hell with Nietzsche and his patronising remark that 'To old age belongs the old man's business of looking back and casting up his accounts, of seeking consolation in the memories of the past, in historical culture.' Herodotus had been dead for something like 2,423 years and I was wading into my fourth decade, but we both still had a spring in our step. As did history itself which, not unlike its father Herodotus, was beyond fashion. History was life's only guaranteed growth industry.

Travelling with a dead man held a number of other, more pragmatic attractions. There would never be any arguments, none of the tedious irritations that come from spending too much time on the road with one person. I wouldn't come to blows with him over pinching the aisle seat on a cramped bus in Greece. His ham-fisted attempts to speak foreign languages, or perhaps his linguistic brilliance, couldn't annoy me. I wouldn't have to lend him money, he wouldn't keep the lights on after I wanted to go to sleep and he would never embarrass me in front of a pretty girl.

I began to see Herodotus all over the place. He wouldn't leave me alone. A newspaper report revealed he had been quite correct in suggesting – contrary to received archaeological opinion – that the Etruscans originally came from Lydia, now western Turkey, before resettling in Italy. DNA analysis confirmed it. It turned out history had proved him right in all sorts of other instances where his account had been dismissed, from sacred prostitution and Assyrian burials in oil to the length of the Royal Road from Sardis to Susa and the size of grain in Mesopotamia.

He started appearing when least expected. One evening he even stole into the final scenes of Ridley Scott's dystopian classic *Blade Runner*. The dying replicant Roy, played by a platinum-shocked Rutger Hauer, was recalling the marvels he had seen in his short life, the time he watched attack ships on fire off the shoulder of Orion, bright as magnesium, the mesmerising sight of C-beams glittering in the dark near Tannhäuser Gate. 'All those moments will be lost in time, like tears in rain,' were his dying words. There it was again, that heart-rendingly human need to record the past, to lend meaning to the meaninglessness of our lives and achievements, to ensure that they were not, in Herodotus' phrases, 'forgotten in time' or 'without their glory'.

There were some nagging questions and a biographical void to contend with. Piecing together the skeletal records of his life, I wanted to know where Herodotus went after Halicarnassus and why, precisely what was his role in the coup against the tyrant Lygdamis and if he really was exiled to Samos. It would be helpful to know how long he stayed on the island he seemed to know so well, where he lived and how he travelled. What about his circle of friends and acquaintances during the sojourn in Athens? Was he a friend of the tragedian Sophocles, who composed a poem for him, and the great statesman Pericles? Did he receive Athenian patronage as Plutarch suggested (in an attempt to make him look like a paid hack)? Might he have delivered a public reading from his *Histories* at the Olympics in an enterprising bid for publicity, as Lucian claimed? How long did he travel around the Aegean and Mediterranean to research his masterpiece, where did he write it, how many years did it take, and did he retire to the Greek colony of Thurii to put brush-pen to papyrus?

There would never be any answers. Herodotus' life was an almost entirely blank canvas, with just the faintest pencil line here and there suggestive of place and movement. None of that mattered, I came to see. The trick would be to take Herodotus wherever I could (as long as it was warm), to places he knew or visited, to those he wrote about, might have dropped in on, recorded in jaunty anecdotes, to cities and monuments, temples, rivers, mountains, deserts. I would take a leaf from his book and give myself the widest possible remit, exploring history and histories, collecting wonders and marvels, plunging into digressions, taking excursions into sex, war and religion, clashes of civilisations, adventures in hubris and nemesis.

Where would we go? Greece, certainly, the heart of Herodotus' world. Egypt was another certainty, notwithstanding the sniffiest suspicions of academics in the so-called 'Liar School' of Herodotus, who treat much of the *Histories*, especially his travel claims, with glacial distrust.

*The Times Comprehensive Atlas of the World* started competing for desk space with various editions of Herodotus, edging out Cicero, Gibbon and Thucydides, overwhelming the squabbling duumvirate of Carr and Elton (who had returned to the fray), giving the *Oxford Dictionary of the Classical World* a decent run for its money, bludgeoning the Cadogan guides to Greece and Egypt into squashed submission and banishing the contemptible Plutarch to the section of my bookshelves reserved for minor writers. This wasn't just an atlas, it was a Herodotean all-terrain vehicle. Coolly, it transformed a mooted expedition dreamt up on a wind-lashed beach into an itinerary of infinite range and possibility.

From its pages rose the splintering backbone of the Taygetus mountains in the southern Peloponnese, jaded Sparta, faded Olympia, the tumbled columns of Corinth, divine Delphi and dreamlike Athens, languidly east across the tepid Aegean to the island of Samos and its trio of architectural treasures that caught Herodotus' eye, on to the Turkish mainland and the Persian empire that was, his hometown of Halicarnassus–Bodrum, the coastal jewels of Miletus, Priene, Ephesus. What else? To Plate 84 and the unfurling of Africa, the sapphire cleft of the Nile hissing through the Western Desert and the roiling dunes of the storm-tossed Sand Sea that curl around the Oracle of Ammon in Siwa, where Alexander confirmed his world-conquering destiny, on to storied Memphis, monumental, many-templed Thebes, a lingering digression to Cairo, self-styled Mother of the World with her age-old history and the flaunting pyramids of Giza that so engrossed Herodotus two-and-a-half millennia ago. Unable to stop myself, I flicked through to Plate 35 and there was the beginning of the world, the birth of civilisation and the dawn of history, Mesopotamia, from the Greek for 'between the rivers'. Hemmed in by the Tigris and the Euphrates, Babylon winked at me challengingly, daring me to visit. On the atlas it was irresistible, but with the war in Iraq it seemed a Herodotean step too far.

There was no doubt about it. A journey was taking root. I started buying maps and books and more maps and more books and gradually retreated into the sun-bleached world of fifth-century BC Greece, North Africa and the Middle East.

My wife, unmoved by the obvious glory of the Herodotean trail, started panicking. 'What about the dog?' she asked.

# PART I
## Turkey

*They are very fond of wine and no one is allowed to vomit or urinate in the presence of another person.*

*Themselves they consider in every way superior to everyone else in the world . . .*

Herodotus, *Histories*, 1.133; 1.134

# I

# Priestesses with Beards

*My first answer therefore to the question 'What is history?' is that it is
a continuous process of interaction between the historian and his facts, an
unending dialogue between the present and the past.*

E. H. Carr, *What is History?* (1961)

WHERE BETTER TO begin a Herodotean voyage of discovery
than in the historian's hometown of Bodrum? In Herodotus'
day, when it was known as Halicarnassus, it was a Dorian town on a
bulbous promontory extending from the south-western corner of
Asia Minor. If you imagine the peninsula as the head of a dragon
poised to strike a wandering whale in the Aegean (the whale being
the Greek island of Kos), then Halicarnassus was the underside of
the dragon's neck, where the mainland torso squeezes into the
promontory.

Two-and-a-half thousand years ago, this coastline was dotted with
Greek cities and was steeped in Greek culture on the margins of Asia.
It wasn't a bad stepping-off point for a man who liked to travel. Egypt
was less than 400 miles away to the south. The islands of the Aegean
and the Greek cities on the mainland – Miletus, Priene, Ephesus –
were on his doorstep. Across the water, beyond the haphazard sprinkling of the Dodecanese and the Cyclades, great Athens glimmered like
a beacon. To his east, the centre of the Persian empire, Sardis, Babylon
and beyond.

Today the resort town is steeped not so much in Greek as in
European culture, both elite and popular. Bodrum is beloved by two
very different types of traveller: at one end of the spectrum are the

primly polo-shirted yachting Euro-bankers and their lustrous wives, on the other British package tourists hunting for sun, sex, beer and, in some cases, a good fight.

An early Herodotean challenge. This may have been his home-town – as the first three words of the *Histories*, 'Herodotus of Halicarnassus . . .', proclaim – but our chatty historian says precious little about it.

There are just seven references to Halicarnassus in 600 pages, and this is one of them. The others don't add much to a picture of the city either, concentrating as they do on people rather than place. He mentions a Halicarnassian athlete called Agasicles who got too big for his boots after winning a bronze tripod and instead of dedicating it to Apollo, as was the custom, took it home and hung it on his wall, which got Halicarnassus struck off temple privileges. More bizarrely, he refers to people east of the city who used to receive warnings of impending disasters 'by the priestess of Athene growing a long beard, a thing which has actually happened on three occasions'. Then there's the cameo part played by the opportunist Halicarnassian mercenary Phanes who escapes from Egypt and shamelessly advises the Persian Great King Cambyses how to invade his former master's kingdom across the desert. He tells us that Xerxes' only female admiral, the doughty Artemisia, was half Halicarnassian. And finally there's the brave Halicarnassian Xenagoras who intervenes in an about-to-be-fatal dispute between Darius' son Masistes and a Persian general whom he's roundly abused ('To call a man "worse than a woman" is the greatest insult one can offer a Persian,' Herodotus explains). Xenagoras' quick response saves Masistes' life.

And, as far as Halicarnassus goes, that's it. This is all very well, and a lot of it is hugely entertaining, as you'd expect from Herodotus, but it isn't much to go on. Understandably, Herodotus tends to go in for more exuberant description when he visits foreign places, which would have been of much greater interest to his less-travelled Greek audiences. They would have been less than riveted, one suspects, by detailed accounts of Halicarnassus.

Biographically, there isn't a great deal to go on, either. The first page of my Penguin *Histories* makes this abundantly clear. 'Few facts are known about the life of Herodotus.' Brief, brutal and incontrovertibly true.

What about clues in the *Histories*? You'd think, with all those 1,086 first-person comments, that he might slip in some personal background, tell us something about his childhood and the problems he had with his parents as a teenager, the late nights and the occasional binges, the feuds and friendships. He could share the early years on the road with us, the scrapes and adventures, the highs and lows of his journeys, but he doesn't. It wasn't his thing. So much left unsaid, unrecorded, forgotten in time. We think about all the gossipy sexual titbits in his work and we wonder about the women he loved and whether he got married and had children. Could there be a Herodotean line somewhere in twenty-first-century Greece, Turkey or Italy? We are left with a host of chirpy asides and gossipy wink-winks that offer a tantalising glimpse of a man on the move.

The *Suda*, a tenth-century Byzantine lexicon, gives us a few biographical crumbs, but it's pretty thin and, besides, its reliability is uncertain. It tells us that Herodotus was the son of Lyxes and Dryo, brother of Theodorus and nephew or cousin of the epic poet Panyassis. He was exiled to Samos by Lygdamis, the tyrant of Halicarnassus. Later, he is said to have returned, assisted in a coup against Lygdamis, only to be sent packing again, this time by his fellow citizens. At some point after this, perhaps following a stint in Athens, he may have joined the fledgling Greek colony at Thurii in the southern instep of Italy, where he may have died (Aristotle knew him as Herodotus of Thurii). It's all a little precarious.

———

The Dorian colony of old is today the land of the laissez-faire summer holiday. Bodrum's promotional guide sets the tone, warning women to expect lots of attention from 'the local Turkish man' and advising them how to minimise it by wearing clothes that do not reveal 'too much naked skin'.

In fact, the sexual free-for-all – undeniably one of the place's chief attractions for the younger generation – is not so far from Herodotus, after all. The *Histories* is vigorous testimony to his boundless fascination with sex. He writes of incestuous sex (father and daughter), divine sex (god and priestess), licentious sex, romantic sex, adulterous sex, comic sex (a king with impotence), animal sex, bestiality (woman and goat) and necrophilia (embalmer and corpse). There's no end of it.

Bodrum's promiscuity recalls Herodotus' notes on the Nasamones tribe of Libya, where 'It is the custom, at a man's first marriage, to give a party, at which the bride is enjoyed by each of the guests in turn; they take her one after the other, and then give her a present ...' Or the Gindanes tribe where women wear leather bands round their ankles, indicating the number of their lovers: 'whoever has the greatest number enjoys the greatest reputation because she has been loved by the greatest number of men'.

The crowds of Pied Piper girls in the skimpiest outfits, trailing shiny-shirted, silk-tongued Turkish admirers behind them, remind me of another passage in the *Histories*. Do these girls' fathers know what their daughters are getting up to at night or are they like the Thracians, of whom Herodotus wrote, 'they exercise no control over young girls, allowing them to have intercourse with any man they please'?

The Bodrum waterfront is the busiest part of town, as it surely was in Herodotus' time. Boats coming in, boats going out. On and off step fishermen, island-hoppers, sailors, shoppers, day-trippers, traders, touts and toddlers, restaurateurs, commuters, businessmen, students, hoteliers, hustlers and sunbathers. Across the water, on a rocky outcrop beyond the leafless forest of jostling masts, the town's most celebrated historical landmark, the fifteenth-century Castle of St Peter, its splendid war-battered bulk jutting out into the sea beneath a boastfully blue sky, marks the central prong in the '3'-shaped harbour. Further off, begin-ning to be lost in the rebounding haze, is the Greek island of Kos, raising her smooth rump from the sea to bask scandalously in the sun.

It is the first reminder of Muslim East and Christian West in close proximity. In Herodotus' time, this was the great fault-line between two civilisations, East and embryonic West at war before Islam and Christianity, those tireless pretexts for conflict, had even been invented. Old rivals Turkey and Greece, Them and Us, the Other and the EU, descendants, metaphorical and literal, of the Persians and Greeks –

Dictatorship versus Democracy – who eyed each other across the Aegean with such suspicion two-and-a-half millennia ago. These warm waters, bristling with navies, foaming with blood and consequence, played host to the world's greatest conflicts of that era, at Marathon, Thermopylae, Salamis, Plataea and Mycale, each battle meticulously recorded by Herodotus. Yet no sooner had the mighty menace of the Persians been rebuffed than the exhausted Greeks, tired of looking east, turned inwards and against each other for the next three decades, Athens and her allies versus Sparta and hers in the Peloponnesian Wars that erupted in the Greek historian's final years and tore that world apart.

Today these scattered islands and the Turkish mainland, too sun-shattered to rouse themselves from Aegean lethargy, go about their dozy business, the once blood-spilling rivalry reduced to competition for tourist euros, pounds and dollars, the odd gripe about divided Cyprus, and Turkish membership of the EU.

Peace has brought plenty. It has paid for the sleek white yachts moored in what looks like a millionaires-only marina, where the only rivalry comes down to size and price tag. The owners go to impressive lengths to show off their impressive lengths and the all-over quality of their tans, posing on decks with the complacency of the very rich while their sun-polished, slim-waisted wives, chic in sunglasses, shop in the nearby boutiques, gliding between Polo, Façonnable, Nautica and Tommy Hilfiger, disappointed by the diamonds in the Turkish jewellers, before reuniting with their husbands to pick at Caesar Salads and sip white-wine spritzers in the Marina Yacht Club. These are the modern aristocrats of Bodrum at play, the soft-skinned second-home crowd from Istanbul and the yachting bankers and hedge-fund managers of Europe. Herodotus would have recognised these global citizens as members of the same elite tribe to which he belonged: footloose, prosperous and confident.

Çanan is an excitable local historian with a dark bob and flashing eyes. When she hears I have come to Bodrum to begin a Herodotean quest, she becomes almost apoplectic with enthusiasm. 'Oh, this is a great idea! No one is interested in Herodotus any more, believe me. I've been trying to get the city to make more of him but they never listen. All they're interested in is making money from sailing and discos.'

She says this in a spirit of despair at the city council's obvious philistinism, as though between making more of Herodotus and making money from tourists there should surely be no contest. She shoots me a warning look. 'Of course, everyone thinks Herodotus was a Greek,' she says, eyeing me carefully to see if I share this delusion. 'He wasn't. He was a Carian.'

In fact, Herodotus' Halicarnassus was a Dorian, not a Carian, town on a highly Hellenised coast. It used the Ionic Greek dialect in its public inscriptions, the same language Herodotus used to write his *Histories*. The non-Greek Carian civilisation, which was subject to Persian rule, came from the hinterland to the east. Regular intercourse between the two communities, the most ardent frequently leading to intermarriage, is thought to have contributed to a cosmopolitanism – already natural to a prominent port town – which shaped Herodotus' enlightened and distinctly ahead-of-his-time views about other cultures. It also led to Greeks with Carian names – such as his father Lyxes and one of his uncles or cousins, the epic poet Panyassis – and Carians with Greek names. Herodotus may have been a multiculturalist before the term existed. But he certainly wasn't a Carian.

The Carians, he writes, were 'by far the most famous of all nations' due to their military service for the semi-mythical Minos of Crete whose conquests spanned the Aegean. Given his interest in strange sexual practices, Herodotus must have been unaware of the legislative pederasty Minos is said to have introduced as a form of population control on the island, because unlike Aristotle he makes no mention of it. Minos is supposed to have separated the men from women and encouraged 'sexual relations among the males', conjuring homosexuals from a captive heterosexual market.

Herodotus goes on to say of the Carians, 'The Greeks are indebted to them for three inventions: fitting crests on helmets, putting devices on shields, and making shields with handles.' He relates that while they claim to be native to the mainland, the Cretans say the Carians were originally islanders who were driven out by the Dorians and Ionians and forced to resettle. Indulging his love of the bizarre, he mentions expatriate Carians in Egypt who 'cut their foreheads with knives' during the festival of Isis at Busiris to show they are foreigners and not Egyptians. He also writes about them *en passant* in lists of the various armies in which they served, describes their role in the revolt against Darius, remarks how a number of them were given land in Egypt by the pharaoh Psammetichus (mid-seventh century BC) to thank them for their military assistance in helping him seize the throne, and gives them a tragically swift finale at the hands of the Persians who defeat them without breaking into too much of a sweat. And that is the end of the Carians in the *Histories*.

One afternoon Çanan and I make an appointment to visit the museum. We walk along the waterfront, past the main drag of bars, restaurants, cafés, shops, motorcyclists and music. After the tyrannical neatness of the marina and yacht club the rest of Bodrum harbour revels in scruffiness and lazy, sun-baked charm: boats and boat-trips for people with less money. Some are weatherworn, recycled fishing boats, brazenly tatty. Others, more picturesque still, are the famous Bodrum gulets, big-bottomed boats with broad beams, rounded sterns, two masts, vast white sails and striped hulls, multi-coloured matrons of the Aegean. Small gangways, advertising daily island trips, lead to the gulets' sterns, many of them crowned with the Turkish flag, white crescent and star on a red background. Fishing nets dry in the sun. Piped music and the sweet smell of suncream waft across the waterfront, mingling with the crowd of pink-skinned sunseekers blinking in the white light.

Çanan, a slim, diminutive woman harmoniously dressed in a black linen dress, wide-brimmed sunhat and Jackie Kennedy sunglasses, winces at the sight of these visitors. 'These people are not interested in Herodotus,' she says darkly, as though this is an unforgivable offence.

We drift on towards the castle past a prominent sign on the seafront:

> Come on our Boat for Fun and Frolic,
> The Captain is an Alcoholic.

Herodotus was probably not a natural Booze Cruise man, though the concept might have amused him. He is easier to picture in Halicarnassus' harbour taverns, talking to sailors about the journeys they had made, the foreign lands they had visited, quizzing them about distances, climates, cultures, monuments and languages, standing a few rounds to loosen their tongues, palling up with merchants and foreign passengers from North Africa, Cyprus, Persia, Palestine and across the Greek archipelago in his efforts to understand and explain the world about him.

The writer of the *Histories* was not, it is probably fair to say, the shy, retiring, solitary traveller with his nose buried in a papyrus, aloof from his fellow men. He would have been out and about, as his writing suggests, engaged and engaging, talking to anyone with a story to tell, collecting facts and folktale fiction, histories, genealogies, legends and anecdotes, entertaining us at every turn. His inquiries and investigations did not consist of analysing, synthesising and criticising other people's research from the comfort of an office and library. He didn't have that luxury. He could never have been an armchair historian even if he had wanted to be because there were no other historians to study. He was the first.

'Here he is!' Çanan grins, interrupting these thoughts.

Outside the museum, which is housed in the castle, a bust is mounted on a stone plinth. At last! Herodotus in the town of his birth. Up to this point, he has proved all too predictably elusive. There is no Bar Herodotus, no Herodotus Hotel – though there once was – nothing in Bodrum to commemorate her most distinguished son.

It is a measure of the desperation of the writer in search of his ancient quarry that such a trivial find should elicit such unbridled joy. I was beginning to think that searching for a Greek hero in Turkey was doomed. The superficially secularised land of Atatürk, founder and first president of the Turkish Republic, might not be able to accommodate such a powerful symbol of Greek civilisation. But here he is, finally, centre-stage no less, guarding the entrance to the museum, a seer-like figure with wide blank eyes, a prominent nose, high forehead and a gently flowing beard. His hair is so neatly trimmed it resembles a skullcap, conferring a prophetic calm. His lips, pressed between moustache and beard, are etched into horizontal neutrality. The sculptor has deliberately omitted both pupils and irises so that the eyeballs are completely plain. Yet rather than dehumanising him the effect is to give Herodotus the austere air of a visionary, blind but all-seeing, unruffled by time, staring out to sea expressionless in stone. Beneath the bust a plaque supplies a potted biography in Turkish and English.

> Herodotos
> B.C. 480–425
> He was from Bodrum (Ancient Halikarnassos)
> He is known as the Father of History

After a few reverent photographs, I join Çanan inside the castle. Like many buildings of a similar vintage it has been rudely bastardised over the centuries. In 1522, fearing an imminent attack from the Ottoman sultan Suleiman the Magnificent, the Grand Master of Rhodes sent some of his knights across the water to fortify the castle in Bodrum. They attended to their task with the sort of zeal that today would land them in prison after a high-profile court case. Casting around for some decent material with which to make their repairs, they headed over to the nearby site of the Mausoleum, once one of the Seven Wonders of the ancient world. First they dug up the steps of white marble above ground level and then, when they had exhausted that source, continued digging below ground level for more stone, ransacking the remains of the monument with a ruthlessness that would have pleased the Grand Master.

> It was thus that this magnificent tomb, which ranked among the seven wonders of the world, after having escaped the fury of the barbarians, and remained standing for the space of 2,247 years, was discovered and destroyed to repair the Castle of St Peter, by the Knights of Rhodes, who immediately after this were driven completely out of Asia by the Turks.

Not Bodrum's tourist guide, but the words of Sir Charles Newton, the British archaeologist who in 1857 became the first person to excavate the Mausoleum properly. Yet who was he to pronounce so piously against the knightly mischief? You could argue (if you felt strongly enough about it) that Newton was an imperialist hypocrite who behaved far worse than the knights because a good deal of his excavations ended up back in London, where they can be viewed today in

the Mausoleum Room of the British Museum. At least the knights
left the fruits of their mausolean pillaging in Bodrum, several hundred
yards away across the harbour.

Çanan leads the way up some steps to an office and introduces me
to Oğuz Alpözen with a deference I have not yet suspected in her. He
is a stern-faced man who looks more prize fighter than museum director. The impression is of a tough who has been shoved into a dark suit
against his wishes. A cowboy string tie hangs around his neck, an
unexpected sartorial flourish in a man otherwise untroubled by
fashion. A permanent frown, together with a pugnacious hauteur and
impatience, suggests he is not going to talk about Herodotus for long.
He has been in the museum almost his entire career, arriving in 1962
as an archaeology student, later becoming its first official underwater
archaeologist and, in 1978, its director.

The walls of his office are covered in framed exhibition posters.
There are piles of books, tables bearing pieces of glass retrieved from
ancient shipwrecks, amphorae, kitschy watercolours of the castle set
against a sea and sky of sickly turquoise. It is the office of a man who
has been immersed (often literally) in history, Herodotus' brainchild,
for most of his life. His present has been the past.

'I had the statue of Herodotus erected at the entrance to the
museum in 1995,' he begins with some pomp. 'He is one of the most
distinguished citizens of Bodrum.'

I ask him whether he would like to see a little more Herodotus here.
The Greek is virtually invisible. Alpözen shrugs.

'I have shown my respect to him. But I have no connection with the
city, really. I am just a lonely old man in his castle.' He says this in a way
which implies he is really a bit of a player. 'Of course, I would like to see
more of him in the town,' he goes on, 'a Hotel Herodotus, for example,
or something like that. You should talk to the mayor about this. When
Çanan wrote to the authorities suggesting we had more recognition of
Herodotus in our town, do you know what their reply was?'

I didn't.

'They said, "We already have a junction named after him."'

This is true. Inland, on a main road high above the harbour, there
is a busy crossroads with a petrol station on one side. I have already

made my pilgrimage to the site, wondering at the time whether this was the most appropriate way for his hometown to honour him. Great men have statues made of them, standing proudly before parliaments and in parks, bestriding avenues, dominating piazzas. Buildings, streets, museum wings and galleries, hotels and restaurants all bear their names. But a road junction? A road junction to remember the man who invented history?

Recollection of the town's snub to Herodotus has animated Alpözen. He never studied him at school, he says, but when he first came to Bodrum he immediately wanted to learn more about the historian. 'Herodotus is very important to me because he's the most important person from this town. That's why as museum director I put him in front of the castle. In the fifth century BC, no one knew what history was until Herodotus came along. Here, in our castle, we make history come alive. It grips visitors and transports them back hundreds of years. Gods and goddesses, kings, queens, knights and sailors from across the ages are brought back to life. There is history in the castle, in the shipwrecks we display in our museum, in the beautiful artefacts they reveal to us, the coins and jewellery, the stories of civilisations that otherwise would be lost to us. And it all began with Herodotus.'

He pauses and smiles. I almost fall off my chair in shock. 'A man came into the museum once and asked to see Herodotus' house. My coffee boy said he didn't know where his house was but he could show him Hotel Herodotus. Now even that has gone.'

The Hotel Herodotus was closed in the Nineties. That leaves a bust outside the castle and a nondescript road junction to commemorate the town's greatest son.

It isn't a case of a prophet without honour in his own country. This isn't his country any more. And that is the point. Herodotus was – Çanan's Carian protests aside – a Greek and his hometown of Halicarnassus is now called Bodrum and Bodrum is in Turkey. Herodotus might have been disappointed by this lack of public recognition but he is unlikely to have been surprised by it. As he noted throughout his *Histories*, different cultures have different customs. The dead are honoured – and buried, embalmed, worshipped even – in different ways in different countries. Empires rise and fall, great cities diminish over time, minnows prosper and grow. A corner of Greek culture has become Turkish. Given the often strained, sometimes downright hostile, bilateral relations between the two countries, Herodotus, the man who recorded the birth of the West, is an unlikely hero for Bodrum.

On the surface, then, there is little evidence of him here. But if you plunge beneath the surface, literally, rather than simply scratching at it, the intangible Herodotus reveals himself – obliquely, indirectly, magnificently – in one of the most spectacular finds of the twentieth century. Displayed in Bodrum's Museum of Underwater Archaeology in the heart of Alpözen's medieval castle, it is the most fitting, unconscious tribute his hometown could pay him. Had he been alive to see it, Herodotus would have been captivated.

In the summer of 1984, some 500 feet below the surface of the Mediterranean, the pioneering American underwater archaeologist (Herodotus would already have been on the edge of his seat) George Bass rested one of his fins on a boulder as he stood in front of the world's oldest shipwreck.

Before him, tumbling down a steep stretch of rocky seabed, loomed the outlines of jars, amphorae and copper ingots, the Late Bronze Age cargo of a ship that sank 3,300 years ago. Bass, founder of the Texas-based Institute of Nautical Archaeology (INA), had been diving along Turkey's Aegean coast for twenty-seven years excavating ancient shipwrecks. He had never come across anything like this. Nor did he, at that stage, have the slightest inkling of just how remarkable the contents of this sunken vessel – carrying what looked suspiciously like a royal cargo – would prove.

The initial tip came from Mehmed Çakir, a young sponge-diver who in 1982 told his captain he had seen 'metal biscuits with ears' on the seabed off the Uluburun promontory, around 130 miles south-east of Bodrum. That set off alarm bells. Bodrum's sponge-divers had specifically been asked to keep an eye out for these biscuits with ears, code for copper ingots produced within a relatively narrow period of

200–300 years within the Bronze Age. No one had ever excavated a boat from that period.

A preliminary survey was carried out in 1983, confirming a fifty-foot vessel from the fourteenth or thirteenth century BC. Looking at the pictures from that early survey, Bass quickly understood the importance of the wreck. 'We're looking at an archaeologist's dream,' he told a colleague.

Dendrochronological dating of a small piece of firewood – technology sadly unavailable to Herodotus during the course of his researches – indicated a date of approximately 1318 BC for the sinking of the ship. That made it the highpoint of the Late Bronze Age, when mankind was beginning to up the technological ante, moving away from bronze to the altogether greater potential – for war, agriculture, life – of iron. The difficulty with these sorts of too-long-ago dates is that they don't mean much to most of us. The Herodotean era is difficult enough to conjure up as it is. This vessel was almost a millennium older than that. The Bronze Age Greeks – or Mycenaeans – who sailed in her were the forefathers of Homer's mythical heroes, men like Agamemnon, Achilles and Odysseus who took to the seas a century later and sailed to Troy.

If we were to step into a time-travel machine today to make a 1,000-year journey through British history, we would have to go back through the shattering twentieth century of the Windsors, the transforming eighteenth and nineteenth centuries of the Hanoverians, across the trauma of the Stuarts and the glories of the Tudors, past the feuding Houses of York and Lancaster, past the Plantagenets, King John and Magna Carta to the opportunist, throne-seizing twelfth-century Norman king Henry I. To get back to the Late Bronze Age of the shipwreck, an Egyptian time-traveller would have to say farewell – probably with some relief – to the pharaonic President Mubarak and hurtle back to Tutankhamun and beyond. The *Uluburun*, as she was christened, was so ancient she made Herodotus look like an arriviste.

Bass assembled his dream team. The INA already had a Turkish base in Bodrum's Museum of Underwater Archaeology (it now has its own elegantly expensive headquarters in the hills above the harbour) so was well placed to survey and excavate the wreck. Over the next decade, his archaeologists made 22,500 dives at the site. The depth of the wreck ranged from 140 to 170 feet, with some artefacts having tumbled down as low as 200 feet beneath the surface. At those depths diving the site was fraught with danger.

From 1984 to 1994, they unearthed an expanding catalogue of treasures from seven civilisations of the eastern Mediterranean. The *Uluburun* contained products from the Mycenaeans, Canaanites, Cypriots, Egyptians, Kassites, Nubians and Assyrians. The 'metal biscuits with ears' were copper ingots shaped like oxhides, the ore for which was almost certainly mined in Cyprus. The cargo contained 354 of them, weighing approximately 10 tons. There was another ton of tin ingots. Mixing the two together would have created enough bronze to equip an entire army.

There was a ton of yellow resin, possibly to burn as incense, stored in 150 Canaanite amphorae. Next came 175 whole ingots of glass, the earliest ever found, in striking cobalt, turquoise and lavender. Among the scattered cargo were logs of Egyptian ebony, ostrich shells, elephant tusks, hippopotamus teeth, tortoise shells with which to make musical instruments, Cypriot ceramics, highly stylised drinking cups in the shape of rams' heads, copper cauldrons and bowls.

The *Uluburun* provided a fascinating window into the timeless, glittering world of women's jewellery. Assuming a substantial quantity of disposable income, Late Bronze Age upper-class woman in the eastern Mediterranean might have adorned herself with gold pendants and medallions bearing images of falcons, hooded cobras and fertility figures. Middle-class girls might have had to settle for something a little more modest, silver bangles, rings of shell inset with glass, signet rings of electrum, beads of agate, carnelian, quartz, faience, ostrich eggshell, Baltic amber and glass. Those who fancied something a little flashier might have plumped for a gold ring with swivel scarab setting. But the most dazzling treasure recovered, the Tiffany diamond necklace of its day, the *ne plus ultra* for the dazzlingly rich girl about town, was the fabulous gold scarab, the only one ever found in Asia Minor or the Aegean bearing the cartouche of Nefertiti, the famously beautiful wife of the eighteenth-dynasty, heretically monotheistic Egyptian pharaoh Akhenaten.

Apart from the jewellery, there were tin and bronze figurines, a golden chalice, duck-shaped ivory cosmetics containers, a trumpet carved from a hippopotamus tooth, bronze awls, drills, chisels, axes and saws. The crew, Cypriot or Canaanite – Bronze Age Phoenicians – evidently fished from the ship, for Bass's team found lead net and line sinkers, together with fishhooks, a harpoon, netting needles to repair the nets, even a bronze trident. Was this an early arms-dealing expedition, Bass's team asked, surveying the mass of tin and copper ingots, the bronze spearheads, arrowheads, swords and daggers?

The *Uluburun* offered a number of answers to the uncertainties surrounding Bronze Age international trade. It seemed likely, according to Bass, that ships like this once plied the Mediterranean on anticlockwise circular trade routes, sailing north-west from Canaanite Syria and Palestine to Cyprus, thence into the Aegean then back – sometimes from as far west as Italy and Sardinia – via North Africa and Egypt.

From a literary point of view there was no contest as to the greatest item discovered on the *Uluburun*: fragments of three notebook-sized folding wooden writing boards or diptychs, recessed to house a layer of beeswax for a stylus to scribble on. One of them, after careful reconstruction, was better preserved than the others, retaining two of its three cream ivory hinges. The inner faces of the boards were etched with crosshatched lines to retain the wax. The Moleskine notebook of its day, it was displayed to full dramatic effect beneath spotlights in its own case in the Bodrum Museum, together with a line from Homer's *Iliad*, Book 6: 'he sent him to Lycia and gave him baneful signs in a wooden writing tablet'.

Herodotus would have been delighted. He would surely have been thrilled to see that ancient Halicarnassus was now the Turkish headquarters of the Institute of Nautical Archaeology, where teams of young divers plunged into history every summer bringing lost fragments to the surface to reveal ever more information about our predecessors. And he would have been fascinated by this find above all others. These wooden tablets were a posthumous compliment from his hometown to the man who gave prose a good name. You couldn't have given him a better present. It was – by far – the world's oldest book.

# 2

# Underwater Herodotus

*Does history repeat itself, the first time as tragedy, the second time as farce?*
*No, that's too grand, too considered a process. History just burps, and we*
*taste again that raw-onion sandwich it swallowed centuries ago.*
Julian Barnes, *A History of the World in 10½ Chapters* (1989)

ONE AFTERNOON IN Bodrum I drop in on Tufan Turanli, the underwater archaeologist who worked with George Bass on the *Uluburun*. He was the diver on the cover of the December 1987 issue of *National Geographic* in which Bass announced the discovery to the world. In the picture he is looking to the right, his face and shoulders partially obscuring the magazine's title. Wearing a natty two-tone dive suit, he clutches what looks like a terrifically heavy four-handled copper ingot. On the seabed to his right are rows of encrusted amphorae illuminated by a powerful light. 'OLDEST KNOWN SHIPWRECK' is the headline.

My first impression of Turanli is more Greek god than Turkish diver. For some reason he makes me think of Alexander the Great. I don't know what Alexander looked like, I know that Turkey and Greece are old enemies, but none of that matters. This is an Alexander, past his prime admittedly, but with the unmistakable whiff of greatness about him. Broad-shouldered, dark-haired, classically handsome and intensely male with a short salt-and-pepper beard, he oozes more charisma than is seemly in one man. His eyes have a faraway quality about them, giving him the simultaneously focused and distracted look of a man who has spent most of his life staring into ancient history. He moves like a languid bear, lovingly dandling his angelic eleven-month-old daughter on his knee and trying to talk about archaeology beneath the waves as she pokes fingers in his eyes, mouth and nose.

Turanli has been involved with the INA since 1975, was appointed director of surveys in 1994 and is now its director in Bodrum.

His house, a stone's throw from the institute, is the sort of place you immediately wish was yours, tucked away in the hills in the breezy Belgravia of Bodrum, a world away from the All-Day English Breakfasts of the seafront. Airy, high-ceilinged and smartly, archaeologically scruffy, it opens on to a fertile jungle of a garden, all bougainvillaea, banana palm, hibiscus and grapevine-shaded terraces, fresh beneath the bossy sun. We sit down for tea. Bodrum stretches beneath us, tumbling down towards the sea in its rush to cool off. Sitting there, I wonder whether there could be a better place to live or a more interesting profession – hobby? – to have than underwater archaeology. Turanli is the sort of man who inspires a career change on the spot.

'What's interesting about shipwrecks is that they're like time-capsules,' he says, fending off an infantile finger from his nostril. 'When they go down, the sands cover them and preserve them for centuries. They can tell us enormous amounts about a particular period.'

Herodotus had had to make do with priests. There must have been times during his travels across the Aegean and Mediterranean when he would have been only fifty feet or so above these ancient secrets of the seabed. How much they would have revealed to him about so many of the foreign cultures which fascinated him. These shipwrecks contained the nuts and bolts of the discipline he had founded. They spoke of wars and empires, armies, dynasties, trade, agriculture, fashion, sex, celebration, religion, sacrifice, ways of life and rituals that had long since changed and which, in his day, remained millennial mysteries obscured by shadowy folklore.

He relied for his historical inquiries on the priests, with whom he appears to have checked in on every trip. He was forever consulting them, especially in Egypt. Priests were to Herodotus as Google is to the early-twenty-first-century information-seeker: a valuable and ubiquitous source of information, not all of it accurate. He described how the priests of Zeus took him around the temple in Thebes (modern–day Luxor), showing him wooden statues and explaining the genealogies of the high priests. Discussing the age and origin of the Greek gods, he cited the authority of the priestesses of Dodona in Greece. In Tyre (the Lebanese town of Sour) he was at it again, travelling there explicitly to ask the priests how old their temple of Heracles was. It was a typically ambitious, unlikely and romantic effort to find out how far the tradition of Heracles went back. Shipwrecks might have helped him pontificate with a little more accuracy.

We wander across to the institute from the perfect house to the perfect office in the late-afternoon sun. Around us are the old – very old – walls of Halicarnassus and acres of green gardens teeming with pink and yellow flowers, olive trees, firs and a carefully clipped lawn. The domed dormitory block seems to have wandered off a Byzantine film set. Misplaced medieval turrets guard the marine archaeologists from imaginary attack. The sun singes the warm Bodrum stone.

In the domed hall of the building is a framed picture of Turanli on the *National Geographic* cover, alongside other pictures and artefacts from the underwater world, an early diving suit, photographs of amphora experts, divers in the depths, wrecks discovered and reconstructed, treasures salvaged, history preserved.

In 1960, Bass, then a twenty-six-year-old archaeology PhD student at the University of Pennsylvania, was asked to excavate what was then the oldest shipwreck in the world, off Cape Gelidonya, south of Antalya. He didn't know how to dive then, but quickly learnt. The vessel, inevitably named the *Cape Gelidonya*, was a twelfth-century BC vessel which had sunk in 90 feet of water.

'Ever since that time,' Turanli continues, 'we'd been looking for a Late Bronze Age shipwreck. We were surveying wrecks and we'd find ten to twenty every year.'

But none of them was old enough. In 1979 the quest began in earnest. The institute gathered eighty-five sponge-diving boats at Bodrum and told the divers they were looking for shipwrecks. 'At first they were confused because they thought we'd be looking for sails on the seabed. We told them, no, we're looking for mounds of pottery, that's how you normally find the wrecks with the amphorae protruding from the sand. The wood of the hull disintegrates in a very short time and then the sand comes in so there's not much of that left. One indicator of a Bronze Age shipwreck is ingots, so we used to tell the divers to look out for metal biscuits with ears too. Then one day this sponge-diver came in, Mehmed Çakir, he said he'd seen something like it in Kaş, Antalya. We went to check it out, saw the remains, there wasn't much on display, and we thought, okay, we'll be finished here in two to three years.'

In the end it took eleven. The size, depth and sheer richness of the cargo in the vessel meant that the team of up to eighteen divers had to dive twice a day for three to four months every year. Due to the nitrogen build-up in the bloodstream at these depths, which can hamper thinking and ultimately cause the bends, the dives were limited to twenty minutes in the morning and twenty minutes in the afternoon.

'That wreck was incredible. It changed all the information we knew about the Late Bronze Age. It was by far the most valuable ship ever uncovered in terms of its cargo and the information it provided. Every moment was exciting, people were bringing up important stuff all around you. You'd go to the lab just to see what had been recovered that day and it was always amazing. I felt privileged to dive the world's oldest shipwreck. The richness of it was mind-boggling.'

On one dive he spotted plates with bones on them. 'The sailors had been having a feast before the ship crashed and sank. The plates had just been lying there, completely still and undisturbed, for over 3,000 years.' In terms of material value they were next to worthless, the humdrum dregs of a sailors' meal. But it was one of the most dramatically human discoveries, a moment suspended in watery time, quite possibly from a very real lull before a storm.

What happened next? What disturbed the sailors' meal? We don't know. Perhaps a violent, unexpected squall broke over the vessel. Maybe the waves pounded over the bulwarks, tearing down the protective wickerwork barrier and flooding into the ship, perhaps water burst in after the vessel hit the rocks. Then the dreadful weight of the cargo, the ten tons of copper ingots and the ton of tin, the twenty-four heavy stone anchors and gravity combined in an irresistible, unassailable force and pulled the royal cargo – and how many men and women? – to the bottom of the sea.

49

Turanli strikes me as a fortunate man, the sort you could end up envying. If you were running the excavation, as Bass was, he was just what you wanted. He was the man with the Midas touch. 'I was lucky to have a lot of gold in my area,' he said. He was allocated one square metre of the wreck to examine and excavate. It wasn't long before he was gasping at the surface with a very serious discovery. One morning he came up holding a small plastic box containing a shiny oval piece of solid gold. It was, hieroglyphic study revealed, the Nefertiti scarab, perhaps the greatest secret offered up by the vessel.

Turanli's delicate caresses, with a brush and an airlift, roused the most beautiful woman in ancient history from a sleep that had lasted more than three millennia. Starved of male company for all this time, Nefertiti willingly opened her arms to him. 'It was fantastic to find that scarab. Gold never deteriorates, you see, it never oxidises, so it shines through at any depth. It was very exciting. We had wanted to find things with writing on them, tablets, stones, anything like that. But there was nothing like that on the ship. The scarab of Nefertiti was the only thing on the entire ship.'

Even after he was moved to another area, Turanli took his good fortune with him, bringing back spears, swords and daggers. He couldn't put a fin wrong. Slowly, over time, dive by dive, month by month and year by year, the *Uluburun* surrendered her secrets one by one.

'Antiquities are history defaced, or some remnants of history which have casually escaped the shipwreck of time,' Francis Bacon wrote in *The Advancement of Learning* (1605). The *Uluburun* shipwreck *is* time, at least as much of it as you can realistically comprehend. Predating Herodotus by the best part of 1,000 years, she is a vessel that encapsulates millennia, seabed-still yet sailing motionless across the centuries to her next – who could possibly say final? – destination in the Museum of Underwater Archaeology. History has steered her this far, carrying her back to the shores of the Aegean and dropping her at the portal of the present. The antiquities she carries, Bacon's remnants of history, are time-travellers from an age so fantastically remote it is known as pre-history, as though that makes any more sense of it. It might as well be called pre-Herodotus.

Nautical archaeology, unlike history, does not have a long pedigree.

Assuming Herodotus as its father, history dates back two and-a-half millennia. Nautical archaeology has been around for less than fifty years.

History, in the Bodrum basement of the INA, is lab work in progress. It isn't history as Herodotus would have written it, but its innovative use of technology to delve deeper into our past and throw open a new, hitherto hidden world is something he would have welcomed. In fact, we have pretty good evidence for Herodotus using all available technology to understand his environment. In Egypt, for example, fascinated by the Nile's alluvial deposits, he recorded measurements from soundings off the coast. You can plot a linear progression across the millennia from sounding ropes to the latest tools of underwater archaeology. There is no reason to believe he would have embraced modern research tools and methods with anything other than full-throttle, Herodotean gusto.

Had he been able to visit Bodrum's Institute of Nautical Archaeology, he would have wanted to know when the next boat was going out. From there it is only the sprightliest imaginative step to see Herodotus going into action, donning his diving suit and scuba gear, spitting in his mask to preserve its transparency, and rolling backwards off the boat, splashing coolly into the liquid aquamarine to begin his investigations.

——

After reading George Bass's article in *National Geographic*, I want to speak to him to check a few things. The article appeared in 1987, but the excavation of the *Uluburun* continued for another seven years. Going back to check details like that must have been nightmarishly difficult, more often than not impossible, for Herodotus. A long conversation with a priest in Memphis was all very well, but how to check the facts of his story several decades later when he finally set about writing up the fruits of his world-spanning research? It was a Herculean task.

I call Bass at his home in Texas to discuss his unusual, briny branch of history. At seventy-three, after forty-six years of underwater archaeology, he has finally hung up his fins, he says, but still spends up to six months a year in Bodrum, where he has a house. He helps the INA out on various business.

Bass says he was 'fated' to be an underwater archaeologist, the sort of language Herodotus used (he has Apollo telling Croesus that 'he had been unable to divert the course of destiny'). It wasn't something he ever planned. In 1958, a New York photojournalist and diver who was writing a book about sponge-divers in Bodrum approached the University of Pennsylvania, saying sponge-divers had located a Bronze Age shipwreck. Would they like to excavate it? The faculty passed it to Bass. He thought, why not? He took a diving course, flew to Turkey and got to work. 'It all began as a bit of a lark.' The *Cape Gelidonya* wreck proved to be early Phoenician, the world's oldest shipwreck. There was no turning back after that.

Bass set up the INA in 1973, initially in Cyprus, ideally located from an eastern Mediterranean and Aegean shipwreck-hunter's point of view. After the Turkish invasion of 1974, the institute was relocated to the US, at Texas A&M University, where it has remained ever since. Bass says he has always been motivated by history, driven by the desire to discover unknown information from the past. He has been fortunate, unlike a good many other academics, that his field of research has tremendous popular appeal. 'People relate to the romance of shipwrecks. Wrecks make history come alive. When I was a child I loved reading about shipwrecks. Like all kids I loved stories about pirates and buried treasure.'

Herodotus, the founder of a new academic discipline, had a bruising time with his invention. His methods were attacked, his history challenged, his integrity and honesty impugned, his reputation traduced. Bass, generally acknowledged as the father of nautical archaeology, experienced similar problems with the rubber-suited infant he brought splashing noisily into the world. Archaeologists were sceptical. Some still are.

'It was a long uphill battle,' he says. 'We were dismissed by everyone except the giants of archaeology who alone had the vision to see that what we were doing could contribute immensely to our knowledge of the past. People used to say to us, "Aren't you the guys who go diving on your summer holidays and bring amphorae out of the sea?" It was very dismissive. They had no idea we were rewriting history.' The *Uluburun* excavation helped shift opinion. 'It made Pre-Classical archaeologists sit up and take notice and realise the incredible importance of it. One of the greatest enjoyments in my field of archaeology has been to rewrite some history through our excavations.'

Rewriting history proved as contentious for Bass as writing it had been for Herodotus. 'With the *Cape Gelidonya* wreck, for example, our conclusions were extremely controversial because we redated the *Odyssey*, pushing evidence for dating it from the Iron Age back into the Bronze Age. Up to that point the eighth century BC had been the accepted date for its composition because Homer makes frequent mention of Phoenician sailors and metal-smiths, who were not thought to be active seafarers as early as the Bronze Age.' People said their conclusions were impossible. 'There was assumed to be a Mycenaean monopoly on sailing because Mycenaean pottery was all over the Mediterranean. Now I'm no good at economics but I knew these Mycenaean sailors weren't going around the Aegean and Mediterranean giving out freebies. There had to be two-way trade going on. I suspected Near Eastern raw materials were the return trade for these manufactured goods. Then the *Uluburun* confirmed our findings. We uncovered a vast invisible trade in which raw materials – copper, gold, tin, ivory – were shipped from the Near East to Greece and manufactured into other products. That was why you didn't see Near Eastern goods in Greece.'

The early 'books' discovered on the *Uluburun* likewise had pushed back dramatically the date for the world's oldest book, Bass said. 'Everyone assumed that because there was only one line in all of Homer's *Iliad* and *Odyssey* referring to a book – "a wooden writing tablet"– that there couldn't have been books before the eighth century BC. The *Uluburun* moved that back four or five centuries to around 1300 BC.'

INA students in Texas still study Herodotus and Thucydides for their descriptions of naval battles. Bass says he had to read a random page of both authors to test his Greek as a student. 'I've never looked at the Persian vessels Herodotus mentions going down in the seas, though.'

I ask him if he thinks humans learn from history. 'One of the things we're not learning, but that we should, is that commerce leads to peaceful relations between people even in times of great turmoil. We see it in the Bronze Age with Greece and the Near East. We see it in the eleventh century AD between Byzantium and the Fatimid Arabs, trading very peacefully. This is something history is trying to teach us.' He's thinking about America and Iran, he says.

---

Herodotus announced at the outset of the *Histories* that he would deal with 'small cities of men no less than of great. For most of those which were great once are small today; and those which used to be small were great in my own time.' These days, the concept of cities rising and falling, of empires coming and going, is a truism, rather like saying the sun rises in the east and sets in the west. It is not a penetrating observation. It was a more original remark, however, in an era when history was in its infancy. He was discerning an important, even fundamental, pattern in human history.

Herodotus' Halicarnassus was a Greek city in a distant corner of the Persian empire. It was neither great nor small. Nevertheless, its fortunes and its size have, over the years, ebbed and flowed in keeping with his observations on history as the great recycler. In the twentieth century alone, Bodrum grew from small to great. Mazlum Ağan, the town's mayor, recalls an idyllic place before the invasion of the tourist and second-home-owning hordes in the latter part of the century altered it almost beyond recognition. 'When I was a child I remember Bodrum as a fishing village with a population of around 5,000. Everyone knew each other. These days the population in the summer is 100,000,' he says.

Ağan has the sort of professorial mien I expected to find in Oğuz Alpözen, the museum director. Someone with a mischievous sense of humour – the Greek gods at play? – has apparently swapped their clothes and characters. Alpözen is stern politician, Ağan kindly bohemian. The museum director wears a suit, the mayor a scruffy brown shirt. Alpözen is master of all he surveys, Ağan timidly overwhelmed by the world. Alpözen looks terrifyingly organised, Ağan endearingly scatty. The museum man is bald, the mayor rejoices in a tousled, mad-professor head of hair.

It reminds me of the famous passage in the *Histories* in which

Herodotus expresses his wonder at the similarly unexpected contrasts and contradictions he encounters in Egypt. Women are out and about in the markets, men are stay-at-home weavers, most priests grow their hair long, but in Egypt they shave their heads, and so it goes on, through circumcision, writing, mourning, animal husbandry, fashion. It is his way of expressing his wonder at the sheer otherness, the foreignness, of Egypt, the pleasing symmetry of opposites, of the ordinary and the extraordinary.

A black-and-white photograph of Bodrum hanging in the mayor's office, taken in 1964, confirms his childhood memories. The familiar arc of the harbour is unchanged, though the waterfront is empty by comparison with the commercial development today. Slender white minarets slimly rise above the whitewashed houses, pushing through a canopy of eucalyptus, olive, pine, palm, oleander, citrus grove, bougainvillaea and morning glory. The castle stands alone on high. But the biggest difference now is the encroachment of houses on the hills, sweeping up from the harbour like an advancing tide. In 1964 most of these slopes were virgin territory, shaded by trees and smothered by plants. In recent years they have surrendered to the developers, whose houses climb steadily higher, a wave of white froth rising towards the summits.

Bodrum has become too developed, according to Ağan. He has walked out of George Orwell's novel *Coming Up for Air*: George Bowling marooned in the present, hanging on to the past. His history has been bulldozed, filled in and forgotten. 'Herodotus would be surprised and angry if he returned today,' he says.

The mayor intends to market Bodrum more widely through its great history. There are plans to conduct more excavations. The Myndos Gate on the western fringes of the town, destroyed by Alexander the Great during his siege of Halicarnassus in 334 BC, is being restored. Only its sides remain, sunk in the ground like a pair of vast, shattered incisors. My hotel overlooks the site and I have spent a couple of hours up on the hill, clambering over the boulders, trying in vain to conjure something up from the neatly cobbled, over-zealously restored site. 'The objective of the project . . . is to contribute protection to our cultural values which are in the risk of to be vanished,' a plaque reads.

People often feel their cultural values are on the point of vanishing, as anyone who has ever listened to a discussion of multiculturalism and immigration will know. Traditions, languages, ways of life are always under threat. To face the onslaught many hang on to history – Herodotus' custom. It is one of our default settings.

In Bodrum, the mayor fears the all-conquering All-Day English Breakfasts that are steadily swallowing up his seafront in a humus-harassing tidal wave of carbohydrate. If the number of cafés that serve them keeps on growing unchecked, his town will be awash in sizzling fat, reeking of bacon, eggs and sausages, teeming with John Bull fatties sweating out beer, black pudding, and vodka and Red Bull. He doesn't like it. 'I don't understand why these tourists want to eat English breakfasts all the time, but I don't think they are interested in Turkish customs and culture. We have to hold on to our history. We want our children and the tourists who come here to know our history. Your Herodotus would understand that.'

If Herodotus failed to provide a lasting description of Halicarnassus, we can fast-forward 400 years or so to the time of the Roman architect Vitruvius whose *De Architectura* provides one of the most detailed ancient descriptions of the city under Mausolos, its fourth-century BC satrap. 'Mausolus, perceiving that Halicarnassus was a place naturally fortified, favourable for trade, and with a convenient harbour, made it his royal residence,' Vitruvius wrote.

> As the form of the site was curved like a theatre, on the lowest ground near the port was placed the *forum*. Along the curve, about half-way up its height, was made a broad street: as it were, a *praecinctio*. In the centre of this street stood the Mausoleum, constructed with such marvellous works that it is considered one of the seven wonders of the world.

Vitruvius' literary mapping of Halicarnassus was critical to another man we have come across in passing, the nineteenth-century British archaeologist Sir Charles Newton. He read the passage carefully again and again, comparing it with other less detailed descriptions of the city, because it provided the best clues to the location of what had once been the greatest building in Halicarnassus, one of the finest in the world, a monument of skyline-challenging dimensions and such epic grandeur that forever after it lent its name and that of the man buried inside it to an entire style of funerary architecture: the mausoleum.

Herodotus would have wanted to know more. As for Newton, he, like Bass, couldn't wait. He wanted to find it and start digging.

Ask anyone to list the Seven Wonders of the ancient world – a list whose origins can be traced back to Herodotus – and most get little further than the pyramids, the only one of the wonders still standing today (which Herodotus discusses in some detail, as we'll see). Perhaps the next most popular is the Hanging Gardens of Babylon and then the Colossus of Rhodes. After that it's anyone's guess. I can't list them myself without a discreet look at my *Oxford Reference Dictionary*. In no particular order they are: the Pharos Lighthouse in Alexandria, the Mausoleum of Halicarnassus, the Temple of Artemis at Ephesus and the Statue of Zeus at Olympia (my *Oxford Dictionary of the Classical World* suggests the walls of Babylon might be a better bet than the Pharos as a bona-fide wonder, but we won't worry about that).

The Mausoleum is the one that interests us here. Herodotus' failure to mention it can be excused. It hadn't even been built while he was alive. It dates to the mid-fourth century BC, seventy years or so after his death, to the reigns of King Mausolos and, after his death, his sister–wife Queen Artemisia. Mausolos, an ambitious ruler who from 377 BC nominally ruled Caria on behalf of the declining Persian empire, took advantage of the centre's weakness and steadily expanded his dominions until he controlled much of south-western Asia Minor. It is not clear whether he started the building towards the end of his life in a fit of grandiloquence or whether it was an incestuous tribute from his devastated wife after he died in 353 BC. What is not disputed is the building's greatness. It was a Graeco-Egyptian mountain of multi-coloured marble columns topped with a pyramid whose crest was graced with the colossal figures of Mausolos and Artemisia in a four-horsed chariot charging across the sky – the whole edifice, according to Pliny the Elder, soaring 140 feet into the heavens.

Had he been alive to see it, Herodotus – compulsive collector of marvels that he was – would probably have had something to say about the Mausoleum. Pliny did. He said the fabulous decoration of the Mausoleum by the sculptors Scopas, Bryaxis, Timotheus and Leochares, each man given one of the four elevations to work on, was the main reason the monument was considered one of the Seven Wonders. The size must have been a contributing factor, too. It would have been visible for miles, dominating the city from every approach, dwarfing every other building in sight, more dramatic than New York's Twin Towers in their heyday. Sailors approaching Halicarnassus would have known their journey was nearing an end once the chariot-pulling horses and their royal riders, sculpted by a fifth artist, Pythios, first reared above the horizon.

Pliny said that Artemisia died before the sculptors had finished their work but that they continued undeterred until it was complete. Why would they do that? Why spend all that time – and possibly their own money – on a monument when the royal patron(s) who had commissioned it had died? It seems the royal desire to leave an unforgettable legacy had unleashed an equally fervent bid for immortality among the sculptors. Conscious of posterity, they wanted history to remember them, said Pliny, 'regarding it as a monument of their own fame and of art'.

No one knows exactly what the Mausoleum looked like because the earliest references to it, such as those from Pliny and Vitruvius, are literary rather than pictorial. Pliny left a fairly detailed account but, like Herodotus, he appears to have made his fair share of mistakes. We can get a pretty good idea, however, from a number of reconstructions and drawings. We can also see some of the best-preserved fragments, including the colossal statues Newton said were Mausolos (ten feet high) and Artemisia (nine feet), in the British Museum.

The British have form when it comes to digging up ruins all over the world and then taking the best pieces back to Britain. They helped themselves to the remains of another of the Seven Wonders, the Temple of Artemis at Ephesus, which Herodotus thought one of the most 'remarkable' monuments in Greece. All that survives on the site today is a solitary column. In Bodrum, they had been warming up to the main event from 1846, when the then British ambassador in Constantinople, Sir Stratford Canning (a.k.a. Lord Stratford de Redcliffe), discovered some of the Amazon reliefs in the castle that he believed belonged to the Mausoleum. For a nineteenth-century Englishman convinced of his nation's superiority to the barbarian Turks, it went without saying that the swarthy, moustachioed Orientals could not be trusted to preserve these important historical objects *in situ*.

'A wish was very generally expressed among the archaeologists and students of art in England, that these reliefs might be rescued from their perilous and obscure situation at Budrum, and brought to England; but it was not till the year 1846 that this wish was carried into execution by the zealous and praiseworthy exertions of Viscount Stratford de Redcliffe, at that time British ambassador at Constantinople,' Newton explained with an obsequious flourish in *A History of Discoveries at Halicarnassus, Cnidus and Branchidae* (1862). 'Having obtained from the Porte [the Ottoman government] a firman authorising the removal of these marbles from the castle walls, Lord Stratford de Redcliffe caused them to be sent to England in H.M.S. *Siren*, and presented them to the British Museum . . .'

First blood to the British. Newton went out of his way to toady up to the Old Etonian diplomat, praising him for 'not forgetting the claims of Archaeology even amid the momentous distractions of the Russian war'. There were good reasons for his transparent sycophancy. Not the least was Canning's assistance in getting another firman from the Turkish government to help Newton launch his own expedition.

The reliefs whetted Newton's appetite for more. As Herodotus would have understood, it wasn't every day you had the opportunity of unearthing one of the Seven Wonders. Once he had overcome the difficulties of getting his hands on funding (£2,000), transport ('Her Majesty's steam corvette *Gorgon*, under the command of Captain Towsey, with a crew of 150 men'), an archaeological team (Lieutenant R. M. Smith, Royal Engineers, commanding the sappers, Corporal William Jenkins, senior NCO, Corporal B. Spackman as photographer and two lance-corporals, one a smith, the other a mason), Newton's first problem was one of location. Where exactly was the Mausoleum? He turned to Vitruvius, who was about as explicit with his directions as one could hope for in an ancient writing almost 2,000 years earlier. 'Along the curve, about half-way up its height, was made a broad street . . .' he wrote. 'In the centre of this street stood the Mausoleum.'

Newton began digging in the middle of the arc, halfway between the Agora on the shore and the Temple of Mars on the heights, on 1 January 1857. Understandably, local residents did not take kindly to a group of imperious Englishmen prodding about the place, digging here and there looking for they knew not what. Then Newton came across fragments of white marble in a field near the house of a man called Hadji Nalban, quickly followed by fragments from a frieze in high relief, one of them – showing a foot – matching friezes previously discovered in the castle. He was getting closer.

He marked out a quadrangle he estimated to be the foundations of the Mausoleum, home-owners only letting him dig with 'great reluctance'. The going was tough. 'Houses and garden-plots hemmed me in on every side, and, as every one of these belonged to a different owner, the difficulties of negotiation were infinite.'

You can imagine the Englishman squatting uncomfortably on the ground with his Turkish hosts and would-be vendors, sweating profusely as he sat through innumerable glasses of tea with Hadji Nalban first of all, the Turk twirling his moustache and assuring him that it would be his greatest pleasure and the most profound honour to sell the esteemed Englishman his house, Allah be praised, only he had to consider most carefully where his family would go, everything was becoming much more expensive in town these days and he, Hadji Nalban, had so many mouths to feed, Allah be praised for blessing him with a large family. So although it would delight him to give the Englishman his house for nothing – because they were brothers now, Mr Newton Pasha understood, not friends – what was he to do about all these expenses? As Mohammed was his witness, he was not a greedy man, and Mr Newton Pasha – who was also married, was he not? – would surely understand how much his wife loved their little house, with its airy rooms, its views on to the harbour and its most excellent location for the markets of the town. Mr Newton Pasha would also understand, would he not – most merciful Allah having perhaps also blessed him with children? – how happy his sons were here, playing in the garden, climbing trees and walking to school every morning. Perhaps Mr Newton Pasha would have another glass of tea ...

And then, when the interminable, knee-stiffening negotiations with Hadji Nalban were successfully completed, there was another family to deal with, and another, and so on. Reading his account, it is impossible not to admire the man's stamina.

Newton's excavations continued, with spectacular success. On the north side of the site he discovered the colossal statue of a bearded Asiatic man in cloak and tunic. With one eye on posterity, perhaps, not unlike the statue's sculptor, he identified the figure as Mausolos. In fact, according to the British Museum, it was probably one of thirty-six such statues standing between the Ionic columns of the peristyle and therefore not Mausolos, but Newton's claim was more romantic. Likewise, the colossal statue of a woman found near by was inevitably Mausolos' queen, Artemisia, glamorous in a figure-hugging tunic and cloak.

One by one, the treasures were exhumed, dusted off, packed away and despatched to England. The discovery of the hindquarters of one of the monument-topping horses caused a sensation. 'After being duly hauled out, he was placed on a sledge and dragged to the shore by 80 Turkish workmen,' Newton wrote. 'On the walls and house-tops as we went along sat the veiled ladies of Bodrum. They had never seen anything so big before, and the sight overcame the reserve imposed upon them by Turkish etiquette. The ladies of Troy gazing at the wooden horse as he entered the breach, could not have been more astonished.' The giant testicles must have brought a flush to a few cheeks. The horse's head joined his nether regions on the boat back to England. Then there was the head of Apollo, alongside Newton's Mausolos and Artemisia, the Amazon frieze, fragments and more fragments.

The excavations made Newton's name. Within three years, having turned down the offer of the Regius professorship of Greek at Oxford, he was appointed keeper of the Greek and Roman section of the British Museum, a position he held for the next twenty-five years. Having discovered one of the Seven Wonders of the World, the rest of Newton's career must have seemed something of an anticlimax, rather like life for Tufan Turanli and George Bass after excavating the

*Uluburun.* He had unearthed so many finds he had to build a new space – the British Museum's Mausoleum Room, completed in 1882, now Room 21 – just to accommodate them.

---

'Believe me, the Mausoleum is unbelievable,' Çanan says with a fervour undimmed by several hundred visits. 'Of course, you must see it.' She is scowling at me.

I have been wondering aloud whether it is worth visiting a comprehensively ruined, post-Herodotus monument.

'Do you think Herodotus would not have been to see one of the Seven Wonders of the World if he had had the chance?' she presses on. 'And in his hometown? Don't be crazy. Come on, let's go.'

So we do. As we walk through the town, sunlight shooting through cobbled streets, bouncing off whitewashed walls, she chatters away, reeling off little-known facts about her beloved Carians. My interest in seeking out Herodotus in and around his hometown opens me to endless Carian broadsides, reading recommendations, unsolicited and impassioned advice on must-see Carian sites, ancient Carian burial techniques, flanking movements in which she reminds me sternly that Herodotus was a Carian, and castigation of the Greeks for claiming him as one of their own.

One of her better stories is the legend that after the death of her husband Mausolos Queen Artemisia used to sprinkle his ashes into her wine. 'She loved drinking and she liked making love so much she wanted his body inside her, even after he had died!'

A fancifully Herodotean anecdote, you could say: all sex and no evidence. That, at least, is the sort of accusation routinely levelled at Herodotus by the Liar School of academics who don't trust Herodotus as far as they can throw him. According to this rather mean-spirited lot, our roving Greek is notoriously unreliable, inaccurate, far too casual with his facts and all too liable to make things up. Some consider him an out-and-out liar, rubbishing his claims, for example, even to have travelled to Egypt. I prefer a more forgiving view: that Herodotus, seeking to do something truly extraordinary, something no one before had ever attempted, had to contend with the sort of difficulties these armchair critics scarcely seem to comprehend, challenges he by and large overcame with the monumentally successful achievement of the *Histories*. He travelled to the ends of the known world with limited resources, recording intricate details of foreign cultures at a time when written records were laughably limited and oral accounts the norm. That his magnificent work should contain numerous errors along the way is only to be expected given the nature of his quest and the time at which he undertook it. Modern academics have been known to make far bigger howlers with much less excuse. It is worth noting, as a parting shot at the Liar School, that a good deal of Herodotean scholarship, unlike the wonderfully breezy *Histories*, is notoriously unreadable. Anyone want to dip into 'Temporal and Causal Conjunctions in Ancient Greek, with Special Reference to the Use of *epei* and *os* in Herodotus'? I thought not.

The setting of the Mausoleum is enough to dispel any doubts about the wisdom of a visit, as exciting for a gardener as for a historian or archaeologist. It is a walled quadrangle of open ground, dripping with jacaranda, pink bougainvillaea, red and lilac hibiscus, Japanese rose and prickly cacti, a wistful garden strewn with ruins and a peaceful retreat from the modern world.

The romance of the place offers floral compensation for the lack of vertical splendour. Where once the Mausoleum thrust into the blue heavens with priapic vigour, today it lies scatters across the ground, the royal erection subdued into flaccid marble. In its more vital years it towered over the entire town, a monument to masculine strength and glory, overlooking the harbour for almost seventeen centuries before being felled by an earthquake in the Middle Ages and subsequently plundered by the knights sent by the Grand Master of Rhodes in 1522. In their original format, with sunlight streaming between them, the thirty-six slender columns helped create the illusion from afar of a marble pyramid floating on air, Mausolos and Artemisia riding trium-phant atop it, charging stallions to the fore, destination apotheosis.

Displays give an indication of how the mausoleum has been envis-aged over the centuries, with thirty-three drawings from 1521 to 1939 showing variations on the pyramidal mausoleum theme, some of them not unlike the top of New York's Trump Building on Wall Street or the upper reaches of Big Ben. But as one of the world's great wonders, it is a disappointment. There is no getting away from it. It is, as a Canadian writer once described it, a hole in the ground.

Çanan doesn't seem to mind at all. For her the ruins, however limited, are the finest proof of what a world-beating culture the Carians once were.

The Bodrum authorities take a different view. They don't think what Sir Charles Newton left them after two-and-a-half years of excavations is good enough. In 2005, Turkish lawyers launched a campaign for the restitution of the Mausoleum and said they were filing a suit against the British Museum in the British courts. Perhaps anticipating failure from that quarter – the artefacts had been conveyed to London with the explicit permission of the Ottoman sultan – the lawyers said they would take their case to the European Court of Human Rights if they couldn't get results in the UK. For good measure they laid a black wreath at the British Museum.

The campaign gathered pace. The following year, a story appeared in the *Turkish Daily News* headlined 'Bodrum Wants its Mausoleum Back'. Eighteen months in the making, an $80,000 documentary called *Ancient Halicarnassus Bodrum* was being shown in the town's cinemas free of charge to stir up a bit of patriotic mausolean pride.

The sixty-minute film, shot on location in the town's historical sites, starred the ageing Lothario and Turkish singer Fedon and the former model Merve Ildeniz as wife of the Emperor Augustus. But it was Herodotus, appearing in a lively animated section, who completely stole the show.

———

Drawn by the name if not the dance floor, I spend my last night in Bodrum in Halikarnas, which describes itself as the most beautiful disco in the world. As wave upon wave of dancers surge across the dance floor, ebbing and flowing from the bar, splashing into discreet corners to enjoy private encounters, I look back on the quest to find my own quarry in his hometown. Herodotus was everywhere and nowhere in Bodrum. In sheer physical terms his great age underlined the difficulty of laying hands upon him. Even the town's oldest monument was no match for his antiquity and today it lay in piles of glorified rubble, brought low by man, nature and time. The Halicarnassus in which he grew up, in whose streets he ran and played and studied, had sunk deep into the limestone, had merged with the soil and disappeared. Only the glittering waters and the amphitheatre of hills above town recalled the backdrop of a city that was once his own.

He left clues. Outside the walls of the castle, fortified by the mausolean pillagers of history, he gazed serenely across the Aegean. Above the town he presided over an otherwise anonymous road junction lost in the roar of traffic. Then, abruptly, he went to ground. To find Herodotus here you had to look beyond the shattered columns, plinths and pedestals, to seek him in ways and places not immediately obvious. Nudged along by the absence of Herodotean references in stone and marble, I came to realise how he made his presence felt where least expected, almost as though it had been decided that I would find him only when I wasn't looking.

Herodotus inhabited the imagination. His spirit haunted the corridors of the Institute of Nautical Archaeology, dived down to the shimmering turquoise depths to examine shipwrecks from vanished civilisations, smiled down indulgently on the sexual adventures of tourists partying on the Aegean coast. Men like Newton, Bass, Turanli and Alpözen were immersed in the discipline Herodotus had invented.

The humanity of Herodotus' views on foreign cultures, the vision of tolerance and openness, remained relevant in the waters that two-and-a-half millennia ago ran with Greek and Persian blood and which today divided distrustful Turkey and Greece. The revelry in front of me represented a freedom of expression and behaviour that continued to separate East from West. One man's disco was another man's diabolic inferno. Yet the dance floor was also where East met West in each other's arms. In the world of the Harvard University political scientist Samuel Huntington, civilisations clashed. In Halikarnas they caressed.

Whistles from the dance floor tear into the night. Red lasers shoot across the sky, the bass boom-booms away. Fountains play over lithe professional dancers in postage-stamp bikinis, drenching them as they whip the crowd into a frenzy. A dancer glides on to the stage, long blonde hair and tiny thong, acres of naked skin glistening in the lights. The throbbing dance floor cheers as one and whistles rise into a crescendo as she slinks towards a cannon pointing at the party. She holds it lovingly in her hands, dipping before it, dancing around it, caressing it, toying with the machine and teasing her hoarse-from-screaming admirers, bottom swaying with the beat. Then she flicks her hair coquettishly to one side, rests one hand on her hip, presses a button and the cannon ejaculates a torrent of white foam in an arc across the dance floor.

Laughter and lusty roars of approval. More whistles. Couples clinch as the foam engulfs them. Drunken men slip and fall to the floor. Halikarnas is a modern marvel in Herodotus' hometown. I can't help thinking he would have enjoyed himself at the Crazy Foam Party.

# PART II

## Iraq

*No one is fool enough to choose war instead of peace – in peace sons bury fathers, but in war fathers bury sons.*

Herodotus, *Histories*, 1.87

# 3

# Fools and Wars

*What experience and history teach is this — that nations and governments have never learned anything from history, or acted upon any lessons they might have drawn from it.*

G. W. F. Hegel, *Lectures on the Philosophy of World History* (1830)

IN JULY 2004, Herodotus took me to Baghdad. And I took him with me.

One word explains the journey to Iraq and it is not Baghdad but Babylon, the ancient city fifty-five miles to the south. A name and place familiar to most of us from our very first Biblical forays – the fabled capital of warring Nebuchadnezzar, Old Testament king of Babylon, conqueror of Jerusalem, slayer of the Jews – yet utterly alien in its inaccessible foreignness. As the king Hezekiah tells the prophet Isaiah of recently arrived envoys: 'They are come from a far country, even from Babylon' (2 Kings 20:14). A city punished by God for building a tower that dared to reach for the heavens: 'Therefore its name is called Babel, because there the Lord confused the language of all the earth; and from there the Lord scattered them abroad over the face of all the earth' (Genesis 11:9).

A name that somehow defines the remoteness of the past and symbolises the troubles of the present – the encounter between America and Iraq – through the destruction of one of the world's greatest heritage sites. If Mesopotamia is the cradle of civilisation, Babylon is its firstborn child.

Babylon appeals because it is a genuinely Herodotean destination. Did he travel there himself? As ever, scholars can't agree. They are divided into two camps: those who believe he was an astonishing world traveller of boundless spirit and energy who should be taken at face value when he claims to have visited these places, and those who argue he simply made up much, if not most, of the travel writing which is interspersed throughout the *Histories*. For his part, in his passages on Babylon, Herodotus implies very strongly he has been there.

My own inclination is to believe him, while retaining a gently raised eyebrow at some of his taller stories. If, in his foreign reportage, we judge him as an ancient travel writer, rather than as a twenty-first-century historian, then the verdict is more favourable. We shouldn't forget that Herodotus is the first great travel writer as well as historian and that travel writing has a long and distinguished tradition of artifice and exaggeration. It often lets its literary ambition get the better of it, valuing a good story or an amusing quote over strict accuracy. If we're going to be literal about it, we could argue there is an inherent dishonesty in some of the best recent examples of the genre in English, from Bruce Chatwin to Sir Patrick Leigh Fermor. And it's also worth remembering, when we're wondering how accurate and truthful Herodotus is about the places he describes and whether he really went to Babylon, that the *Histories* were probably written to be delivered in public. When we attend lectures, we want tall stories, we want drama. When we're listening to a mountaineer discuss his latest expedition, we want frostbite and arguments in raging snowstorms, we'd like a broken leg, disaster on the summit, an avalanche on the descent, perhaps an abortive rescue mission, maybe a death while we're at it, above all we want triumph and tragedy for this is an intoxicating cocktail. There's nothing worse than the bloodlessly teetotal story that everything went to plan, the expedition was successful and no one was hurt. Herodotus knew that and he understood that he was out to entertain as well as educate. The most eloquent tribute to his success is the fact that he is still in print today, 2,500 years after he was first published.

Either way, whether he actually visited Babylon or simply culled information about the place from as many sources as he could muster, the point is that Herodotus devotes a good deal of time and effort to writing about the city. He provides us with one of the earliest descriptions of Nebuchadnezzar's capital, an urban marvel that once boasted one, possibly two, of the Seven Wonders of the World. He discusses the famous Babylonian tradition of brick-baking and explains how the city's walls – possible candidates for Seven Wonders status – were built. As you might expect, he does a spot of temple-hunting and, just as inevitably, compiles a wide-ranging survey of Babylonian life and customs: religion, agriculture, medicine, marriage markets, prostitution and a deliberately startling overview of strange sexual practices, etiquette and hygiene.

Babylon, in other words, is an essential destination in the Herodotean itinerary. If the ancient site is the main physical attraction of a journey to post-Saddam Iraq, a challenging Ultima Thule on the trail of Herodotus, then war is its equally compelling conceptual counterpart. Conceptual because it offers the opportunity to test some of Herodotus' views and observations in the crucible of conflict.

War, above all the defining struggle between Greek city-states and the rapacious Persian empire over the reigns of its kings Cyrus, Cambyses, Darius and Xerxes, forms the narrative spine of the *Histories*. In the very first sentence Herodotus says he will be looking at 'great and marvellous deeds – some displayed by Greeks, some by barbarians'. He is going to try, he tells us, 'especially to show why the two peoples fought each other'. He was writing at a time when the Peloponnesian Wars were overshadowing his world.

From April 2003, the war in Iraq, the most controversial in a generation, was doing the same thing. It thrust itself to the heart of international affairs, watched by the world with growing horror. Herodotus, for all his fascination with war, was really a bit of a peacenik, which is why he wrote that no one would choose peace over war. Yet President Bush had done just that. This was his personal conflict. He had chosen war – a very big one – instead of peace, and American and Iraqi fathers were burying their sons daily.

All the elements of the war in Iraq carried an unmistakably Herodotean echo: they sounded the enduring themes of empire, imperial over-reach, the sensible limits of power, cultural confrontation and the clash of civilisations, democracy versus dictatorship, West versus East, religion, greed, hubris and its consequences. Who could forget the now infamous moment on 1 May 2003, when Bush landed on the USS *Abraham Lincoln* aircraft carrier, emerging from a navy jet in full flight suit with helmet tucked under his arm to raucous hoo-rahs from the assembled troops before giving a rousing victory speech beneath a banner that read 'MISSION ACCOMPLISHED'? 'Major combat operations in Iraq have ended,' Bush began. 'In the Battle of Iraq, the United States and our allies have prevailed.' The *Washington Post* called it 'the ultimate self-destructing image of victory'. It was the defining act of hubris in a conflict that was only just getting under way and would kill many more Iraqis and Americans. The Herodotean world-view suggested that hubris led to nemesis – destruction – and the example of Iraq seemed, from afar, only to confirm it.

Further study required greater proximity. Once I had established there would be no marital nemesis in the event of my own departure for Iraq, had persuaded my wife that this was bona-fide service in the cause of Herodotus (and my bank balance) if not quite of spreading freedom and democracy to benighted parts, I flew to Baghdad.

How did we get here? How did we end up with the war in Iraq? Herodotus offers some telling parallels. In his world, wars tend to begin only after kings and emperors have ignored all the warnings.

The wise adviser pops up regularly in the *Histories* to give these warn-ings and counsel against war. It is Herodotus' favourite literary device to underline the gravity of decision-making, the folly of unstoppable arrogance and the tragic inevitability of fate. He has a character called Artabanus, fraternal adviser to Darius, his brother and king, warning against war with the Scythians, blood-drinking Eurasians who lived in the Black Sea and Caspian Sea region. He 'did his utmost to make him abandon the enterprise, on the ground that the Scythians were such difficult people to get at. Good though the advice was,' says Herodotus, 'it had no effect upon Darius.' The Persian king ignores him and in 513 BC presses on with his ruinous war in what is now Ukraine.

Darius marches into the empty steppes but finds his enemy is always one step ahead, one moment withdrawing before him, the next attack-ing his flanks and rear before disappearing into the endless wastes again. Darius is unable to master the art of nomadic warfare. The Scythian cavalry launches skirmishing raids, falling on the ravenous Persian foraging parties and worsting the invaders. Eventually, after incurring severe losses, Darius is ignominiously harried out of Scythia by an elusive army whose hit-and-run tactics prove his undoing. Humiliatingly for the man who would rule the world, he is forced to retreat under the cover of night. The campaign is a failure.

So much for Artabanus' shrewd advice to Darius. It is simply ignored. This tends to be the fate of anti-war advisers. Their wisdom is disregarded, indeed that is their point. They serve as a reminder of what might have been.

Later, Artabanus appears again, this time advising his nephew Xerxes against war with the Greeks. He recalls his earlier advice to Darius and how his brother dismissed it to his cost. This time, the enemy contemplated is 'a nation greatly superior to the Scythians: a nation with the highest reputation for valour both on land and sea'. He outlines the formidable risks inherent in Xerxes' policy for war. 'I urge you, therefore, to abandon this plan; take my advice and do not run any such terrible risk when there is no necessity to do so.' In the run-up to April 2003, many argued there was no necessity for America to invade Iraq. Artabanus goes on to give a classically Herodotean warning against overweening pride:

> You know, my lord, that amongst living creatures it is the great ones that God smites with his thunder, nor does he allow them to show off. The little ones do not vex him. It is always the great buildings and the tall trees which are struck by lightning. It is God's way to bring the lofty low. Often a great army is destroyed by a little one, when God in his envy puts fear into men's hearts, or sends a thunderstorm, and they are cut to pieces in a way that they do not deserve. For God tolerates pride in none but Himself. Haste is the mother of failure – and for failure we always pay a heavy price.

Furious, Xerxes excoriates Artabanus for his 'cowardice and lack of spirit' and says the only reason he isn't going to kill him is that Artabanus is his uncle. He ignores the advice. But in taking on the Greeks Xerxes has bitten off much more than he can chew. After a

Pyrrhic victory at Thermopylae, his forces are cut to pieces at Salamis in 480 BC and again in 479 at Plataea and Mycale, defining battles which bring his massive expedition to a sorry close. The invaders from the East are repelled, their adventures in the West over. Greece, land of freedom and democracy, is triumphant. And Herodotus' wise adviser Artabanus is vindicated.

One afternoon in London, I was talking to the Dutch writer Cees Nooteboom about his latest book, a collection of travel essays. As rain leaked from a leaden sky outside, our conversation drifted on to the Iraq war. All of a sudden Nooteboom brought up the wise adviser. The context was Napoleon's disastrous war against Russia in 1812. 'When Napoleon wanted to go to Moscow, Talleyrand said, "Don't do it. It'll be a catastrophe." What did Napoleon do? He fired him. The problem for Bush was that he didn't even have a Talleyrand.' Like Herodotus' Darius and Xerxes, Napoleon and Bush had landed themselves in a quagmire of their own making.

Bush's principal advisers, the most powerful people around him, did not advise against war. In the Dick Cheney–Donald Rumsfeld camp, restraint and diplomacy were not the order of the day. The juggernaut of war with Iraq started revving up amid the fall-out from 9/11 and, with Vice-President Cheney, Defense Secretary Rumsfeld and his deputy Paul Wolfowitz at the advisory wheel, the engine got louder and louder. 'Powell might have expressed some opposition to the war, but he was no Talleyrand,' Nooteboom said.

The absence of a Talleyrand or Artabanus figure counselling the American president against war with Iraq was one thing. But if Bush was unable or unwilling to find a Herodotean wise adviser in the White House, he was certainly aware of anti-war opinion: on the streets of Washington, in foreign capitals and parliaments, in the UN, above all in the international media.

---

Did history, brainchild of Herodotus, have any wise advice on Iraq? What, if any, were the predictive powers of a subject that looked backwards rather than forwards?

On 19 February 2003, the *Guardian* published a survey of views on the impending war from leading historians on both sides of the Atlantic. Though the verdicts were varied, the weight of opinion, as you would expect from the *Guardian*, was anti-war. Most disputed the historical analogies being made by both the pro-war (Munich 1939) and the anti-war (Suez 1956) camps. The Bush and Blair governments were portraying anti-war opinion as appeasement of a dangerous dictator who threatened world peace. Some of their opponents regarded the looming conflict as another Suez, an imperial fiasco revisited.

'I don't think it's a case either of 1939 or of 1956,' Simon Schama argued. 'I'm allergic to lazy historical analogies. History never repeats itself, ever. That's its murderous charm. The poet Joseph Brodsky, in his great essay "A Profile of Clio", wrote that when history comes, it always takes you by surprise, and that's what I believe, too.'

Schama went on to make a fairly clear and thoughtful forecast which suggested that there *were* some discernible outcomes of the invasion, that history wouldn't necessarily take him by surprise. First, the war would be easy to win. No surprises there. What concerned him most, however, was that there had been extraordinarily little debate about a post-war settlement. This led him to predict 'a teddy bears' picnic for terrorism'. It was a remarkably prescient forecast from a man who believed that history was a series of surprises.

At Yale, Paul Kennedy sounded another cautionary note. There were shades of Artabanus' 'Haste is the mother of failure . . .' in his warning. In the absence of a second UN resolution authorising war, Kennedy said military action would be a *folie de grandeur* likely to backfire. As for how long the American military remained in Iraq after the invasion, history offered a significant parallel. When Gladstone's government intervened in Egypt in 1882 to uphold order against anti-Western Muslim firebrands, Kennedy noted, it claimed it would leave Iraq soon. 'As it turned out, Britain didn't leave for another 73 years.'

The lessons of history: it's a portentous phrase, but what exactly does it mean? What are these lessons? We're always told that politicians should learn from the past and condemn them because they never do (as if the rest of us are any better at using history to regulate our behaviour). The *Guardian*'s brief survey of historians showed that history offers no certain paths to enlightenment. The nineteenth-century

French philosopher Ernest Renan was quite right, surely, when he wrote that 'Getting history wrong is an essential part of being a nation.' Or of being human, he might have added. If there are lessons to heed from studies of the past, they are a gloriously subjective pick-'n'-mix. Take what you will and dispute the rest. Whatever you want to draw from a particular historical event to suit your intended course of action is legitimate. Anything suggesting the opposite course of action, however, is a false analogy.

Historians themselves are not shy in acknowledging the limitations of the 'learn from history' thesis. 'History never repeats itself, so anyone looking for parallels between the present situation and past events is likely to be disappointed,' said Richard Evans of Cambridge University, who considered the parallels with both Munich and Suez specious. 'I belong to the school that doesn't put much trust in historical precedents,' said Norman Davies, a fellow of the British Academy and of Wolfson College, Oxford. 'They only show that no precedent ever fits exactly and that history never quite repeats itself.' Michael Burleigh at Stanford agreed. 'Historical analogies are rarely useful,' he argued. He predicted a quick war that Iraqis would regard as 'liberation'.

In an article in the *New York Times* on 5 January, Michael Ignatieff wrote the following passage whose message could have come straight from Herodotus.

> What every schoolchild also knows about empires is that they eventually face nemeses. To call America the new Rome is at once to recall Rome's glory and its eventual fate at the hands of the barbarians. A confident and carefree republic – the city on a hill, whose people have always believed they are immune from history's harms – now has to confront not just an unending imperial destiny but also a remote possibility that seems to haunt the history of empire: hubris followed by defeat.

Ignatieff reminded his readers that the great English historian Edward Gibbon – following Herodotus – had argued that empires lasted as long as their rulers took care not to overextend their natural borders.

Bush's vision of the course of history was different. 'We meet here during a crucial period in the history of our nation, and of the civilised world,' he told an audience of 1,400 at a black-tie dinner hosted by the American Enterprise Institute in Washington on 26 February 2003. 'Part of that history was written by others; the rest will be written by us.'

It was as though Bush and America could simply lift themselves above the forces and currents of history and impose themselves upon it as its sole master, unchecked by other forces, untroubled by unintended consequences. The president's remark reminded me of the famous passage in Herodotus in which Xerxes vents his fury on the Hellespont – the ancient name for the Dardanelles – after a storm has smashed up the bridges constructed for his troops to cross over from Asia into Europe. 'Xerxes was very angry when he learned of the disaster, and gave orders that the Hellespont should receive three hundred lashes and have a pair of fetters thrown into it,' Herodotus wrote. 'I have heard before now that he also sent people to brand it with hot irons.'

As the countdown to war in Iraq gathered pace, the warnings mounted. And in these warnings, history cast a long shadow over the future. In March, Dominique de Villepin, the elegantly tailored French foreign minister, a latter-day Talleyrand, recalled Europe's own history of conflict in a warning to America not to rush to war. The implication was that the United States, with a less traumatic history of war – with less history, period – was less inclined to exhaust every diplomatic option to avert conflict.

Bush, like Darius and Xerxes before him, like Nooteboom's Napoleon and every other wartime leader we can think of, dismissed all this anti-war advice. He had his own trusted advisers who wanted war and they carried the day. Like the God of Genesis, they wanted to remake Iraq and the Middle East in their own image. They wanted to break from the region's dictatorial past and forge a democratic future. They wanted to make history.

———

The war against Saddam, as many commentators, historians and politicians had predicted, did not last long. It began on 20 March. Saddam's government fell on 9 April.

History, however, did not disappear in the euphoria of victory. Writing in the *Washington Post* on 20 April, Paul Kennedy summoned it to caution against the glib neoconservative assumption that America could remodel the Middle East along democratic lines. 'To be sure, history never repeats itself exactly, but it often deals hard blows to those who ignore it entirely,' Kennedy insisted, advising caution, scepticism and humility. Humility seemed almost entirely absent from Bush's mission to topple Saddam. There was a swagger about the wartime president which offended not only critics of the war but many of its supporters.

For a brief honeymoon period in 2003 American forces were indeed looked upon as liberators in Iraq. The ease with which Saddam's regime was overthrown seemed to justify Bush's bold attempt to write history. The hawks were in the ascendancy. Democracy was infectious, after all. The talk was of Iran next. And then Syria. It did not take long, however, for a vicious insurgency to take root which cooled the enthusiasm of the president and his advisers to start new wars in the Middle East. It challenged some of America's most basic assumptions about invading the country and contested Bush's determination to place himself beyond the bounds of history.

When Bush announced the end of 'major combat operations' on 1 May, the American death toll stood at 139. In May and June another sixty-seven American soldiers were killed. Bush was unrepentant. On 2 July, he said, 'There are some who feel . . . they can attack us there. My answer is bring them on. We've got the force necessary to deal with the security situation.'

In July another forty-eight American soldiers were killed. By the time I flew to Baghdad a year later, on 14 July 2004, the Americans were losing an average of sixty soldiers a month. Clio, the muse of history, was flaunting her 'murderous charm' in classically Herodotean style.

⸻

Baghdad International Airport. It used to be called Saddam International Airport but Saddam is history now.

Hot metal and blinding light. Forty-four degrees Celsius. Hairdryer wind. The roar of generators, jet engines and machinery. Palm trees swirling through the shimmering waves. Black Hawk helicopters overhead, blades ripping through the air, dust clouds surging in the down-draught. A parking lot filled with armoured four-wheel drives, bonnets boiling in the sun. Groups of security teams waiting for their passengers. Guns and sunglasses. Sirens in the distance. Sporadic gunfire. Grit in my mouth, eyes and ears. Sweat pouring down my back into the waistband of my boxers. Fear in my stomach. A fury of noise, heat and light.

Two American men from a team sent to collect me. Their mission is to drive me to the protective bubble of the International Zone. Both wear black wraparound sunglasses (or Wiley X low-profile ballistic eye protectors) and what look like cut-off helmets, also black. Matching black M4 rifles suspended from a clip on their chest, already bulging with magazines, medical packs, identity badges, combat knives and radios. Glock 17 pistols in their thigh holsters. Tactical combat trousers festooned with pockets. The black vest they wear over their body armour is made by an American company called Blackhawk. Its motto: 'Honor as a way of life'.

One steps forward and shakes my hand. I can see myself in the reflective lenses of his sunglasses. I don't look very military. He does. 'Welcome to Baghdad, sir. Please step this way for your security briefing,' he begins. 'My name is Matt and I'm your team leader today. This afternoon we will be travelling in a convoy of three armoured vehicles into the Eye Zee [he means the International Zone]. There is only one way into the Eye Zee and that is via Route Irish. You will be in the principal's vehicle in the middle. Please have your seat belt fastened at all times. We have a lead vehicle in front and a gun-truck in the rear. I will be travelling in the lead vehicle.'

The heat is all over me. My shirt is sodden. There's so much sweat running down into my linen trousers it looks as though I have wet myself. Matt looks preternaturally cool.

'Our route from BIAP into Baghdad is dangerous. The bad guys have been attacking it a whole lot recently. They may attack us today. If they do, we have B6 armour in these vehicles to protect us. It will stop automatic fire but it will *not* stop RPGs or VBIEDs and it may not stop IEDs.* If we lose a vehicle, if one of the Toyotas goes down, you are to stay in your vehicle. Do *not* attempt to leave the vehicle on your own. I repeat, do *not* attempt to exit the vehicle by yourself. This is the way to get killed. We will take care of the situation. If we have to debus, follow the instructions of the team leader in your vehicle and do exactly what he says. If everything goes okay, our journey should take us around twelve minutes. Please ensure you are wearing your body armour and helmet at all times. Good to go?'

'Excuse me?'

'Are you good to go?'

'Oh sorry, yes.'

I have been fixated on this seven-mile stretch of road for weeks, ever since accepting a job with a British security company in Baghdad to set up a nationwide civil affairs programme. I'm not thinking of the schools and hospitals I'm here to help, I'm wondering if we will even make it to the International Zone. I'm thinking about what Matt just said about the recent spate of attacks on the road and how the armoured vehicle offers no protection against suicide car bombers. I'm remembering the newspaper articles describing Route Irish as 'Ambush Alley' and 'the most dangerous stretch of road in the world'. I'm wondering what I'm doing here when this is a war zone – fourteen months after the speech on the USS *Abraham Lincoln*, Bush's Mission has still not been Accomplished – and all the men around me are ex-military and I'm the only one who isn't. I'm wondering whether this particular part of the Herodotean quest is strictly necessary and I'm thinking of my wife and nine-year-old stepdaughter saying goodbye to me back in London in tears.

I sit in the back. In the front the driver and the man in the passenger seat with an M4 rifle are talking about a suicide bombing at the 'Assassin's Gate' checkpoint on the edge of the International Zone earlier that morning. Ten people were killed. They speak about it as office chitchat, round-the-water-cooler gossip.

* Baghdad International Airport; Rocket-Propelled Grenade; Vehicle-Borne Improvised Explosive Device (car bomb); Improvised Explosive Device. A war zone is a world of acronyms, most, though by no means all, TLAs or Three-Letter Acronyms.

'I don't get these dudes at all,' says the driver, whose name is Shane. He has a sun-whitened goatee beard and is in his early thirties. 'What's the point of blowing yourself up for a load of virgins who don't even exist? Y'know what I mean? Think about all that pussy they're missing out on right here. That's what they should be concentrating on, getting laid in *this* world. Leave the next till later.'

'That's the whole problem,' says his colleague Carl. No goatee. 'They're not *getting* any pussy. When was the last time you saw a disco in downtown Baghdad? These boys don't get to fuck. They reckon if they blow up you, me and some other Jews and Christians, Allah's going to lay on some hot chicks for them. Seventy-two virgins, dude.'

'Sure, but would you wanna gamble on that if you weren't getting any? Seems kinda extreme to me. Strapping on explosives because they can't get laid. And what happens when they find out that it's all bullshit?'

Carl sighs. Weary how–can–you–expect–me–to–answer–theological– crap–like–that resignation. 'Dude, I'm not a fucking Muslim.'

'Fuckin' ragheads,' says Shane.

I scarcely think about these remarks. I don't relate them to Herodotus' astonishingly tolerant views about other people's religions and his respect for different cultural traditions around the world because my mind is on the road. Our three-vehicle convoy drives out of the airport into the rest of what is known as Camp Victory, Coalition headquarters in Iraq. I remember this first instance of Victory only because of its Orwellian ring. There are other references here, too. Herodotus on doomed imperial adventures collides with the bleakly black humour of *Catch-22*. I haven't yet encountered Freedom and Liberty, but soon there will be no avoiding them.

Sharp metallic click-clicks as the three men around me – two in the front, one in the back – load their weapons. We are approaching the beginning of Route Irish. A sign outside warns us we are leaving a secured area. The war is not over. Weapons should be locked and loaded. Convoys must consist of a minimum of three vehicles. There is a last radio check between the cars. Matt's voice comes on. 'Let's roll,' he says. 'Eyes on.'

'Hoo-rah,' says Shane. 'Bring it on!'

Hotter than ever beneath the body armour and helmet. Outside, palm trees wilt. There is a statue of what looks like a giant angel–soldier, a fascist sculpture straight out of Mussolini's Italy.

We pick up speed and soon the palm trees in the central reservation become charred stumps. They have been cut down by the American army to deny attackers cover from which to shoot up convoys. Nothing behind us. An expanse of rutted tarmac. Melting. The rear gunner is keeping the traffic back several hundred yards. A Minimi machine gun poking out of the boot – together with occasional display of clenched fist and orders to 'BACK OFF!' – concentrates minds. The lead vehicle in our convoy weaves from side to side, pulling alongside Iraqi vehicles and waving them off to the side of the road. From time to time the rear vehicle speeds up, flashes past us and directs traffic out of our way. We are travelling faster and faster now, but not so fast I can't see the faces of the moustachioed drivers whose journeys we have disrupted. They have a range of expressions: nervous, neutral, studiously indifferent, hostile. Some turn their faces away from us. None of them are smiling. Their reaction helps me understand why there is an insurgency. Within a few months of arriving in Baghdad, I will think that, if I was an Iraqi, I would join it.

We pass a dead dog on the verge and I pray it doesn't conceal a roadside bomb. In the world of the insurgent explosive expert, dead dogs are the latest thing. But there's no explosion and we race on, arrowing through traffic, Moses parting the waves. Western culture in the driving seat. Over-paid and over-confident. Seventy miles an hour now, up to eighty. Iraqi cars peeling away before us. It feels like a computer game, swerving, racing, braking hard, avoiding vehicles, pushing those who get in our way off the road, only the stakes are higher. Houses line our route on either side. Shane tells me he was shot at from this area a few days ago. No one was hurt. 'The bad guys can't shoot straight,' he says.

The central reservation narrows to a sliver, the road curves to the right, we slow down and then we are suddenly static in a line of vehicles – army Humvees, white Toyota Land Cruisers, black GMC Suburbans, armoured personnel carriers – queuing to enter the checkpoint. We are on the threshold of arrival. We are entering a world of concrete blast walls and razorwire, a border that divides Us from Them.

'This is the worst bit,' says Carl. 'Just when you think you're back in one piece, some asshole with a beard blows himself up right next to you. And the thing that sucks most about it is there ain't nothing you can do. They get into position in the line, between a couple of nice-looking American cars, wait until they're right next to the soldier on the checkpoint, press the switch and then . . . BOOM!' He throws his arms out in a theatrical explosion. He's not talking to anyone in particular but it's obvious the remarks are meant for me, the new guy, the sucker in the back for whom car bombs and suicide bombers are not yet part of the daily routine of life in Baghdad, who has not yet consigned them to the category of black humour as a way of coping with the daily horror. Trying not to listen, I pick up a copy of *Stars and Stripes*, the American military's newspaper, which is lying on the seat next to me.

'Car bomb in Baghdad kills 10, wounds 40' is the headline. In the picture on the cover there are five helmets resting on five rifles above five framed portraits of soldiers and five pairs of desert boots standing on camouflage netting. Dog tags hang from the rifles. The portraits show the faces of five young American men. Most of them are smiling. One is holding a rifle. Another seems to be holding candyfloss up to the camera, obscuring half of his face. There is a pair of candles on a table that looks like an altar. Behind it are the American and German flags, next to what is probably a military flag. 'Last farewell – Germany memorial honors five 1st ID GIs killed in Iraq' is the caption. The five men were killed in Samarra on 8 July in a mortar attack on the Iraqi National Guard headquarters.

I don't want to know any more about the car bomb but find myself turning to page three to read more. A column on the right-hand side of the page catches my eye. 'U.S. deaths in Iraq'. The death toll of American servicemen and women is 880. Britain has lost fifty-nine, Italy eighteen, Spain eight, Bulgaria and Poland six each, Ukraine four, Slovakia three, Thailand two, Denmark, El Salvador, Estonia, Hungary, Latvia and the Netherlands one each. The Coalition of the Willing. There seems to be something accusatory about the sentence 'Since

May 1, 2003, when President Bush declared that major combat operations in Iraq had ended, 742 U.S. servicemembers have died – 542 as
a result of hostile action and 200 of non-hostile causes.' As though the
military felt let down by the politicians.

Next to the deaths column is the main story, 'Bomb blast shakes
Baghdad'. It opens: 'A suicide attacker detonated a massive car bomb
Wednesday at a checkpoint near the British Embassy and headquarters
of the interim Iraqi government, killing at least 10 people and wound-
ing 40, including a U.S. soldier, authorities said.' I scan past several
paragraphs reporting the separate assassinations of a provincial governor near Mosul (a hand-grenade and machine-gun attack) and an
official in the industry ministry (drive-by shooting as he was leaving
his office) until the car-bombing story continues. 'The morning
suicide attack outside the main gate of the International Zone was the
worst in Baghdad since the United States transferred sovereignty to
the interim Iraqi government on June 28.'

I stop at the last sentence. It makes me think of a radio interview I
heard a few weeks earlier, when an anti-war commentator was arguing
that the Americans were in no position to transfer sovereignty because
Iraq had never lost its sovereignty in the first place. The Americans
had never taken it because you couldn't take someone else's sovereignty. It wasn't yours – or theirs – to take. By definition.

> The explosion shook buildings throughout central Baghdad at about
> 9:15 a.m., when a suicide bomber detonated a car packed with 1,000
> pounds of explosives.
> 'We were thrown on the ground. Then I saw many dead people on
> the ground,' witness Alla Hassan said. Black and gray smoke billowed
> from the blast site, leaving a crater two yards wide and a yard deep in
> the road. The charred remains of five cars stood by a protective blast
> wall that had been partially destroyed. Two other trucks and a car lay
> smouldering nearby.

So much detail about just one day in the Iraq war in just one newspaper. Each new conflict more comprehensively recorded than the last.
Newspaper and magazine reports, television news, radio broadcasts,
books, letters, speeches, emails, blogs, photographs, films. Protective

technology for the past, wrapping it up in layer upon layer of information for future historians to pore over. Herodotus had to make do with a lot less than this. History has become easier and infinitely more complicated.

The man next to me, who is called John, up to now a strong, silent type, notices the car-bomb story I'm reading. He whistles through his teeth. 'Jesus, that was a big one,' he says. 'I was in the office when that went off. The whole place shook. Pieces of the ceiling came down and everything. Assassins Gate again. We were just about to go into town. A few minutes later and we'd have been fucked. Danny and me, we went to have a look at it later. Blood everywhere. A second bomber came in a few minutes after the first one, killed the ambulancemen and policemen just as they were getting the place under control. Fuckin' assholes, man.'

Suddenly, a scream outside.

'STOP! STOP!'

My stomach tightens again. Something very bad is about to happen. A soldier is pointing his rifle at the man driving a car just in front of us. The Iraqi has moved forward before being called by the soldier on the checkpoint. I don't want to watch but I can't take my eyes off him. The man must be a suicide bomber. He stops. Another soldier is looking at him through binoculars. Long, time-telescoping pause. How is this going to unfold? In a hail of blood and metal? The soldier with the binoculars lowers them and says something to his colleague who now waves the car forward.

'You understand STOP?' he shouts at the driver. The Iraqi looks terrified. The second soldier searches the car. 'Next time, don't FUCKIN' move until I say you can go!' He shows him a clenched fist. 'This means STOP!'

He waves him through. The dilapidated vehicle limps into the International Zone, a scrawny mongrel compared with the muscular, four-wheel-drive thoroughbreds driven by the Americans.

We are next in line at the checkpoint. Only yards from safety now. The soldier waves us forward. Shane, Carl and John show him their security badges through the windows. Carl opens his door because the windows in an armoured vehicle do not open.

'These hajjis are going to get themselves killed,' he says to the soldier.

'If they don't stop at checkpoints, they will,' the soldier replies. 'I'll fuckin' shoot them.' He waves us through. 'Have a good day,' he says. 'Be safe,' Carl replies.

We are in. The ordeal is over.

Mesopotamia has become the International Zone. History compressed. Miles and miles of razorwire, sharply glinting in the sun. Everything apart from the palm trees seems to be grey. Concrete blast walls everywhere you look, dividing compound from compound, building from building, even separating driving lanes in the approach to the checkpoints. Guardhouses. Bulletproof glass. The infrastructure of the war on terror. The architecture of freedom. The checkpoints, manned by Marines, are located every few hundred yards even though we have reached the bosom of the American presence in Iraq, symbolically headquartered in Saddam's republican palace on the banks of the Tigris.

Land of the fertile crescent, bounded by the Tigris and Euphrates, home to mankind's earliest beginnings. This is the realm of Herodotus, the birth of history and the desert city of Babylon. Adam and Eve's Garden of Eden is said to have been in southern Iraq. Baghdad, seat of the Abbasid caliphate, once known as Dar as Salam, the House of Peace, now runs with blood. Bodies are being found in the Tigris every day. Most have been shot in the head. Their arms are bound. Many have been tortured. Their bodies betray the marks left by their torturers. Holes made by electric drills. Bruises from beatings. Skin peeled off. Ears removed. Eyes gouged out.

I don't know it yet but these three square miles on the banks of the Tigris will be my home for the next year. I am halfway to Herodotus.

'Welcome to hell,' says Shane.

# 4

# Baghdad, Evangelicals and Mocking Madmen

*War makes rattling good history; but Peace is poor reading.*
Thomas Hardy, *The Dynasts* (1904)

IN BODRUM, HERODOTUS emerged most clearly through living history. His spirit presided over the pioneering band of nautical archaeologists and their history-changing underwater discoveries, seeped through the crumbling marble stones of the Mausoleum and stood on guard outside the castle. It was in the study of the past, pulsing strongly beneath the surface of everyday life in a modern tourist resort, that he was most discernible in his hometown. If this was the Herodotean splash in Bodrum, there was also a gentler ripple spreading out across the sun-bright waters disputed by historically squabbling Greece and Turkey, a liquid reflection of Herodotus' portrait of clashing Greek and Persian civilisations in the Aegean.

In Baghdad it was different. Before leaving for Iraq, Babylon was my main goal. There are only so many places Herodotus writes about in the *Histories* with a level of detail suggesting he had visited them himself, and Babylon, which he describes with a sense of sheer wonder and delight, is one of them.

But I was also drawn to Babylon in the same way that nineteenth-century explorers were attracted to the Nile. They were searching for its source, tracing the elusive beginnings of the world's greatest river as it oiled its way through palm-studded sands. Babylon was history's equivalent of those dark clumps of oozing soil, as close to the source of human civilisation as one could hope to approach, seat of a world-spanning empire which had given its name ever after to denote greatness, untold wealth and ostentation, not to mention decadence and outright debauchery. The *Oxford English Dictionary* described the Chaldaean capital as 'the mystical city of the Apocalypse', an irresistible siren to any traveller. If I'm honest about it, I was also attracted by Babylon's desert-bound exoticism, by the chance to travel to a once cosmopolitan city whose links to the outside world had recently been severed. A veil had been drawn across Babylon, and what could be more tempting than the opportunity to draw that veil aside and stare upon her naked form?

To Baghdad, on the other hand, I gave little thought. The Iraqi capital, former jewel of the Islamic world, home of the Abbasid caliphate that held sway from 750 to 1258, was interesting in its own right. But in the world of the *Histories* it wasn't even an impostor. It didn't even appear for the very simple reason that it didn't exist at the time. Which is why, at this stage, I regarded the city only as a diverting stepping-stone towards the historied Herodotean prize less than sixty miles to the south.

And yet. Herodotus introduced himself in Baghdad before I could even contemplate a journey in an armoured convoy to Babylon.

---

I was having dinner one evening in the heart of Saddam's old head-quarters, a vast ballroom–canteen in his high-kitsch presidential palace in Baghdad. The Americans called it the DFAC (Dining Facility). Naively, I had been looking forward to local Iraqi and Arab cuisine, fresh humus and tabouleh, fatoush, baba ghanoush, lamb kebab, shish taouk, bulging olives and succulent dates, perhaps even the occasional Iraqi delicacy of masgouf, fish from the Tigris and Euphrates marinated in lemon and tamarind juice and grilled whole on an open wood fire. Herodotus hailed this region as the richest grain-producing country in the world, also mentioning its dates, sesame oil, wine and honey. None of these local foods, I soon discovered, was an option under Halliburton's subsidiary Kellogg Brown and Root (KBR), which supplied all our food and drink, trailers, beds, desks, televisions, linens, laundry and cleaning services, air-conditioning units, pens, stationery . . . You could barely eat, drink, breathe, shit, work, sleep or shop without using an expensively contracted KBR service.

This was an American war serving American food to American soldiers and American contractors. Other members of the Coalition of the Willing (once you got past Britain the list looked pretty thin) were welcome in the DFAC, but the deal was that DFAC food, flown in from abroad, was American in style, substance and size: fried chicken, burgers, hot dogs, limp vegetables boiled into sad submission; under-seasoned meat microwaved into oblivion; crunchy factory salads notable only for their lack of flavour.

Although it took me by surprise, Herodotus would have understood the situation immediately. He probably wouldn't even have batted an eyelid (though he would have had a good deal of fun writing about the Americans' eating habits, tastes, appetites, manners and waistlines). The simple point was that Americans thought their customs – in this case cuisine – were best. Why eat weird Iraqi food when you could have a Sloppy Joe and chilled soda instead? You could venture outside to try your luck in what was known as the Red Zone – a small group of us, rebels against the War on Terror's official lexicon, called it Iraq – but in the end most people tended to prefer a hamburger, fries and Coke inside the International (or Green) Zone to humus, fatoush and kebab (and a possible bullet in the head) outside.

This evening I was having dinner alone. A weary-looking, middle-aged Iraqi man, also alone, shared the table a couple of places down from me. Between us, propped against a bottle of Buffalo Bob's Extra Spicy Everything Sauce (an essential condiment given the lack of flavour anywhere), was a little gold-and-black leaflet, not much larger than a couple of business cards. It was called 'The Pilgrimage' and on the cover it had a picture of the Kaaba at Mecca, Islam's holiest place, the sacred cube of granite Muslims believe was built by Abraham and his son Ishmael. A devotional blur of pilgrims swirled around it. The Koran enjoins all able Muslims to make the pilgrimage or *haj* to Mecca at least once in their lives. It is one of the five pillars of Islam. I picked up the leaflet and started reading. My Iraqi neighbour spotted me but carried on munching away on his fried chicken without enthusiasm.

Inside was a cartoon story. A group of Muslims are returning from the pilgrimage to Mecca on board Flight 727 to Heathrow. The lead character is a pious and respected man called Dr Abdul Ali. Suddenly, there is a problem. 'We have an EMERGENCY!' the pilot barks to air traffic control. Flight 727 has only one landing gear locked down. The passengers are instructed to prepare for an emergency landing. 'Dr Ali, I'm AFRAID to die,' the man next to him whimpers. 'Be of courage, my brothers,' he replies. 'If Allah wills it, we may be in paradise in just a few minutes.' The plane crashes. All 246 people on board are killed. Next an angel appears, lifting Abdul Ali out of the fire. Now we see the distraught relatives waiting for their loved ones on the ground. A woman asks, 'Why?' 'It was the will of Allah,' her companion replies. 'Thankfully, their sins were forgiven because they performed the *haj*.'

Alas, it is not so straightforward. Dr Ali assumes the winged angel is taking him express to paradise as they hurtle across a starry, sci-fi sky. But no. First there is some celestial bureaucracy to contend with, a heavenly dose of health and safety. The angel has to see whether his charge's name is in the Book of Life. Would you believe it, it isn't. Dr Ali's having a day from hell. He doesn't know it yet, but hell is where he's going. 'Depart from me, ye cursed, into everlasting fire,' a giant, enthroned God commands him. (There is a helpful asterisk at this point, indicating that God's words are taken from Matthew 25:41.) But Dr Ali isn't going to accept it just like that. 'No, wait! I'm supposed to stand before Allah,' he says. 'Who are YOU?' You have to admire the man's pluck. He's not taking his banishment to the everlasting inferno lying down. The Almighty booms back: 'I am the Lord Jesus Christ, to whom is given all judgement [John 5:22]. Because Mohammed rejected Me, he is not in Heaven.' God is in full fire-and-brimstone mood now. 'And Allah is a satanic counterfeit. He is one of many false gods that have deceived millions.' Dr Ali is understandably confused by all this, not to say a bit miffed. It's not fair, he counters, no one ever told him the truth, he was simply following the religion of his family. God isn't having any of it. He's heard all these lame excuses before. He reminds Dr Ali that when he was a medical student, a Christian tried to show him the light, tried telling him that the only way to heaven was through faith in Jesus Christ. But Abdul Ali, as he then was, didn't listen. So now he's toast. 'You must pay the penalty for your own sins,' God pronounces. And off to hell he goes.

The final picture is of Dr Ali, sweat – or are they tears? – pouring down his face. Perhaps he's already in hell. 'Dear Reader ... like Abdul Ali YOU have been told the truth,' the leaflet says. 'Your religion will NOT get you into heaven. Jesus is the ONLY way. Will you trust him as YOUR personal Saviour? Your eternal destiny hangs in the balance.'

On the last page was a sort of sign-up-for-Christianity-as-the-only-passport-to-heaven pledge. It included a guide to prayer which began, 'Dear God, thank you for showing me what You think about Islam. *I also reject it!*'

I put the leaflet down mildly shocked, though probably not quite as taken aback as Dr Ali appearing before an unexpectedly Christian God. After a few weeks in Baghdad, I was growing used to the daily reports – and sounds – of car bombs, suicide bombings, attacks on American soldiers and civilians, kidnappings and beheadings of contractors and so on. I no longer stared in disbelief at civilians wearing two holstered pistols to lunch. The International Zone had its own micro-culture in which the normally strange soon became strangely normal. The abrupt discovery of Christian missionary work in Baghdad took me completely by surprise. I looked across at my Iraqi neighbour.

'Perhaps this is the first time you have seen this?' he asked. His English was lightly perfumed with an Iraqi accent. It had a courtly style that evoked 1950s England: tweed and starch.

'I've never seen anything like it,' I replied, slightly embarrassed.

We introduced ourselves. Fadel was a Baghdad University professor working for the American State Department in the US Embassy. He looked a beaten man, a flat football, as though the life really had been kicked out of him. Instead of offering me his card, he pulled out another leaflet from his breast pocket, this time green and black, and passed it to me. 'I think you will like this one even more,' he said.

There was a white star and crescent on a green background. 'Allah Had No Son' was the title. An angry, bearded Muslim overhears an American boy asking his father what the congregation of men in a mosque courtyard are doing prostrating themselves. They look like rows of turtles. 'They're praying to their moon god, son,' the father replies dismissively. The Muslim is enraged and threatens to kill them for the remark. He boasts that a Muslim flag will fly over the White House by 2010. 'It will be the end of Christianity in America,' he snarls. 'Think it's impossible? England was our first target and the Islamic religion is bringing England to her knees.' The illustrator had excelled himself in drawing a face so thoroughly menacing and evil that it would have sent small children diving under their duvets in terror to escape it – perhaps also leaving them with the indelible impression that all Muslims were killers.

In due course, however, and much to our surprise, Mr Angry Bearded Muslim is persuaded that Islam is a false religion based on the pagan worship of the Sabean moon god. He accepts that Allah is just an idol, one of 360 in the Kaaba, and is converted to Christianity. 'O, God, I've been deceived. Allah is a false god, Mohammed is not Your prophet and the Koran is not Your holy book. I trust You as my Saviour. Come into my heart, Lord Jesus.' Exit stage left, tears streaming from his eyes, on a divinely inspired mission to convert his errant Muslim brethren. 'It may cost you your life,' the American warns him sympathetically. No matter. 'It will be worth it, because I'll be with my loving Father in heaven for all eternity (see Luke 9:23–24),' the game new convert replies. The tract ends with a reading recommendation for those who want to discover 'more of the truth about Islam': *Islamic Invasion* by Dr Robert Morey.

'Unbelievable,' I said. 'Must be evangelicals.'

'Some of the language is regrettable, I agree, but I don't think it is quite as bad as al Zarqawi slitting Christian and Jewish throats in the name of Islam [Abu Musab al Zarqawi, leader of Al Qaeda in Iraq, was killed by American forces in 2006]. His methods of conversion are even less subtle than those of our evangelical friends here. And this is terrible for us Muslims because people in your country and in America and the West, they think we are all like this. Bloodthirsty killers and terrorists. These Al Qaeda leaders are evil men but also very brilliant because they make Jews and Christians hate Muslims more and more and this is exactly what they want. They use mosques to store weapons and plan attacks and then, when American soldiers raid the mosques to catch the terrorists, they tell the people the Americans are attacking their religion and that this war is a war against Islam.'

I asked him if he shared this view. He frowned. A pair of salt-and-pepper caterpillar eyebrows made a dash for it down his forehead.

'No, no, I do not think this at all, of course not, but unfortunately more and more of the people are saying this. They hear about the attacks on mosques, they see pictures of the minarets damaged by the American army in Fallujah, they see all the innocent Iraqis being killed in Tikrit, Ramadi, Baghdad, Mosul, all over the country, and they start to believe the bad propaganda. It is very dangerous. Sometimes I think the Americans do not understand how dangerous it is to offend our religion.'

Herodotus alert, in the heart of America's headquarters in Iraq, over a hamburger with an Iraqi academic. Fadel's description of American soldiers raiding mosques and offending Islam, however innocently, recalled one of the most important passages in the *Histories*. It's one which provides us with the clearest indication of Herodotus' passion for religious tolerance.

It comes in Book 3 and the context is Cambyses' invasion and conquest of Egypt in 525 BC. The Persian Great King has been forced to abandon his campaign against Ethiopia due to abysmal planning and the resulting lack of provisions for his army. Herodotus goes on to discuss what he calls the Persian king's 'maniacal savagery' in Memphis. The bloodshed begins with a calculated assault on the Egyptians' religion when Cambyses sees the city celebrating the appearance of Apis, the sacred bull of Memphis. He wants to know why the people weren't celebrating when he first visited their city but have waited until now, just after he has lost a large part of his army in the Egyptian desert. 'They replied that a god had appeared amongst them; he was wont to reveal himself only at long intervals of time, and whenever he did so, all Egypt rejoiced and celebrated a festival. Cambyses' answer to this was, that the men were liars, and as such he had them executed.'

Religious tolerance is not high on his agenda in Egypt. Next he calls in the priests, questions them about Apis and orders them to bring him the bull.

The priests brought the animal and Cambyses, half mad as he was, drew his dagger, aimed a blow at Apis' belly, but missed and struck his thigh. Then he laughed, and said to the priests: 'Do you call that a god, you poor creatures? Are your gods flesh and blood? Do they feel the prick of steel? No doubt a god like that is good enough for the Egyptians; but you won't get away with trying to make a fool of me.' He then ordered the priests to be whipped by the men whose business it was to carry out such punishments, and any Egyptian who was found still keeping holiday to be put to death. In this way the festival was broken up, the priests punished, and Apis, who lay in the temple for a time wasting away from the wound in his thigh, finally died and was buried by the priests without the knowledge of Cambyses.

After this initial display of aggression, Cambyses embarks on a killing spree. First of all, he has his brother Smerdis killed. Then, bloodlust up, he kills the younger of the two sisters he has married in defiance of local custom. According to the Egyptian version of the story, Herodotus says, 'Cambyses, in a fury, kicked her; and, as she was pregnant at the time, she had a miscarriage and died.'

A brother and sister down. The bloodshed is purely familial up to this point. Poor old Prexaspes is next to get it in the neck. Or at least his son, the king's cupbearer, is. Cambyses suddenly recalls an earlier comment from Prexaspes that the people thought their king was a bit of a tippler, 'too fond of his wine'. Cambyses says to Prexaspes, 'You see your son standing there by the door? If I shoot him right through the middle of the heart, I shall have proved the Persians' words empty and meaningless; if I miss, then say, if you will, that the Persians are right and my wits are gone.' He draws his bow, fells the boy and orders the body to be cut open and examined. The arrow is found to have pierced the heart. Cambyses laughs hysterically. 'Now tell me if you ever saw anyone else shoot so straight.'

The mayhem continues with further desecration of sacred sites. According to Herodotus, Cambyses 'broke open ancient tombs' and examined the corpses inside, went into the temple of Hephaestus and 'jeered at the god's statue', and 'entered the temple of the Cabiri, which no one but the priest is allowed to do, made fun of the images there ... and actually burnt them'. Herodotus is astonished. The crime is so awful there can only be one explanation for it. The Persian king must have been unhinged. Why else would he insult another people's religion?

> In view of all this, I have absolutely no doubt whatever that Cambyses was completely out of his mind; it is the only possible explanation of his assault upon, and mockery of, everything which ancient law and custom have made sacred in Egypt. For if anyone, no matter who, were given the opportunity of choosing from amongst all the nations in the world the beliefs which he thought best, he would inevitably, after careful consideration of their relative merits, choose those of his own country. Everyone without exception believes his own native customs, and the religion he was brought up in, to be the best; and that being so, it is unlikely that anyone but a madman would mock at such things.

You can see Herodotus on stage, hamming it up and working himself up into a lather of incredulity in front of his transfixed audience. He's enjoying every minute of it. Mocking another religion? Who would do such a thing? His conclusion that Cambyses' insanity is 'the only possible explanation' for the outrage strikes the early-twenty-first-century reader as quaintly naive. Today we are inured to religious hatred and persecution across the world. We see zealous intolerance in the Balkans, Kashmir, Egypt, Lebanon, Palestine and Israel, in Northern Ireland, Saudi Arabia, Pakistan, Iraq, Iran, Afghanistan, America, the UK, US, France, Turkey, China, the Philippines, the list is endless.

Herodotus' message is even more timely and relevant today than it was two-and-a-half millennia ago. But it goes unheeded, as it always has and as it always will, because history teaches us that we do not learn from history, that we fight the same wars against the same enemies for the same reasons in different eras, as though time really stood still and history itself as moving narrative was nothing but an artful illusion.

Everyone is instinctively loyal to his national customs, Herodotus goes on.

> There is abundant evidence that this is the universal feeling about the ancient customs of one's country. One might recall, in particular, an account told of Darius. When he was king of Persia, he summoned the Greeks who happened to be present at his court, and asked them

what they would take to eat the dead bodies of their fathers. They replied that they would not do it for any money in the world. Later, in the presence of the Greeks, and through an interpreter, so that they could understand what was said, he asked some Indians of the tribe called Callatiae, who do in fact eat their parents' bodies, what they would take to burn them. They uttered a cry of horror and forbade him to mention such a dreadful thing. One can see by this what custom can do, and Pindar, in my opinion, was right when he called it 'king of all'.

Herodotus is referring to his contemporary the great lyric poet who wrote,

> Custom, the king of all
> Of mortals and immortals,
> Leads, justifying that which is most violent
> By its very powerful hand.

'This passage is sometimes seen as an example of the tolerant attitude of Herodotus towards other lands, a type of cultural relativism,' a footnote in my edition tells me. 'Herodotus may indeed be tolerant but the point in Pindar seems to be that custom is a tyrant, compelling people to behave in a certain way.'

An indication, in other words, that multiculturalism can be a double-edged sword. Tolerance of different customs in Western societies is admirable, particularly when compared with the repression practised against minorities in many developing countries. It runs into difficulties, however, when someone else's customs call for the very destruction of Western societies and their freedoms. We can't, unfortunately, seek out Herodotus on this. Such problems were yet to appear. But we can speculate that, had he been around to grapple with the conundrum posed by Islamist militancy in Western societies, he would have been a powerful and eloquent advocate against it in the op-ed pages of national newspapers, in television studios and probably in his own blog. It seems reasonable to assume he would have identified the ideology of Al Qaeda and its sympathisers as a threat to the West, and one that needed to be engaged, confronted and defeated, more in the marketplace of ideas, perhaps, than on the battlefield. I think he would have opposed the Iraq War, objecting to pre-emptive action and arguing it was a dangerous case of imperial overstretch that would inevitably result in nemesis. But he surely would have had no truck with those who sought to demonise Islam – or Christianity. He would have understood only too clearly from personal experience the seismic dangers inherent in a clash of civilisations.

The profound loyalty attached to customs, as identified by Herodotus, is such that you break open tombs (Cambyses) or raid mosques (the American military in Iraq) at your peril. Customs are not passing whims. They evolve over time, harden over history into cultural cement. They become defining, all-important badges of identity, for nations, tribes, religions, individuals. Herodotus knows this, understands the need to recognise and tolerate differences, appreciates the danger of riding roughshod over other people's traditions.

'The Americans are not interested in our history,' Fadel continued. 'Unlike many of my countrymen, I think they came here with good intentions but they seem to believe they can just sweep all our past to one side as if it doesn't matter and install democracy overnight.'

He told me about his neighbourhood in Baghdad, where the Americans had recently established an elected Neighbourhood Advisory Council or NAC. 'Of course it's good to have democracy and elections, but we already have tribal authority exercised through our sheikh. Suddenly we have two leaders in the community and now there are problems all the time because no one knows who is in charge. Everyone respects the sheikh but the Americans are giving all the money to the NAC. They don't like the tribal system. They say it's not democratic. They disapprove of the sheikhs having all this hereditary power without any elections. The problem is, it's part of our culture. It's a custom which goes back long before America or Britain even existed.'

Over the months in Baghdad, these cultural collisions became customary. The template of freedom and democracy didn't always fit as neatly as its ideological architects had hoped in Iraq. In which case they pushed harder and forced it. It was like an imperial default setting. Contrast this with Cyrus, whose more enlightened behaviour after capturing Babylon saw him later revered by Jews as a messiah.

The American gospel of free-market capitalism brought with it its own faith-filled preachers in the form of the Office of Private Sector Development, an organisation founded on perversely optimistic assumptions that looked increasingly incongruous as the fires of the insurgency consumed ever greater swathes of the country. Earnest seminars on strengthening liquidity, asset monetisation and managing market transparency, held against the fearful baritone of car bombs, rocket and mortar attacks and staccato small-arms fire, belonged more to an Evelyn Waugh satire than to twenty-first-century nation-building.

Then there were the fantastically well-paid Women's Rights and Equality consultants. One of them, an Iraqi-American woman called Zeinab, who was less evangelistic than some of her colleagues, became a friend. Her Iraqi side saw the funny side of it. 'It's all bullshit,' she confessed to me once. 'Contractually, I'm not even allowed to leave the Green Zone for security reasons, so how much empowering Iraqi women am I going to do stuck inside this bubble? We're creating a national assembly where 25 per cent of the politicians will be women, and you know what, we don't have anywhere like that proportion of women legislators in Congress and I bet you Brits don't in your parliament, either. And nor does any other Western democracy I know about. But, hey, it's going to work here, because we say so. Never mind about Iraqi culture, history or anything.'

The British were not much better. In their case, they knew more than the Americans. About everything. This was abundantly true among the brisk army officers who believed their experience in Northern Ireland gave them unique insight into an insurgency that was daily breaking new ground in terms of its utter, beheading brutality and, frankly, made the Troubles in Ulster look like a half-hearted scrap in a children's playground. The Americans had no history, the British argued, no tradition of empire and peacekeeping overseas, they didn't understand other cultures like the British did, weren't able to build rapport with the Iraqis, had no idea how to win hearts and minds. Of course, if the UK was running the show, they wittered on, it would all be different. They spoke with the overconfidence common to fallen empires. History had removed much of the swagger, but the hubris was hanging on.

'You asked me a moment ago if I thought this was a religious war,' Fadel said. 'Well, I don't think it is. There are all sorts of other reasons for this war. But many Iraqis do feel President Bush is attacking Islam. They listen to the language he uses, they listen to his call for a crusade, and they remember the history of Islam and the West. History matters very much here.'

On 16 September 2001, five days after the attacks on the Twin Towers, Bush warned Americans they were in for a long struggle. 'This crusade, this war on terrorism, is going to take a while,' he said. An international uproar, especially loud in the Muslim world, quickly followed. A couple of days later, the president's spokesman Ari Fleischer was wheeled out for damage-limitation purposes. 'Any connotations that would upset any of our partners, or anybody else in the world, the president would regret if anything like that was conveyed,' he said, as though the notion of Muslims being offended by the use of the word crusade was slightly fanciful.

In one sense, it was a minor gaffe. In the largely non-Muslim West, the word crusade is not considered so offensive. Over the past thousand years it has managed to shed much of its historical baggage in general usage so that outside discussions of the eleventh-, twelfth- and thirteenth-century attempts to retake Jerusalem from the Muslims, we understand it more in the sense of the *Oxford English Dictionary*'s 'vigorous movement or enterprise against poverty or a similar social evil' or as a 'personal campaign undertaken for a particular cause'. Many would excuse Bush for what might have been – claims of presidential Christian fundamentalism notwithstanding – a simple slip of the tongue. Yet Muslims, with a more narrowly historical definition and understanding of the word, are unlikely to be so forgiving. Victims tend to have longer historical memories. If the leader of the Western world used the word crusade in the context of launching a war on terrorism, was it any wonder that many Muslims considered this a war on Islam?

The episode was a reminder that history doesn't just belong in the corridors of otherworldly academe. It isn't something to be dismissed lightly, to be brushed under the carpet without a thought. It is a vital force, as integral to decision-making in the worlds of international affairs, statesmanship and war as contemporary politics. In 2007, the History & Policy initiative was launched in London with a view to introducing historical advisers to British government departments. Professor David Cannadine, director of the Institute of Historical Research, said: 'I believe Whitehall departments should have historical advisers and the government should have a Chief Historical Adviser' to improve policymaking. It was Herodotus' wise adviser revisited.

If it is a mistake to seek solutions in history, it is equally unwise not to search for suggestions. To use a maritime analogy, historians are a little like the local pilots that ships' captains use to guide them into ports and harbours around the world. These professionals have an intimate understanding of the terrain below the water, they are familiar with all the shipping lanes, contours, channels, sandbanks and other obstacles. Their local knowledge and navigational expertise provide a reasonable assurance of safety. One could argue that Bush's neocon advisers were like the unhinged ship captain who says, to hell with the pilot, I'll just ram through anything that gets in my way. They were attempting to put themselves above history, to remake and rewrite it in Iraq: tear down all the bricks and start building again from scratch. Perhaps it was the comprehensive failure to understand the unique history of Iraq – every nation prides itself on a distinctive history – that lay at the root of American failure in that country. Maybe, as some of the defenders of the war argued (taking their cue from Zhou Enlai's famous remark in 1972 that it was 'too early to tell' the impact of the French Revolution), it was premature to offer firm historical judgements.

Herodotus would simply observe that hubris tends to lead to nemesis and, however lacking in sophistication that explanation may be, however quaintly old-fashioned it might appear, the argument has an enduring appeal. It is limited, certainly, but it accords with our basic instincts.

Had Herodotus been working as President's Bush's speechwriter or spokesman, quite possibly he would have thrown his hands up in despair at the president's announcement of a crusade. As an observer of the war in Iraq he would have been deeply saddened by the conflict, disturbed by American and British arrogance and equally horrified by the slaughter of 'infidels' at Muslim hands. We suspect he would have been struck by the tragedy of a vicious civil conflict pitting one group of people with one set of customs (the Sunni) against another group with slightly different ones (the Shia). The historian in him would certainly have deplored the looting of the National Museum in Baghdad. He would have been troubled, above all, by the poisonous effect the war has had on relations between the Muslim world and the West, a toxic blast that has corroded common ground, helped entrench prejudices on both sides of the civilisational divide and made future confrontation, conflict and terrorism more likely. And, had he lived to see it, he would have been utterly devastated by the destruction of Babylon.

———

I had a theory: that the road to Babylon led through Baghdad. Time spent in the developing world had taught me the lesson that provincial permission often required capital approval. Without it, historical quests – Herodotean or otherwise – could be doomed before they began. The Iraqis were meant to be running Iraq, but everyone knew the Americans were the real power. Then again, in Hillah and Babylon the Poles were supposed to be in charge. Were they?

It had the potential to be a multilingual minestrone, a Babel of confusion (not unlike Saddam's forked-tongued daily newspaper *Babel*). Which was, thematically, just as it should have been, because the Biblical Tower of Babel was thought to be based on the heaven-grazing temple tower – or ziggurat – of Etemenanki in Babylon, the 'House of the frontier between heaven and earth'. In his account of Babylon Herodotus described it, less evocatively for once, as 'a solid central tower'. I was happy to put up with as much confusion as Babylon could throw at me. As long as I could get there.

The National Museum of Iraq, repository of the nation's history, legacy of the British Orientalist Gertrude Bell, seemed a sensible place to start. I made an appointment to see Dr Donny George, its director, and, several days later, on an intensely bright morning cracking with heat, we punctured the Green Zone bubble and set off in a three-vehicle armoured convoy. The first sight of a stiff summer sky in piercing cornflower blue was a heart-lifting inspiration every morning. I was more used to sagging grey skies that leaked and leaked and wore you down. But with the insurgency showing no signs of abating, only reaching new levels of surreal viciousness with every week that went by, the stabbing heat and crystalline light seemed also to reek of danger. There was a ferocity about the temperature that complemented the savagery of the suicide bombers who ripped through crowds in a maelstrom of boiling metal and molten rain.

The convoy was commanded by Team Leader Luis (pronounced Lou-ees), an improbably languid, barrel-chested Cuban-American colleague with the sort of glamorously hypogean voice that evoked nightclubs, velvet jackets, cocktails, dim lighting and cigars and was designed expressly to get women into bed.

Sometimes I forget, but not everyone is interested in history. I had been thinking that Luis and his team, who were more used to taking out American army engineers to visit ministries and inspect infra-structure projects, might relish the change in routine. They would inevitably share my enthusiasm for visiting a museum that housed some of civilisation's greatest treasures but was otherwise closed to the public, a huge, unlikely-to-be-repeated treat. It wasn't to be. Inside the Land Cruiser there was a conspicuous lack of interest in the museum, offset by a considerable interest in women, ambushes, magazines about women, pictures of women with no clothes on, small-arms attacks, women in Baghdad generally, roadside bombs, available women spe-cifically and suicide bombers. The priority was staying alive – and talking about women.

I wanted to talk to George about getting to Babylon and also to see if there was anything we could do with a modest budget of $10,000 to help his museum, which had infamously lost so many artefacts shortly after Baghdad fell to American forces. History had walked out of his doors in April 2003. Some of it had found new homes with private dealers, others had gone to unscrupulous collectors, some reappeared later in auction houses and even, in the most brazen cases, on eBay.

Nothing is ever very clear in war. After the initial outcry around the world at the loss of a reported 170,000 items, it later emerged that nothing like that number had been stolen. The museum had, in fact, removed much of its collection to bank vaults and other hiding places before the war began. There were rumblings against George, in particular his Baathist background, and murmurings of an inside job. In the *Guardian*, David Aaronovitch criticised 'the credulousness of many western academics and others who cannot conceive that a plausible and intelligent fellow professional might have been an apparatchik of a fascist regime and a propagandist for his own past'. During a conversation with George's then boss, Dr Abdul Aziz Hameed, chairman of the State Board of Antiquities and Heritage, on 14 December 2004, I was told that 15,000 items were missing, still a terrible loss.

George was a short, pear-shaped man, a jovial, welcoming Weeble, a slimmed-down Iraqi version of the English actor Richard Griffiths, complete with matching moustache. He had an air of merriment about him, and a twinkle in the eye that made me think of Father Christmas. He had probably never dressed up as St Nicholas, but the religion was right. He was one of the more prominent members of Iraq's tiny Christian community, part of the Assyrian Church of the East. That connection unlocked another historical doorway which led, of all things, to the See of Babylon, said to have been founded by the Apostle St Thomas and regarded as the origin of the Assyrian Church of the East. He normally worshipped at St George's Church in Baghdad, where he had been married, he told me, but it had been damaged in a recent terrorist attack and was now too dangerous to attend.

Herodotus' generalised observations on religion – each man thinks his own is the best – were being confirmed across the country in pools of blood. Like Syria and Jordan, Iraq had long been proud of the peaceful coexistence between its Muslim majority and Christian minority, but Christians were being attacked in their droves. Churches had been bombed in Baghdad and Mosul, Christian-owned shops selling alcohol and music had been firebombed and Christians were receiving leaflets warning them to stop 'corrupting Islamic society'. The era of religious tolerance that would have delighted Herodotus – under secular Saddam – was over.

Though he was obviously busy, George insisted on showing me around his museum. I needed no encouragement. It had been closed since the first Gulf War in 1990 and had never opened again. No one had decorated it during that time, either, and the fabric of the building, invaded by termites long before the Americans arrived, was decaying steadily. As we walked along, Luis padded discreetly behind us with his M4 rifle, oblivious or indifferent to the history around him. Now and then, like many government buildings in Baghdad, the place came under fire. Occasionally I made way for him so he could listen in on George's commentary.

'Go ahead, man, you do your history thing,' he growled. 'I want to make sure *you're* not history.'

My abiding memory of the visit is of dust and closed doors, locked gates, sealed storehouses and regret. The museum Gertrude Bell had laboured so hard to establish had, less than a century later, given up the ghost. It was a mortuary for history. We ambled disconsolately through neglected galleries, shafts of sunlight lancing through the gloom, illuminating dancing motes of dust thrown up by our funereal procession. The museum had lost its grip on the present. Blurring time, it was falling back into the past, becoming part of the history it contained. The treasures of classical antiquity were suffocating. So, too, some of the greatest artefacts ever culled from the Muslim world, fruits of Islamic jihad when Baghdad was the illustrious, sparkling-domed capital of the Dar al Islam, seat of the Abbasid caliphate. Now imperial hubris, jihad and greed had snatched many of those treasures back and dealt the museum a fatal blow.

I remember a magnificent pair of Assyrian statues glowing gold in the light, winged bulls from the palace of Sargon in Khorsabad, standing tall like bearded sentinels, aloof from the chaos outside. I can picture George bobbing about enthusiastically before an arch-shaped panel of glazed bricks in faded green and brown, rich with floral and geometric decorations and pictures of animals, telling me they were the oldest decorated bricks known to man, from Fort Shalmaneser in Nimrud. There were gorgeously ornate statues of deities, stone *mihrabs* (a *mihrab* is an internal niche in a mosque indicating the direction of Mecca in which the faithful should pray), friezes and tablets and statues hidden in darkened corridors and unlit galleries, surrounded by piles of masonry and plaster, the odd wheelbarrow, broken windows, half-finished scaffolding. The cradle of civilisation had been shattered.

I had experienced something similar before in Afghanistan, when I visited the Kabul Museum after the fall of the Taliban. A tearful curator led me through a sad series of empty galleries, pausing here and there to show me ancient Buddhist artefacts smashed by the turbaned iconoclasts. He had managed to preserve them for years during the dark days of the Russian invasion and the factional mujahideen fighting that followed their withdrawal a decade later. Then the Taliban came along and non-Islamic history was just something to destroy. For the greater glory of Islam.

On an earlier trip to Afghanistan, I had marvelled at the colossal Buddhas of Bamiyan, 125- and 180-feet statues sculpted into sandstone cliffs almost 2,000 years ago, with the same sense of wonder as the countless visitors and pilgrims who had come to see them before me. Weeks later, after condemning them as unIslamic, the Taliban blew them up in one of the more shocking assaults on history of recent years. Religion, despising Clio's studied indifference to the chronological story of man's worship of God over the centuries, its lack of preference for one band of zealots over another, had taken offence and wreaked havoc.

I mentioned Gertrude Bell to George while we were walking through the museum. Like many British visitors to Iraq, I was fascinated by a woman whose name is permanently inscribed in Iraqi history. Inevitably, there were historical parallels between the British invasion of Iraq and the American-led campaign eighty-six years later. 'We shall, I trust, make it a centre for Arab civilisation and prosperity,' Bell wrote to her father as British troops entered Baghdad in March 1917. The optimistic neocons said the same sort of thing.

Bell was also a Herodotus fan. In 1903, then aged thirty-four, she was travelling alone in Asia Minor. She began by visiting Smyrna, Ephesus and Pergamum. Moving on to Sardis, the opulent capital of Croesus before Cyrus took it from him in 546 BC, she turned to the Greek historian as her guide. 'I was delighted I had Herodotus so fresh in my mind,' she wrote. In 1927, Bell's brilliant colleague, archaeologist and lifelong friend, the 'wandering scholar' David Hogarth, in his last public speech as president of the Royal Geographical Society, said that he was looking forward to 'spending quite a respectable portion of Eternity in talking to Herodotus'.

'Ah, Miss Bell,' George said wistfully. 'She was a very great lady.' He spoke her name tenderly as though recalling a lover from a golden era. He led me to a section of wall in the entrance lobby on which a large square outline was visible. Whatever it was that had been attached there originally had been removed. 'This is where Miss Bell should be,' said George. 'We're trying to have her returned to the museum where she belongs. She's part of our history.'

George said the bust and plaque had been sent to the holy southern city of Najaf for safekeeping prior to the 2003 invasion. Later, I offered to help restore Gertrude Bell to her rightful home in Baghdad and a team was sent to bring her back. Unfortunately, the museum in Najaf had been taken over by the Mahdi Army of firebrand cleric Muqtada al Sadr and our infidels were told to clear off, empty-handed.

Through the museum she founded, Bell had sought to preserve the antiquities of – in reverse historical order – Iraq, Mesopotamia, Babylonia and Assyria and their earlier, Biblical incarnations of Sumer and Akkad. It was a hugely important, unifying act for the new nation she had helped create, giving Iraq a shared history – national life-blood – for the first time. Her achievements were commemorated in a bronze plaque which had hung on the wall in front of us, together with a bust by Anne Acheson. I later tracked down a picture of the plaque *in situ*, in a volume of Bell's personal papers. It read:

GERTRUDE BELL

Her memory the Arabs will always hold in reverence and affection.
She created the Museum in 1923
Being then Honorary Director of Antiquities for the Iraq
With wonderful knowledge and devotion
She assembled the most precious objects in it
And through the heat of summer
Worked on them until the day of her death
On 12th July, 1926
King Faisal and the government of Iraq
In gratitude for her deeds in this country
Have ordered that the Principal Wing shall bear her name
And with their permission
Her friends have erected this Tablet

We said farewell to Bell and returned to George's office. He said the $10,000 donation I was offering – a drop in the ocean of international funding that he was more accustomed to dealing with – could help renovate one of Baghdad's oldest buildings, owned by the museum and used to house its archives on Haifa Street, which had become the city's most dangerous road. It was a small contribution to preserving Baghdad's endangered history. But that morning, once we had finished our tour of the depleted galleries, he was more interested in talking about Babylon.

He was apoplectic about the damage done to the site since the invasion. Although it was the Americans who had decided to construct a military base at Babylon, just outside the town of Hillah, in April 2003, George blamed the Polish forces, to whom the site had been handed over in September, for its physical destruction (the Poles, naturally, blamed the Americans). He wanted them to provide compensation, which seemed a forlorn hope. Recently he had spoken to a Polish colonel who admitted his men had scraped off some topsoil to make parking lots in the camp.

'If a farmer did this to Babylon, we'd put him in jail,' George said, scarcely able to believe such thoughtless philistinism. 'He told me it was "nothing much, just a bit of topsoil". We're talking about Babylon here. What did he think he was doing? In 1987, when I was a field director at Babylon, the electricity department wanted to build a room for a transformer. We told them they weren't allowed to dig any foundations. Scraping off less than ten centimetres of soil we discovered a Parthian plate from 200 AD, a beautiful, delicate piece of pottery. You find things like that in Babylon. You're standing a few centimetres above the history of the world. It's mankind's greatest heritage site. You don't just start digging it up to make more room for your tanks.'

George said the Poles had dug two huge trenches, fifty and eighty metres long respectively, in the south central area of the site. 'This is the most sacred area of Babylon, the main temple, priests' houses. What they were doing wasn't archaeology. They were excavating to make parking lots. I mean, can you believe it?'

Wars shape history, define its contours, give it form and substance, reroute it, dispose of old powers and bring new ones to the fore. Yet in Babylon war seemed not to have shaped history so much as to have erased it. That the world seemed to be so surprised – as well as justly horrified – by the violent rape of the site is evidence of our inability to see ourselves as nothing more than a tiny part of a historical continuum, a frozen still in a film spanning untold millennia. This is now, we say, the present. We have nothing to do with history. We stand apart from it. We are modern and civilised. It shouldn't happen in the twenty-first century, we insist, as though now renders null and void the sorry history of human behaviour in war.

The Polish and American soldiers and the Iraqi looters, who had all played fast and loose with civilisation's greatest historical site, were digging away, scraping, stealing and selling just as their ancient-world counterparts had done.

You see the same thing happening in Herodotus. Indulging his love for the dramatic moment over strict historical accuracy as we would understand it today, he stages a conversation between Cyrus and Croesus, shortly after the Persian conqueror has taken the Lydian capital of Sardis after a two-week siege. One empire is making way for another. World-changing history is being made. Flushed with his success, Cyrus kicks off the victory celebrations by condemning his rival to death. Croesus is clapped in chains and placed on a pyre. There, the man whose name came to define wealth beyond our most exuberantly avaricious dreams – rich as Croesus – ponders his spectacular downfall.

How he wishes he had listened to the wise man Solon who, on an earlier visit to Sardis, had been conspicuously unimpressed by the magnificent capital, making light of Croesus' legendary wealth and good fortune. 'Often enough God gives man a glimpse of happiness, and then utterly ruins him,' Solon warned, and now, as the flames lick around him, Croesus remembers these nuggets of wisdom every king in the world should heed.

Pride, once again, has brought about a man's ruin. But no. Cyrus learns of his rival's brink-of-death repentance and is sufficiently moved by it to order a dramatic, last-minute reprieve. Spared this exquisitely painful execution, the defeated monarch is in an understandably reflective mood. Surveying the scene around him, he sees the Persian soldiers ransacking the rich city he has just lost. He begs Cyrus for permission to speak. The Persian nods encouragement.

'What is it', he asked, 'that all those men of yours are so intent upon doing?'

'They are plundering your city and carrying off your treasures.'

'Not my city or my treasures,' Croesus answered. 'Nothing there any longer belongs to me. It is you they are robbing.'

These days, with our more inclusive ways (and love of emotive platitudes) we might say those who defiled Babylon and Sardis were robbing humanity of its shared history. But it's unlikely the soldiers, the men who owed their allegiance to Cyrus or President Bush, ever thought that. Soldiers are like locusts. They consume everything that is put in front of them. Some of the more legacy-minded celebrate their actions for future generations to discover. The Marines who scrawled graffiti all over Babylon, including memorably banal messages such as 'Cruz chillen' in Saddam's spot' and 'Hi Vanessa. I love you. From Saddam's palace' were adding their own records, displaying the common impulse to inscribe their names and those of their loved ones in history.

I asked George how I could visit Babylon, what I would need in terms of permission. He laughed sadly and rocked in his chair. The Weeble wobbled but it didn't fall down. It was a lot easier for me, who had ridden into Iraq on the coat-tails of the Coalition and had access to a fleet of armoured vehicles and colleagues working in a security company, to get to Babylon than it was for him, director of the National Museum. To his great dismay the Poles still controlled the site. Getting inside, once I reached Camp Babylon, would be a formality. As for official permission, I was just in time. The Poles were about to hand the site back to the Iraqis, at which point Babylon would once again close its doors to the outside world to take stock of its most recent battering and audit the latest losses in its time-stretching history.

On the way back from the museum we drove through the capital at high speed, mounting and crossing central reservations at will, driving along streets the wrong way to avoid dangerous traffic jams. Baghdad flew past in a haze of resentful faces and burnt rubber. I was buzzing after our VIP visit to the museum, bristling with excitement about the trip to Babylon.

'How about that, then, Luis?' I said, feeling full of it. 'Not bad for a morning's work? A private tour of the Baghdad Museum. Beats going to the Ministry of Electricity, doesn't it?'

But history, Iraqi or otherwise, held no interest for Luis. He was as unimpressed as Solon had been in Sardis. He looked at me in the mirror. 'Just a bunch of fucking stones, man,' he said.

# 5

# Babylon

*Human blunders, usually, do more to shape history than human wickedness.*
A. J. P. Taylor, *The Origins of the Second World War* (1961)

BABYLON FIRST LOOMS from the beige desert plain and prods into our consciousness in around 1792 BC, a spectacularly long time ago. For once we can be reasonably specific with the date. It marked the beginning of the reign of Hammurabi, one of Babylon's two most famous kings. He's known, above all else, for his promulgation of a fairly uncompromising code of laws which bear his name and which sit today in the Louvre in Paris in the impressive form of an eight-foot stela of carved black diorite.

There are other ways of contextualising 1792 BC. We might calculate, for example, that Hammurabi's reign began roughly 1,300 years before Herodotus was born. About half as much time as separates the early twenty-first century from Herodotus. It seems a little presumptuous for this prolific Babylonian lawmaker and monarch so comprehensively to predate the Father of History, but perhaps the presumption is Herodotus'. It was awarded posthumously, so we shouldn't blame him for it, but the Father of History moniker draws a neat line between the pre- and post-Herodotean worlds, as though consigning anything that happened before the *Histories* into the realm of non-history. Hammurabi didn't even get the title Father of Law. You could argue that his achievements are remembered in the popular expression 'written in stone', which is possibly the case, but it's really not very much in terms of name recognition and you couldn't ever prove it anyway. So much for capricious Clio.

Before we start feeling too sorry for Hammurabi, we need to check in with our chronology again. Brilliant though this trailblazing, territorially acquisitive, irrigationally enlightened king undoubtedly was, he's much too early for us. We may be interested in his laws, most of which seem to end in the ominous phrase 'he shall be put to death', but anyone who can make Herodotus look so much younger by comparison falls outside this discussion.

We'll put Hammurabi and his formalised control-freakery to one side, use him as the most convenient marker of Babylon's vast antiquity and then fast-forward a millennium or so – make that 1,188 years – until we're just about in the Herodotean orbit. We'll stop in, say, 604 BC, which happens to be the date at which Babylon's even better-known king, Nebuchadnezzar II, Old Testament anti-hero, succeeded to the throne.

He, too, predates Herodotus, by over a century, but his importance here is in the terrific building programme he orchestrated, the fruits of which so impressed the Greek historian. It was Nebuchadnezzar's imperial frenzy of construction which resulted in the most glorious city of the ancient world, a dazzling urban vista of towering temples, shrines and palaces clad in blue-glazed tiles, resplendent in gold, silver and bronze, all encircled by city walls so massive, said the Greek geographer Strabo, that two chariots, each drawn by four horses, could pass each other with ease on the road that ran atop them.

'Babylon lies in a wide plain, a vast city in the form of a square with sides nearly fourteen miles long and a circuit of some fifty-six miles, and in addition to its enormous size it surpasses in splendour any city of the known world,' Herodotus' ten-page description of Babylon begins. 'It is surrounded by a broad deep moat full of water, and within the moat there is a wall fifty royal cubits wide and two hundred high.'

Nebuchadnezzar's fame or notoriety in the Western world owes more to the Bible than to our history books. He's forever popping up doing dastardly deeds in Kings, Chronicles, Ezra, Jeremiah and Daniel, with cameo appearances in Nehemiah and Esther. He's as Old Testament as they come, an exemplar of thieving, slaying, kidnapping idolatry, a mighty, rich, slightly deranged, Jew-killing, temple-bashing despot, the incinerator of Shadrach, Meshach and Abednego for whom there is no such thing as too many graven golden images. Daniel 3:1–2 gives us a graphic impression of his passion for building and opulence:

> Nebuchadnezzar the king made an image of gold, whose height was threescore cubits, and the breadth thereof six cubits: he set it up in the plain of Dura, in the province of Babylon.
>
> Then Nebuchadnezzar the king sent to gather together the princes, the governors, and the captains, the judges, the treasurers, the counsellors, the sheriffs, and all the rulers of the provinces, to come to the dedication of the image which Nebuchadnezzar the king had set up.

The Babylonian king's subjects were subsequently ordered on pain of death by incineration in a 'burning fiery furnace' to worship this gold-god. Wisely, they quickly adapted to their king's peculiar religious tastes. As a child, I remember staring awestruck at a picture of this golden idol in my illustrated Bible.

Nebuchadnezzar's more enduring success – which lasted longer than either his golden images or other monuments – was the publication of his architectural legacy for posterity. His inscriptions followed the tradition of Babylonian kings in relating their building achievements rather than their military record. Not that this in any way implied a show of monarchical modesty. You cannot accuse Nebuchadnezzar of hiding his light under a bushel. In one inscription he talked about tearing down two gates on the celebrated 'Processional Way', the most important street in Babylon, leading from the inner city through the Ishtar Gate and onwards to the Bit Akitu, the 'House of the New Year's Festival':

> I laid their foundations of mortar and bricks and with shining blue-glaze tiles with pictures of bulls and awful dragons I adorned the interior; mighty cedars to roof them over I caused to be stretched out, the wings of the gates of cedar wood coated with bronze, the lintels and the door knobs of brass I fastened into the openings of the gates; massive bulls of bronze and dreadful, awe-inspiring serpents I set up at their thresholds, the two gates I ornamented with great splendour to the amazement of all men. In order that the onslaught of battle might not draw nigh to Imgur-Bel, the wall of Babylon.

Nebuchadnezzar wanted history to record his transformational work in burnt-brick-building and his boasts were virtually ubiquitous for Babylonians, whichever way they looked. They must have been heartily sick of them. He granted himself titles such as 'Nebuchadnezzar, king of Babylon, the judicious prince, shepherd of the widespread people, who like the sun-god oversees the totality of the lands, who determines right and justice, who destroys evil-doers and criminals'. He completed the most celebrated monument Babylon had ever seen, a construction so hubristically horizon-dominating it became the most famous building in the world, a byword for mankind's god-rivalling arrogance.

> As to Etemenanki, the ziggurat of Babylon, of which Nabopolossar, king of Babylon, my father, my begetter, had fixed the foundation – and had raised it 30 cubits but had not erected its top, I set my hand to build it. Great cedars which were on Mount Lebanon in its forest, with my clean hands, I cut down, and placed them for its roof. The gate of Ea, the gate of Lamassu, the gate of Plenty, the gate of Vision, its huge gates about Etemenanki as the day I made brilliant I fitted them in, huge cedar beams for their roof I fitted into place . . .

The rush of building came, as it often does in history, against a background of military conquest. The campaigning began even before he succeeded to the throne. As son and heir of Nabopolossar, Nebuchadnezzar led the Babylonian army into Egypt in 605 BC, routing his enemy at Carchemish, then again at Hamath, after suffering serious losses. In 597, his forces attacked Jerusalem, taking its leaders captive after one of the Bible's better-known sieges. According to the Book of Kings, he:

> carried away all Jerusalem, and all the princes, and all the mighty men of valour, even ten thousand captives, and all the craftsmen and smiths: none remained, save the poorest sort of the people of the land.
>
> And he carried away Jehoiachin [the king of Judah] to Babylon, and the king's mother, and the king's wives, and his officers, and the mighty of the land, those carried he into captivity from Jerusalem to Babylon.
>
> And all the men of might, even seven thousand, and craftsmen and smiths a thousand, all that were strong and apt for war, even them the king of Babylon brought captive to Babylon.

Kidnapping was going strong in Iraq almost three millennia before the beheading thugs of Al Qaeda took to it with such throat-slitting gusto. Where Nebuchadnezzar led, the godless jihadis followed.

Master of Palestine and Syria, Nebuchadnezzar retook Jerusalem in 586 after the Egyptians had been impudent enough to seize it from him, and then put the city of Tyre under siege. In 571, after holding out bitterly for thirteen years, it fell to him. He returned to Egypt, less successfully this time, in 567. By the time of his death in 562, after a masterful reign of forty-two years, he had built upon his father's military successes to establish a powerful empire with Babylon as its unparalleled capital. At three square miles, its size alone was worthy of legend.

Nebuchadnezzar's immediate successors came and went in a whirl-wind of bloodshed and underachievement, three in the space of six years. It was the fourth, Nabonidus, who made more of an impression, ruling from 555 to 539. He was not related to the royal family and came to the fore instead in a military coup, one reason why he turned to history so frequently to legitimate his reign, portraying it in inscriptions as part of Babylon's smooth continuum of religious devotion and architectural munificence. But for all his shamelessly self-serving respect for history, he was unable to do much about the arrival of an infinitely greater history-maker before his city walls in 539. Cyrus had his own designs on posterity – and took Babylon by the sword.

I have sex on my mind when I arrive at Babylon. Nothing to do with my companions on the drive down from Baghdad, two men with guns and a retired British brigadier. Nothing to do, either, with the comely blonde Polish archaeologist whom I bump into after jumping over several rolls of razorwire laid around the main entrance to the site in a desultory attempt to keep out intruders.

No, sex has bubbled up because I have been reading Herodotus *en route*. After the adrenaline-filled exit from Baghdad, a high-speed and swervy business which always concentrates the mind and quickens the heartbeat, I settle down in the back seat with the *Histories*. Outside, the motorway miles stretch with pitiless horizontality across a landscape of litter, squat, square houses, date palms, desert and the occasional shepherd boy or girl driving their tousled flocks along the verges, heads shaded beneath shabby scoops and twirls of cotton. The sun burns the plain into oblivion.

To the south lies the Biblical land of Shinar (Sumer) where some of the earliest humans settled and learnt for the first time how to build with baked mud bricks. As Genesis 11: 2–3 records, 'And it came to pass, as they journeyed from the east, that they found a plain in the land of Shinar, and they dwelt there. Then they said to one another, "Come, let us make bricks and bake them thoroughly." They had brick for stone, and they had asphalt for mortar.'

Herodotus has been discussing the curiosities of Babylonian medicine. The city's population, he tells us, did not enjoy access to a good local GP.

> They have no doctors, but bring their invalids out into the street, where anyone who comes along offers the sufferer advice on his complaint, either from personal experience or observation of a similar complaint in others. Anyone will stop by the sick man's side and suggest remedies which he has himself proved successful in whatever the trouble may be, or which he has known to succeed with other people. Nobody is allowed to pass a sick person in silence; but everyone must ask him what is the matter.

Scarcely pausing for breath, barely allowing us time to digest this magnificently haphazard approach to healthcare, he goes on to observe that the people bury their dead in honey and their funeral dirges remind him of those you hear in Egypt. And then suddenly, completely out of the blue (to the extent that sex is ever a surprise in Herodotus), he comes out with the following ejaculatory – or perhaps post-coital – aside: 'When a Babylonian has had intercourse with his wife, he sits over incense to fumigate himself, with his wife opposite doing the same, and at daybreak they both wash. Before they have washed they will not touch any household utensils'.

What a picture! No high-pressure rainforest shower to blast away the dirt, no moisturising shampoo for dry or damaged hair, no exfoliating soap to peel away the dead skin. No deep bath in which to luxuriate and relax those aching muscles after such a strenuous sexual encounter. Husband and wife have to hunch over a pathetic little fire to perfume their exposed genitals in clouds of sweet incense, wafting the smoke over their nether regions while making sure they don't crouch too low and singe them. What on earth would their children have made of it if they caught a glimpse of their parents behaving so oddly? 'Mummy, why are you burning your bottom?' their baffled little daughter might have asked. And the last sentence, that snippet of domesticity, utterly brilliant. A little extra detail from a virtuoso storyteller. No chopping up garlic and onions or sweeping out the kitchen until both of them have scrubbed up nicely.

Outside, Iraq's melting horizons of flashing mercury speed by. Heat seeps into the vehicle like gas, overpowering the air-conditioning whose whirring gives way to a whimper. My clothes are starting to stick to me and I taste salt in my mouth. It is too hot to speak. Closing my eyes, I retreat down the cool corridor of history and see Herodotus on stage again, working his wide-eyed audience like an old pro. Once he's started on sex, there's no stopping him. It's too good to pass up. And sex and foreigners: a deliciously titillating combination.

'There is one custom amongst these people which is wholly shameful,' he says, pausing coquettishly. The consummate tease. What is it, his audience wants to know? What Babylonian practice can be so low, so depraved that it elicits outright disapproval from this wonderfully tolerant, non-judgemental man? He continues: 'Every woman who is a native of the country must once in her life go and sit in the temple of Aphrodite and there give herself to a strange man.' A snigger or two in the back row. A nudge and a knowing glance here and there. No one can take their eyes off Herodotus.

Many of the rich women, who are too proud to mix with the rest, drive to the temple in covered carriages with a whole host of servants following behind, and there wait; most, however, sit in the precinct of the temple with a band of plaited string around their heads – and a great crowd they are, what with some sitting there, others arriving, others going away – and through them all gangways are marked off running in every direction for the men to pass along and make their choice.

No! Surely it cannot be? A sexual supermarket for Babylonian men with neatly laid-out aisles? It's too good to be true. The Greek men in Herodotus' audience are all Babylonians now. They love this story.

> Once a woman has taken her seat she is not allowed to go home until a man has thrown a silver coin into her lap and taken her outside to lie with her. As he throws the coin, the man has to say, 'In the name of the goddess Mylitta' – that being the Assyrian name for Aphrodite.* The value of the coin is of no consequence; once thrown it becomes sacred, and the law forbids that it should ever be refused. The woman has no privilege of choice – she must go with the first man who throws her the money. When she has lain with him, her duty to the goddess is discharged and she may go home, after which it will be impossible to seduce her by any offer, however large.

You only get one chance, boys, so make it count, Herodotus seems to be saying. Choose carefully. And it doesn't even matter if you're dirt-poor with hardly a bean to your name. You still get the girl.

I like to think of a slave in the audience at this point. I know, a slave would never have been at a snooty symposium like this, you're thinking, it's anachronistic, inaccurate, plain wrong. What's he talking about? And you'd be right. Your scepticism would be entirely justified. But indulge the thought if you will, in the spirit of some of Herodotus' infinitely taller tales and digressions. All right then, I picture a hoary man of toil fantasising about his master's sumptuously soft-skinned wife. If only he was Babylonian, he thinks! How he would enjoy her, ripping off her gown and tumbling about in the grass with this high-handed aristocratic beauty, her dark ringlets cascading down a swan-like neck. He would show her! How sweet it would be to take her, even if just the once. And what a glorious insult to his master. The slave's lost in a blissful, escapist reverie now and he misses Herodotus' playful punchline, delivered in a way which suggests he doesn't find this practice 'wholly shameful' at all: 'Tall, handsome women soon manage to get home again but the ugly ones stay a long time before they can fulfil the condition which the law demands, some of them,

---

* The Babylonians would have known and worshipped the Greek goddess Aphrodite as Ishtar.

indeed, as much as three or four years.' It's a long time to wait to be prostituted to a complete stranger.

---

Agnieszka Dolatowska would not have had to hang around so long. One of three Polish archaeologists attached to the Multinational Division headquartered in Camp Babylon, she is an attractive woman with wavy blonde hair, a light sprinkling of freckles and an air of windswept dreaminess. She is neither tall nor slender – the French would call her *costaude* rather than svelte – but she would have been considered handsome enough to avoid having to languish in the Temple of Aphrodite for three or four years.

If the practice really existed, of course. It is time, once again, to confront Herodotus' reliability. In 1986 the archaeologist Dr John MacGinnis published 'Herodotus' Description of Babylon', an article in which he acknowledged the story of temple prostitution in Babylon had caused 'much controversy'. Many, if not most, academics think the whole thing was a typically Herodotean fantasy. MacGinnis is less inclined to dismiss it out of hand. He argues there were temple employees who may have been prostitutes and notes that the Babylonian goddess Ishtar (a nymphomaniac who was said to have managed a sexual bout with 120 men without so much as pausing for breath) 'assumes the specifically sexual role as the Prostitute and Mother of Love-making'. Augustine, he adds, also refers to sacred prostitution in *De Civitate Dei*. 'It seems that a genuine tradition is recorded,' MacGinnis concludes.

Agnieszka, who has a PhD in the archaeology of death, is doing her afternoon rounds, part of the daily routine to check everything in Babylon is in order (it isn't). She walks along using a black-and-white staff as a walking stick. It resembles an oversize magician's wand. If she could, she would wave it to restore Babylon to its unscathed glory. Though she seems overtaken by melancholy, an understandable reaction in a youthful archaeologist contemplating the destruction of Babylon, meeting her is a happy coincidence because there is no one else to act as guide. Babylon is in the heart of a war zone and isn't open for business. She can spare an hour to show me around.

We begin next to the Ishtar Gate. Here, almost certainly, we are treading in the serially victorious sandalled footsteps of both Cyrus and Alexander, who took Babylon in 539 BC and 331 BC respectively. Assuming they had wanted to make the appropriately triumphal entrance after their hard-won conquest, this is where it would have begun. Here, too, in my own mind, at least, my suede desert boots, submerged in the dust and history of Babylon, are scuffing along in the phantom footprints of Herodotus.

He introduces his account of Babylon towards the end of Book 1, in the context of Cyrus' invasion of Babylonia – which he, like most ancient writers, wrongly calls Assyria. The story begins with Cyrus crossing the River Gyndes and seeing 'one of his sacred white horses' swept away to its death in front of him. What follows next is a harbinger of Xerxes' Hellespont-whipping tantrum much later in the *Histories*: 'Cyrus was so furious with the river for daring to do such a thing, that he swore he would punish it by making it so weak that even a woman could get over in future without difficulty and without wetting her knees.'

We will pass over Cyrus' sexist aside and examine what he did next. First, he halted the army's march on Babylon, split his army in two, marked out 180 channels on each side of the river and 'ordered his men to set to work and dig. Having a vast number of hands employed, he managed to finish the job, but only at the cost of wasting the entire summer. Then, having punished the Gyndes by splitting it into 360 separate channels, Cyrus, at the beginning of the following spring, resumed his march to Babylon.' There is something ominous about this punishment of a river. Interfering with nature, in the Herodotean worldview, is a recipe for disaster. We have been warned.

Since the city had enough provisions to last many years, says Herodotus, Cyrus was despairing of success with his siege of Babylon until one of his men came up with an outlandish – they always are in the *Histories* – suggestion: drain the Euphrates until its level was so low the army could force an entrance along the riverbed. This, like the Gyndes-bashing story, smacks of the fantastic (it 'is not to be accepted', the Penguin footnotes caution, though MacGinnis considers it a possibility. Who to believe?). Cyrus liked the sound of this cunning plan, had the Euphrates diverted into a lake, and the Persian army marched into the city to take it, the water lapping only up to the soldiers' thighs. Cyrus had conquered two rivers and a city.

But Cyrus wouldn't have made his putative triumphal entrance through the gate we pass through for the simple reason that it is a replica. After several years of excavations, the original and best-known entrance to Babylon was carted off by German archaeologists in 1914, together with the lion's share of the lions in relief that once decorated the walls of the Processional Way and now stand in the sanitised safety of the Pergamon Museum in Berlin. Most Iraqis consider that looting. Turks feel likewise about the relocation of friezes and statues from the Mausoleum of Halicarnassus to the British Museum, Greeks about their loss of the Elgin Marbles. If archaeologists have a weakness, it is that they take liberties with other people's history.

The reproduction of the Ishtar Gate is a pristine slice of Legoland, a blue-tiled backdrop for Marines to pose before in photographs emailed to loved ones at home: digitised history from Iraq. I have travelled halfway across the world into a disturbingly vicious war-zone to see this. Things can only look up from here. They do. Sections of the Processional Way, having shed their glazed revetment, glow rather than sparkle in the bullying blaze of light, giant teeth of sun-burnt bricks decorated with Nebuchadnezzar's 'awful dragons', bulls and what look like a pair of unicorns in relief. Once brightly coloured, they have all faded into the colour of brick but have lost none of their lithe-limbed elegance. One of the famous dragons is missing a large chunk of its neck, a painful and all-too-visible example of the looting that has happened since the fall of Saddam.

'What's happened here is a crime,' Agnieszka says.

She must have had many conversations with people arriving in Babylon scandalised by the recent damage. She must have explained to these visitors again and again that Saddam had a much more pernicious effect on the city with his monomaniacal reconstruction efforts; that had the Coalition not secured the archaeological ruins the looting by Iraqis would have been much worse; that the Poles have been responsible guardians of Babylon since taking over from the Americans in September 2003. They have sponsored the reconstruction of the local museum, have fenced off the most vulnerable archaeological areas, are monitoring the site daily and have even placed cameras among the ruins to make sure nothing more is looted. I wonder what she knows and whether she is telling the truth as she knows it. Perhaps she is making – or even making up – her own history. She is an archaeologist attached to Polish forces in Camp Babylon, probably less influential than even the most junior officer on the base. A general who wanted more space for his tanks or armoured vehicles, a helipad here, a car park there, would not have bothered to ask her permission before sending in the diggers and gravel.

A colony of pigeons lands among the high-walled ruins of the Processional Way. Every few minutes they take off in a flutter, only to land on another parapet a few moments later to rest in the sun and shit all over history. The sound of their flapping echoes along the walkway like a muffled round of applause, an ironic congratulation for the latest round of Babylon's desecration. It reminds me of the clapping of sheepskin gloves on the sideline of school rugby matches three decades ago, amid the tracery of frozen breath hanging in the air.

The sun wouldn't allow that to happen here. It sucks up my breath, dry-cures my skin and fires the life out of a landscape of crushed parchment. It is so hot the sky can barely contain it. I stare across the remnants of the city, besieged on all sides by a foreign army of occupation – tents, temporary accommodation, armoured vehicles, helicopters, soldiers – and search in vain for any structure imposing itself on the skyline.

Like any visitor to Babylon, I want to see the Tower of Babel, even though deep down I know it has long since descended from its heavenly heights. Herodotus offers a characteristically graphic description of this luminous beacon as the centre of the temple of the god Bel. He was known as Marduk by Babylonians and his temple was called Esagila.

> The temple is a square building, two furlongs in each way, with bronze gates, and was still in existence in my time; it has a solid central tower, one furlong square, with a second erected on top of it and then a third, and so on up to eight. All eight towers can be climbed by a spiral way running round the outside, and about half-way up there are seats and a shelter for those who make the ascent to rest on. On the summit of

the topmost tower stands a great temple with a fine large couch on it, richly covered, and a golden table beside it. The shrine contains no image and no one spends the night there except, as the Chaldaeans who are the priests of Bel say, one Assyrian woman, all alone, whoever it may be that the god has chosen.

He can't help dropping in another piece of sexual innuendo. This time he's reporting godly libidinousness and, good historian that he is, distances himself from the tale he's been told: 'The Chaldaeans also say – though I do not believe them – that the god enters the temple in person and takes his rest upon the bed.' With the woman of his choice, no doubt.

Agnieszka says what I have known all along, but dreaded hearing confirmed: the sky-scraping Tower of Babel has long gone. Some say it was badly damaged after Cyrus' invasion of 539 BC. Certainly by the time Alexander the Great took Babylon in 331, it was in pieces. The Greek conqueror planned to reconstruct it at a later date and the debris of the tower was removed to prepare the site. And then, while staying in Babylon again in 323, he spoiled these ambitious plans by dying suddenly.

Babel-hunting Gertrude Bell was more fortunate than me (or so she claimed), despite visiting Babylon as late as 1911. 'I rode off with a guide, and lunched on the top of the Tower of Babel,' she wrote in a letter on 10 March. 'You know what it was? It was an immense Babylonian temple dedicated to the seven spheres of heaven and the sun god. There remains now an enormous mound of sun-dried brick, with the ruins of a temple to the North of it and on top a great tower of burnt brick, most of which has fallen down. But that which remains stands up, like a finger pointing heavenwards, over the Babylonian plain and can be seen from Nejef to Babylon.'

Nebuchadnezzar, as his inscriptions make plain, wanted to rebuild his father's ziggurat of Etemenanki, as his Babylonian subjects knew our Tower of Babel, and he managed to pull it off, if Herodotus' account is anything to go by. Alexander wanted to do the same but his untimely death proved a stumbling block too far for the bricklayers. And then, millennia later, an Iraqi leader who saw himself as another Nebuchadnezzar was filled with similar desires to be remembered in history as The Man Who Rebuilt the Tower of Babel. This time an expensive war with Iran intervened and Saddam's priorities shifted from architecture to Armageddon. Babel has not been rebuilt.

Saddam might have failed to resurrect the tower from its horizontal slumber but most of the Babylon I walk through with Agnieszka today is of his, rather than Nebuchadnezzar's, vintage. The dictator put the comprehensive rebuilding programme in the reluctant hands of Dr Donny George among others (whatever the archaeologists' reservations, they kept them to themselves; Saddam had a way with words).

Nebuchadnezzar made his mark with stunning, convention-challenging architecture which defied technology and awed the world. Saddam's approach was simpler. Rebuild on top of whatever ruins remained, make a new city and don't worry about what the original incarnation looked like. It is, as one writer christened it, Disney for a Despot. Through an archway on the Processional Way, piled on to an artificially raised mound overlooking the entire site, I glimpse Saddam's monstrous four-storey palace, which is meant to resemble a ziggurat but in practice is more low-budget Gotham City with a touch of Dubai.

Nebuchadnezzar's boasts in burnt brickwork had a magnificent architectural foundation. Those of his twenty-first-century imitator, who had one of Nebuchadnezzar's palaces 'restored', are vainglorious:

> This was built by Saddam Hussein, son of Nebuchadnezzar, to glorify Iraq.

> In the reign of the victorious Saddam Hussein, the president of the Republic, may God keep him, the guardian of the great Iraq and the renovator of its renaissance and the builder of its great civilisation, the rebuilding of the great city of Babylon was done in 1987.

Dictators are no slouches when it comes to history. Saddam had what one psychologist called a 'Nebuchadnezzar Imperial Complex'. Symptoms of this rare historical condition included posing for portraits standing in a copy of Nebuchadnezzar's war chariot and even appearing alongside Nebuchadnezzar in the sky over Baghdad as part of a night-time laser show. In 1979 Saddam was quoted as saying, 'Nebuchadnezzar stirs in me everything relating to pre-Islamic ancient history. And what is most important to me about Nebuchadnezzar is the link between the Arabs' abilities and the liberation of Palestine. Nebuchadnezzar was, after all, an Arab from Iraq, albeit ancient Iraq ... That is why whenever I remember Nebuchadnezzar I like to remind the Arabs, Iraqis in particular, of their historical responsibilities. It is a burden that should ... spur them into action because of their history.' What he really meant was that the Arabs – like his other historical hero Saladin – should retake Jerusalem, and put the Jews to the sword.

Nebuchadnezzar's Babylon, like Saddam's, was a monument to his vanity (that is one aspect of historical continuity in the city's story). Hence the inscriptions such as 'The fortifications of Esagila and Babylon I strengthened and made an everlasting name for my kingdom.'

You do not need to be an archaeologist or historian to spot where one man's building programme ended and the other's begins. The remains of Nebuchadnezzar's brickwork can be seen at the bottom of the temple walls, a crumbly frontier of masonry extending up to three feet from the ground. The original bricks were laid with bitumen as mortar, a process which Herodotus selects for special notice. He says the bitumen came from a city called Is, eight days' journey away on a tributary of the Euphrates, and describes how the outer wall of Babylon was built: 'While the digging was going on, the earth that was shovelled out was formed into bricks, which were baked in ovens as soon as a sufficient number were made; then, using hot bitumen for mortar, the workmen began by revetting with brick each side of the moat, and then went on to erect the actual wall.' MacGinnis says Herodotus gets the details of this process 'exactly right'.

On top of the Nebuchadnezzar-era bricks and bitumen Saddam's builders piled bricks that less than twenty years later are cracking. At the join of the old and the new yellow sand is leaking out like pus from a wound, as though Saddam has inflicted a terrible internal injury on these creaking walls. The weight above is too much to bear. It is a bad job and it isn't going to last, but at least history has been given a new lease of life.

The Iraqi art historian Dr Lamia al Gailani doesn't think much of Saddam's restoration either, but tells the *New York Times* she has been won over by her compatriots' enthusiasm for it. 'It is not just about Saddam's time,' she says. 'Ruins in Iraq are ugly for most people. Ordinary Iraqis want something they can be impressed by like this.' There is something in this line of argument. Saddam was cavalier with Babylon, damaged it incalculably in its very rebuilding, but he at least restored some vertical vigour to the place. Babylon had long ago been brought to earth, besieged by wars, weather and time. The looting and levelling in 2003 were merely the latest attack on the shrinking fabric of the city. Saddam, in his crude, dictatorial fashion – another aspect of continuity in the Babylon story – reclaimed a piece of history and brought it forcibly into the present. Archaeologists might have been horrified by what they saw as his destruction of the ruins but they cannot be the sole stewards of the past. In his brutal way Saddam provided another layer of history for future generations to pore over and condemn, some perhaps even to praise.

Apart from Saddam's grotesque or inspired rebuilding – take your pick, to me it looks like Barratts-home with battlements – there is only so much ancient Babylon to look at. I would like to spend several more days at least here, but Agnieszka can only spare an hour and in any case I have to leave later this afternoon because the military convoy to Diwaniyah, in which I have managed to secure one of the last available places, departs shortly.

Before we say goodbye, Agnieszka takes me to the statue of the 2,600-year-old Lion of Babylon, something else Saddam restored, with greater sensitivity. We stop *en route* among some teetering cliffs of bricks so precariously overhanging there is little danger of them surviving much longer without some sort of Saddamite rebuilding. Scattered around my feet are tiny fragments of brick. An inner voice urges me to slip one into my pocket. 'Go on,' it whispers, 'take some history home with you.' Then another one chimes in. 'Don't you dare.' I pick up a piece and agonise. Agnieszka must have seen me. 'What will be left of Babylon if everyone takes a stone home?' she asks pointedly. I open my hand and let it drop to the ground, feeling disappointed and virtuous.

The grizzled old lion is snub-nosed after a group of Turkish soldiers tried to blow him up a century earlier, mistakenly thinking there was some gold inside the statue, according to one account. He is mounted on a pyramidal plinth in the centre of a middle-England, Barratts-home patio and looks as though he is having the time of his life, having athletic sex with a woman beneath him. The woman seems to be enjoying it, too, if her raised knees and one hand caressing the lion's flank are any guide. 'Iraqis say this is why they are so strong,' says Agnieszka. 'The lion mating with a woman symbolises the birth of Iraq.'

A young Marine in desert fatigues, black, wraparound sunglasses and sunhat approaches us as we contemplate this picture of Babylonian bestiality. He is chewing gum. 'Excuse me, Ma'm, I got a question for you,' he says. 'Which way's the Hanging Gardens?'

——

The Marine's faith in its longevity is touching, but Babylon's most famous water feature has long since dried up and disappeared. In fact, some archaeologists believe it never really existed, at least not in Babylon or on the epic scale in which it was described by some of Herodotus' successors.

Diodorus the Sicilian, the first-century BC Greek historian, records that this most elusive of the Seven Wonders was 400 feet square. It was, he says, born out of one man's love for a woman. 'There was likewise a hanging garden (as it is called) near the citadel, not built by Semiramis, but by a later prince called Cyrus, for the sake of a courtesan, who, being a Persian, they say, by birth and coveting meadows on mountain tops, desired the King by an artificial plantation to imitate the land in Persia.' Other accounts agree that the lush, gravity-defying gardens were a gift from a monarch to his homesick consort but that it was Nebuchadnezzar who gave them to his wife Amyitis, daughter of the king of the Medes. Either way, it was one of history's more romantic and technologically challenging presents.

Strabo, writing a little later, gives us a detailed architectural description of what this vast mountain of greenery must have looked like climbing up from the parched desert plain:

> The shape of the garden is a square, and each side of it measures four plethra. It consists of vaulted terraces, raised one above another, and resting upon cube-shaped pillars. These are hollow and filled with earth

to allow trees of the largest size to be planted. The pillars, the vaults, and the terraces, are constructed of baked brick and asphalt. The ascent to the highest storey is by stairs, and at their side are water engines, by means of which persons, appointed expressly for the purpose, are continually employed in raising water from the Euphrates into the garden. For the river, which is a stadium in breadth, flows through the middle of the city, and the garden is on the side of the river.

All of which makes Herodotus' failure even to mention the Hanging Gardens a mystery.

———

Hanging Gardens aside, Herodotus' account of Babylon is admirably detailed. He covers everything from its general geography, the construction of the outer wall and the street plan of the city to the main crops grown (wheat, barley, millet, sesame and dates), the various uses of the palm tree (food, wine and honey), religious, medical and sexual practices and the types of boats used to navigate the Euphrates. Though we can never be entirely sure, there is a weight of evidence here which suggests he visited the city in person.

According to MacGinnis's forensic study, Herodotus is right about the general geography of Babylon, its rainfall, canals, irrigation, main crops, uses of the date palm, boats, double walls, quay wall, gates, brick-making, ziggurat tower, upper temple, lower temple, worship of Bel, streets, bridge, seals, Nebuchadnezzar's Median Wall, staffs, clothes and drinking water of the Persian king. He's also correct in saying that knowledge of the sundial and the gnomon (its shadow-maker) came to Greece from Babylon. He is wrong about the technique of palm fertilisation and the length and height of the city walls (most writers would be even today) and mistakenly calls Babylonia Assyria (only one classical writer, Claudius Ptolemaeus, consistently gets the two right). He makes a number of errors in his potted history of Babylon, in particular attributing its architectural glories to a queen called Nitocris rather than King Nebuchadnezzar. MacGinnis says Herodotus' description is 'obscure' about the three- to four-roofed houses, burial in honey, the stairway of the ziggurat, temple prostitution, auctioning girls, laying out the sick, a nearby village called Ardericca, and fish-eating among three of the clans.

'In short,' he concludes, 'we may be astonished at the accuracy of the account; and when noting that Herodotus' saying in 1.193.4, "I shall not record the height to which the sesame and millet grows . . . because no one who has not been to Babylonia would ever believe me", is a virtual acknowledgement that he had been there, I find no possible remaining reason to doubt that he did.'

Perhaps we can leave it at that.

———

We cannot bid farewell to Babylon without having one last session on sex. Herodotus would approve of the digression, I think, not least since it is in his honour. Our Greek historian has been describing local dress (think linen tunics and woollen cloaks); coiffure and toiletries ('they grow their hair long, wear turbans, and perfume themselves all over'); walking sticks (everyone has one, with a carved picture of 'an apple or rose or lily or eagle or something of the sort' on the top). Then, all of a sudden, he breaks off with the customary Herodotean that's-enough-of-this-time-for-something-different device: 'I will say no more about dress and so forth,' he announces abruptly, and then returns to one of his favourite crowd-pleasing subjects. Cue more sex.

Renewed shuffling on seats. This Herodotus chap is pretty damn good, some of the men think. No end of racy stories. Sex in foreign cultures, prostitution, genital peculiarities in the animal kingdom (he has delighted in regaling them with details about the camel's back-wards-pointing genitals). He's got it all. Herodotus says he wants to talk about Babylonian 'practices' and without further ado describes what he calls an 'ingenious' local custom that sadly is no longer observed.

In every village once a year all the girls of marriageable age used to be collected together in one place, while the men stood round them in a circle; an auctioneer then called each one to stand up and offered her for sale, beginning with the best-looking and going on to the second best as soon as the first had been sold for a good price. Marriage was the object of the transaction. The rich men who wanted wives bid against each other for the prettiest girls, while the humbler folk, who had no use for good looks in a wife, were actually paid to take the ugly ones, for when the auctioneer had got through all the pretty girls he would call upon the plainest, or even perhaps a crippled one, to stand up, and then ask who was willing to take the least money to marry her – and she was offered to whoever accepted the smallest sum.

It's always the same, the poorer men in his audience grumble, the rich always get the best. Of everything. The biggest houses, best land, finest clothes, choicest food, most beautiful wives. There's no justice.

Alas, such marvellous marriage arrangements are no more, Herodotus tells his audience in a tone of regret: 'This admirable practice has now fallen into disuse and they have of late years hit upon another scheme, namely the prostitution of all girls of the lower classes to provide some relief from the poverty which followed upon the conquest with its attendant hardship and general ruin.'

I spot a man in the audience at this point nudging his anachronistic wife (who wouldn't really have been there). He's been chortling away at every one of Herodotus' Babylonian sex stories. His wife has had it with him. 'Prostitution of all the lower-class girls, hey?' he says, grinning stupidly. 'The fellow's right. It *is* ingenious!'

His wife doesn't reply. Calmly she collects her belongings, stands up, slaps him in the face and storms out. For once Herodotus is lost for words.

---

I entered Babylon with an invading army and now I leave in the last available Coalition convoy. The occupation forces are moving on. Camp Babylon is closing down and Polish and American forces are relocating south-east to the town of Diwaniyah. The desecration of Babylon, for the time being at least, is over.

I hitch a ride in one of the few unarmoured Humvees and immediately feel uncomfortably exposed. It's too late to do anything about it. I'm lucky to get a seat. Body armour has been hung over the doors, almost as an afterthought, to provide a modicum of protection, but serves only to underline how vulnerable the vehicle is. We set off in an untidy straggle like a snake slithering away from trouble. The end-of-an-era atmosphere hangs heavily in the air. I am a short-term impostor but these men have been here for months in what will be a shameful footnote in Babylon's history. Everyone knows the Iraqis can't wait for the invaders to leave this place, the symbol of their country's unrivalled history. Most of the soldiers couldn't care less. They have just been doing their job.

Babylon is dissolving behind me into my personal history, a fleeting encounter with Herodotus in a city stormed by Cyrus, lead man in the starring quartet of the *Histories*. My only chance to visit it has been in the midst of a war pitting East against West – which bears, in other words, the echoes of the Persian Wars Herodotus describes. Babylon, in the thousands of years since he wrote about it, has become a one-word code for luxury, extravagance, decadence, confusion, sexual licentiousness and abandon. You could say Herodotus' early focus on sex in Babylon has left an indelible mark on its reputation as a more upmarket version of Sodom and Gomorrah. The closest we come to it today, perhaps, is Hollywood – without the walls, Tower of Babel and monumental temples.

'Dudes, get this,' says one of the sergeants in the Humvee, turning to me. I see a dusty self-portrait in his wraparound sunglasses. 'Justin, you'll like this, these guys are Brits. Check out our farewell-to-all-this-bullshit song.'

He pushes a button on his portable stereo and a tinny voice vibrates through the sand-smothered speakers. It is an anthem of my childhood. Boney M. 1978.

> By the rivers of Babylon,
> There we sat down
> Ye-ah we wept,
> When we remembered Zion . . .

The wind rushing through the Humvee snatches some of the music away, but I know the words. They have lodged in my memory and cannot be removed. The soldiers hoo-rah and whistle. 'Rock 'n' roll, baby!' one of them screams, kicking off another round of celebrations. Their time in Babylon has come to an end. They are a step nearer home.

The 'Rivers of Babylon' lyrics were directly lifted from Psalm 137, a melancholic meditation on slavery by the Jewish captives in Babylon, sitting on the banks of the Euphrates. They are enslaved in a foreign land, far from their home, where their captors mock their religion and demand they entertain them with 'one of the songs of Zion'.

'How shall we sing the Lord's song in a strange land?' they reply, utterly bereft. The Babylonians are foreigners, no part of the covenant God made with Abraham. These barbarians have laid waste to Jerusalem, and the Jews, missing their religion, longing for their temples, urge each other not to forget what happened in their homeland, to remember their tormentors' orders to raze the holy city to the ground – 'Raze it, raze it, to its very foundation!' Now they wish only vengeance upon their captors. This is no New Testament turn-the-other-cheek response to their humiliation and captivity because we are in the fire-and-brimstone Old Testament world of an eye for an eye, tooth for a tooth. But all this bloodlust proved too much for Boney M, otherwise so faithful to Psalm 137. The group wisely left out the final verses.

> O daughter of Babylon, who are to be destroyed,
> Happy the one who repays you as you have served us!
> Happy the one who takes and dashes
> Your little ones against the rock!

According to Jewish tradition, the Psalms were written by King David, most righteous of the kings of Israel, some time around 1000 BC. The prayers of the Jews of Psalm 137 were answered, albeit half a millennium later, with the fall of Babylon to Cyrus. Showing a touch of Herodotean enlightenment, the Persian allowed the Jewish population to return to Jerusalem and ordered their temple to be rebuilt. The Jews considered his behaviour towards them so just that he earned the unusual accolade, as we have seen, of being designated a Messiah in the Tanakh, the only Gentile to enjoy such an honour.

The road slides south, a dull grey ribbon pasted across the desert plain. Boiling horizons come and go, flowing like liquid in the heat.

As we leave it behind us, I try to fix Babylon in my mind, feeling the links weaken with the widening miles. The story of Babylon is an ebb and flow of slaughter and mercy, war and peace, a microcosm of human history. It is a story of greed, hubris, empire and religious persecution, also one of human civilisation, prodigious wealth, monumental architectural achievement, religious tolerance and yes, of course, sex, Herodotean and otherwise. It encapsulates humankind's finest and most deplorable characteristics and burst on to the front pages of newspapers around the world during the Iraq war precisely because it is hallowed as the source of our history. The birth of human civilisation belongs to us all.

Reports of soldiers filling sandbags with earth containing archaeological fragments, of armoured vehicles crushing sixth-century BC bricks on the Processional Way, of looters gouging out pieces of dragons from the original foundations of the Ishtar Gate, of digging, levelling, compacting and gravelling on what was a sacred historical site disgusted the world.

Dr John Curtis, keeper of the Department of the Ancient Near East at the British Museum, was invited to visit Babylon a month after my visit, in December 2004, prior to its formal handover by Coalition forces to the Iraqi authorities in January. In his report he acknowledged that a military presence in Babylon served a useful purpose to prevent looting in the early days after the war. 'But it is regrettable that a military camp of this size should then have been established on one of the most important archaeological sites in the world. This is tantamount to establishing a military camp around the Great Pyramid in Egypt or around Stonehenge in Britain.'

Virtually inconceivable, in other words. The understated language only accentuates the horror at what the occupying forces have done. 'Months of war that ruined centuries of history,' was the *Guardian*'s headline. War, history's perennial rapist, its most savage sculptor, has struck again. It has descended on Babylon 2,542 years after Cyrus' triumph, and another piece of the past has been chiselled away, another layer of history added.

Boney M's lyrics drill into the rushing desert air. On the seat beside me, my tatty copy of the *Histories* lies next to the butt of an M4 rifle and a couple of clips of ammunition. Its back cover is face up and as we bump along away from Babylon I can see the bouncing orange script with the famous Herodotean epigram: 'No one is fool enough to choose war instead of peace – in peace sons bury fathers, but in war fathers bury sons.'

It is time to get away from all this. Time to leave Iraq and revisit the country which most fascinated Herodotus with its constant surprises, bizarre customs (some of them sexual) and humbling history.

It is the place in which Herodotus revealed his joyful embrace of other cultures most clearly, a society whose sophistication and antiquity startled him into re-evaluating the Greeks' adamantine faith in their own supremacy at a time when this was akin to heresy. The fact that it is a nation at peace not war only adds to its appeal. Herodotus is taking us to Egypt.

# PART III

## Egypt

*About Egypt I shall have a great deal more to relate because of the number of remarkable things which the country contains, and because of the fact that more monuments which beggar description are to be found there than anywhere else in the world. That is reason enough for my dwelling on it at greater length.*

Herodotus, *Histories*, 2.35

# 6

## Memphis and Thebes: Tall Stories and Self-Immolating Cats, or No Sex in Temples, Please, We're Egyptian

SWINDON: *What will history say?*
BURGOYNE: *History, sir, will tell lies as usual.*
George Bernard Shaw, *The Devil's Disciple* (1901)

THE ROAD TO Egypt runs through the Fens. Sheikh Ali Gomaa, Grand Mufti of Cairo's Al Azhar, the highest seat of religious learning in the Islamic world, is making an historic visit to Cambridge University to deliver a speech with an unmistakably Herodotean ring: 'Building Bridges of Understanding', part of an interfaith dialogue between East and West.

No Grand Mufti has ever visited the university before and it is standing room only in the faculty of divinity. Dog collars and crucifixes mingle with skullcaps and *hijabs*. The auditorium is crackling with anticipation, student excitement tempered with pious gravitas.

Gomaa, soberly dressed in a long black kaftan and simple white hat that matches his beard, has an air of high-minded austerity about him. He surprises his audience with an eloquent denunciation of terrorism. 'I am here with you today to tackle the issue of terrorism and extremism in order to build bridges of understanding between the Muslim world and the West,' he begins. Terrorists are criminals, not Muslim activists, he says, making his case with multiple references to the Koran stressing the importance of peace and mercy. There should be no compulsion or violence in religion.

He says he speaks on behalf of the vast majority of the 1.3 billion Muslims worldwide who are 'ordinary, peace-loving, decent people'. He is here 'to repudiate the actions of a misguided criminal minority' who see inevitable conflict between East and West. The Islamic world is rich in history with a cosmopolitan and humanitarian world view. 'We see ourselves as a people who have absorbed a multiplicity of civilisations; we have been exposed to and assimilated the great civilisations of the Persians, Indians, Chinese, and Greeks into our cultural and intellectual life, and we benefited from all of them as well as contributing to them.' He concludes with a rousing appeal for greater education, the most powerful weapon against extremism. The applause is deafening. The divinity faculty has never heard anything like it.

With his first assignment over, the Grand Mufti moves on to Ridley Hall, the theological training college, for a more relaxed talk alongside his old friend the Anglican Bishop of Egypt, Mouneer Anis, a smiling vision of maroon splendour. The lecture room is bursting with religious goodwill. Serenely he discusses the 1,035-year history of Al Azhar, the institution of the Grand Mufti (he is Egypt's eighteenth) and its role in issuing fatwas (120,000 in 110 years, an average of three a day, governing all aspects of human behaviour), and stresses, to considerable chuckles, including his own, that his sermons never last more than twenty minutes. Beyond that, people don't listen. The would-be vicars have been warned.

I catch the Grand Mufti later that evening in his room in the Garden House Hotel. An ever-hovering diplomat from the Egyptian Embassy, slightly suspicious of Herodotus, volunteers to translate.

There is no reason why the Christian West and Muslim East cannot coexist peacefully, Gomaa argues. 'We utterly refute Huntington's theory of a clash of civilisations. It contradicts the law of God and His creatures. He created day and night, male and female, heaven and earth, everything to complement each other not conflict with one another.' The relationship between the West and Islam during the past half-century has been a great improvement on the first half of the twentieth century, when much of the Muslim world was occupied by European countries while there was no Islamic presence in the West. He is an optimist.

Dialogue between the faiths is essential, he says, rubbing his beard thoughtfully. He considers terrorism a passing crisis. 'History demonstrates that terrorists do not survive more than one or two generations.'

Continuing dialogue and education are the best way to overcome it. 'In dialogue we search for common ground. Where there is knowledge, there is better understanding and wherever we find ignorance we find blind fanaticism.'

I can see Herodotus applauding wildly. Gomaa, an academic who has published more than thirty books, is familiar with our Greek friend. He says he has an Arabic copy of the *Histories* in his library. The book on Egypt was translated into Arabic in the late nineteenth century. 'There are different interpretations of Herodotus. Some studies say he was an evil man, others that he was a deep thinker. Some claim he called for interaction between civilisations, some think he was a symbol of bigotry who was against everything that wasn't Greek. I consider him a great thinker.'

A clerical yawn and a diplomatic scowl indicate the interview with the Grand Mufti is over. He wishes me well for the journey to Egypt, we pose for a photograph (so that our meeting will not be 'forgotten in time') and then Herodotus and I disappear into a watery winter night.

---

It is the mid-fifth century BC. Herodotus, in his mid- to late thirties, weary from his long voyage by sea, sets foot on African soil for the first time. Long has he waited for this moment, for the opportunity to visit the ancient kingdom of Egypt, land of boundless antiquity. The country is labouring under the Persian yoke, following the conquest of Cambyses in 525 BC, but life along the Nile valley goes on unchanged, as it has for thousands of years. Like today's tourists, he has an itinerary in mind. He has dreamt of sailing up the Nile to learn more about this mysteriously majestic river. He is already fascinated, having discussed the subject with the captain, by how far out from the coast the silt from this life-giving river pours forth. He has seen the ship's crew take soundings showing 'eleven fathoms, muddy bottom', a day's sail from the coast, to prove it. There is plenty more to discover. Maybe he will make it as far south as the First Cataract and talk to people about the unknown source of the great river. Memphis is a must, so too the august city of Thebes and – if he can find a good guide and fellow travellers to make the thirsty trek – the elusive desert oasis of Siwa which Alexander the Great will make famous a century later on a history-changing journey to confirm his divine destiny with the Oracle of Ammon. Perhaps, if there is time, he will travel up the delta to Bubastis to visit a particularly magnificent temple. Then there is the astonishing Labyrinth, the temple of Athene in Sais, the Greek *emporion* or trading colony at Naucratis, on the Canopic branch of the Nile, where he can rub shoulders with some of his more commercially minded country-men. He has heard lurid tales of Egyptian mummification that he would like to investigate. And, it goes without saying, he will make the pilgrimage to the magical, sky-grazing pyramids of Giza.

His heartbeat quickens as he contemplates the treasures ahead. So much to see and learn. But first he will rest after the long journey by boat. All around him the sounds, smells and sights of the port are new and utterly foreign. The sun streams down and rebounds off the waters with an intensity he has never known. A throng of Egyptians hurries up to him as he stands there, squinting in the blinding light, offering him their services in a language he cannot understand. The captain of the boat has warned his passengers about this before disembarking. Have nothing to do with these touts in the port, he advises his captive audience, smiling to himself. I'll fix you up with the best guides in Egypt. I've already negotiated a special price. Herodotus adjusts his tunic, makes sure he's got everything (the ancient-world equivalent of passport–wallet–mobile–keys check), and steps off into the blazing unknown.

Many Greeks have made this journey before him. Many have visited the sites that will so captivate him. But no traveller has returned from Egypt with so much information about the country's history, geography, religion, politics, its culture and customs, sacrificial rituals, manners and morals, flora and fauna, architecture, agriculture and diet, sex, burial practices and the mummification process – and then written about it. Herodotus' landmark research here, unchallenged in its scope and detail, will prove one of the finest achievements of his life. It will provide the world with the greatest store of information on Egypt until the nineteenth century.

I have returned to Egypt to seek out Herodotus, but I have also come back because, in the words of the old proverb, 'He who drinks the water of the Nile is destined to taste its sweetness again.' I first tasted the waters as an eighteen-year-old hungry to learn Arabic. Cairo devoured me and I allowed myself to be swallowed up whole, for there is no resistance to this most all-consuming of cities. It was overpowering, suffocating, intoxicating, impossibly splendid, darkly squalid, monumentally inspiring, spirit-lifting, maddening, arrogant, whisperingly seductive, intimidating, insouciant and always totally compelling, for better or worse.

When I was not immersed in the encyclopaedia-sized tome of Modern Standard Arabic, fretting with enclitic pronouns and indefinite genitive plurals, I traipsed around the pyramids by day and by night, groping around their stuffy, sweat-filled chambers, meandered dutifully down the polluted passageways of the Egyptian Museum, got lost among the checkerboard splendours of Islamic Cairo with its rambling *suq*s and ferocious merchants, drifted idly down the oily Nile, staring up at the dazzling puffed-up lateen sail of a felucca piloted by a captain high on hashish, trundled around the crowd-thronged tombs and temples of Luxor, hiked up biblically trembling Mount Sinai to meet the hoary monks of St Catherine's and fell in love with a country that has been welcoming – and enthralling – visitors for many millennia. There is nothing new or unusual in any of this. Egypt, Oum al Dounia, the Mother of the World, has been collecting travellers' superlatives from as far back in history as anyone can imagine, so long ago in fact that you might as well consider it the beginning of time itself.

Herodotus was no exception. He was so taken by Egypt he devoted an enormous chunk of the *Histories* to it. It's the longest digression in the book, in fact, as though he got so carried away he just couldn't stop. It was simply too interesting not to dwell on 'at greater length'. How these people lived! In my travelling edition, Book 2, the Egyptian section, runs to 174 pages, a shade under a third of the *Histories*. This is rather a lot, particularly when you consider Herodotus' main objective – as he expresses it in his first sentence – is to explain why Greeks and Persians came to fight each other. There is a clue to his devotion of so much space to Egypt and the Egyptians in that very same sentence. He is interested, he says, in 'great and marvellous deeds', *erga megala te kai thomasta*, and these marvels range way beyond the battle-fields of the Persian Wars, from stupendous temples and human adventures to curious sexual practices and the workings of the Nile. Herodotus is awarding himself a licence to thrill – and be thrilled.

The truth is that, like so many visitors to Egypt before and since, he was overcome by the place, by monuments whose splendour was unrivalled 'anywhere else in the world'. It was a humbling admission from a man who came from a culture that luxuriated in the architec-tural grace and sophistication of its own monuments and tended to consider itself a cut above the uncouth barbarians who surrounded Greece.

And if there were more monuments that beggared description in Egypt, there were more tall stories too, a number of them vouchsafed by the ubiquitous priests consulted by Herodotus throughout his travels. He wastes no time in reporting them. On the very first page of Book 2, after the briefest introduction to Cambyses, son and heir of the great Persian king Cyrus, poised to invade Egypt in 525 BC, he's off. The subject in question: which is the oldest race in the world? Right up the budding historian's street.

'The Egyptians before the reign of Psammetichus [664–610 BC] used to think that of all races in the world they were the most ancient,' he writes. Then, when Psammetichus became pharaoh, he came up with 'an ingenious method' to determine whether this was indeed true. 'He took at random, from an ordinary family, two newly born infants and gave them to a shepherd to be brought up amongst his flocks, under strict orders that no one should utter a word in their presence.' The shepherd was instructed to keep them in a lonely cottage and take a goat in from time to time so that they had enough milk. Psammetichus wanted to see which word they would speak first. Two years later, in walks the shepherd and both children run towards him saying the word 'becos'. At first he doesn't report this but when they repeat the word every time he visits, he lets his master know.

Psammetichus ordered the children to be brought to him, and when he himself heard them say 'becos' he determined to find out to what language the word belonged. His inquiries revealed that it was the Phrygian word for 'bread', and in consideration of this the Egyptians yielded their claims and admitted the superior antiquity of the Phrygians.

In fact, the Phrygians, who settled in Asia Minor from around 1200 BC, were arrivistes by comparison with the Egyptians who at that time were already on their nineteenth dynasty. But Herodotus is going on what he's told and he's doing his best to track down the most reliable sources available. 'That this was what really happened I myself learnt from the priests of Hephaestus at Memphis, though the Greeks have various improbable versions of the story, such as that Psammetichus had the children brought up by women whose tongues he had cut out,' he explains. 'The version of the priests, however, is the one I have given.'

And from there he's off again, leaping from one subject to the next in giddy exuberance, religion, astronomy and geography, at breakneck speed. How the Egyptians were the first to divide the year into twelve parts, first to bring into use the names of the twelve gods (Zeus, Poseidon, Apollo, Hera, Athene, Artemis, Ares, Demeter, Hephaestus, Aphrodite, Hermes and Dionysus), first to assign altars and images and temples to them and to carve statues in stone. As a rule, he's careful to attribute the information to the priests. 'There were other things, too, which I learnt at Memphis in conversation with the priests of Hephaestus, and I actually went to Thebes and Heliopolis for the express purpose of finding out if the priests in those cities would agree in what they told me with the priests at Memphis,' he writes. Not unlike a journalist corroborating his sources.

———

When Herodotus visited Persian-administered Egypt, Memphis, though it had declined in status to a provincial capital of the empire, was nevertheless on a par with the ancient city of Thebes in terms of architectural grandeur and cosmopolitan glamour. He mentions it a number of times. Greeks lived here, he reports, together with Indians, Canaanites, Medes, Scythians, Sumerians and Kurds. The priests told him the city had been built by King Min (also known as Menes, who is thought to have founded the First Dynasty of Egypt in around 3000 BC), who diverted and dammed the Nile and raised his capital on the land that had been drained. Herodotus also provided the clues to the city's ultimate disappearance. The Persians governing Egypt kept a close watch on the dam at the elbow of the Nile there 'for should the river burst it, Memphis might be completely overwhelmed'. In time, the city was indeed overtaken by the Nile, dams or no, worn down by the annual deposits of silt that accumulated until the whole place had been submerged, reclaimed by the relentless river from whence it had risen. Today, a few lonely muddy mounds, interlaced with barbed wire, weary palms and acacias and a recumbent colossus of Ramses II, abandoned by the British Museum, are all that is left. Ramses has given up the ghost and so has his once magnificent city. Memphis and her memories sit sadly on the west bank of the Nile, in the shadow of the megapolis of Cairo which lurks fifteen miles to the north and threatens further encroachment. However hard it shines here, the sun can't quite dispel a sense of gloom.

'Muslims are very pessimistic about living among the ancient ruins of non-Muslim civilisations,' my guide Galal says as we wander around the site. 'It comes from a *hadith*. When the Prophet was passing Sodom and Gomorrah, he covered his head and told his followers, "Go quickly, these people were destroyed by God, I can hear their screams in hell." This is why Muslims don't like having their mosques or houses next to ancient ruins.'

When you walk around ancient sites with a trained Egyptologist and guide like Galal, a self-confident and fluent young man who knows his subject, you are, to a certain extent, at his mercy. Herodotus was probably in exactly the same position when he was visiting the monuments or deep in priestly tête-à-têtes. 'A good guide should have the courage and honesty to say he doesn't know something,' says Galal, 'but a lot of guides find it easier just to say anything, even make it up.'

I ask him if he knows of any tall stories told by guides, the sort of nonsense that from time to time came Herodotus' way. He smiles. 'Min, the ancient fertility god, is always seen with his penis erect in reliefs.

You can't miss it. It's huge. Now you only ever see him with one arm and some guides tell their groups that his arm is missing because a king cut it off, after Min impregnated all the women in Thebes with his seed while the king was away fighting with his army. The king returned, got mad with Min, and made him choose between having his arm or dick cut off. Later, the king realised Min had done a good thing because the war had wiped out so many young men and Min had sired only male children to replace them. Now the guides never say which king it was or anything. It's a myth. The whole story is rubbish. The only reason you don't see his left arm is because it's hidden in his gown.'

Guides should always show the greatest cultural sensitivity, Galal says. 'American men don't like to be touched, for example, if you do this you could be considered gay. In Egypt, it's normal for men to kiss each other. Americans don't like their kids to be touched, but Egyptian girls love picking up blonde children and kissing them. This might not be acceptable.' He sighs complacently. 'The thing is even if you're a bad guide, eventually they'll like you because they come to depend on you completely.'

His last words are twenty-first-century Herodotus. 'You always have to be aware of other people's customs.'

---

If Memphis no longer attracts the streams of visitors it once did, an Egyptian itinerary that doesn't include Luxor – Herodotus' Thebes, seat of pharaonic power from the sixteenth to the eleventh centuries BC – is virtually unthinkable today. For whereas the Nile has erased Memphis from the face of the earth, Luxor still boasts 'more monuments which beggar description' than anywhere else in Egypt, remnants of a city that represented the apogee of New Kingdom grandeur and excess. For once Herodotus is, as the notes in my *Histories* put it, 'strangely silent' about the monuments of Thebes.

Strange because you'd expect him to be in his element here, dissolving into paroxysms of excitement at yet another temple with thunderous pylon façades, soaring statues and mysterious inscriptions. Yet there is nothing, for example, on Karnak Temple with its feast of obelisks and the sky-dimming columns of its *Death on the Nile*

Hypostyle Hall, not a word about the fabulously revolutionary Mortuary Temple of mighty queen–pharaoh Hatshepsut hewn from the mountain, no mention of the Ramesseum and the jaunty reliefs of dog-faced baboons with hearty erections. Why this is so we can never know.

His most vivid piece of reporting in the city is also one of the most memorable. He is trying, with the help of the priests, to chart the genealogy of the pharaohs on the one hand, and establish their mortal – as opposed to divine – ancestry on the other. Why he does this will become clear in a moment. 'They declare that three hundred and forty-one generations separate the first king of Egypt from the last I have mentioned – the priest of Hephaestus – and that there was a king and a high priest corresponding to each generation.' Take three generations as one hundred years, he goes, on, showing us his calculations like a good maths student, so 300 generations make 10,000 years, add forty-one generations × 33.3 years and you get a total of 11,340 years, 'during which time, they say, no god ever assumed mortal form'.

So far so good. Having established that, he's keen to show how his illustrious sixth-century predecessor Hecataeus of Miletus, who laid the foundations for historical research, got it all wrong (some things never change; historians have been doing this ever since). A spot of one-upmanship.

> When the historian Hecataeus was in Thebes, the priests of Zeus, after listening to him trace his family back to a god in the sixteenth generation, did to him precisely what they did to me – though unlike Hecataeus, I kept clear of personal genealogies. They took me into the great hall of the temple, and showed me the wooden statues there, which they counted; and the number was just what I have said, for each high priest has a statue of himself erected there before he dies. As they showed them to me, and counted them up, beginning with the statue of the high priest who had last died, and going on from him right through the whole number, they assured me that each had been the son of the one who preceded him. When Hecataeus traced his genealogy and connected himself with a god sixteen generations back, the priests refused to believe him, and denied that any man had a divine

ancestor. They countered his claim by tracing the descent of their own high priests, pointing out that each of the statues represented a 'piromis' (a word which means something like 'gentleman') who was the son of another 'piromis', and made no attempt to connect them with either a god or a hero. Such, then, were the beings represented by the statues; they were far from being gods – they were men.

There he rests his case. Wow, you think, what a superb bit of empirical research. Good on Herodotus. Ahead of his time as ever. Rather mean to poor old Hecataeus, perhaps, but he's made his point. And then, just when you're thinking how terrifically modern he is, out comes the following passage:

> Nevertheless, before their time Egypt was, indeed, ruled by gods, who lived on earth amongst men, sometimes one of them, sometimes another being supreme above the rest. The last of them was Horus the son of Osiris – Horus is the Apollo, Osiris the Dionysus, of the Greeks. It was Horus who vanquished Typhon and was the last god to sit upon the throne of Egypt.

Beware the dangers of spending too much time with priests.

— — —

Or pharaohs. Who have never really disappeared from Egyptian life. Friends in Cairo have warned me that my time in Luxor may coincide with a presidential visit and pharaoh–presidents have a nasty habit of shutting down roads and valleys and tombs. Normal life comes to a complete standstill. Pharaohs like to be reminded of their absolute authority. They take comfort in demonstrations of their mastery of the common people. Picture the countless throngs of workers assembled to build the mortuary temple of Ramses II, compulsive builder bar none, and imagine the pride that would have swelled in his breast as he watched them toiling away in the oven-like heat for his greater glory.

Today it is in the interest of security, rather than architectural grandiloquence, that thousands upon thousands of Egyptian policemen and soldiers have been brought out, standing for hours on end, for mile upon mile, with their backs to the road, guarding the president against an invisible (and almost certainly non-existent) threat. I lose count of the number of these poor creatures standing in the middle of luminous green fields in the shadowless sun. Other lonely colleagues stand on rocky precipices in the mountains that rear above the Valley of the Kings like startled waves. Only pharaonic power could muster such an astonishing show of strength and only a pharaoh could tolerate such a staggering waste of human time. A pharaonic policeman's lot is not a happy one.

A few lines from the Egyptian writer Alaa al Aswany's novel *The Yacoubian Building* come to mind. A politician is explaining to an aspiring candidate why there's never any need to fix elections because the people are congenitally loyal to whichever government is in power. 'The Egyptians are the easiest people in the world to rule,' he explains. 'The moment you take power, they submit to you and grovel to you and you can do what you want with them.'

This ruthless display of power becomes more striking when news eventually breaks out – hours later, by which time the policemen and soldiers have wilted – that the president has decided to travel to the Theban necropolis on the west bank of the Nile by helicopter rather than motor cavalcade. Like a god from the sky he drops on the ancient monuments, a wonder for the *fellahin* peasants to behold as they scratch away in their fields in age-old drudgery. There was no need for all these policemen and soldiers to line the roads for eight hours, after all.

The president has been admiring the subterranean splendours of his predecessors' tombs. I follow in his wake, down into the tomb of Ramses IV, past reams of Ptolemaic and Coptic graffiti, a fury of scribbles and crosses, past the ram-headed god Amun and scenes from the *Book of the Dead*, till I reach the square sarcophagus of glistening pink granite. For a moment I can see the sculptors chiselling away at this block, peering in the gloom that is only relieved by a flickering flame from a lamp burning sesame-seed oil and animal fat to minimise the choking smoke. I can smell the sand-specked sweat dripping off the workers' shoulders as they crane their necks upwards to paint the protective sky goddess Nut stretched across the stone ceiling in an indigo heaven. For an instant I can picture the artisans working together on scenes from the *Book of Caverns* and the *Litany of Ra*, etching hieroglyphics in red, tracing green pastels alongside details in brown, blue and yellow and gossiping about one of their colleagues' shapely new wife, grumbling about pay and returning to their homes in Deir al Medina after their two-week shift has ended. And then, just as I have hauled them from the forgotten sleep of three millennia, the picture disappears in a flash, interrupted by a toothy tomb guardian soliciting a bribe from a hapless Japanese tourist.

Dear old Herodotus. If only he'd been able to see the eye-popping treasures of the Valley of the Kings, indicated by a roadside sign which reads 'YOU ARE IN THE EMBRACE OF THE HISTORY'. You can only imagine his hyperactive joy, scurrying from one royal tomb to the next, beavering away through the dynasties: a long morning on Ramses I to IV, VI, VII, IX, X, XII, then, after a quick lunch, on to Seti I and II, the woman–king Hatshepsut (a marvel in her own right), Tuthmosis I to IV, boy–king weakling Tutankhamun, Amenophis II and III, Horemheb . . . He was fascinated by the dynasties that came and went in the kingdom of the sun god. More than half of Book 2 consists of a Herodotean – that is, madcap, freewheeling and totally engaging – history of one pharaoh to the next, from King Min to Amasis. Sadly for Herodotus, the archaeologists had yet to reveal these resting places of the pharaohs.

That they would have fascinated him there can be no doubt. And yet, for all their stately pomp and august scale, the royal tombs are disappointingly impersonal. They are ideological statements in stone, monuments of relentlessly religious and political convention. After a while, in fact, they become tedious. The more personal, rough-and-ready Tombs of the Nobles, though less visited, are far more thrilling.

I find myself returning several times to a tomb high on the southern hillside of the village of Sheikh Abd al Gurna, overlooking successively the Ramesseum, the iridescent, Nile-girdling belt of green and the distant desert. It belonged to Sennefer, mayor of Thebes under King Amenhotep II in the late fifteenth century BC. Sennefer was a busy man and a big noise. In addition to his duties as mayor, he doubled up as 'Overseer of the Granaries and Fields, Gardens and Cattle of Amun'. He also found time to serve as high priest of Amun in Menisut. No wonder he could get away with calling himself the 'Great Confidant of the Lord of the Two Lands'.

After the stylised austerity of the royal tombs, his resting-place is an extraordinary feast of colour and character, hidden away down a treacherously steep stairwell of crudely hacked limestone. The human touch is everywhere. Where the ceilings of the royal tombs are immaculately chiselled to within an inch of their lives, here it is a craggy mountainscape of troughs and peaks, teeming with vines traced in green, brown and black. Stand underneath this bountiful trellis and you can almost feel the grapes dripping on to you. If the brightness of the colours and the rustic finishing come as a refreshing shock, the gloriously personal, romantic scenes of Sennefer and his beautiful wife Meryt, 'Chantress of Amun', are utterly arresting. In the many domestic scenes that line the walls, the couple can barely take their eyes – or hands – off each other.

Meryt is a rangy, gracefully rounded woman in a dress of sleek, diaphanous linen. While her husband has a dark complexion and goatee beard, her pale, lustrous skin is offset by thick black hair elegantly held in place by a floral diadem. A lotus bud is resplendent on her forehead. Sweetly she offers her husband dishes of fruit, papyrus flowers, a gold necklace and a scarab of gold and lapis lazuli to speed his passage into eternity, staring into his eyes with the rapturous flame of first love. In one scene they hold hands beneath the succulent, shade-giving vines, in another, radiant with beauty, she snakes an arm tenderly around his waist. He caresses her wrist, shoulder and fingers. She is his stalwart partner in life. Everything they do, from worshipping their gods to munching fruit and sailing undaunted into the afterlife on a boat laden with provisions, they do together, their eyes locked in the tenderest of embraces. Daily tasks and pleasures are shared in innocent enjoyment, cocooned in their flourishing arbour. They look inseparable. It is a life-affirming place and we respond so acutely to it because in steadfast Sennefer and his loyal wife Meryt we see ourselves, an unconscious reminder of what it is to be human. We see a man and a woman deeply in love 3,400 years ago and we empathise with them because we know exactly how they feel.

Now and then, you get the impression that it was a bit of a struggle for Herodotus to get the information he wanted in Egypt. The problem was he was a Greek tourist who didn't speak the language. The clearest example of the sort of difficulties he faced comes when he visits the famous Labyrinth at Hawara in the central Fayoum. 'I have seen this building, and it is beyond my power to describe it,' he begins, before describing it. 'It must have cost more in labour and money than all the walls and public works of the Greeks put together ...' But he confesses there's a limit to what he can report.

> I went through the rooms in the upper storey, so that what I shall say of them is from my own observation, but the underground ones I can speak of only from report, because the Egyptians in charge refused to let me see them, as they contain the tombs of the kings who built the labyrinth, and also the tombs of the sacred crocodiles.

Herodotus had to contend with these sorts of challenges daily. If you think about it, it's really not that surprising that the Egyptian priests should restrict the movements of a strange foreigner poking about in some of their most sacred sites and asking interminable questions. It is only to be expected. Try it today and many Egyptians think you're a spy.

Take mummification. The ancient art of embalming is probably less controversial than, say, nuclear-weapons technology. As non-contentious research goes, you'd be hard pressed to think of something better. But try to fix an interview with the director of Luxor's Museum of Mummification and no one knows which way to look. Not allowed. Absolutely forbidden. An edict has come from On High. From faraway Cairo. From the office of Dr Zahi Hawass, secretary general of the Supreme Council of Antiquities. Dr Hawass, they say, has prohibited anyone in Egypt from speaking to foreign writers or journalists without his personal approval. It seems odd for a country whose government frequently boasts of its 7,000-year-old history (historians usually reckon on 5,000) to allow one man to monopolise it. To sew up Egyptian history, as it were, all by himself. Strange in a country that relies so heavily on its fabulous heritage to promote tourism, lifeblood of the economy. And it turns out that Dr Hawass is not available to approve an interview with the mummification man. He's out of the country having an operation. 'I hope he comes back in a sarcophagus,' says one of my grumpier acquaintances in the Valley of the Kings. There are mutterings that Dr Hawass is doing rather well for himself out of Egyptian antiquities.

My interest is purely Herodotean. I'm not trying to steal Egypt's latest mummification technology on behalf of MI6. I haven't been sent by Mossad to sabotage Luxor's newest museum. I'm just trying to test the reliability of what Herodotus wrote about Egyptian mummification. Totally absorbed by this unusual custom, as he knew his audiences would be, he researches it, learns how it's done, explains the different techniques that vary according to cost and then presents us with his findings:

> The embalmers, when a body is brought to them, produce specimen models in wood, painted to resemble nature, and graded in quality; the best and most expensive kind is said to represent a being whose name I shrink from mentioning in this connection; the next best is somewhat inferior and cheaper, while the third sort is cheapest of all. After pointing out these differences in quality, they ask which of the three is required, and the family of the dead man, having agreed upon a price, go away and leave the embalmers to their work.

You can see the embalmer's suddenly grave expression as he addresses the bereaved family, trying to steer them towards the most expensive model. 'Of course, it's your choice, sir, I know these are hard times, but the cheapest way is a little, how can I put it, messy. It doesn't last as long, either, which can be a problem. Had a terrible case the other day . . . But don't let me influence you. No, you must choose the model that suits you and I'm sure you'll want to do your best by your lovely wife. You were very close, weren't you? Such a charming woman . . .'

Herodotus then explains the most expensive treatment:

> The most perfect process is as follows: as much as possible of the brain is extracted through the nostrils with an iron hook, and what the hook cannot reach is rinsed out with drugs; next the flank is laid open with a flint knife and the whole contents of the abdomen removed; the cavity is then thoroughly cleansed and washed out, first with palm wine and again with an infusion of ground spices. After that it is filled with

pure bruised myrrh, cassia, and every other aromatic substance with the exception of frankincense, and sewn up again, after which the body is placed in natron, covered entirely over, for seventy days – never longer.* When this period, which must not be exceeded, is over, the body is washed and then wrapped from head to foot in linen cut into strips and smeared on the underside with gum, which is commonly used by the Egyptians instead of glue.

What luxury! Good stuff if you can afford it. And if you can't, how about the middle-class option? It differs in that 'no incision is made and the intestines are not removed, but oil of cedar is injected with a syringe into the body through the anus which is afterwards stopped up to prevent the liquid from escaping'. After a session of natron pickling, the anus is uncorked (with a pop?) and the oil is drained off. Its effects are so powerful that flesh, stomach and intestines rush out in liquid form, leaving only skin and bones.

The poor have to dispense with all this high-end embalming. Never mind pure bruised myrrh and the finest spices known to mankind, the cheapest method 'is simply to clear out the intestines with a purge and keep the body seventy days in natron'. That's your lot, you nasty little peasant.

Herodotus' passage on mummification would have had his Greek audiences hanging on his every word. There is no reason to suppose they would have been any less fascinated by this uniquely exotic process than we are today. But just in case their interest is flagging – it's been a long morning in the symposium, after all, and a few stomachs are rumbling in the back row – he drops in this brilliantly vivid, and shocking, titbit.

When the wife of a distinguished man dies, or any woman who happens to be beautiful or well known, her body is not given to the embalmers immediately, but only after the lapse of three or four days. This is a precautionary measure to prevent the embalmers from violating a

---

* Natron is a naturally occurring deposit of sodium carbonate, sodium bicarbonate, sodium chloride and sodium sulphate found in salty lake-beds. Its name comes from the western Egyptian town of Wadi Natrun, where natron was harvested from the earliest times. Its water-absorbing qualities made it an excellent compound for use in mummification.

corpse, a thing which is said actually to have happened in the case of a woman who had just died. The culprit was given away by one of his fellow workmen.

Hang on to the corpse, then, until the bitter-sweet pong deters even the most shameless necrophiliac.

Eventually, the director of Luxor's Museum of Mummification agrees to a strictly off-the-record interview. He is intensely uncomfortable about it and you feel for him. Such is the power of the poor man's boss 2,500 years after Herodotus was writing about free speech and equality before the law.

I read him the mummification passage, asking him every few moments whether the information is correct. He nods repeatedly. The removal of the brain via the nostrils, tick, an incision on the left flank, tick, use of myrrh and other spices, tick. Correct about linen – 375 strips required, with a total length of 138 metres, amulets inserted between the layers. Herodotus is less accurate about the length of the natron pickling process. It would have taken forty days, not seventy. The mummification process as a whole would have taken seventy days, which perhaps explains the confusion. The anal cedar oil injection was used for animals, not humans, he says. And as for necrophiliacs' delight, he's never heard of it. Scurrilous! Overall, he's highly impressed with Herodotus' account, not least because he says it would have been extremely difficult to get that sort of detailed information as a foreigner travelling around Egypt in the middle of the fifth century BC.

'I think he was a good man,' he says. 'He spoke to the priests a lot because they were the most important class, an aristocracy, with the best information and records. Obviously he knew how to deal with them because you can see how much detail they provided him with. Maybe he even entered temples with their permission, although normally this would have been forbidden.'

It makes you wonder. Who was Herodotus travelling with? Had he lined himself up the best guides available (as I have)? Were they bilingual or how otherwise did he get by? Some of the information he compiles, for example on the roll-call of Egyptian pharaohs – an early Ladybird guide to the dynasties of Egypt – is highly detailed and would have required a good deal more expertise than the local guide who could spin tall stories about the pyramids.

The museum director dutifully recommends Dr Zahi Hawass's book *Secrets from the Past* in case I need any more information, and the awkward interview is over. On the way back to my hotel I mull over how difficult it seems to be getting Egyptians to speak freely. My guide Refaat, a quietly spoken, studious man thin as a reed, looks at me reprovingly. 'You're starting to sound like Herodotus,' he says. 'He was always complaining, too.'

———

For the past few days walking up and down Luxor's corniche, the glimmering Nile has been reminding me that it is time to take Herodotus on to the water, to join him in his studies of a river that has fired the imagination of mankind from the earliest days.

Herodotus is not afraid to admit he's baffled by its behaviour. What particularly interests him is its mystifying annual flood, which he reports as beginning in the summer solstice and lasting a hundred days before subsiding once again and remaining low throughout the winter until the next summer's flood. He does his best to discover why this is so but for once his usual correspondents fail him. 'About why the Nile behaves precisely as it does I could get no information from the priests or anyone else,' he says. He then summarises (and rubbishes) three far-fetched theories posited by 'certain Greeks, hoping to advertise how clever they are'. First, that summer north winds block the water flowing into the Mediterranean, as suggested by Thales, the sixth-century BC philosopher and polymath. Second, that the Nile flows from 'the Ocean' which encircles the earth, as Hecataeus believed. Third, that melting snows empty into the sources of the Nile, as mentioned in Anaxagoras, Aeschylus and Euripides.

Having comprehensively dismissed this trio of theories, Herodotus is then sufficiently rash (engagingly so) to advance his own explanation, 'that during winter the sun is driven out of his course by storms towards the upper parts of Libya'. He develops this fanciful hypothesis for a couple of pages, opening himself to greater ridicule in the eyes of modern readers, who may know that the annual flood is caused by nothing more exotic than the monsoon rains that fall on the Ethiopian plateau and flow into the Blue Nile and Atbara rivers.

So much for the flooding. Next he wants to discuss the most enduring question: where does the river come from? 'Concerning the sources of the Nile, nobody I have spoken with, Egyptian, Libyan or Greek, professed to have any knowledge, except the scribe who kept the register of the treasures of Athene in the Egyptian city of Sais. But even this person,' Herodotus adds in a caustic aside, 'though he pretended to exact knowledge, seemed to me hardly serious' with his declaration that the springs of the Nile flowed from between two conically shaped mountains close to Syene, near Thebes (Luxor), and Elephantine (Aswan). 'On this subject I could get no further information from anybody. As far as Elephantine I speak as an eye-witness, but further south from hearsay.'

Herodotus' failure here is hardly surprising. The quest for the source of the Nile, one of the great riddles of exploration, continued for centuries. It was only in the fifteenth and sixteenth centuries that Europeans first set eyes on Lake Tana and the mountains to its south that form the source of the Blue Nile in Ethiopia. The source of the White Nile proved even more elusive, discovered on the northern shores of Lake Victoria by the British explorer John Hanning Speke as late as 1858. The story didn't even end there. Explorers, always an argumentative lot, have continued searching for the 'true source' of the Nile into the early twenty-first century with expeditions to the 'remote source' of the Blue Nile deep in the Nyungwe rainforest of Rwanda. Perhaps we should just applaud Herodotus for getting into the spirit of the quest and sailing as far south as Aswan. As far as the *Histories* was concerned, this was a sideshow. The Nile had nothing whatsoever to do with the Persian Wars. It was simply too magnificent a marvel to ignore.

Of course, when Herodotus visited Egypt in the middle of the fifth century BC, there were no dams at Aswan and the annual flooding of the great river continued unchanged as it had since the dawn of time.*

---

* References to the Nile, and its mighty floods, abound in the Bible. Jeremiah 46:8: 'Egypt rises up like a flood, And its waters move like the rivers; And he says, "I will go up and cover the earth, I will destroy the city and its inhabitants." '

Two dams, the first British-built between 1899 and 1902, the second a Soviet-Egyptian construction of the Sixties, put an end to that age-old cycle, creating one of the largest lakes in the world and completely changing the fabric of Egypt. The landscape of the delta during the natural floods would have been less land than river. As Herodotus writes, 'When the Nile overflows, the whole country is converted into a sea, and the towns, which alone remain above water, look like the islands in the Aegean. At these times water transport is used all over the country . . .' If that seems odd to us today, it is only because our memories are so short. In the sweep of Egyptian history, the high dams and absence of annual floods are the novelty rather than the norm.

To learn more, I make a beeline for Mohammed Talat Abdul Aziz, chairman of the High Dam and Aswan Dams Authority, a jolly, middle-aged man in an office the size of an imperial suite. Among the thick jungle of palms and plants, the models and maps of the Nile, several monitors show various images of the great grey dam curled up in the sun like a basking snake. Others flash figures from around the country. He introduces himself, points to one of the screens and declaims grandly, 'I hold all of Egypt's water in my hands!' Then he chuckles. 'You know, without the dam there would be no Egypt! Our share of the Nile is 55.5 billion cubic metres and because there are no other dams to the south we have more than 90 billion cubic metres during the floods. If that amount of water came down into Egypt without a dam, both sides of the Nile would be flooded and Egypt would disappear.' Or return to its seasonally submerged landscape of old.

What does he make of Herodotus' comments about Egypt being 'the gift of the Nile'? Some Egyptians don't like it at all. 'What about all the other countries the Nile flows through?' one asked me in irritation. 'What about Sudan, Ethiopia, Tanzania, Kenya, Burundi, Rwanda and Uganda? Eight countries but only Egypt has created such a civilisation and all the monuments that go with it. Herodotus should have said Egypt was the gift of the Nile *and* the Egyptians. He gives us no credit.'

Mohammed takes a more relaxed view. 'Other countries on the Nile have rains, in Egypt we have none. We depend completely on the

Nile for our water. We have always had to control and use the water and this has helped our civilisation develop, so Herodotus was quite correct. The Nile is the heart of Egypt, its lifeblood.'

The new dams also revolutionised Egyptian agriculture and the rural economy. Herodotus, entranced by the Nile, reckoned that 'As things are at present these people get their harvests with less labour than anyone else in the world . . . they have no need to work with plough or hoe, or to use any other of the ordinary methods of cultivating their land; they merely wait for the river of its own accord to flood their fields; then, when the water has receded, each farmer sows his plot, turns pigs into it to tread in the seed, and then waits for the harvest.'

A slight exaggeration, perhaps, but the fundamentals were true. Each flood brought with it deposits of the marvellously life-giving silt. What the dams, by ending the single annual flood, allowed were multiple harvests with a regulated year-round supply of water. 'Before the dam, you'd have one harvest a year,' says Mohammed. 'In years when the Nile flood was low, we'd suffer from famine, as you know from your Bible, the story in Genesis when seven thin cows come out of the Nile and eat seven fat cows, a sign that feast would be followed by famine. Now you have three crops a year and production has trebled.'

And yet despite this revolutionary upset the scenes along the banks of the Nile still strike the visitor as utterly timeless as he floats down the river. When you get away from the towns of Luxor and Aswan, dodging the behemoth Nile cruisers, you escape the modern world and sail blithely into the many-layered past. As Lady Duff Gordon wrote in 1863, 'This country is a palimpsest, in which the Bible is written over Herodotus, and the Koran over that. In the towns the Koran is most visible, in the country Herodotus.' Children and old whitebeards bump along dusty paths on flabbergasted donkeys and permanently aggrieved camels, trotting past green-glowing fields on their way to market. On the river egrets break upon the skyline in a blinding ripple of applause, disturbed by a flotilla of white-sailed feluccas whose sails twist and billow like fluid sculptures. Ducks take off in a flash of pale feathers, ibis spear through the busy sky, cows graze with the stupefying languor that the Nile induces. Palms whisper in the breeze. The ponderous river slides by beneath granite boulders, a steaming band of silver slicing through the desert. Green and grey herons join the aerial dance, with grebes and yellow-billed storks, cranes, Nile Valley sunbirds, painted snipe and plovers, descendants of the birds revered by the ancient Egyptians and traced with such care on the walls of their tombs and temples.

Although the crocodiles that Herodotus spends so much time discussing are gone now, driven south by the Aswan dams, our itinerant Greek is still an amusing, if erratic, guide to Egyptian wildlife. 'Other animals avoid the crocodile,' he says, 'with one exception – the sandpiper or Egyptian plover; this bird is of service to the crocodile and lives, in consequence, in the greatest amity with him; for when the crocodile comes ashore and lies with his mouth wide open ... the bird hops in and swallows the leeches. The crocodile enjoys this, and never, in consequence, hurts the bird.'

I take a felucca bound for Kom Ombo, once a centre of worship of the snout-faced crocodile god Sobek. In between sunlit snoozes that are interrupted regularly by a spattering of chilly Nile spray, I leaf through Book 2 of the *Histories*. What my edition calls the 'nadir of Herodotean zoology' is his description of a hippopotamus, complete with 'horse's mane and tail, conspicuous tusks, a voice like a horse's neigh'. He probably based this wild portrait on the creature's Greek name, which means 'river-horse'. It is difficult not to be amazed by the range of fact (and sometimes fiction) Herodotus records in Egypt. Sometimes it's the sober voice of an encyclopaedia, at others it's Lonely Planet on acid.

———

A small selection of Herodotus on tour, culled from a couple of days on the Nile.

On age-old good manners: 'There is another point in which the Egyptians resemble one section of the Greek people – the Lacedaemonians: I mean the custom of young men stepping aside to make room for their seniors when they meet them in the street, and of getting up from their seats when older men come in.'

On the prohibition of sex in temples: 'It was the Egyptians who first made it an offence against piety to have intercourse with women in temples, or to enter temples after intercourse without having previously washed.'

On a curious case of bestiality: 'In this province in my lifetime a goat had intercourse with a woman, in full view of everybody – a most surprising incident, which became publicly known.'

On how the Egyptian celebration of the phallic festival of Dionysus differs from the Greek: 'Instead of the phallus they have puppets, about eighteen inches high; the genitals of these figures are made almost as big as the rest of their bodies, and they are pulled up and down by strings as the women carry them round the villages.'

On self-immolating cats:

> What happens when a house catches fire is most extraordinary: nobody takes the least trouble to put it out, for it is only the cats that matter: everyone stands in a row, a little distance from his neighbour, trying to protect the cats, who nevertheless slip through the line, or jump over it, and hurl themselves into the flames. This causes the Egyptians deep distress.

On a morbid custom at plutocratic Egyptian dinner parties:

> When the rich give a party and the meal is finished, a man carries round amongst the guests a wooden image of a corpse in a coffin, carved and painted to look as much like the real thing as possible, and anything from eighteen inches to three foot long; he shows it to each guest in turn, and says: 'Look upon this body as you drink and enjoy yourself; for you will be just like it when you are dead.'

On the birth of horoscopes, a prelude to Roman astrology: 'The Egyptians were also the first to assign each month and each day to a particular deity, and to foretell by the date of a man's birth his character, his fortunes, and the day of his death . . .'

Probably the most famous passage in Book 2 is Herodotus' discussion of 'opposites', how everything about Egypt, from its climate and its customs to the workings of the Nile and its people, is completely different from the rest of the world. What is lovely about it is the sense of his delight at these peculiarities. There is nothing scornful or dismissive in his tone. The Egyptians, he begins, 'seem to have reversed the ordinary practices of mankind'.

> For instance, women attend market and are employed in trade, while men stay at home and do the weaving. In weaving the normal way is to work the threads of the weft upwards, but the Egyptians work them downwards. Men in Egypt carry loads on their head, women on their shoulders; women urinate standing up, men sitting down. To ease themselves they go indoors, but eat outside in the streets . . . Elsewhere priests grow their hair long; in Egypt they shave their heads. In other nations the relatives of the deceased in time of mourning cut their hair, but the Egyptians, who shave at all other times, mark a death by letting the hair grow both on head and chin. They live with their animals – unlike the rest of the world, who live apart from them. Other men live on wheat and barley, but any Egyptian who does so is blamed for it . . . Dough they knead with their feet, but clay with their hands – and even handle dung. They practise circumcision, while men of other nations – except those who have learned from Egypt – leave their private parts as nature made them. Men in Egypt have two garments, women only one. The ordinary practice at sea is to make sheets fast to ring-bolts fitted outboard; the Egyptians fit them inboard. In writing or calculating, instead of going, like the Greeks, from left to right, the Egyptians go from right to left – and obstinately maintain that theirs is the dexterous method, ours being left-handed and awkward.

We're all different, he's saying. We all have our own ways of doing things, our own customs. Some things foreigners do may strike us as weird or unseemly, but doubtless our own traditions seem odd to others, too. The richness and diversity of human life is something to cherish, not to fear or despise.

Herodotus was as fascinated by the natural world as by man-made monuments and Egyptian history. He couldn't resist offering his audience a portrait of what the Greeks called the pebble lizard, *kroke dilos*, which gave us the word crocodile. He describes it quite correctly as a four-footed amphibious creature which lays and hatches its eggs on land. 'It has eyes like a pig's but great fang-like teeth in proportion to its body . . .' he continues, slipping up with his observation that it has no tongue (it does) and a stationary jaw (it doesn't). Then, after the comments on the friendly, symbiotic relationship of the leech-seeking plover and the crocodile, he gets on to the animal's religious significance:

> Some Egyptians reverence the crocodile as a sacred beast; others do not, but treat it as an enemy. The strongest belief in its sanctity is to be found in Thebes and round about Lake Moeris; in these places they keep one particular crocodile, which they tame, putting rings made of glass or gold into its ears and bracelets round its front feet, giving it special food and ceremonial offerings. In fact, while these creatures are alive they treat them with every kindness, and when they die, they embalm them and bury them in sacred tombs.

Kom Ombo looms high on a sandy hill on the east bank of the Nile, a confident cluster of columns and an amalgam of two temples, one dedicated to the worship of Haroeris , the older falcon-headed Horus, solar god of war, the other to Sobek, the crocodile-headed god of fertility and creator of the world. We can excuse Herodotus for not mentioning it because it was only built a couple of centuries after his death, during the Ptolemaic dynasty of the second century BC when our travelling historian would have been intrigued to discover Egypt rejoicing in Hellenistic rule, a time of cultural and military glory.

Two millennia have passed but the flying vultures painted on the ceiling of the pronaos are still decked in joyful red, white and blue, the colours of their magnificent plumage softened but not eclipsed by time. My guide points out a relief depicting what he says is the world's earliest record of surgical instruments, a collection of scalpels and suction cups, scales and saws, lances, retractors, chisels and various dental tools so awful they make you wince.

Step inside the bijou Roman chapel of the goddess Hathor, let your eyes grow accustomed to the darkness and slowly a roomful of mummified crocodiles appear before you like a vision. And there, in the snarling fangs, the timeworn scales and, if you can see them, the pig-like eyes, is a tiny reminder of Herodotus.

Black geese fly overhead into a sunset of wind-ruffled pink clouds that hang completely still in the sky. The sun sinks into the desert, singeing the sandstone cliffs and sucking down plumes of golden light on to the sands sloping above the river. The river's modest green skirt fades into darkness and the history-shrugging timelessness of the Nile returns. Silhouettes stiffen. Palm trees bristle. Felucca captains lower the sails and haul out their cudgel-oars to row home. Naked masts point to the glittering stars sprinkled across a steely sky. For a few moments they are transformed, with the slanting hypotenuse yard-arms, into clusters of right-angled triangles. Now the Nile is a slick of pitch-black oil, stained with the smudged glares of reflected lights. *Muaddins* from their minarets call into the gloaming, urging the faithful to prayer. Some details change – Allah has displaced the crocodile-headed Sobek – but man's worship of an unknown god continues. For a moment we wait as the Nubian skipper Ali attends to the call of nature. He hoists up his voluminous *galabiya*, squats on the deck and pees into the Nile. Then, with a vigorous fart, we are off into the night.

# 7

# Herodotus in Hollywood (and the Sahara)

*HISTORY, n. An account, mostly false, of events, mostly unimportant,
which are brought about by rulers, mostly knaves, and soldiers, mostly
fools.*

Ambrose Bierce, *The Cynic's Word Book* (1906)

As the crow flies, it is 350 miles from Cairo. Oh to be the eter-
nally short-cutting crow, flying high over the Great Sand Sea! In
real life it is a lot further away, half as much again. To get there from
the Egyptian capital, first you have to travel north-west through the
small town of Wadi Natrun (supplier of the natron used by ancient
Egyptian embalmers, then west along the Mediterranean road to
Mersa Matruh, before diving south another 200 miles on a dubious
road across a featureless limestone desert until, after many bone-
crunching hours, a mystifying flash of water and mile upon mile of
green palms surrounded by roiling rocks and dunes tell you that you
have finally arrived in the remote (and deeply Herodotean) oasis of
Siwa, home to one of the ancient world's most celebrated oracles. The
first sight of it is unforgettable.

---

Many visitors break their journey to Siwa by stopping at the El
Alamein War Cemetery to pay their respects to the dead, honouring
those who fell in the Western Desert campaigns of the Second World
War. It is a moving place, fifty acres carpeted in beige headstones that
brighten into blinding white beneath the desert sun. Clusters of
crimson and mauve hibiscus strike a surprising note of serenity among

lines of graves that are laid out with crisp precision. There is an echo of Herodotus (and Ecclesiasticus, from where it was borrowed) in the legend 'Their name liveth for ever more', a recognition that the sacrifice made by these men must never be 'forgotten in time'. Above the entrance to the cloister the dedicatory inscription pays tribute to the soldiers, airmen and naval forces who 'turned the tide of the war', a reminder of Herodotus' determination to ensure that great deeds 'may not be without their glory'.

The sea of loss is overwhelming, row upon row of young men felled in conflict. There are 7,367 burials in the cemetery, in addition to the 603 cremations and the 11,874 soldiers and airmen with no known grave, whose names are inscribed beneath a slender stone cross on the Alamein Memorial, unveiled by Field Marshal Montgomery on 24 October 1951. The words on the top of the headstones are briskly official, detailing the man's name, age (if known), number, rank and military unit next to an engraved regimental or services crest and the date of his death. On the bottom, beneath a large crucifix, is a smaller space for the bereaved families to add personal tributes.

84782 DRIVER
I. PARK
ROYAL ARMY SERVICE CORPS
4TH OCTOBER 1942 AGE 21
SO HE PASSED OVER
AND ALL THE TRUMPETS
SOUNDED FOR HIM
ON THE OTHER SIDE

6285910 L. CPL
H. M. CHEESEMAN
THE BUFFS
15TH AUGUST 1941
HIS LIFE A BEAUTIFUL MEMORY
HIS DEATH A SILENT GRIEF.
SADLY MISSED BY ALL

Many fell during the battle of El Alamein that raged for a fortnight from 23 October to 4 November 1942. Allied victory in what was one of history's most ferocious battles led to the final expulsion of Axis forces from North Africa in April the following year.

556861 TROOPER
P. V. HARRIS
THE ROYAL WILTSHIRE YEOMANRY
ROYAL ARMOURED CORPS
KILLED ON 24TH OCTOBER 1942 AGE 25
GREATER LOVE
HATH NO MAN THAN THIS;
THAT A MAN LAY DOWN
HIS LIFE FOR HIS FRIENDS

2936192 PRIVATE
M. M. NEWTON
THE ARGYLL AND
SUTHERLAND HIGHLANDERS
KILLED ON 24TH OCTOBER 1942 AGE 21
FOR YOU REST, LAD
FOR US MEMORIES.
MOTHER AND DAD

1122275 GUNNER
A. HESELTINE
ROYAL ARTILLERY
3RD NOVEMBER 1942 AGE 21
FOR HONOUR
LIBERTY AND TRUTH
HE SACRIFICED
HIS GLORIOUS YOUTH

And then there are the 821 graves honouring the unidentified dead.

A SOLDIER
OF THE
1939–1945
WAR
KNOWN UNTO GOD
★

There is no memorial, though, to the soldiers who lost their lives in a much earlier campaign in the Western Desert. The most disastrous expedition across the Sahara took place around 2,467 years before the battle of El Alamein. What little we know about it comes from Herodotus.

In Book 3 he tells the story of Cambyses' turbulent Egyptian campaign. The date is about 525 BC, still fresh enough in living memory for Herodotus, who was travelling in Egypt barely seventy-five years later, to report upon with some confidence. Having conquered the Nile Valley, the Persian king has now moved to Thebes, from where he is launching fresh expeditions, one against the Ethiopians to the south, the other, a formidable force of 50,000 men, against 'the Ammonians' of the desert to the west. Herodotus never refers to Siwa, only to 'the oracle of Ammon in Libya' and the people who live there, 'the Ammonians', whom he supposes quite logically to have taken their name from the famous oracle 'for Amun is the Egyptian name for Zeus'. Cambyses' soldiers are sent with orders to 'reduce them to slavery, and burn the oracle of Zeus'. Such unholy intentions do not augur well in Herodotus' world. According to the Greek, the Persian king had already 'lost his wits' and was behaving like 'the madman he was', having launched a fatally ill-prepared expedition against Ethiopia that went so badly that his men, having exhausted their supplies in the Nubian wilderness south of the cataracts at Aswan, were reduced for survival to choosing one man in ten to be eaten by his fellows. The conquest of Ethiopia had to be abandoned.

The expedition against the Ammonians in Siwa proved far worse. Herodotus' story of what happened inspired one of the world's greatest archaeological riddles, unsolved to this day.

The force which was sent against the Ammonians started from Thebes with guides, and can be traced as far as the town of Oasis [Kharga] . . . seven days' journey across the sand from Thebes. The place is known in Greek as the Islands of the Blessed. General report has it that the army got as far as this, but of its subsequent fate there is no news whatever. It never reached the Ammonians and it never returned to Egypt. There is, however, a story told by the Ammonians themselves and by others who heard it from them, that when the men had left Oasis, and in their march across the desert had reached a point about mid-way between the town and the Ammonian border, a southerly wind of extreme violence drove the sand over them in heaps as they were taking their mid-day meal, so that they disappeared forever.

Thus ended the most catastrophic lunch in the annals of desert picnicking. Generations of Egyptologists and archaeologists have dreamt of finding Cambyses' lost army ever since, none more enigmatic than the Hungarian aristocrat we met briefly earlier, Count László de Almásy, aviator, explorer, soldier and sometime spy, whose action-packed life inspired the Herodotus-loving protagonist of Michael Ondaatje's novel *The English Patient*. A recent study suggested that, in addition to astrology and necromancy, Almásy's exotic interests may have embraced Occult Templarism with its tradition of 'satanic practices and blasphemies, including the worship of a huge androgynous idol called Baphomet in phallic-cult orgies, involving sodomy and fellatio'.

Be that as it may, in 1934 Almásy discovered an intact Greek amphora between Dakhla Oasis and the Bir Abu Mungar well. He believed Cambyses had stockpiled supplies of water along the marching route across the Great Sand Sea. In 1935, driving north from near Farafra Oasis, he came across a number of hollow pyramids of stone the size of a man, apparent cairns that stretched for at least ninety miles towards Siwa. When he was 155 miles south of Siwa, he was engulfed by a searingly hot sandstorm that lasted eight days. He was lucky to escape alive. Convinced that Cambyses' army had been wiped out by such a storm, he hoped to continue his explorations, only for the Second World War to intervene. Almásy died in 1951. Recent archaeological finds in the Western Desert, including arrowheads and a dagger near Siwa, together with textiles, weapon fragments and human remains, have offered tantalising glimpses of Cambyses' lost army, but final confirmation has proved elusive. The riddle of the sands remains.

A journey to Siwa, then, was no small undertaking in the ancient world. When visitors today moan about the rigours of their day-long drive, having enjoyed a sandstorm-free lunch of fresh fish and calamari in Mersa Matruh, they might remember that the more direct journey across the desert from the Nile – as taken by Cambyses' army – was once a matter of life and death.

The temple of the ram-headed Libyan–Egyptian god Ammon and the famous Siwan spring Herodotus describes already justify a visit to this far-flung oasis, but there is another, quirkily Herodotean reason for making the long trek across the Sahara. Siwa has a reputation as a bastion of illicit homosexuality. Illicit because this ancient settlement is a conservative place and Islam does not look favourably, to put it mildly, on homosexuality. In certain quarters a sense of shame lingers about the oasis to this day. In others, especially among gay foreign tourists, lustier concerns prevail. Siwa is featured on gayegypt.com, for example, which unequivocally recommends it as 'one of the best cruising places in the world'. The urge to investigate is irresistible.

It is a strange tale, so perhaps it's only appropriate that it has a weird beginning. It all started with town planning and a well-meaning regulation that had far-reaching consequences. Until well into the nineteenth century, the Siwan elders prohibited anyone from building their houses outside the fortified walls encircling the original settlement of Shali, for fear of the regular Bedouin raids across the desert. Mohammed Ali, founder of the modern state of Egypt (whom we will meet in Greece), sent soldiers to occupy Siwa in 1820, ensuring the town's security against these invaders. By 1826, the elders, by now presiding over a town of tottering eight-storey houses and streets so narrow that if two donkeys met in the street one had to reverse awkwardly into a home, finally gave their permission for houses to be built beyond the walls.

At the bottom of the strictly hierarchical Siwan society were the *zaggalah* (club-bearers), poor young men akin to feudal serfs, who worked on the landowners' groves of date palms and olive trees by day, and who by night were security guards, hence their name. According to Siwan custom, the *zaggalah*, who were not allowed to marry before the age of forty, were forbidden from entering the city walls, lest they encounter the girl of their dreams who might – perish the thought – already be married. No prospect of a dark-skinned Lady Chatterley's Lover here.

With time on their hands, no girls to party with and nowhere to go, the *zaggalah* had to make their own fun. At night they took to meeting *en masse* in the deserted groves and gardens, drinking draughts of the local firewater *lagbi*, fermented juice from the date palm. Friends whipped out their flutes and drums, riotous music rang out beneath the stars and in the flickering light of campfires svelte young men danced away. Over time, the innocent fumbles and furtive clinches developed into something more enduring.

Homosexuality among the *zaggalah* became such an institution in Siwa that gay marriage contracts were drawn up specifying the dowry payable to the younger partner – generally a boy – who was considered the 'wife'. They were still being written openly as late as 1928, when the practice was outlawed after a rare visit from King Farouk, who reminded the tribal elders of their Islamic heritage and berated them furiously for condoning the town's 'certain vice'. It was said to continue underground, however, until the early 1950s.

In a 1991 paper on the universality of incest, the American psychohistorian (what would Herodotus have made of that?) Lloyd de Mause wrote:

> Pederastic marriages and pederastic prostitution have been so widespread in Siwa until just recently that everyone is accustomed to the proposition that men normally love boys more than they do women, saying: 'They will kill each other for a boy. Never for a woman.' Muslim holy men (imaam) regularly have boys available for sex, saying the ingestion of the imaam's semen is necessary for absorbing his spiritual powers, sometimes even extending to formal marriage with the boy.

The controversy refuses to go away. A book on Siwan customs published in 2001 by Fathi Malim, a twenty-seven-year-old local anthropologist, caused a terrific uproar and almost led to his tribe disowning, expelling and disinheriting him, the fiercest sanctions in such a traditional tribal society. His crime was to have laid bare some aspects of Siwan society the elders thought it improper to reveal. Although the book tiptoed delicately around the issue of homosexuality, Malim was still forced to white-out several passages considered offensive by the tribal elders. One revealed how a groom whose wife does not bleed on their wedding night cuts his hand and bleeds on to the sheet to prove she was a virgin. Another detailed how a husband and wife who commit adultery are made to divorce, given sixty lashes with an olive branch (wonderful irony) and then fined 10,000 Egyptian pounds. The only possible reference to homosexuality in the book is the poem entitled *The Poet*:

> You could beat me with an iron bar
> But I will still love my boyfriend . . .
>
> All those who love him
> Feel as if their liver is burning in a fire . . .
>
> Oh, beautiful boy, please do not sin
> Be kind to us, lovely boy
> Oh, beautiful boy, be kind to us
> You are the medicine for our wounds
> Before we die, find us
> We will love you more and more.

My driver Bahaa, a laconic fortysomething with a love of the desert, has a dim view of Siwans. He regards them, with the withering perspective of the superior Cairene, as provincial primitives. I ask him whether the old tradition of homosexuality continues. 'Why not?' he replies dismissively. 'These people fuck donkeys. I'm serious. I once heard two teenage boys discussing fucking a donkey. It's completely normal for them. They're not allowed to do anything with girls before they get married so they've either got each other or donkeys.'

It is true that contact between young men and women before marriage is almost unthinkable. Women in Siwa flit like phantoms through the streets and groves, shrouded in the all-encompassing blue cotton sheet or *tarfottet*, embroidered with silk, that resembles a more decorative and colourful version of the Afghan *burqa*. Their faces are permanently covered. They remind the visitor how different Siwa is from the rest of Egypt, a cultural independence forged by geography, treasured and defended in the Siwi language, proclaimed in local dress and quietly maintained in age-old customs and, however violently Islam disapproves of it, an enduring belief in magic.

One evening I head into the town centre to hunt out Fathi Malim. Twilight falls gently through the palms. Donkey carts driven by young children rush by in a flurry of raised arms and beatings, blue-parcelled sisters and mothers perched on the back like an afterthought. The main square of Siwa stretches out beneath the illuminated ruins of Shali. By night the abandoned old town is a magical mountain of twisting alleys and crumbling, jagged walls and houses made from *karshif*, the local soil that glitters with rocks of salt. Paths wind and steps climb past shattered-teeth silhouettes to a broken house reincarnated as a lonely watchtower on a windy summit. The new town spreads and sparkles beneath a crescent moon lodged in a swirling, ink-stained sky that Van Gogh might have painted. Shali is derelict now, left long ago, but it lords it above the new town like an inescapable memory.

Fathi Malim is easy to find. A red-and-blue sign reads 'Siwa Information Center and Internet Service Author's Shop Mr Fathi Malim'. A young man with a beard and hunted look in his eyes sits in a shop whose shelves are lined with copies of *Oasis Siwa from the Inside: Traditions, Customs and Magic*, a local bestseller to the chagrin of the town's elders. A semicircular section of a date palm trunk sits on his desk, inscribed with the legend 'Mr Fathi Malim'. Next to it is another which reads 'Anthropologist'. Lest there be any doubt that this is indeed the anthropologist Fathi Malim, a third announces the happy synthesis, 'Fathi Malim Anthropologist'.

Malim says there is less magic practised in Siwa today than in earlier times because people are more educated now. But it still happens. Curses are used by jealous rivals to prevent girls getting married and men and women from having children. There are a couple of practitioners of black magic in Siwa who are widely feared. My eyebrows must involuntarily twitch because Fathi fixes me with a look of deadly seriousness. 'No one in Siwa can say they don't believe in magic,' he warns me. Three weeks ago, a thirty-two-year-old man from Siwa got lost in the desert. For three days his friends and family looked for him with cars and donkeys, driving up and down calling for him with megaphones. Then they found him under a tamarisk tree. He told them he had spent three days eating and drinking with the jinn spirits. 'This happens every year. The jinn approach people in the form of their friends or family and then Satan lures people into the desert.'

He tells the story of his sister falling to the ground once when the Koran was being recited. 'She fainted and then her body was shaking.

It took her half an hour to wake up and then, when I was going to put the television on, she screamed "No! Please don't do it!" because the Koran was being recited on a religious programme. Satan and the jinn had taken her over and they can't stand the holy words of the Koran.'

The section on magic is one of the longest and, for a Western reader, most unusual in Malim's book. 'The occult and the supernatural have a very strong presence in the oasis,' he writes, giving details of how sorceresses used to raid graves to extract various body parts – brain, liver, left arm, bones, hair, fingernails – from which to make their magic potions. The most common spells cast are those to bring about divorce, illness, infertility and love. A groom's wedding-night nerves are unlikely to be calmed by his knowledge that a popular spell, usually requested by a jealous rival, is to transform his penis into a vagina so that he is unable to consummate the marriage. How (short of popping a discreet Viagra) to protect oneself against this magic? Holy water from Mecca must be sprinkled around the bedroom before the couple go to bed and the bride must wear a (rather unromantic) *hijab* veil to protect her from Satan.

After the furore over his book, Malim would rather not discuss homosexuality in Siwa. He blames a lot of the 'gay Siwa' controversy on an earlier book on the oasis written by the late Ahmed Fakhry, a history professor at Cairo University, who made much of it. The unpleasant experience with his first book has taught him a lesson. He won't write anything sensitive again. His next project is a lavishly illustrated Siwan cookery book containing eighty-eight recipes. 'I don't think there will be a problem with this,' he says nervously.

Apart from the Oracle of Ammon, Herodotus refers specifically to one other landmark in Siwa. As so often in the *Histories*, it is a crowd-pleasing marvel.

> They have another spring there, of which the water is tepid in the early morning and cools down toward market time; by noon it is very cold, and that is the moment when they water their gardens; then, as the days draw towards evening, the chill gradually goes off it, until by sunset it is tepid again; after that it gets hotter and hotter as the night advances,

and at midnight it boils furiously. Then, after midnight, the process is reversed, and it steadily cools off until dawn. The spring is known as the Fountain of the Sun.

Siwans used to know it as Ain Gubah, the Well of Jupiter. Today, with a canny eye on tourist income, they call it Cleopatra's Spring, though there is no evidence whatsoever that the doe-eyed Egyptian queen ever set foot here. 'I tell visitors that Antony and Cleopatra bathed here with no clothes on,' the Alexandrine owner of a café next to the bubbling water chuckles. 'I tell them anything and they believe it because they want to.'

Harmless enough, you might think, though enough to make the high-minded Frenchman Alain Blottière, author of a romanticised portrait of Siwa, apoplectic. 'It would have been better to have avoided such a pathetic falsehood just a few hundred metres from the temple of the oracle where, for centuries, people have come in search of the truth,' he huffs. 'If one wanted to ensure its prestige in the eyes of casual visitors, it would have been more than sufficient to point out that it was regarded as a marvel of the natural world by the ancients.' Apart from Herodotus, he notes, the spring attracted comment from Aristotle, Lucretius, Diodorus, Ovid, Quintus Curtius, Arrian and St Augustine. None of whom, it might be remarked, is quite as exotic as Cleopatra, but never mind.

The spring is the largest in Siwa and one of the most romantic open-air swimming pools in the world, collected within a circular stone wall sixty feet in diameter and fringed by a garland of date palms beneath the wide desert sky. Bubbles rise up like chains of diamonds from the rocky depths. Craters, mountains and zigzagging fissures, magnified by the crystalline clarity, mark the unruly bottom that is twenty-five feet below. A couple of boys hurl themselves into the fizzing water, their cries rebounding and echoing within the stone surround. I slip into the limpid waters, agog at the thought of swimming in Herodotus' slipstream. A drooling Bahaa, dressed like an urban gangster with wraparound shades, Chicago White Sox satin bomber jacket, moustache and permanent scowl, is less interested in Herodotus than the more compelling prospect of watching two giggly young

Double-headed bust of the historians Herodotus (left) and Thucydides (right), Museo Archeologico Nazionale, Naples

*Above:* Herodotus' hometown of Halicarnassus, now the Turkish resort town of Bodrum on the Aegean coast. The fifteenth-century Castle of St Peter, built from the ruins of the Mausoleum of King Mausolos, one of the Seven Wonders of the World, crowns the promontory jutting into the harbour

*Left:* A bust of Herodotus outside the Bodrum Museum, the only trace of the Greek historian – with the dubious exception of a road junction - in the town

*Right:* Taking liberties with other nations' histories. In 1857, the British archaeologist and inveterate pillager Charles Newton began excavating the Mausoleum of Halicarnassus, which dates to the mid-fourth century BC. Here he supervises the raising of a colossal lion from Cnidus, now in the Great Court of the British Museum

*Below:* An eighteenth-century Austrian interpretation of what the Mausoleum might have looked like in all its glory

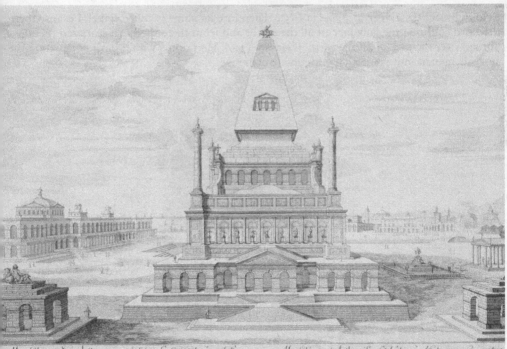

Mausoleum der Arthemisia welches sie hat erbauen lassen ihrem Ehegemahl dem König Mausolo zu Halicarnasso inlaren zwischen dem Tempel Venus und den Königlichen Pallast

Mausolée qu' Arthemisie fit bâtir à Halicarnasse entre le Temple de Venus et le Palais Royal en memoire du Roy Mausole son epoux

*Left:* Dr Donny George, former director of the National Museum, in front of an arch-shaped panel of glazed bricks with floral and geometric patterns and pictures of animals, the world's oldest decorated bricks (ninth century BC), from Fort Shalmaneser in Nimrud

*Above:* An Assyrian human-headed winged bull from the palace of Sargon in Khorsabad, late eighth century BC, National Museum, Baghdad

*Below:* Brueghel's *Tower of Babel* (1563). 'Therefore its name is called Babel, because there the Lord confused the language of all the earth; and from there the Lord scattered them abroad over the face of all the earth' (Genesis 11:9). Herodotus would have understood the story as human hubris meeting with divine nemesis

*Above:* Aswan, Egypt, from Elephantine Island, Herodotus' southernmost point during his exploration of the country and his quest for the source of the Nile. 'As far as Elephantine I speak as an eye-witness, but further south from hearsay,' he wrote

*Right:* Felucca captain Ali on the Nile. The river, particularly its seasonal floods, fascinated Herodotus. 'About why the Nile behaves precisely as it does I could get no information from the priests or anyone else,' he confessed

*Above:* The Temple of Luxor, ancient Thebes. Of the Egyptians Herodotus wrote, 'They are religious to excess, beyond any other nation in the world'

*Left:* The famous fragment of the colossus of the pharaoh Ramses II from his mortuary temple, Luxor. Diodorus, the first-century BC Greek historian, transliterated the pharaoh's cartouche as 'Ozymandias', inspiring Shelley's eponymous sonnet describing a 'half sunk ... shattered visage' lying on the sand. 'My name is Ozymandias, king of kings: Look on my works, ye Mighty, and despair!'

*Above:* Siwa, the ancient oasis 350 miles west of Cairo

*Right:* The Oracle of Ammon, Siwa, one of the most prestigious in the ancient world. Seeking confirmation of his divine, world-conquering destiny, Alexander made a death-defying journey to consult the oracle in 331 BC

Sand Sea, Siwa. Herodotus tells the story of the Persian Great King Cambyses' army, marching across the desert to attack the oasis in about 525 BC and being wiped out by a ferocious sandstorm. Generations of archaeologists have hunted in vain for the lost army ever since

Fountain of the Sun, Siwa, now known as Cleopatra's Spring. According to Herodotus, 'the water is tepid in the early morning and cools down toward market time; by noon it is very cold ... at midnight it boils furiously'. In fact, it is only warmer or colder to the touch, depending on the time of day and the air temperature

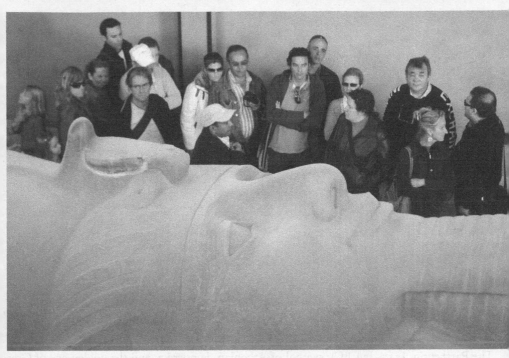

A recumbent Ramses II at Memphis, Old Kingdom capital of Egypt

An eighteenth-century engraving of the pyramids of Giza. In one of his taller stories Herodotus described how the pharaoh Cheops prostituted his daughter to raise funds for the construction of his Great Pyramid (c. 2500 BC). When he visited the pyramids in about 450 BC, they were almost as distant from his time as he is from our own

PYRAMIDES ÆGYPTIACÆ.

The Parthenon, (447–432 BC), symbol of Athenian democracy and the golden age of Greec Herodotus records how Xerxes' invading army stormed the Acropolis and burnt it to the ground in 480 BC

The Spartan king Leonidas at Thermopylae by Jacques-Louis David, who began the paintin in 1800 and finished it in 1814. What we know of the glorious defeat of the 300 Spartans i 480 BC we owe to Herodotus, who described the epic confrontation in riveting detail

The statue of Leonidas at the Thermopylae memorial

The view from the hill on which the Spartans made their last stand. 'Here they resisted to the last, with their swords, if they had them, and, if not, with their hands and teeth, until the Persians, coming on from the front over the ruins of the wall and closing in from behind, finally overwhelmed them with missile weapons'

*Left:* The Tholos in the Sanctuary of Athene Pronaea, Delphi

*Below:* The Treasury of the Athenians at Delphi, built to commemorate the Athenian victory at the battle of Marathon in 490 BC

Above: Olympia, where
Herodotus may have given live
performances of his writings

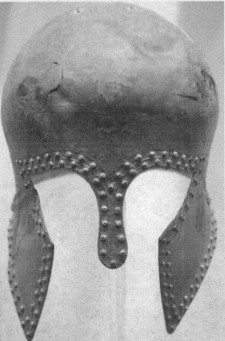

Right: Hoplite helmet,
Archaeological Museum,
Olympia. The collection includes
the helmet dedicated to Zeus by
Miltiades, the victorious general
mentioned by Herodotus at the
battle of Marathon

Herodotus singles out the island of Samos for 'three of the greatest building and engineering feats in the Greek world' carried out during the reign (c. 535–52 BC) of the expansionist tyrant Polycrates

*Left:* The Temple of Hera, 'the biggest of all Greek temples known'

*Below:* The breakwater 'which runs out into twenty fathoms of water and has a total length of over a quarter of a mile'

The extraordinary Eupalinos Tunnel, 1,133 yards long, bored through Mount Kastro from both ends simultaneously, designed to bring a secure supply of water to the town of Samos

The English writer and Second World War hero Sir Patrick Leigh Fermor at his home in Kardamyli, in the Peloponnese

East meets West. A church on the easternmost point of the island of Samos, with the Turkish mountain of Mycale in the background. The battle of Mycale in 479 BC, possibly on the same day as the battle of Plataea, brought Xerxes' ill-fated invasion of Greece to an end

Japanese girls undress by the side of the pool. Lascivious eyes follow their every move.

It is just as Herodotus described it: warm in the early morning, cooler under the desert sun, then ever warmer as the hours slide by and the temperature falls. Only it is not the water that changes temperature, of course, but the air outside, making the water seem cooler or warmer to the touch, depending on the time of day. And boiling furiously? Not quite. Perhaps the bubbles fooled him.

———

The most famous visitor to the Oracle of Ammon, Lord of Counsels, arrived in February 331 BC, about a century after Herodotus' death. It had taken his party eight tormenting days to reach the oasis just from the coast, four of them without water after a sandstorm had engulfed them. His name was Alexander. He was twenty-four years old and already had defeated Darius III at the battle of Issus. Legend has it that he had come to ask the oracle whether he was the son of god. Confirmation of his divine ancestry would provide heavenly endorsement of the world conquest to follow.

A path winds gently up through a fortified *karshif* gatehouse, past a bulbous minaret in the same material, to the rocky outcrop of Aghurmi on which the ruins of the oracle he came to consult still sit, overlooking the green immensity of Siwa. The unearthly glory of this miraculous oasis – life in the midst of death – must have fuelled Alexander and other truth-seeking visitors over the centuries with faith in the oracle's supernatural powers. To the north the sun-singed escarpment of limestone, folded in shadow; to the east the flashing jewel of Lake Aghurmi; Jebel Mawta, mountain of the dead, to the west and beyond it the incomprehensibly vast mirror of Lake Siwa; to the south the snub-nosed mountain Jebel Dakrur, the whole panorama overwhelmed by a floating sea of feathery palms that melt eventually into the crashing ocean of army-crushing dunes, wave upon glittering wave of the Great Sand Sea.

How long the Temple of Ammon has withstood the onslaught of time. Yet how unstable it looks today, perched above the abandoned village of fanged houses on a perilously flaking limestone cliff. The lower reaches are falling away like sheets of paper so that the whole site is overhanging. The final approach to the oracle is through a series of three square stone entrances, the last opening on to the innermost shrine, an unremarkable rectangular room perhaps nine feet wide by eighteen, roofless and empty. Enfolded in this tiny space you stand here in the footsteps of Alexander the Great and countless other seekers of destiny, his mythical ancestors Heracles and Perseus among them. Today the ruination of the monument has laid bare its secrets, revealing a detail unseen by Alexander: a narrow passage running behind the right-hand wall perforated with rows of little holes through which the priest's otherworldly voice rang out as though all-powerful Ammon himself – and no mere mortal – was answering.

The Oracle confirmed that Alexander was indeed the son of a god. His world-conquering rampages could begin.

***

Sheikh Fathi Kilane plucks a satsuma from the coffee table in front of him, peels it deliberately, rearranges his burgundy *shenna* skullcap with one hand, breaks off a segment of the fruit with the other and pops it into his mouth with a sigh that widens into a yawn. Somewhere deep in the innards of this large house a baby bawls into the night.

Some of the State Department Americans I knew in Iraq would have called this a 'sheikh-up', a meeting with the tribal leaders. Sheikh Kilane, a kindly man in his mid-fifties, is sitting in his main reception room alongside the younger, taller and more voluble Sheikh Omar Rageh of the Awlad Moussa tribe, whose elongated face reminds me of that sleek-cheeked monotheist pharaoh Akhenaten.

There are eleven tribes in Siwa that owe their allegiance to twelve sheikhs, the largest tribe – Kilane – having the privilege of two sheikhs, one of whom sits in the national parliament. 'We are the symbols of the tribe,' says Kilane, 'solving all the problems people have in their lives.' Crime is low in Siwa, he goes on, so most of these problems concern agricultural issues, with disputes over land, water and irrigation pre-eminent. Anything involving the government must also go through the sheikhs.

We discuss the *zaggalah* question, which prompts Kilane and Rageh to launch into their own tongue for a couple of minutes. Voices are raised. It's still controversial. 'They did these things,' says Rageh at last. 'I want to be honest about it with you. They were very poor, they worked for food, they couldn't marry until they had saved enough money which was not until they were forty to forty-five. The *zaggalah* were uneducated men, I am sure you find people like this in Scotland, drinking in the streets and doing wrong things. They drank to forget. The Siwans then were Muslims in name only, they didn't know anything about Islam. Then King Farouk came and built a mosque and school and the people's education improved and so now there are less people doing these things.'

Kilane picks up another satsuma and disposes of it remorselessly, happy to let the younger man do the talking. I ask them why Fathi Malim's book was censored. 'There were some things we didn't like in it, but we didn't want to twist his arm so we found a solution to remove certain passages. There was a big meeting of all the sheikhs. Some things in the book were not true, you see.'

Kilane acknowledges that black magic remains a problem in Siwa. The tribal and religious leaders are doing their best to stamp it out. 'It comes from Morocco and Sudan. We're fighting it, the imams are trying to get the devil out of men and women. A week ago I found a woman practising magic against a man. I made her pay the man's expenses to go and get cured, so it cost her 27,000 Egyptian pounds which is a big fortune here. To test whether there is a jinn inside someone I read from the Koran and if there is, the person shivers. Sometimes the jinn will answer, blaming someone else for the magic, lying and trying to cause fights between people. In some rare cases the imam beats the feet of the person, burning the jinn by reading the Koran and then pricking the sufferer's feet with a needle so that Satan leaves the body through the drops of blood.'

Modern life, with the arrival of television (only introduced in 1986), cars and mass tourism, is exposing Siwa to a host of new influences. The traditional Siwan life, as recorded in Fathi Malim's book, is under threat. 'We don't want to become like Sharm el Sheikh where you can't tell which man is Bedouin and which is from Cairo,' says Rageh defiantly. 'The whole country is changing but we're holding on to our traditions and customs.' Herodotus would have understood.

———

The sun slips behind the dunes and hisses into the horizon, casting a golden veil across their shifting shapes. The soft scoops of caramel darken into fearful silhouettes. Lights flicker in the ancient town. The tumbledown ruins of Shali twitch into life. An interlude in this impossible oasis draws to a close.

Herodotus in the desert. The natural home of storytellers. The desert campfire, Lawrence wrote, was the Arabs' university, the place they learnt 'the news of their tribe, its poems, histories, love tales, lawsuits and bargainings'. One of the most piercing moments in the film *The English Patient* is set around a campfire in the Egyptian desert. It's pure Herodotus.

Kristin Scott Thomas, playing the wife of the explorer Geoffrey Clifton (Colin Firth), is telling a story beneath the stars. She takes one from the *Histories*, the dark tale of the Lydian king Candaules who, brimming with braggadocio and convinced his wife is the most beautiful woman on earth, instructs his favourite bodyguard Gyges to watch her undressing and admire her naked one night. Candaules' servant is horrified but has to go along with it. The queen spots him hiding in her bedroom but says nothing to her husband. Next morning she summons the luckless Gyges and addresses him icily. Kill Candaules and become king with me as your wife, or be killed for gazing upon what you have no right to see, she says. Gyges kills Candaules and becomes king of Lydia. There is an awkward silence as Herodotus' story ends. Firth looks uncomfortable. Ralph Fiennes, playing the Herodotus-loving Almásy, and Scott Thomas lock eyes across the fire. Looming infidelity simmers among the sparks.

After the film was released, thousands rushed out to buy the *Histories*, drawn by the inscrutable Almásy and the vicious romance of the desert. One university bookstore in the US reported sales up 450 per cent. Twenty-four centuries after his death, Herodotus had finally achieved his Hollywood moment.

# 8

## Cairo, Mother of the World

*Clio, the muse of history, is as thoroughly infected with lies as a street
whore with syphilis.*
Arthur Schopenhauer, *Parerga und Paralipomena* (1851)

ENCOUNTERS WITH A secretly gay movie star, a flirtatious Pakistani
Egyptologist with a passion for Herodotus, a Muslim Brotherhood
Islamist arguing for greater women's rights, the combative bestselling
novelist Alaa al Aswany, a soft-skinned belly dancer in a dingy night
club, the Egyptian Museum's Daddy of Mummies, a compulsively
name-dropping pioneer of interfaith dialogue, the hamster-like head
of the Anglican Church, Egypt's most famous – or infamous – single
mother, an unorthodox, pyramid-theorising mathematician, the stun-
ningly feline director who infuriates the religious establishment with
sex and immorality in her films, a perennially pessimistic political scientist, the mournful wife of Egypt's jailed, ailing opposition leader, the
formerly jailed democracy activist Saad Eddin Ibrahim, a professional
dancer who dances with a candelabra of blazing candles on her head,
madly brave demonstrators at a rally against police torture, tales of
gynaecologists making a killing refurbishing young women's broken
hymens, of free-spirited girls fellating in veils, of policemen raping
protesters by thrusting batons into their backsides, rumours of stray cats
being exported for thousands of euros as rare pharaonic breeds – Cairo,
the mother of civilisation, is the ultimate Herodotean destination and
distraction, a digression on a monumental scale. All the world is here.

But first we must begin with the pyramids which, in the absence of
Cairo (which hadn't been born yet), is exactly what Herodotus did,

dutiful tourist and seeker of marvels that he was. Of all the many continuities we can lay our hands on in this Herodotean miscellany, the fascination with the pyramids must be one of the most fascinating. Of all the many marvels in Egypt, the pyramids are generally held to be the most marvellous. No other monument on the planet is as instantly recognisable, none so identifiable with the country that produced it. The ancients included them among the Seven Wonders and to this day they are the only survivors. For many it is a lifetime's ambition simply to set eyes upon them.

Herodotus was the first to describe their construction, sparking a debate that has lasted ever since. How exactly were they built? How many workers were needed to finish this staggering project? Were slaves used? How long did it take? What sort of mathematical calculations would have been necessary? How did they attain such purity of form, such wondrous perfection, such geometrical accuracy? Herodotus would have been astonished to see how this interest in the pyramids has evolved, over time, into a limitless obsession. How, for instance, someone we might consider an arch-rationalist like Sir Isaac Newton dabbled in pyramidology (not to mention alchemy), how the nineteenth-century Scottish Astronomer Royal Charles Piazzi Smyth believed the proportions of the pyramids were inspired by the Christian God. How the zanier outpourings of pyramidology (or pyramidiocy as it is also known) offer otherworldly explanations such as that championed by the onetime Swiss hotelier Erich von Däniken who since the Sixties has been convinced – and convinced tens of millions of others in his books and films – that the pyramids of Giza were built by visiting aliens flaunting their superior technological wizardry. It was the modern age, not the ancient world, which suggested that the pyramids predicted, among other events, the First World War, the Second Coming of Christ and the rise of the Third Reich, and which posited an alignment between the pyramids and the so-called 'Face on Mars'. Pyramid fashions come and go in a technicolor parade of cranks, gurus, occultists, black magicians, mystics and mediums, necromancers and sun-worshipping New Agers. The pyramids of Giza really are mind-boggling.

Herodotus' two-page description of them is a model of understatement by comparison. He opens with a dig against the pharaoh Cheops, builder of the Great Pyramid that bears his name, who, he says, 'brought the country into all sorts of misery' by closing temples, forbidding people to practise their religion and forcing the population into slavery. Many of the slaves were made to transport blocks of stone from the quarries. He says work was carried out in three-monthly shifts, each shift comprising 100,000 men. 'It took ten years of this oppressive slave labour to build the track along which the blocks were hauled – a work, in my opinion, of hardly less magnitude than the pyramid itself.' The pyramid itself took twenty years, he goes on, describing its dimensions with remarkable accuracy.

Now picture the scene. Herodotus, clutching his traveller's papyrus jotter with sweat-sticky hands, surveys the pyramids of Giza. They dominate the desert plateau in a way unthinkable today, when Cairo laps at their feet like a greedy ocean. The Greek is in a state of great excitement, he's never seen anything like them (no one ever has). He's hanging on his guide's every word, committing the stories to memory, noting down as much as he can. The Egyptian guide to the pyramids, as a breed one of the world's greatest storytelling hustlers, spins a sensational tale for his tourist. Perhaps Herodotus has told him he's researching a book or preparing material for a series of lectures on Egypt. Whatever, the guide tells him just the sort of story he's dying to hear.

No crime was too great for Cheops: when he was short of money, he sent his daughter to a brothel with instructions to charge a certain sum – they did not say how much. This she actually did, adding to it a further transaction of her own; for with the intention of leaving something to be remembered by after her death, she asked each of her customers to give her a block of stone, and of these stones (the story goes) was built the middle pyramid of the three which stand in front of the great pyramid. It is a hundred and fifty feet square.

Entertaining nonsense. Imagine how many satisfied clients she would have had to find. To give you an idea, the Great Pyramid contains 2.3 million blocks of limestone, each one weighing 2.5 tons. That's a lot of tricks.

It's worth pointing out this story does not go down well with Egyptians. The anecdote about Cheops renting out his daughter as a hooker because he's run out of stone and the remark that Egypt is 'the gift of the Nile' account for the defensive, occasionally downright hostile, reaction to our man.

There's one last Herodotean anecdote on the Great Pyramid which is about as reliable as the first. Perhaps his tip-seeking guide was over-doing it again.

An inscription is cut upon it in Egyptian characters recording the amount spent on radishes, onions and leeks for the labourers, and I remember distinctly that the interpreter who read me the inscription said the sum was 1,600 talents of silver. If this is true, how much must have been spent in addition on tools and bread and clothing for the labourers during all those years the building was going on – not to mention the time it took (not a little, I should think) to quarry and haul the stone, and to construct the underground chamber?

You can see how his mind works. The inscription is a discovery for him. It sets off a train of thoughts, flights of fancy, exactly the sort of reaction we have 2,500 years later when we stand in the shadows of these magnificently incomprehensible shapes, set in the sands like a row of uneven teeth. The Great Pyramid, largest of them all, was built around 2467 BC. When Herodotus saw them, they were already over 2,000 years old, a similar gulf of time to that which separates our world from his. Yet his response to them is just like our own. And that seems to be one of the greatest, time-shrinking marvels of all.

――――

An article in *Al Ahram* newspaper on ancient maths and the construc-tion of the pyramids. Assem Deif, a maths professor at Cairo University, suggests that ancient Egyptians must have possessed a much greater degree of sophistication in maths than has hitherto been recognised. They couldn't have built the pyramids without it. 'The Giza pyramids offer definitive evidence of the ancient accuracy of measuring,' he writes. 'Built in the middle of the third millennium BC, shortly after the first known evidence of Egyptian writing, they predate by 600

years any early mathematical tools.' He offers some startling Great
Pyramids facts to support his argument.

1. The sides agree in length to within 0.01 per cent.
2. The 350-foot descending passage deviates from a central axis by less
   than a quarter of an inch horizontally and just one-tenth of an inch
   vertically. 'This compares with the best laser-controlled drilling of
   today.'
3. The casing stones covering the pyramid are so perfectly aligned
   that the mortar-filled joints are just one-fifteenth of an inch wide.
   The Egyptologist Flinders Petrie (1853–1942) argued that such
   phenomenal precision was beyond the capabilities of modern
   technology.
4. It is said to be the most accurately aligned structure on earth, facing
   true north with only three-sixtieths of a degree of error. Deif says
   that the misalignment in the Paris observatory is twice that.
5. A Japanese team came to Giza in the early Nineties to construct a
   pyramid using modern technology. They gave up, after concluding
   it would take 1,000 years.

I meet Professor Deif for a coffee one morning. He says his article
has caused a stir. He's been inundated with correspondence from all
over the world. 'I've had a successful career, I've written lots of books,
I've never had a reaction like this,' he says, baffled by the fuss, but
obviously enjoying it. Such is the pyramids' talismanic hold on our
collective imagination. Their obvious perfection is a shocking challenge to our inbuilt notions of superiority over the dusty ancients.

He says the Greeks got the credit for inventing mathematics as we
know it, a new science culminating in the groundbreaking treatise –
and history's most successful maths textbook – Elements, written by
Euclid of Alexandria, the father of geometry, somewhere around
300 BC. Yet where did all the expertise come from originally?
Pythagoras, Thales, Eudoxus and Archimedes, to name just a few
Greek mathematicians, all worked in Egypt, some of them for many
years. Deif reckons that Egyptian mathematics was simply absorbed
into the body of Greek mathematics during the Hellenistic period.
At this point he leaves layman's territory behind, veering off on a

distinctly mathematical tangent which, with O Level maths a blissfully distant memory, I struggle to follow. He mentions a couple of important Egyptian mathematics texts, one dating to 1890 BC, the other to 1650 BC, both containing a number of problems of varying complexity, but sufficiently difficult to lose me in a whirring vortex of isosceles trapezoids, pyramid frustum volumes and unfathomable calculations about rectangular co-ordinates on limestone ostracons. His point is that, although the textual evidence has largely disappeared, we know that Egyptians had been practising mathematics for an awfully long time before the Greeks arrived.

'Alexandria was like a Greek institute in Egypt, the library attracted the greatest minds of the time. Science was written in Greek, all that knowledge flew to Greece. Then, once the great fire at Alexandria had destroyed the library, everything was lost, 700,000 scrolls or volumes gone up in smoke . . .' – he throws up both hands – 'just like that. Hieroglyphs and hieratic script on fragile parchment and papyrus didn't survive, so that left everything in Greece. It's very clear to me,' he adds. 'The West considers Greece the cradle of civilisation. It prefers the mother of civilisation to be European, not African. But the knowledge the West regards as coming mostly from Babylon and Greece is beyond any doubt inherited from the ancient Egyptians.' Herodotus would have got up and applauded.

---

Guides still tell tall stories at the pyramids. They probably always have. They know storytelling pays. Within a few minutes of arriving in Giza, I have attracted an army of hustlers. Young men, spotting that I am not part of a large group, and am therefore undefended, charge forth. On foot, on horse, on camel. Reflexively I check my wallet. After a month in Egypt I'm beginning to feel I've become a *baksheesh* ATM. The traveller in Egypt can barely move without a tip. I'm offered camels, horses, photos, papyrus, never-before-seen tombs, lost treasures and – in whispered asides – women who will do anything – 'ANYTHING!' – for foreign tourists. When I say I'm after something a little more historical, one tells me that pharaonic workers were much stronger than modern men so they could lift the massive stones to the top during the construction of the Great Pyramid. Another says the pharaoh was buried upside down, feet pointing to the stars. One of them shares a joke.

A competition between Egyptian, British, French and American intelligence to catch rampaging wolves in a forest. First in are MI6. Twenty minutes later, they return triumphantly through the trees with a dead wolf. Next are the Americans. They come back in an hour with their trophy. The French take two hours. The Egyptians go in last, quietly confident. Nothing is heard from them for an hour. Time passes. Two hours, twelve hours. Two days. Eventually a team of rescuers goes in to find out what has happened. They find the Egyptian spies standing over a rabbit pinned to a tree. 'Confess!' the officer is screaming at the bloodied animal, beating it with a stick. 'Admit you're a wolf!'

The tallest stories these days tend to have a ring of truth about them. And it is the Egyptian guides, rather than the foreign tourists, who speak about them with a sense of wonder bordering on disbelief. How sun-worshipping American New Agers descend on Giza once a year, dressed in white, holding hands in a circle and praying before indulging in wild sex, then slipping into the Great Pyramid at midnight to make their pilgrimage through the granite darkness of the Great Gallery to the millennial stillness of the King's Chamber for a bout of soul-searching and exploration of their consciousness.

Suddenly the atmosphere turns poisonous. One moment come-my-friend-ride-camel/horse/calèche hustle, the next fear, suspicion and hostility. The sight of my notebook proves fatal. 'Don't talk to him,' one of them hisses to a younger man approaching us. 'He's recording us.'

Moments later my translator and I are engulfed in a scrum of glinting-eyed Giza Mafiosi. I am a spy, a foreign investigator compiling evidence of guides behaving badly, I'm going to report them to the police, get him out of here, I'm persona non grata at the pyramids. A tourist policeman on a threadbare camel trots over to find out what's going on. Voices are raised. Some pushing around. A scuffle. My translator is becoming frightened. The gang of men pressing around us in an intimidating circle are making nasty threats. The blood-red sky darkens. It's time to leave.

Hind al Hinnawy is a modern-day marvel. We meet in her parents' home in the Moqattam Hills, a prosperous eastern suburb overlooking the seething city below. She is a striking woman with large almond eyes and swept-back hair, fine-boned and birdlike. The low-cut, figure-hugging black top and a denim mini-skirt worn over black tights and high boots announce that she is an upper-class Egyptian woman, a sleek pharaoh's queen in shades.

In 2005, the twenty-seven-year-old costume designer scandalised Egyptian society – and much of the Arab world – by having a child out of wedlock and then going public by filing a paternity suit against Ahmed al Fishawy, a famous actor and outwardly religious scion of a movie-star family. Conventional Egyptian mores dictated a discreet abortion but Hinnawy refused to go quietly. Lina, the two-year-old, adorably tousle-haired fruit of their union, is being dandled on her knee.

Hinnawy claimed that she and Fishawy had contracted an *urfi* marriage, a secret, sex-sanctioning arrangement favoured by the young (and married men who don't want to feel guilty about screwing their mistresses). Premarital sex remains taboo in Egypt. Fishawy initially denied any relationship, but the television talk show in which he gave advice to devout Muslim youth was abruptly cancelled. 'Newspapers and television cameras were chasing us around everywhere we went and Ahmed said he didn't know me, maybe he'd met me twice – can you imagine? He said to me, "You're scandalising me, you're destroying my reputation, now I'm going to destroy yours. The Prophet Mohammed said the son of a sin cannot be given his father's name, I'm just obeying God."'

Hinnawy lost the first stage of the battle. The court ruled against her because she had no evidence of the *urfi* marriage. After she got pregnant, she says, Fishawy asked for her copy of the *urfi* contract, telling her he was going to have the papers registered officially. She never saw them again. Under pressure, Fishawy subsequently admitted they had had an affair, but not a marriage. He then refused to comply with the court order to take a DNA test. She says he also tried to discourage her from having the baby, arguing it was a sin against Islam. 'It seemed stupid to me. He was trying to be religious but he drank alcohol and was sleeping with other women while he was married to me. Then a religious scholar called me up out of the blue and said, "You're a very weak woman. The best thing for you to do is throw yourself off a ten-storey building. You have nothing to live for."'

Another religious sheikh advised the couple to sacrifice five camels each and fast for sixty days. Only then would God absolve them of their sins. The Grand Mufti Ali Gomaa (whom we met in Cambridge), head of Egypt's highest theological authority, Dar al Ifta, the House of the Fatwa, weighed into the debate, urging Fishawy to recognise the child on the grounds that the marriage had been valid and that he therefore bore a responsibility towards his child. 'My father said he'd support me with the last drop of his blood, but my mother didn't talk to me until I was six months pregnant.'

Hinnawy describes both parents as liberals. Her father is a university economist, her mother a psychology professor. Their liberalism was put under the severest test as the fight between their daughter and her onetime boyfriend was played out in the national media. Her father was told he had a loose daughter with no values. Her mother's family severed all contact, her father's side became distant and aloof. Egyptian society, says Hinnawy, prefers hypocrisy to public disgrace.

Although her motivation was questioned – some considered her a gold-digger – she says she was simply fighting for her daughter's official recognition. A woman in Egypt cannot obtain a birth certificate for her child without the father's consent. 'A man can get it without documents, just his ID. He can name the mother of the baby and just get it. A woman can't, even with a marriage certificate. The father must come or the grandfather. The certificate can't be issued without the father's name.' Fishawy refused to give the baby his name. 'After the first stage, Ahmed was very happy. There were pictures of him in all the papers. He said the ruling showed he was a good Muslim and an upright man. I was destroyed. I had no papers for Lina, nothing to show that she existed.'

In May 2006, Hinnawy appealed the court's ruling. 'The whole country was speaking about it. My lawyer told me to take Lina to court, to show her to the judge. I was so scared. I knew the ruling would either be the end or the beginning of my life. I went to court, together with Ahmed, and the judge asked us a lot of questions about our relationship, how many times we had had sex, had we discussed not having babies, and so on. Normally it would take four years to get the ruling. For us, it took one day.' The judge ruled in Hinnawy's favour. 'My whole life changed that day. I got sixteen copies of the birth certificate and gave them as presents to my supporters.'

Hinnawy then enrolled at the American University in Cairo to read a masters in women's studies. The experience has galvanised her. She says she now wants to devote her life to women's rights. 'I just feel there's hypocrisy everywhere. I have the feeling that I'm living among plastic people, people who aren't real. On the one hand you've got all these people pretending to be religious and then there's this whole scene of sex parties, people drinking and smoking, where everyone is *yallah*, come on, let's have sex.'

She shows me a recent text message from Fishawy. 'Look at this. He calls Lina "your amazing daughter". He wants to meet her to tell her she's illegitimate. He says, "It's Allah's orders, not mine. If you don't believe it we're worshipping two different gods." And there he is still pretending to be a good Muslim while he carries on drinking and having sex with other girls.'

Lady Macbeth stares down at us spookily from a Shakespeare poster on the nursery wall. 'The problem these days is that we're always talking about religion. Egyptians are getting more religious on the outside, but it's all fake. These days, it's really rare to find a girl who hasn't had sex before marriage. It's a secret, though, of course. They'll deny it. It's *haram*, against our tradition. I'm just one of the few who admits it. The horrifying thing is that lots of girls believe it's their fault if they get pregnant. Some girls commit suicide, some kill their babies. Can you believe it, there are hymen repair operations for 500 Egyptian pounds? I've got friends who are gynaecologists making a fortune from this. It's a whole industry. Everyone's talking about the veil and Islamic values. It's a lot of rubbish. There are girls in veils giving blowjobs in parked cars in Moqattam.'

What would Herodotus have made of it? Outwardly pious Egyptian girls giving head in car parks. You can bet he would have written about it for a start. But perhaps, putting oral sex to one side, he wouldn't have been surprised to discover that religion remains centre-stage in Egyptian life, governing many aspects of society, culture, politics and even the economy. 'They are religious to excess, beyond any other nation in the world,' he wrote of the Egyptians, people we now consider ancient but who were, of course, entirely contemporary to him. Are they excessively religious today? Is there something about Egyptians that makes them inherently receptive towards religion, in the same way that Orwell pronounced that English civilisation was bound up with 'solid breakfasts and gloomy Sundays, smoky towns and winding roads, green fields and red pillarboxes'?

Outward displays of religiosity certainly are on the rise. A growing majority of Egyptian women wear the *hijab* veil. More and more are taking to its all-enveloping black cousin the *niqab*, which covers the entire face bar a slit for the eyes, historically not a garment worn by Egyptian women. Increasing numbers of men sport ostentatious *zabiba* 'raisins' on their foreheads, bumpy calluses that advertise to the world how zealously they perform their five daily prayers. The long-banned Muslim Brotherhood, an avowedly religious political party, is growing in popularity. The desert road from Mersa Matruh to Siwa is lined with Islamic exhortations to drivers: Praise God, God is great, and so on.

Yet this random collection of developments may be less an Egyptian than a broader Islamist trait. It may reflect political as much as religious conditions, an act of defiance against Western values, say. The *hijab* might be worn for any number of reasons. A woman might wear it simply in submission to the Koran's call for women to 'draw their veils over their bosoms'. It might be worn, as one Egyptian woman told me she used it, to ward off groping men on the bus to work, out of obedience to a husband who insists upon it, by poor women who can't afford expensive hairdos, or even, as Hinnawy says, to enable a woman to perform oral sex on a willing boyfriend without losing the virtually sacrosanct image of conventional piety.

As Herodotus understood, sometimes it is wise not to delve too deep in matters of faith. 'I am not anxious to repeat what I was told about the Egyptian religion for I do not think that any one nation knows much more about such things than any other,' he wrote.

The *hijab* and the *niqab* come up a few days later during a conversation with Abd al Monem Abu al Futuh, a senior official in the Muslim Brotherhood and general secretary of the Arab Medical Union. Smartly suited with a white shirt, striped tie, neatly clipped white beard and rimless spectacles, he looks more World Bank technocrat than the dangerous Islamic fundamentalist the government considers him.

'You must distinguish in the West between what is required in Islam and what is invited, like the *hijab*,' he says. 'There is nothing in Islam or sharia law to impose the *hijab*. If you force a woman to be decent in her dress, she'll do it because you're oppressing her, or to please you, not because she's sincere before God. It's just promoting hypocrisy. If a woman comes into a room without a *hijab* and a man looks sternly at her, that's a form of terrorism.' He says his wife and three daughters all wear the *hijab* of their own choice. 'If they don't want to wear it, no problem. I never imposed it in the first place. My relationship with my wife is based on honesty, free discussions and arguments . . .' He creases into a smile. 'And occasional mutiny!'

As for the *niqab*, he dismisses it curtly. It has no relation with Islam. I try to draw him out on a historical analogy between the Egyptian president and ancient pharaohs. He has suffered personally under the present regime, serving five years in prison during a clampdown on Islamists in the late Nineties in what he says were 'inhumane conditions'. He is openly scathing of government oppression, corruption and its manipulation of religion (through the Grand Mufti's Al Azhar, among other organisations), but he won't have any of my Herodotean gambit. 'Trying to link the pharaohs and today's heads of state is incorrect because different contexts, circumstances and beliefs apply.' He's being a bit too literal, I think.

———

I wonder what Dr al Futuh would make of Inas al Deghedy, Egypt's most controversial film director and the leading woman of Arab cinema. Films such as *Diaries of a Teenage Girl*, *Cheap Flesh* and *Search for Freedom*, dealing with rape, sexual problems, hymen-repair surgery and relationships between the sexes, have transfixed Egyptian audiences and horrified the soberly robed clerics who regard her as society's arch-corrupter. They have also won her cinematic laurels all over the world.

Deghedy is magnificently attractive, beautifully coiffed, expensively dressed and languidly self-confident. There is a formidable feminine challenge to the patriarchal Egyptian society in her very style and bearing. When we meet late one evening in her sleek modern offices, I imagine trim-bearded Islamists gulping in her wake, overwhelmed by her sexuality, emasculated by her charisma. She is a full-figured, fire-breathing lioness with long dark eyelashes, a mane of flaming hair, gold-glitter make-up, deep brown eyes, plump red lips and long pink fingernails. A large opal ring, diamond clusters and gold earrings glint in the spotlights.

'Some men are afraid to come near me,' she purrs. I try not to gulp. 'I don't try to hide my femininity, I'm proud of it, I show it. I'm strong and I have a good mind.' She swivels in her chair, tilts her head to one side and strokes an earring. 'The media gives a very bad image to emancipated women in the Arab world. Some men fight me because they think I'm a loose woman, they know I influence the younger generation. Lots of girls aspire to be like me, to be feminine, have a career. They tell me they don't want to be oppressed by anyone. Be your own person, I tell them.'

She says her films explore taboos that have been constructed in a culture dominated by men. 'Society teaches us that sex is *haram*, that women aren't meant to enjoy sex, whereas it's the opposite for men, they can do what they like. Mothers often tell their daughters that sex is no good to strike fear into the girls' hearts, but the girls are still curious, of course, they discover sex, make mistakes like getting pregnant or contracting an *urfi* marriage. The next thing you know they're having an operation to repair the hymen so they can still be virgins when they get married properly.'

I ask her how she gets on with the censors. As far as Egyptian society is concerned, much of her work is too hot to handle. 'The strange thing now is that the public is stricter than the censors. You have the fundamentalists, the Islamists, women in veils, who go to the cinema, summon the manager and warn him that unless he cuts the risky scenes out of the films, they won't bring their families to the cinema any more. After

*Diary of a Teenage Girl* came out, even though the censors had approved it, objections were raised in the people's assembly and I was asked to remove certain scenes. It was the first movie to be put on trial.'

What about Herodotus' remark about Egyptians being excessively religious? She jumps in her seat. 'It's true! These days Egyptians are more religious than the Saudis, where Islam originated. I agree 100 per cent, there's too much religion here. Some people just use the Koran to shut down debate. We're supposed to take the spirit of the Koran. Some verses were inspired by certain circumstances, like those that talk about infidels. As long as you don't touch the essence of the religion, the five pillars of Islam, then you have the freedom of *ijtihad*, interpretation.* I think Herodotus is absolutely right. We've got much too much religion in Egypt.'

———

A final farewell to Herodotus on the banks of the Nile. Salima Ikram, the high-spirited professor of Egyptology at the American University in Cairo (the sort of place our man would have found so useful), is one of Herodotus' greatest fans. Ikram is a leading authority on animal mummies and Egyptian funerary archaeology. She bobs with animation at the merest mention of Herodotus, eyes aglow, pearl necklace bouncing up and down from her black V-neck jumper, gold bracelets jingling on her wrists as her arms fly this way and that to emphasise a point. Behind her, silently sombre by comparison, are two framed prints of animals from the Middle Kingdom tombs of Beni Hassan, outlines of copulating gazelles, sharp-nosed jackals, long-necked quasi-dinosaurs, a sulking leopard, a rhinoceros lookalike and a jaunty hound.

'I love Herodotus, I adore him! The poor man's been much maligned but so often proved right. At the pyramids, for example, he wrote about the underground tombs and he was spot on. He might be the Father of Lies, but which historian isn't? If the soi-disant historians think they're any better, they're full of bullshit.' This is no fusty

* The five pillars of Islam are: *shahadah*, the profession of faith; *salah*, the requirement to pray five times daily; *zakah*, alms-giving to the poor; the *haj* or pilgrimage to Mecca; *sawm*, the annual month-long fast of Ramadan.

academic. She's getting in to her stride now, throwing herself back in her chair and swinging her legs on to her desk. A Herodotean coquette. 'He's a travel writer, really. You can imagine him at the pyramids, the whole place reeking of piss, no camels but lots more donkeys, loads of palanquins carrying VIPs around, lots of graffiti from the pharaonic and Hellenistic period, guides spinning these far-fetched stories and dear old Herodotus taking it all in, agog with excitement. I think he's quite wonderful, charming, he's an absolute riot, a great storyteller, the best way to get people to read history. All Egyptologists in Pakistan read him, but you know what Egyptians are like, they're fed all that nationalist stuff about foreigners so he's not so popular here, the "Egypt is the gift of the Nile" thing, but you know what, it is! The flood plain's here, not in Nubia. It was simple geology and he got it right. The Egyptians are ridiculous because, until the Rosetta Stone, Herodotus was the Bible of Egyptology.* Of course you can't take him hook, line and sinker, but the more confident you are with him, the more you get out of him.'

Though he's more in vogue now, with our interest in foreign cultures and the rise of social history, Herodotus has long suffered by comparison with Thucydides. Ikram's eyes roll towards the ceiling. 'Oh please! Okay, so Thucydides is a finer historian, but he's so dull, so tedious, oh my God, I'm going to shoot myself! And Plutarch calling him the Father of Lies, he must have been very jealous – I've been allowed into more temples than you. Can you imagine? It was like a pissing contest! The thing I love about Herodotus is that you can take him to the beach and he's a rollicking good read. He's much more human. He's like a cheerful pal going off on this great trip and telling you about it with all these wonderful stories, getting confused along the way.'

We compare notes on mummification and Luxor. The mention of mummies lights another touchpaper. A pair of dark crescent eyebrows leaps up in enthusiasm. The pearls jump up in tandem. 'I've got some

* The translation of the Rosetta Stone by the pillaging French Orientalist Jean-François Champollion in the 1820s proved the decisive breakthrough in deciphering Egyptian hieroglyphs. The stone was inscribed with the same text, a decree from the second-century king Ptolemy V, in three languages, hieroglyphic and demotic Egyptian script and classical Greek.

mummified rabbits downstairs if you want a look. I didn't want to kill cats so I thought I'd use Flopsy, Mopsy and Tufty and follow Herodotus' recipe. I was particularly keen on doing the enema. People thought it was rubbish, they said it wouldn't work. The poor rabbit had a pipette stuck up its arse, then some turpentine – Herodotus would have had juniper oil – and then it was plugged with linen. You know what? It works. Herodotus was right. Again. The most important thing to remember is not to stand behind it when you pull the plug out and all the insides squirt out. Whoooosh! Very messy! I'll never forget it. I almost lost two students.'

The sky twists into a carpet of ruffled crimson above the Nile. Herodotus prepares to leave Egypt for the last time. He's going back to Greece. We don't know how long he has been travelling across the country but his exhausting journey has been a triumph of discovery. He might even have a bestseller on his hands.

The ship's captain greets the returning Greeks in the party with a knowing smile. Well, how was it? Come on, what was it like? Didn't I tell you the Egyptians were a load of thieving, hustling, sun-worshipping, stinking barbarians? Not at all, thinks Herodotus, shaking his head quietly in the stern. They're the most extraordinary people on earth.

# PART IV

## Greece

*There is the Greek nation – the community of blood and language, temples and ritual, and our common customs.*

*The Greeks have never been simpletons; for centuries past they have been distinguished from other nations by superior wits.*

Herodotus, *Histories*, 8.144; 1.60

# 9

# Athens, City Hall of Wisdom

*History is philosophy from examples.*
Dionysius of Halicarnassus, *Ars Rhetorica*, first century BC

I AM ITCHING TO get at the priests, in the spirit of Herodotus, but my first port of call in Athens is a potentially enlightening, possibly deadly, three-day conference. 'Ancient Greece and Ancient Iran: Cross-Cultural Encounters'. It has Herodotus all over it. And in it. A modern-day version of a fifth-century BC symposium and a good way, perhaps, to acclimatise to Greece. 'You might even get a few lines out of it for your book,' says Chris, an academic friend of a friend of a friend who is helping organise the conference. He sounds doubtful.

I decide to dip in and out. Lectures on 'Pseudo-Aristotelian Politics and Theology: From Rome to Qom' and 'The Adaptation of the Achaemenid Griffin in a Macedonian Tomb-painting and a Sikyonian Mosaic' can be missed. 'The Death of Masistius and the Mourning for his Loss (Herodotus 9:20–25)' sounds a little specialist but at this early stage in Greece anything with the word Herodotus in the title is on, even 'The Settlement of Artaphernes–Mardonius in Herodotus as an example of imperial nostalgia'.

The conference opens on a mild November evening. The antiquated auditorium, a hangover from the Seventies, is packed to the rafters with beards, turbans, professorial tweeds and priestly cassocks. Jostling television crews are on hand to record the moment. Speakers come and go in a blizzard of acronyms. The National Hellenic Research Foundation (NHRF), whose boxy headquarters are playing host to these largely Greek and Iranian scholars; the Iranian Cultural

Heritage and Tourism Organisation (ICHTO); the Institute of Greek and Roman Antiquity (KERA); Musée Achéménide Virtuel et Interactif (MAVI); UNESCO. It is not so much an ivory tower as an academic Tower of Babel.

The talk is of exchange and solidarity, dialogue and civilisation. As if to embody this cultural cross-fertilisation, a bearded Greek Orthodox priest sits alongside a bearded Iranian mullah in the front row, both men clicking away at their worry beads. Dr Seyed Taha Hashemi Toghrajerdi of ICHTO speaks ponderously of economic, military and religious exchange, of how Alexander's victory over Darius III was not a lasting spiritual defeat for the Iranians. 'I told you a lot of it would be bloody boring,' says Chris. Several conference-savvy academics make a beeline for the exit as waves of mellifluous Farsi roll over the audience. Toghrajerdi winds up his address: 'May the two great powers that helped define history and civilisation play a role in shaping the future of the entire world.' A polite ripple of applause.

Mohammed Reza Darbandi, cultural counsellor from the Iranian Embassy in Athens, sounds a more political note. Greece is really an Eastern country, he says, and shares much in common with Iran. Both countries are deeply religious, warm and hospitable, both are block-aded by the West. He discusses Montesquieu's observations on Alexander the Great adopting Persian customs: 'He resisted those who wanted him to treat the Greeks as masters and the Persians as slaves; he thought only of uniting two nations and wiping out the distinc-tions between the conquerors and the vanquished.'

A diminutive Professor Vassos Karageorghis, a chirpy, silver-haired Greek Cypriot whom I like as soon as I listen to him, criticises the introversion of Greek academe. No universities in Greece or Cyprus have ever created chairs for the study of the civilisations of Egypt, Assyria, Phoenicia, the Near East, the Americas or the Far East, he notes. And then my ears really prick up.

'In this respect we have to follow the noble tradition of one of our great historians, Herodotus, who was convinced that in order to understand the reasons which caused the Greco-Persian wars he had to study profoundly the achievements of both. Modern scholarship has given Herodotus his rightful place in modern historiography as a broadminded researcher who had the intellectual curiosity to get to know the peoples he was writing about.'

Profoundly ahead of his time, in other words. How disappointed he would surely have been to see scholars from Greece – the nation he was the first to define, 'the community of blood and language, temples and ritual, and our common customs' – turning their back on the study of other cultures 2,500 years after his breathtakingly 'broadminded' researches. I make a note to grab a few minutes with Karageorghis later.

There is a final Herodotean flourish from Dr Miltiades Hatzopoulos, an amusing and self-deprecating man who says that writing his welcoming address triggered memories more than fifty years old of what Persia meant to a Greek schoolboy. Some words and expressions from Herodotus and later authors had passed into everyday speech but now mean something completely different. 'For example, the word *satrap*, a Persian governor, which figured as a compliment to a lady in a popular song called *rembetico*, which nice boys were not supposed to know, had somehow acquired for me the connotation of a generously endowed lady who could completely subjugate her lover.'

He concludes with the first technical Herodotus gag I have ever heard.

'The single historical event that most impressed Greek schoolboys half a century ago was the glorious defeat of the Spartans at Thermopylae. No wonder, for Greeks no less than Iranians are prone to celebrate defeat. Unfortunately, Herodotus had retained the Laconian dialect of Leonidas' speech in the famous answer of the Spartan king to the envoy of Xerxes who had demanded the immediate surrender of the Spartan army's weapons: *Molon labe*, come and take them. A Greek schoolboy could readily understand *labe*, take, but the aorist participle of the uncouth verb βλωσκω sounded utterly foreign to him. So the boy in my brother's class who was asked to narrate these memorable events confidently related how Leonidas, in order to reply to Xerxes' demand, mustered the little Persian he knew and pronounced *molon labe*.' The lad didn't realise it was Greek. Titters among the audience. A suitably scholarly joke. 'Unbeknown to him, the anonymous schoolboy, though he had never heard anything about the

Indo-European family of languages, was advancing the hypothesis of a close linguistic affinity between Greeks and Persians that made communication possible. It is because we believe that communication between peoples, Greeks and Iranians, Easterners and Westerners, is both possible and profitable that we have come together today in order to explore the cross-cultural encounters between ancient Greece and ancient Iran.' Prolonged applause. Herodotus would have approved.

The odd thing about Hatzopoulos' story is that the great *molon labe* moment is nowhere to be found in Herodotus. It comes from the rather more obscure work, *Laconic Apophthegms*, traditionally attributed to Plutarch. Ask most Greeks where the famous one-liner comes from, however, and everyone will answer Herodotus, because that is what they were taught at school. Herodotus has made the Thermopylae story his own.

The chuckles subside. This is not a crowd, I suspect, that would have thought much of the Hollywood film *300*. Certainly not the Iranians. Tehran reacted furiously to the Hollywood epic, which depicts many of the Persians facing Leonidas at Thermopylae as grotesque monsters and Xerxes as an effete, heavily made-up pervert with numerous body piercings. Chris interrupts these thoughts. 'Quicker we get out of here, the quicker we can get a cross-cultural glass of wine,' he says. 'I can't listen to any more of this stuff.'

There is no wine. The organisers of the conference have decided that having alcohol would be insensitive in front of their Iranian guests. Cross-cultural encounters only go so far.

---

You can tell if someone is a Herodotean. There is a sparkle in the eyes and a flash of fun. Perhaps even a dash of mischief (you don't get that with Thucydides). Professor Vassos Karageorghis is one. He is a tubby, genial man, nattily dressed in a dark-grey suit with a red-and-blue striped tie. Unlike most of his more po-faced colleagues here, he exudes bonhomie and is constantly smiling. I could be wrong, but I have him down as an irrepressible Herodotean.

A snatched conversation over coffee with him:

'One could understand the absence of chairs for the study of foreign civilisations if there was no scope for it, but we're part of the EU now. Greek students and the public should be exposed to foreign civilisations. How can you understand the Mycenaeans, for example, unless you know something about Egypt, the Levant and Anatolia?'

He says the move by Western scholars in the nineteenth century to dissociate modern Greeks from their classical ancestors put Greeks on the defensive, where they have remained ever since. Political geography narrowed historical horizons even further. 'After independence the Greeks were confined to a small territory in the Balkans, whereas in the classical world they spread from Marseilles to Anatolia. This caused a lot of introversion, what we call *endostrefia*. Herodotus was the first to look beyond the Aegean. Sometimes he relied on hearsay, but he was always trying to find out more. Remember his opening sentence – he was trying to understand both sides, Greek and Persian. He was the first to have an interest in foreign civilisations. He was trying to understand the whole world. Of course, he would feel let down to see such a lack of interest in other cultures in Greece today.'

He summarily rubbishes those who deplore Herodotus for his unreliability. 'Who can claim complete accuracy? We all make mistakes and have lacunae in our work. I have a huge respect for Herodotus. He was so ahead of his time in trying to go as profoundly as he could into other civilisations to make comparisons between them.' So he is a bona-fide Herodotean, then? His face creases into a broad grin. 'I took Homer and Herodotus as a special subject at University College London from 1948 to 1952. As soon as I read Herodotus, I was converted.'

The Masistius story, which features on the first day of the conference, is classic Herodotus. It takes us back to the summer of 479 BC. Greek and Persian forces are manoeuvring for position and skirmishing in the run-up to the battle of Plataea. The Greeks are on the parched lower slopes of Mount Cithaeron. Beneath them, camped on the banks of the River Asopus, are the Persians under their general Mardonius.

Among the Persians there is a sense of foreboding. Although they are as numerous as the sands of the desert, they are about to face the largest hoplite army ever put into the field, around 40,000 committed

Greeks. A Theban collaborator hosts a large banquet for the most distinguished Persians and Thebans. One of the Persian guests, probably in his cups, starts weeping, turns to his Greek neighbour, a man called Thersander, and referring to the Persian guests around them and the soldiers by the river tells him that 'in a short time from now you will see but a few of all these men left alive'. Thersander is shocked. Shouldn't he be saying this to Mardonius, the Greek asks him?

'My friend,' the Persian replies, 'what God has ordained no man can by any means prevent. Many of us know that what I have said is true yet, because we are constrained by necessity, we continue to take orders from our commander. No one would believe us, however true our warning. This is the worst pain a man can have: to know much and have no power to act.'

It is a remarkable passage summing up some of Herodotus' essential beliefs: divine fate, the consequences of failure to listen to prophetic warnings and the contrast between freedom and subjection. Herodotus then names the man who told him this story – Thersander – one of only three times he does so in the entire *Histories*. It is Herodotus the travel writer–reporter again, out and about interviewing the veterans of 'the great and marvellous deeds' he is chronicling.

Mardonius sends his cavalry commander Masistius to dislodge the Greeks from the high ground. The Persians are having by far the better of it, Herodotus says, until the Greeks are reinforced by a detachment of 300 Athenians and a body of archers. Masistius, astride 'a Nisaean horse with a bridle of gold and other splendid trappings', rides out bravely at the head of his men. His horse is shot in the side, rears and throws him to the ground. The Athenians fall on him and, after a fierce struggle, kill him. 'The reason why they could not kill him at once was the armour he wore,' Herodotus explains, zooming in on the detail, 'a corslet of golden scales under his scarlet tunic. No blow upon the corslet had any effect, until at last a soldier saw how it was and struck him in the eye.'

As soon as the Persians see the Greeks have their commander's body, they are beside themselves. They charge and, being a larger force, overrun the Athenians and seize back the body. The Greeks reinforce again, and, with overwhelming numbers, retake Masistius' bloodied corpse for the last time. The dejected Persians slink back to Mardonius and report the loss of their commander: 'they shaved their heads, cut the manes of their horses and mules, and abandoned themselves to such cries of grief that the whole of Boeotia was loud with the noise of them'.

The Greeks gloat. 'They put Masistius' body on a cart and paraded it along the lines. It was certainly worth looking at, for Masistius was a tall and splendidly handsome man – this was why they did it – and men broke their ranks to get a sight of Masistius.'

This is the only significant account of the death and mourning of a Persian in the Persian Wars and once again Herodotus comes up trumps. He presents Masistius as a true hero, a noble man of great virtue and bravery, who led from the front at enormous risk to his own life. There are no pejorative words, no cultural condescension. Masistius is of such stature, both moral and physical, that he is of interest to the entire Greek army. Herodotus chooses to emphasise the stellar qualities of a Persian warrior whose death triggers unprecedented mourning from Mardonius down to the common soldier. It is one of the many remarkable cross-cultural encounters in the *Histories*.

***

The lion of the conference is not Masistius, however. Nor is it Herodotus, though I like to think his spirit hovers benevolently over us for the three days. It is Professor Pierre Briant, whose splendidly pompous title – chair, History and Civilisation of the Achaemenid World and the Empire of Alexander, Collège de France – reflects one of the larger egos among this confusion of scholars. He is a physically imposing and handsome man, with a windswept thatch of salt-and-pepper hair and an aura of greatness. His less celebrated peers take a dim view of him.

'Wanker,' says one.

'Dietetically barbarous,' says another. 'Doesn't eat cheese or fish.'

'Bet he would have liked a glass of wine, though.'

'I'll never understand how he wrote 600 pages about Darius III without knowing the slightest thing about him.'

Briant has the unique honour of addressing the conference twice. First he delivers the opening lecture, a gallop through the history of

Western judgements of the Persians, almost uniquely unflattering, he says, summarised as a long slide into decadence from the time of Cyrus onwards. Montesquieu set the tone with his 'Oriental despotism', a tradition picked up by William Loftus, John Gillies and the German historians Niebuhr and Heeren. John Stuart Mill is spared criticism for his famous observation that the battle of Marathon was a more important event for English history than the battle of Hastings.

It is his second lecture, however, that really hits the Herodotus alert button. It is an introduction to the virtual museum he has created, the online Musée Achéménide which opens up the world's finest Achaemenid collections to scholars and the general public alike. Herodotus was a modern man, an insatiably curious pioneer committed to using the latest technology available to research his history. In his time it was priests and papyrus scrolls. In the dawn of the twenty-first century it is projects like Briant's virtual museum.

He plays film clips from its website about Cyrus' conquests, a potted history of his empire, pictures of his royal tomb at sun-bleached Pasargadae, reliefs and stately monuments, fortresses and palaces, sacrificial sites roamed over by shepherds and their flocks. Researchers can access the digitised Achaemenid collections from fifteen of the world's leading museums, including the British Museum, the Bibliothèque Nationale, the Louvre and the Cairo Museum.

> Wherever you are in the world, if you have a high-speed internet connection, you can enter the virtual museum and start creating your own archive for whatever it is you are researching. You can look at coins, reliefs, statues, travellers' drawings, jewellery, weaponry, everyday items. We're bringing together historical artefacts that have been separated and scattered across the world and we're putting them in one place for everyone who's interested in seeing them and studying them.

He selects a relief panel with barely discernible decoration and then zooms in steadily, until first the outline of a figure emerges and then, as he continues clicking, the minutely detailed features of an enthroned king, complete with hair, pointed beard and crenellated crown. He does the same again, this time with a coin from the British Museum's Great King collection, revealing the head of Athena in a crested helmet decorated with olive leaves, on the obverse side a Persian satrap with extravagant head-dress. The magnification is thrilling and draws appreciative murmurs from the assembled scholars, who for a moment have managed to suppress their jealousy of the great Frenchman.

It is an impressive creation, a powerful tool for historians that would have thrilled Herodotus, just as he would have been entranced in Bodrum by the Institute of Nautical Archaeology's underwater researches in the Aegean. Our fascination with our past, our boundless amour-propre, is the engine that drives this questing narrative forward, harnessing the power of new technology to probe deeper into the story of humankind's time on planet earth. The desire to know more about our ancestors is one of the most profoundly human instincts.

Briant exits the stage to rousing applause. Acolytes, especially the prettiest young women in the auditorium, close in around him, determined to share a private Achaemenid moment with this distinguished scholar. I run the gauntlet of sharp female elbows and penetrate this inner sanctum as he is sweeping out of the conference room. 'What do you think Herodotus would have made of your virtual museum?' I ask, feeling faintly ridiculous.

He looks me up and down – whether out of disbelief at the stupidity of the question or my cheek in accosting him like this it isn't clear. A couple of seconds pass. Then, just as I am preparing to receive a few *bons mots* for my notebook, he gives a magnificently disdainful Gallic shrug, turns on his heels and strides out without a word, leaving me staring at the back of a grey tweed jacket.

———

The thing about Herodotus is that he doesn't really belong in academic circles. He's much too fun for that. And, in most cases, for them. The man who crafted the elegantly breezy prose of the *Histories* would have choked on his olive reading today's Herodotean studies. Try this for instance:

> If one broadens the notion of authorial presence to include not only the overt first-person pronouns and verbs but also all of the places where the authorial 'I' is effectively present as a tacit register of authoritative control over what is being recounted, as narratology has taught us now to do, the picture one forms of Herodotus' authorial

interventions is more complex than this initial binary separation into narrator and focalised logoi suggests.

Herodotus wouldn't have put up with that. To quote a line from Richard Evans's rambunctious volume *In Defence of History*, one of the books I have been humping around this ancient archipelago:

> Most history books are hopelessly unreadable. Professional historians publish works that no sane person would attempt to read from beginning to end; works that are designed explicitly for reference rather than for reading. They usually lack the kind of literary ability that would make their work rival that of minor poets or novelists. If they had it, no doubt most of them would be writing poetry or fiction.

★

High in the howling wind, the Parthenon sits complacently atop the Acropolis, presiding over a sea of white rooftops. I have broken free from the conference to wander across town. It is endlessly agreeable to drift along the streets of Plaka, tourist trap and neighbourhood of the gods, counting the different views of the suddenly close Parthenon that rears up from changing perspectives in the shifting light. The trick is to incline your head a few degrees towards the skyline, ignoring the shop windows teeming with busts of Pericles and Plato, Hercules and Hera, Neptune, Athena and all their capricious chums (but no Herodotus!), tourist phalli, vases depicting fine-boned, buggering Greeks, and all the other touristic delights and simply admire the architectural snapshots of the nineteenth century that are regularly interrupted by glimpses of something infinitely older. And after an hour or two in Plaka, I am drawn ineluctably to one of the most instantly recognisable monuments in the world, a place that would have been familiar to Herodotus, who writes about it in the *Histories*.

Today the highpoint of classicism looks down on a brutalist sprawl. There are other acropoleis in Greece – in Argos, Thebes and Corinth – but this is *the* Acropolis. There are many other temples in Greece, too, but there is only one Parthenon. It is the most famous temple in the world, admired as much for its architectural grace as for its representative power. These sun-bronzed columns are symbols of the cradle of democracy. As a sign announces, 'The great temple of Athena Parthenos 447–432 BC. Highest achievement of ancient Greek classical art and the most significant and representative moment of Athenian democracy at the height of its glory.'

This is exactly what a latter-day Athena – tall, fiercely beautiful, flaming locks – is telling her American charges on a chilly afternoon. The west side of the Parthenon is suspended before us in a sagging sky. 'Was it really democracy?' a woman in a Stars and Stripes sunhat asks sceptically.

'Historians date the birth of democracy in Athens to this time—'

'What about women's rights?'

'Well, these were only the beginnings and—'

'And immigrants?'

'Of course, there were some groups that—'

'And all the slaves?'

'It's true that not everyone participated, but—'

'Okay, so really it was a bunch of rich white guys running every-thing.'

'Just like the US, then,' a middle-aged man in a baseball hat chuckles. His wife elbows him in the ribs.

Athena looks deflated.

If Athens was the world's first democracy, Herodotus was its first literary witness (putting to one side, a little unfairly, the playwrights Aeschylus and Sophocles). He was the man who recorded this history-making moment for posterity. We can date this revolutionary political flirtation with the common man – not, as our aggrieved American tourist correctly notes, woman – to Cleisthenes, the Alcmaeonid aristocrat and leading figure of Athens who, in 508 or 507 BC, broadened the franchise as part of a series of political reforms. It was he, says Herodotus, 'who bribed the priestess at Delphi'. It is worth noting in this brief discussion of fledgling Athenian democracy that Cleisthenes emerges as much a populist, gerrymandering opportunist as democratic hero. In other words, from its earliest days, from Herodotus' survey of its embryonic beginnings, democracy was no miracle cure. It was flawed from the start.

First some background. Athens has just been freed from four decades of tyranny, first under Pisistratus (the anal-sex man we met earlier), who seized power in 546 BC, then under his son Hippias who ruled from 527 until 511 or 510. Hope, suddenly, is in the air. 'Athens had been great before,' says Herodotus; 'now, her liberty won, she grew greater still.' He describes the birth of democracy without fanfare. It's boiled down to six words and comes in the context of a power struggle between Cleisthenes and Isagoras, 'son of Tisander, a man of reputable family'. Blink and you'll miss it.

'These two were rivals for power, and Cleisthenes, who was getting the worst of it, *took the people into his party.*' My 1936 edition says he 'called to his aid the common people'. To this day no one really knows precisely what this expression means or how it was put into practice, but it is clear that Cleisthenes gave the people some sort of voice in government in return for their support.

Either way, there it is. Almost over before it's begun. The messy birth of Athenian democracy and Herodotus as literary midwife again. It is strangely satisfying in this era of democratic disenchantment to see Herodotus' healthy scepticism about political motives 2,500 years ago. Cleisthenes didn't embrace the smelly hoi-polloi out of the goodness of his heart, didn't take 'the people into his party' or call them 'to his aid' from any desire to spread freedom, he did it because he was 'getting the worst of it' in a naked fight for power. Remember, this is a priest-bribing politician on the make. In any case, the people – *demos* – had made their political debut.

When it comes to evaluating this new system of government in Athens, Herodotus seems to be interested not so much in arguments about freedom, ethics and the common good as in a more hard-headed assessment of what works. And it turns out that the removal of the tyrant dynasty in Athens and the introduction of more popular government coincides with a renewed supremacy on the battlefield.

The Spartan king Cleomenes, who has been plotting to install Isagoras as tyrant in Athens, has attacked the city and occupied the Acropolis. After being blockaded there for two days, says Herodotus, a truce is agreed and the Spartans withdraw. But all know now that Sparta and Athens are at war. Cleomenes soon returns to the fray and Athens faces a formidable alliance of Spartans, Boeotians, Corinthians and Chalcidians. The situation looks grim, but differences begin to emerge among the invaders. First, the Corinthians decide to leave, unsettled by Spartan plans to restore the Athenian tyranny, then Demaratus, one of the two Spartan kings, decides to follow suit, leaving Cleomenes in sole command. Athens watches this 'inglorious dispersal of the invading army' in relief and is hell-bent on revenge. First the Athenians march against the Boeotians and trounce them. Then they engage the Chalcidians in Euboea (Evia) and rout them, too. Hundreds of prisoners are kept in chains and later ransomed for 200 drachmas apiece.

Herodotus the journalist then adds a wonderfully vivid piece of reportage:

> The fetters they were bound with, the Athenians hung up in the Acropolis; they were still there in my time, hanging on the walls which the Persian fire had scorched, opposite the shrine which faces westward. With a tenth of the ransom money they had a chariot-and-four made in bronze and consecrated it as an offering to Athene. It is the first thing you see on the left as you pass through the Propylaea on the Acropolis.

The 'Persian fire', of course, is a lasting reminder of the Persian Wars, when Xerxes stripped the Acropolis bare in 480 and burnt much of Athens to the ground.

Herodotus is in no doubt why Athenian fortunes have been reversed so quickly. His analysis would bring a smile to any free-market Thatcherite. No Marxist he.

> Thus Athens went from strength to strength, and proved, if proof were needed, how noble a thing freedom is, not in one respect only, but in all; for while they were oppressed under tyrants, they had no better success in war than any of their neighbours, yet, once the yoke was flung off, they proved the finest fighters in the world. This clearly shows that, so long as they were held down by authority, they deliberately shirked their duty in the field, as slaves shirk working for their masters; but when freedom was won, then every man amongst them was interested in his own cause.

Self-interest is a powerful thing.

But Herodotus is no mug about democracy. He's acutely conscious of its shortcomings. Only a few pages after his apparent endorsement, he has Aristagoras, the tyrant ruler of Miletus, deceiving the Athenians in a master-class of demagoguery. Having been sent packing by the Spartan king Cleomenes, he's trying to rally Athens to join the Ionian revolt against Darius (499–494 BC, prelude to the Persian Wars) and uses every argument he can muster. Herodotus' observation that Aristagoras 'promised everything that came into his head' has a sadly familiar ring to those of us used to listening to politicians tell us what they'll do for us come election time. Swayed by his smooth words, the Athenians agree to send twenty ships to Ionia. 'These ships were the beginning of evils for Greeks and barbarians,' Herodotus writes with a Homeric flourish, a warning of terrible things to come. In three words, the Persian Wars.

Yet if democratic–demagogic Athens was partly to blame for this cataclysmic conflict, it was also responsible for ultimate victory, says Herodotus (despite an initial, thoroughly inglorious attempt to seek an alliance with Persia):

> one is surely right in saying that Greece was saved by the Athenians ... It was the Athenians ... who having chosen that Greece should live and preserve her freedom, roused to battle the other Greek states which had not yet submitted. It was the Athenians who – after the gods – drove back the Persian king ... they stood firm and had the courage to meet the invader.

So by the time the foreign invaders had been overwhelmed in the concluding battles of Plataea and Mycale in 479, free Greeks had prevailed over Persian tyranny. As Leonidas tells Xerxes in the film *300*, 'The world will know that free men stood against a tyrant, that few stood against many . . .' But, to borrow a phrase from Wellington, it was a damn near-run thing. Athens might have been the birthplace of democracy, but that was no guarantee of success. A ragtag band of noisy, feuding island-states and statelets had come perilously close to destruction. Greek culture, the foundation of Western civilisation, had stood on the brink. Herodotus was only too aware that tyranny – not democracy – had provided the unity and strength to make Persia the most formidable power on earth.

There is a remarkable passage in the *Histories* in which Herodotus turns political philosopher. It's known as the Constitutional Debate and sees three Persian nobles discussing the best – or rather least bad – form of government. One by one, they consider the merits of democracy, oligarchy and monarchy before putting their respective cases to the vote. What's particularly interesting about the discussion is that it's history's first ever example of political theory. Anywhere. Remember, Plato was only a toddler by the time Herodotus died in around 425–420 and Aristotle was one of Plato's students. Once again, Herodotus is in pioneer territory. In the words of the Italian historian Arnaldo Momigliano, 'there was no Herodotus before Herodotus'.

The context is the aftermath of the counter-coup in around 521 BC against Smerdis and Patizeithes, the Magi usurpers of the Persian throne after Cambyses' death. Seven Persian conspirators have revolted against the two leading Magi, the hereditary caste of priests – the 'wise men' of the Bible – and killed them in the royal palace at Susa. Five days later, after mopping up the remaining Magi throughout the city, the conspirators meet to decide what sort of government they should have.

Otanes, one of the wealthiest Persian nobles, is the first to speak. He urges popular government, on the grounds that monarchy corrupts. The time has passed for any one man among them to have absolute power. Monarchy has no place in 'any sound system of ethics' because it 'allows a man to do whatever he likes without any responsibility or control'. He adds: 'The typical vices of a monarch are envy and pride . . . . These two vices are the root cause of all wickedness: both lead to acts of savage and unnatural violence.' The great problem with monarchy is that it relies on the character of one man and that character, corrupted by unchecked power, becomes dangerously fickle. There is a fine line between monarchy and tyranny. Worse still, Otanes continues, a monarchy 'breaks up the structure of ancient tradition and law, forces women to serve his pleasure, and puts men to death without trial'.

So what form of government would he suggest for the mighty Persian empire? Wait for it. The rule of the people. *Isonomia*, or popular government, literally equality before the law, a system in which the people in power cannot rule unchecked. He doesn't use the newer word *demokratia*, but this is as close as you can get to what we would understand as democratic government.

> Under a government of the people a magistrate is appointed by lot and is held responsible for his conduct in office and all questions are put up for open debate. For these reasons I propose that we do away with the monarchy, and raise the people to power; for the state and the people are synonymous terms.

A Persian nobleman recommending democracy in the sixth century BC? It doesn't seem very credible and certainly wouldn't have to Herodotus' Greek audiences. This looks like a quintessentially Greek debate, in fact, but suspend your disbelief for a moment. Look at this whole episode as Herodotus flexing his political-philosophy muscles rather than as a strictly historical account of Darius' accession. The debate is a literary device.

Next up is fellow conspirator Megabyzus. He agrees they should abolish the monarchy but disagrees with handing power to the people. 'The masses are a feckless lot – nowhere will you find more ignorance or irresponsibility or violence.' It would be intolerable, he says, to exchange 'the murderous caprice of a king' for 'the equally wanton brutality of the rabble'.

Megabyzus would have had a difficult time of it in twenty-first-century Britain. Not for him the proletarian vulgarity of parliamentary democracy, trades unions and *Big Brother*. He's got no time for the common people. Let Persia's enemies – that is, the feeble Greeks – practise this form of government if that's what they want, but we seven should choose 'a certain number of the best men in the country, and give *them* political power'. Oligarchy – or, strictly, aristocracy – is the way forward. His suggestion is not entirely disinterested. 'We personally shall be amongst them, and it is only natural to suppose that the best men will produce the best policy.'

Silence. All eyes turn to Darius, son of Hystaspes, the governor of Susa. Darius, still in his twenties, is emerging as the young pretender to the Persian throne. He shares Megabyzus' distaste for the wretched masses and doesn't think much of oligarchy either. It leads to rivalries and 'violent personal feuds' between the oligarchs, triggering civil wars from which 'the only way out is a return to monarchy – a clear proof that monarchy is best'. As long as the man at the helm is the best available, what form of government could be better? 'His judgement will be in keeping with his character; his control of the people will be beyond reproach; his measures against enemies and traitors will be kept secret more easily than under other forms of government.' Who could Darius be thinking of? Does he have someone in mind?

The debate ends. The four conspirators who haven't spoken take a vote. The result is unanimous. Darius' argument wins the day. Democracy is out. Persia will be ruled by one man.

This being Herodotus, there's a limit to how long he can discuss something serious without throwing in the fantastical. So back to the Persian conspirators, who must choose who among them will be king. They agree to meet at dawn the following day, get on their horses on the outskirts of Susa and the man whose horse neighs first after sunrise wins the throne. A bizarre way to select a monarch, perhaps, but there we are.

The ambitious Darius rushes off to his groom, Oebares, and tells him of the agreement. If that's all there is to it, this ancient-world Jeeves replies, then consider it done, my lord. Nothing could be more straightforward. Oebares takes 'the mare that Darius' horse was particularly fond of' and ties her up on the outskirts of the city. Then he brings up the stallion and walks him round and round the mare, driving the poor horse to distraction until finally he allows the lusty beast to mount her and take his pleasure.

Dawn the next day. The would-be kings are riding through the suburbs, steely glint of absolute power in their eyes. Ancient Persia meets *The Good, the Bad and the Ugly*. When they reach the spot where the mare had been tethered – and mounted – the previous night, Darius' stallion suddenly gives a mighty snort. Simultaneously there's a flash of lightning and a thunderclap from the heavens. Destiny has spoken. Darius is the new king. All bow before him.

Herodotus is not done. Before he signs off on this fanciful little story, he tells his spellbound audience that there is another, earthier version told by the Persians. According to this one, Oebares rubs his hand all over the mare's genitals then hides it in his breeches. The next morning he thrusts his stinking hand under the stallion's nostrils and Darius' oversexed horse neighs triumphantly. 'In this way Darius son of Hystaspes became king of Persia.' Only Herodotus could combine high political theory with tales of horse sex.

Two-and-a-half-thousand years later, Greeks are still passionate about their democracy. An intensely independent lot, they have an uneasy relationship with authority and don't like being told what to do. Take smoking. Huffy health ministers tell the people that cigarettes are harmful, quickest way to the grave, must be stopped, but the freedom-loving Greeks don't give a hoot. They keep puffing away, everyone from fresh-cheeked children to wrinkled crones. Better to die of lung cancer and remain free than obey the bossy government's orders.

So much for smoking, as Herodotus might have said. Strikes and protest marches are further indications of the enduringly fierce attachment to democratic rights. Greeks strike and take to the streets at the drop of a hat.

One of the most hallowed dates in the calendar is 17 November. Ostensibly, this is a march in memory of the 1973 Athens Polytechnic uprising against the military regime of the junta under George Papadopoulos. Hunkered down on their campus, the students began by going on strike (only in Greece could students strike. They still do. They were occupying universities during my visit, locking themselves in and refusing to let anyone in. They'd been doing it for months. No question of lectures. High-school students caught the bug and were striking too). With the self-dramatising flamboyance of youth they called themselves the 'Free Besieged', in honour of the poem of the same name written by the nineteenth-century Greek national poet Dionysios Solomos, a tribute to the siege of Missolonghi, cornerstone of the Greek fight for independence. Then they set up a radio station and started broadcasting across the city: 'Here is Polytechneion! People of Greece, the Polytechneion is the flag bearer of our struggle and your struggle, our common struggle against the dictatorship and for democracy!'

This was not a message the junta appreciated going out on the airwaves. The students had to be stopped. The city lights were switched off and at 3 a.m. on the morning of 17 November an AMX 30 battle tank crashed through the steel gate of the Polytechnic. In the ensuing chaos, more than twenty people were killed. The bloodshed set in motion a series of events that led, via the calamitous Turkish invasion of Cyprus in 1974, to the collapse of the junta, the return of a former prime minister, Constantine Karamanlis, and parliamentary elections later that year. Democracy was restored.

Greeks have been marching through Athens on 17 November ever since, their route finishing in front of the American Embassy where things frequently turn violent. I say the demonstration is ostensibly in memory of the uprising because over time it has evolved into as much of an anti-American, anti-capitalism protest as a commemoration of the student uprising. Many Greeks are instinctively anti-American and hold the US responsible for its support of the junta (as well as many, if not most, of the world's ills). Dislike of the Nixon administration has been followed by dislike of most of its successors.

At a dinner party a couple of nights before 17 November one of the *grandes dames* of Greek broadcasting has warned me on no account to join the march. 'My dear, you really have no idea. Of course you can't go. It's very dangerous. You can't speak Greek and if the mob find out you're British, it could get very ugly. A lot of them are socialists and communists, you know.' Perhaps I am becoming a bit Greek, because as soon as the Medusa-like matron tells me I mustn't go on the march, I know I have no option but to join it. Would Herodotus have missed such an important event in the capital of a foreign country in which he was travelling? Something that might shed some light on that country's people? Not a chance.

Being British, I arrive at the Polytechnic two hours early. Being Greek, the protesters arrive two hours late. Another Herodotean clash of customs. Three o'clock means different things to the British and Greeks. It gives me time to beetle about the Archaeological Museum next door while they get ready.

In the opening galleries, with the *kouroi* statues of naked youths and their far-off 'Archaic smile', we are teetering on the edge of Herodotus' world. The last of the *kouroi* date to around 490 BC. 'The new era that begins for Greece and particularly Attica after the victorious Persian

Wars will lay a new base for sculptors and lead the way to the splendid Classical art,' a notice reads. And a new era of Athenian democracy and the golden era of Greece, a period which Herodotus – with the good fortune of being born in the right place at the right time – was perfectly placed to observe.

Anything that dates to Herodotus' time is instantly exciting. How about the sublime bronze of a rippling Poseidon (or Zeus) poised to throw his trident (or thunderbolt) in about 460, when Herodotus would probably have been around thirty? The Thermopylae section is like an electric shock. There, in a small glass case, are arrowheads and spearheads from the battlefield. It's scarcely possible. Archaeological treasures from one of the most famous, poignant, history-changing battles in the world. Imagine, if you are British, the thrill of coming face to face with war trophies from the battle of Hastings, say. A defining moment of British history a millennium ago. Norman conquest and one in the eye for King Harold. And then compare that with these scattered pieces of metal, clearly sharpened for destruction, the few remnants from a terrifying encounter that helped reshape the world, never mind the fortunes of one nation. That 2,500 years ago played a rallying role in the subsequent Greek triumph over the Persians, a victory that ushered in Western civilisation, freedom and democracy. Who knows – and it is the sort of schoolboy thought that quickens the historical imagination like nothing else – one of these very arrowheads could have killed the brave Spartan king Leonidas.

A notice next to these extraordinary artefacts hails the Greek self-sacrifice as 'a shining example of belief and dedication to duty and higher moral values and ideals', a glorious deed commemorated in the epigram written by the poet Simonides and carved on the tomb of the fallen heroes:

> Go tell the Spartans, passerby,
> That here, by Spartan law, we lie.

Ruskin considered these the noblest set of words ever uttered by man.

While I'm standing lost in these romanticised thoughts about ancient warfare, Western civilisation and freedom there comes, wafting through the airy galleries, the distant chanting of the protesters. Inside, these totems of nascent democracy, signs and sculptures from an ancient world on the cusp of seismic change. Outside, the sounds of democracy being practised with a thoroughly Greek, freedom-loving robustness. And more than that, another little twist. Here in the bosom of Western democracy, the democracy-loving demonstrators are marching against the world's greatest democracy. Enough to confuse and amuse even Herodotus.

A swelling crowd is milling about the Polytechnic campus. Everyone's smoking. Lots of noise. Chanting. An invisible man on a megaphone driving himself to a fever pitch of anti-Americanism. An old man in a beret, neatly turned out in shirt and tie, holding a noose in one hand and a placard in another. 'Death to the whore America!' I try not to look too British or American. Banners. Posters. Pictures. Hammers and sickles. Clenched fists. Some tell Bush to go home. 'Stop the war.' Others tell Prime Minister Kostas Karamanlis to get lost. 'We need jobs not bombs.' Others want communism not NATO. A solitary pro-Palestinian. A stall selling books: Trotsky's *Fascism: What It Is and How to Fight It*; *Feminism and the Marxist Movement*; *Che Guevara and the Imperialist Reality*; *Malcolm X Talks to Young People*; *Israel: A Colonial Settler State?* My favourite is *Cuba for Beginners*. *The Working Class and the Transformation of Learning: The Failure of Education Reform under Capitalism* is probably not a page-turner.

The *koulouria* (sesame-bread rings) sellers are doing a roaring business at 0.5 euros a go. A young man smeared in mud is crawling along the street on all fours, filmed by some friends. Student film project, perhaps, a protest against world slavery under imperial America. I approach one of the prettier girls I have seen on the campus and ask her why she's here. 'In 1973 the students marched for bread, freedom and democracy,' she says. 'Today we are fighting for the same thing. We want education to be free and the government is changing the law to force us to pay. The Greek people are starving, the students have to work or they cannot afford to study and if they work it is very difficult to study and pass the exams.' Not unlike the lot of your average American student, perhaps, but it's not the moment to suggest it.

She excuses herself to place a few red carnations on a recumbent statue, a monument inscribed with the names of student martyrs killed in the early 1940s. Photographers come and go. The megaphone haranguing continues. Outside the campus the streets have been closed to vehicles, shops are shuttered and a strange calm prevails. The quiet before the storm, presumably. A helicopter buzzes overhead.

We start shuffling along towards the beginning of the march. There's a greater urgency about things now. Leaders of the various groups boss their followers about this way and that. Forward a bit on that side with the banner, back a bit, pull it tighter, that's right. The Greeks know how to do this. They're the oldest protesters in the world. A student leader marches up and down with a megaphone, whipping up his throng into an ecstasy of outrage. Redundant traffic lights flick in a silent cycle from orange to red to orange to green. Here and there a moped scoots past. Passersby grip their shopping bags more tightly and hurry away. The streets around us are empty. In a city that never sleeps, that is disconcerting.

A large group of bikers arrives, carrying armfuls of red flags which they distribute among their group. They are a faintly menacing lot, each man carrying a motorbike helmet on one arm, brandishing a flag in the other. There's something wrong with the flags, too. They're much too short and too broad and they look like cudgels. I take a few photographs as inconspicuously as possible but then one of the toughs in a biker jacket decorated with BMW and COMPAQ logos – perhaps not an anti-globalisation protester – spots me. He barks something, a hundred grimacing faces turn my way, then he rushes at me with a raised cudgel-flag and a blood-curdling roar that in cooler moments might have reminded me of the ancient *eleleu!* war-cry. I stop taking pictures.

Then we're off. I hang back a bit, keeping my distance from the red-flag brigade after this exchange. The marchers have their different groups, most of them with their own megaphone man who maintains discipline and leads the chanting. There are mild-mannered, middle-aged socialists, young Marxist revolutionaries, anti-war firebrands. Most of the march is uneventful but the atmosphere is building up to something. Suddenly there is a series of pistol cracks and the acid whiff of tear gas in the air. The marchers don bandanas but within minutes we all have hot, streaming eyes.

By the time we close in on the heavily fortified American Embassy – sensibly closed for the day – night has fallen, which gives those bent on violence greater anonymity. Hundreds of riot police are drawn up in tight lines between the marchers and the Embassy. We are on the brink of confrontation.

More tear gas rockets into the crowds and the sky is lanced with home-made missiles raining down on the police. Flashing Molotovs are thrown into the mix, the cue for the red-flag posse to charge. They race forward in a blur of flailing fists and flag-cudgels, hoplites in helmets, beating anything foolish or unlucky enough to stand in their way. There is a frightening randomness about their attack, directed less against the police specifically than against anyone who might give them a good fight or who looks deserving of an impromptu beating. It is not a good time to be British. Smashed bottles zing through the air, a shop window explodes in a hail of glass. The police charge back, homing in on roving packs of red-flag bikers with windmilling batons and renewed volleys of tear gas. With eyes burning beneath a red polka-dot handkerchief, I beat a discreet but determined retreat.

Maybe the broadcaster was right. There are better places to be than on the streets of central Athens on the evening of 17 November. But she was wrong about one thing. Herodotus is with me in spirit. He's been with me all evening.

---

I've been neglecting the priests, I know. The cross-cultural conference, Athenian democracy and the 17 November march have intervened. But we're going to get to them now. I haven't rushed to them immediately because, intrinsically interesting as Greek priests and the Greek Orthodox Church are to anyone studying Greece, things have moved on a lot since Herodotus' day. He was a priest obsessive for a very good reason. They were the ones with all the information. This is why he was always sucking up to them wherever he travelled. Mind if I have a look at that papyrus showing the pharaonic dynasties of Egypt? Any chance we could have a chat about how long you've been worshipping Hercules in this temple, good priest? And so on. In Herodotus' time, information was the preserve of a tiny minority. In our era, it's never been so democratic. In short, priests aren't what they were.

But a Greek priest is still interesting for a number of reasons. The history of the Greek Church runs parallel to the history of Greek independence and identity. There are Herodotean themes of religion and freedom to explore. There's the nagging question of why Greek intellectuals are so vehemently opposed to the Church. And then there's the impossibly juicy fact that the Greek Orthodox Church is run by Archbishop Christodoulos, an ultra-conservative who has publicly referred to the Turks as 'barbarians'.* It doesn't get more Herodotean – given the old historian's explicit interest in Greeks and barbarians – than that.

In a speech that provoked a diplomatic storm with Turkey in 2003, the archbishop harked back to Athanasios Diakos, a Greek national hero killed by the Ottomans during the struggle for independence. 'They impaled him,' he told his flock, 'those who want today to get into the European Union.' They – the blood-soaked Ottomans of 1821, not the Turks of today – now wanted to join the EU. It was an astonishingly crude and manipulative use of history to serve nationalist purposes. As far as Archbishop Christodoulos was concerned, there was no question of forgiving or forgetting. Greeks could not share political union with the murderers of Diakos. It was as simple as that. 'The barbarians cannot become part of the Christian family because we cannot live together,' he said. So much for Christian goodwill towards all men and cross-cultural encounters with one's neighbours.

It's not easy to make an appointment with the archbishop's office. After repeated attempts have failed, I tell his staff that everyone, especially writers and intellectuals, keeps telling me what an awful institution the Church has become: how corrupt, lazy and disgustingly rich it is, more concerned with keeping priests in a certain style than attending to the needs of the poor, uninterested in offering spiritual guidance, narrow-minded, mean-spirited and xenophobic. There is a pause on the other end of the line. Theologically ignorant and illiterate,

* Archbishop Christodoulos died in Athens in January 2008.

I add. A meeting is arranged with Father Timotheos, Christodoulos' spokesman, for the following morning.

The archbishop's office is a genuinely palatial building a stone's throw from the Mitropoli, Athens Cathedral. It is a quiet, prosperous-looking neighbourhood teeming with ecclesiastical bling: shop windows gaudy with magnificently lurid vestments, robes and dalmatics, sparkling candelabra and crucifixes, medallions, incense burners and thuribles, oil candles, votive cups, gold-leaf icons, diptychs and triptychs, praying ropes and worry beads, cufflinks, amulets, silver, gold, anything and everything your most discerning, well-heeled and worldly priest could ever need.

Father Timotheos is a bald but bearded Rasputin, beavering away at his desk like a senior civil servant, laying waste to the documents in front of him with the scourge of a fluorescent yellow marker-pen. A crick-necked Virgin Mary stares at him reprovingly from an icon behind his desk.

We begin with some history. This is where, in its own mind at least, the Church derives much of its authority and legitimacy within Greek culture, and a good deal of its self-belief, too. 'The Church played a crucial role in Greek history from before the fall of the Byzantine Empire,' Father Timotheos says. 'Ties with the people were very strong during the Muslim occupation and after the fight for liberation and independence. Many priests gave their lives in the struggle. It was the Church that kept alive Greek identity and Greek history.'

The special role played by the Church in that all-defining struggle for independence goes some way to explaining its undoubted interest in matters temporal. Few Christian Churches can have spilled so much of their own blood in a national cause in recent times. Political struggle is in the Greek Orthodox Church's DNA. 'Intellectuals talk about the Church's interference in political life but we cannot talk about interference,' Father Timotheos goes on. 'The constitution gives the Church of Greece a very precise position in Greek society as the prevailing religion in Greece for historical reasons.' The Church is like a valiant old general rewarded for his distinguished war record with a political sinecure where he can rest on his laurels and twirl his moustache. Its privileged position has important consequences for Greek society. It means that to be fully Greek you really need to be part of the Orthodox Church. The Church is, as the writer Takis Michas told me one morning over coffee, 'the cement of ethnic identity', Greece's 'social glue'. Without it you can come unstuck.

Given the extraordinary centrality of the Church to Greek life, the security of its status in a country where in Father Timotheos' estimate 94 per cent of the people belong to it, why the need to bash the Turks? 'When the archbishop is asked about the relationship between Europe and Turkey, he gives his opinion. It's not just Christodoulos, it's also Pope Benedict. It's not a question of being anti-Turkey, it's about the Christian identity of Europe. Many intellectuals interpret this as being anti-Turk. It's not. It's pro-Christian Europe.'

Is it possible to be pro-Christian Europe without calling one's Muslim neighbours barbarians? Father Timotheos shakes his head. 'No, this is not true. The archbishop has spoken about people involved in the atrocities against our people, meaning the Turks against the Greek population during the Muslim occupation. It doesn't mean the Turks are barbarians. He doesn't use the word [he does], but you can't hide the truth. Too many Greeks were slaughtered during the five centuries of Muslim occupation. The archbishop believes, as does the pope, that one of the foundations of Europe is the Christian faith. The other two pillars are ancient Greek literature and philosophy and the legal system of the Roman Empire.'

Why do Greeks still call Istanbul Constantinople? Does this indicate some deep-seated inability to move on, to accept that the city is lost to them for ever? 'It's everyone's right to call it what they like. Historically it's Constantinople for the Greeks and the Turks call it Istanbul.* Most Greek intellectuals say the Greek people dream of retaking Constantinople,' Timotheos continues, 'but that's in the past.'

He's more concerned with what he sees as Turkey's denial of religious freedom to Greek Christians to worship in the Church of Holy Wisdom, the incomparable Aghia Sophia, successively a church,

* In fact, even Istanbul is thought to derive from the Greek expression, Εις την Πόλιν, Is tin Polin, 'to the city', Poli being the name by which Greeks referred to Constantinopolis, which we better know as Constantinople, the City of Constantine.

mosque and now a museum. Yet as this was the beating heart of the Orthodox Byzantine empire for the best part of a millennium – and therefore highly Greek and Christian – it seems wildly unrealistic to expect secular Turkey to hand back such a landmark building to the tiny Greek flock in Istanbul. What about the 500 years from 1453, when Sultan Mehmed II took Constantinople and converted the Aghia Sophia into a mosque complete with four, sky-lancing minarets? Does that Muslim history not count? But then, 1453 – the shattering, heart-rending fall of the Byzantine empire – still burns in the hearts of millions of Greeks, a date that dare not speak its name.

Greeks hardly go to church these days. Many only ever interact with it in the time-honoured ritual of weddings, baptisms, funerals, feast days and festivals, Christmas and Easter. Religion to a lot of Greeks may be little more than a superstitious flick of the fingers crossing oneself when passing a church, but few would deny the entrancing hold the Orthodox faith has across the country. And no one, probably not even the Church's fiercest critics, would ever argue that intellectuals were closer to the people, more in touch with their daily concerns, than the Orthodox Church. This lasting truth probably explains the often intemperate tone of the criticism.

Herodotus would recognise a familiar human trait in Father Timotheos' final remarks. 'The archbishop believes that the origin of the Christian faith is the Orthodox Church. As far as the Orthodox Church is concerned, we have the truth of religion.' No one else comes close. You could say Christodoulos has history on his side. After all, Rome blew it with the schism of 1054, the final rupture between the Latin Church and Constantinople, a date that marked the still unhealed division of Christianity into Western Catholicism on the one hand and Eastern Orthodoxy on the other. As for the dreary, upstart Protestants, they're barely worth talking about: the schismatics' schismatics, an endlessly splintering babble of Adventists and Anabaptists, Calvinists and Charismatics, Pentecostals and Presbyterians, Lutherans, Quakers, Anglicans, Baptists, Unitarians, Methodists ... no wonder the Orthodox Church sees itself as the sole true protector of the Christian flame.

And no wonder, also, because everyone, as Herodotus loved to point out, thinks his own customs are best.

# 10

# Herodotus Meets Aristotle

*Indeed, history is nothing more than a tableau of crimes and misfortunes.*
Voltaire, *L'Ingénu* (1767)

MY TRAVELLING HERODOTEAN library is expanding fast. Like
Cyrus' acquisitive Persian empire, it is devouring new frontiers
and damning the consequences. The Persian Great King's considera-
tions were global. My worries are for my Globetrotter, an elderly
suitcase struggling to cope with this literary assault. The thing is,
wherever I go, perfect strangers press another volume into my hands.
There's my friend Paul Cartledge's celebrated study *The Greeks*,
former Prime Minister Tzannis Tzannetakis' travelogue on India, a
guide to Samos, a book about the founder of modern Egypt
Mohammed Ali Pasha's house in Kavala, several volumes of new
history textbooks, an elegant coffee-table book illustrating the religious monuments of Xanthi, Henry Miller's *The Colossus of Maroussi*.
The latest additions to the literary empire squeeze in alongside various
Herodotus editions, Patrick Leigh Fermor's *Mani* and *Roumeli*, Richard
Evans's broadside *In Defence of History* (a bust of Herodotus on the
cover but, scandalously, not a single reference to him in the text),
*Thermopylae* (another Cartledge) and Tom Holland's impressively
heavy *Persian Fire*.

The generous literary gifts from strangers are one of my most
remarkable – and entirely unexpected – experiences in Greece. What
could be more appropriate in the land that provided the foundations
of Western literature, philosophy, political theory, history? And one in
which the tradition of *philoxenia* – expressing love to a visitor or

224

stranger; in a word, hospitality – has been refined over the millennia into such a humbling art form.

The only volume I leave behind, with a sense of shame and guilt, is a Greek ultra-nationalist history of the Turkish invasion of Cyprus, and it isn't just because the book is in Greek.

I meet its writer, Stavros Karkaletsis, on one of my first days in Athens. He is a spokesman for Giorgios Karatzaferis, leader of the far-right Popular Orthodox Rally or LAOS party, and I want to talk to him about Turkey to explore some parallels between the ancient Greeks' views of the Persians and modern Greeks' views of the Turks. The fact that I have to go to an extremist political party for such a perspective shows how unrepresentative such views are, which is revealing in itself.

Karkaletsis, an affable, hyperactive man with an open-necked yellow shirt and hairy chest, is obsessed by Turkey. The first thing he did on getting married, he tells me, was to take Turkey to the European Court of Human Rights for illegal occupation of his wife's house. What a start to the honeymoon! Quite what his new bride made of this he doesn't say. Perhaps she thought it romantic. She is a Greek Cypriot from the north of the island. The case is ongoing.

Karkaletsis has an almost comical ability to insert the Turks into any subject we discuss and then say something negative about them. When I tell him I am writing about Herodotus, his eyes narrow into distrustful slits. 'What did our friends in Turkey tell you about Herodotus? Let me guess. I think they told you he was a local man, a Carian or something like that.* He was Greek, of course, but they can never admit that. According to the Turks, there were no Greeks on the Aegean coast, just local people.'

I tell him I have been having a grand time in Greece, bowled over by the hospitality. The writer Sofka Zinovieff and her Greek husband Vassilis have adopted me and are supplying Herodotean leads left, right and centre. New friends Alexandra and her fellow academic Mairi have suggested useful lines of inquiry, another new friend and his Greek wife have offered to take me to Thermopylae. I'm drinking

---

* See p. 36: 'everyone thinks Herodotus was a Greek'.

retsina like it's going out of fashion. Life could hardly be better. Karkaletsis nods. 'Greece is a nice place, but if only we had Sweden or Portugal on the other side of the Aegean and not Turkey.'

He discusses some of LAOS's overarching principles. First, the party is against Turkish entry into the EU. Greece will be finished demographically if three or four million Turks move in. Second, LAOS supports EU political union as long as national cultures are respected. Next, 'We are strongly anti-American.' He pauses. 'We are totally anti-American,' he adds, lest there be any doubt. Then his eyes narrow again. 'We are also anti-British.'

With 5 per cent support, LAOS is the fourth party after Pasok, New Democracy and the Communists. The American State Department's latest human rights report attacked it as an ultra-right organisation. 'They say we are anti-Semitic but we are not. We just criticise the crimes of Israel, for example the invasion of southern Lebanon. They used to call us the Greek Le Pen. We are not. There is a party even more extreme than us, the Greek National Front.' This is one of the most amusing uses of the word 'even' I have ever heard.

On immigration, Karkaletsis deplores the 'waves' of immigrants flooding the country. At around two million, Greece has the highest number of immigrants, legal and illegal, in Europe, he claims. This represents 16–18 per cent of the population. LAOS wants a limit of 5–10 per cent. 'Then we will make them legal. Not Greeks,' he adds quickly. Legal immigrants will not be naturalised.

The one thing Karkaletsis is positive about is the Church. 'The Orthodox Church is extremely important. It's anti-globalisation, anti-American and anti-Turk.' He doesn't say what it is for.

'Many Turks speak of splitting the Aegean fifty–fifty. This is unacceptable. Many of the islands, like Samos and Lesbos, are totally Greek. The Turks have no demographic base in the Aegean. They use Hitler's *Lebensraum* argument, saying the Greek islands are so close to the Turkish mainland that they can't breathe. Every day they make psychological war against us, in the Aegean, above Samos, flying F-16s. They say, okay, Samos is Greek but the airspace above it is Turkish. They're crazy!'

From there we jump to a notional Turkish invasion of Britain. 'I think you'd agree that if they did that, changed the culture, made a third of the population refugees through ethnic cleansing, then that would be a war crime. And you think if they invaded Britain and then wanted to join the EU, Britain would agree? We have right on our side.'

I ask him about the songs that Greek conscripts sing about Turkey during boot camp. He smiles. 'There are many.' He remembers two from his own time in the army. Neither does particularly well in translation.

> Fire! Fire!
> To the Turkish dogs!
>
> Into the Turkish village I jump
> With my parachute,
> Take two Turkish girls
> And fuck them!

Before we say goodbye, he gives me a copy of his book about Turkey and Cyprus. He flicks through it to show me pictures of Turkish atrocities. There is a desecrated cemetery with smashed tombs and crosses, streets and houses destroyed by fighting. The images are terrible, but the insistence on Turkey as unspeakable villain is relentless.

Greeks and Persians, Greeks and Turks. Herodotus reached beyond the standards of his time, made the effort to study 'barbarian' cultures and admire what he found good in them. That he was able to cast a dispassionate eye on Persia, the country which only recently had acted the aggressor and invaded Greece with the largest army the world had ever seen, speaks volumes about his enlightened spirit.

'Just look at this. This is what we're dealing with.' Karkaletsis shows me another picture of a ransacked church, badly burnt by fire. Jesus has had his arms amputated, his crucifix lies in smithereens on the floor. 'It's a complete catastrophe,' he says. 'This is Turkish civilisation. I say this not as a Greek but as a historian. They're barbarians.'

---

A happier literary discovery awaits. One afternoon, my academic guide Chris and I bump into his friend Marianna Koromila, the popular historian, writer and broadcaster. She invites us to her apartment overlooking the Acropolis and the original, white-marbled Olympic stadium.

Koromila is a chain-smoking force of nature, a mass of flaming hair and charisma. Her apartment resembles a fragile model city viewed from above, teeming with skyscrapers of teetering books. The straining bookshelves have long since been filled. Among the Persian rugs and throws and stacked-up pictures, the piles of books and magazines, *objets* and treasures, prowls Xanthos, a huge, slavering dog that looks more Great Dane than the Labrador Koromila claims he is.

She whips out a bottle of firewater. 'Here, we will have a drink.' It's a bit early for me (another way of saying it is not my custom), but when in Athens . . . 'I like Herodotus very much,' she says. 'He's great.' She pauses to light a cigarette and have a drink. 'You know, it was only recently that he became popular again. The *Histories* appeared in a pocket-book edition in 1970, it was a real shock because up to then books had only been for the rich and intellectuals, then these volumes came along and they were very cheap, ten drachmas each, the same price as a newspaper or packet of cigarettes. You know, I think I have something that will interest you,' she says and retreats to inspect a bookshelf. Her fingers run briskly along it like pistons then stop abruptly. 'Aha!' she says. 'Here he is. This is what I was looking for.'

She pulls out a tatty, obviously very old, volume, a hardback in muted pink, and starts leafing through the first few pages. 'That's it. 1836. Andreas Koromilas. My great-great-grandfather. The first edition of Herodotus in modern Greek.' She walks across to a picture on the wall of a handsome, nineteenth-century villa. Above the tall, arched windows on the ground floor are the prominent signs MAGASIN and IMPRIMERIE. 'This is his old house, the first one built on Syntagma Square. It's only two floors because King Otto told him not to build a third floor, he said it would ruin his view down to the port of Piraeus! This was where Andreas set up his publishing and printing house before fleeing to Aegina when it became too dangerous to stay in Athens. Homer came first, of course, in 1835, then Herodotus was second.'

She reads from the introduction. 'This will be very interesting for you, I think, yes, you see, he says he published Herodotus to inspire the Greeks in the age of the struggles against the Ottomans. If you're interested, come back one afternoon before you go and I'll make you a copy.'

As we leave, slightly the worse for wear, she gives me her encyclopaedia-sized magnum opus, *The Greeks and the Black Sea*. It's been sitting on my desk in Norfolk ever since, handsomely sandwiched between the 1936 edition of the *Histories* and a bookend from one of Saddam's palaces in Baghdad.

---

Koromila is right. Her great-great-grandfather's edition of the *Histories* is fascinating. I go through a copy of it a month later with Antigoni, a new, highly argumentative friend who has taken me under her Aristotelian–Herodotean wing. We have spent the morning driving out to Delphi. We don't see eye to eye on Herodotus or much else. In fact, we lock horns almost immediately. The battleground is drawn as soon as she makes her opening pronouncement on Herodotus, anathema to anyone who believes there is romance in history.

'What you've got to understand about Herodotus, Justin, is that he's not a man. He's a text.'

For me this is unthinkable. It makes me see red. Okay, so all we really have to go on is the *Histories*, but what a treasure trove it is. Herodotus the man shines forth on almost every page. Wry, amusing, intelligent, deft, humane, chatty, ingenious, cosmopolitan, teasing, moral – the many facets of his personality are laid bare in his prose. I mark Antigoni down as a postmodernist – all the world's a text – but it turns out she's a philologist, which seems to amount to the same thing. 'Really, I am an Aristotelian,' she corrects me firmly, 'but you can't say that when people ask what your job is so I just say I'm a philologist.'

Either way, none of the discussions about what Herodotus might have been like are real. It's only the text that counts. We have been arguing *en route* to Delphi, Antigoni weaving terrifyingly all over the road while she munches on a *tiropita* cheese pie. 'I'm a bloody rationalist,' she says, swerving to avoid a dead animal. 'I'm not crazy for all these fantastical stories like Croesus boiling up a tortoise and lamb to test the oracles and things like that. The most important thing about Herodotus is not that he's a cosmopolitan or the things you're talking about. It's his message, know the limits of the human condition. It's nothing to do with don't exploit other people, be nice to them, that's Kapuściński's Christian, humanist nonsense.* Completely ridiculous. No, Herodotus is saying, don't think you'll be happy for ever and don't place yourself above the gods.'

We talk about Greece and Turkey. She knows a Turkish girl who is dating a Greek man. 'They were having an argument one day and he said to her, "Thank God we're not the Turks' slaves any more!" Can you believe it? Was he there? What does he know about it? This is how they teach the Turkish occupation in Greek schools. They call it slavery.'

The war in Iraq comes up. Antigoni, as anti-war as the next Greek, is horrified that President Bush had the effrontery to justify the invasion of Iraq with a reference to Herodotus' famous contemporary. It's sacrilege to trespass on Greek history to defend a policy few Greeks could stomach. 'Can you believe Bush used Thucydides to justify the war in Iraq?' she says, narrowly missing an oncoming lorry overtaking a tractor. 'You know, *the strong do what they can and the weak suffer what they must* . . . Greeks were furious about this. It was only one idea among many in Thucydides and we don't even know he approved of it. You think Bush had ever heard of Thucydides, let alone read him? He got his history wrong. He should have listened to Herodotus and what he said about the foolishness of war.'

We spend an hour or so zooming up and down the terraces of Delphi. In between lectures on the Oracle, Antigoni berates me constantly for not concentrating properly. I'm scribbling in my Moleskine and taking pictures. She's used to more attentive students. 'You're not listening,' she says disapprovingly.

She's right. I'm trying to have my Delphi moment, the lamentable lot of the writer reaching out for history like Tantalus with the elusive fruit and water receding from his reach, trying to shut everything out and imagine Herodotus in this ethereal mountainscape. Beneath us,

* Ryszard Kapuściński's *Travels with Herodotus* was the Polish writer's last book, published in England shortly after his death in 2007.

below these twin fangs of rock that enclose the sacred site, the lower slopes of Mount Parnassus are locked in shade before tailing off into the sun-stung haze of the Pleistos Valley, studded with olive trees and the green lances of cypresses. The setting is preternaturally beautiful, precisely why the Greeks chose it as a place in which to honour Apollo and Dionysus and consult the all-knowing Oracle. Herodotus knew this place, almost certainly would have visited it, and writes about it with authority and exuberance.

Sometimes he overdoes it. Take the breathless story of how Delphi managed to withstand Xerxes' invasion of 480 BC, starting with the miraculous appearance of 'sacred weapons' in front of the shrine. Either he has been taken in by the priestly propaganda or he's happy to recycle the myth to entertain his audience:

> It is marvellous enough that weapons of war should move of their own accord and appear upon the ground outside the shrine; but what occurred next is surely one of the most amazing things ever known – for just as the Persians came to the shrine of Athene Pronaea, thunderbolts fell on them from the sky, and two pinnacles of rock, torn from Parnassus, came crashing and rumbling down amongst them, killing a large number . . .

The Persian troops panicked and were cut down by the Delphians as they fled. The great shrine and its untold wealth were saved. Then the travel writer–journalist's final flourish. The I've-been-there-myself moment: 'The rocks which fell from Parnassus were still there in my time; they lay in the enclosure round the shrine of Pronaea, where they embedded themselves after crashing through the Persian troops.'

A house-sized boulder still lies insouciantly amid the ruins of the temple of Athene Pronaea, remnant of the divine thunderbolt or more prosaic landslide. It doesn't matter. This is Herodotus' rock and I run my hands over it.

'Hey, Justin, are you listening? My God, you're just like Herodotus,' Antigoni says. This is not intended as a compliment. 'Taking notes everywhere you go, behaving like a tourist, only half understanding what's going on around you. I should call you Herodysseus. By the way, you must read the first few verses of the *Odyssey*.'

Tell me, O muse, of that ingenious hero who travelled far and wide after he had sacked the famous town of Troy. Many cities did he visit, and many were the nations with whose manners and customs he was acquainted . . .

'Herodotus wants to join this Homeric tradition. He travels far and wide and he studies different nations and their manners and customs. Are you writing this down? Good. You should also know that Herodotus is the first to incorporate the hubris-leads-to-nemesis argument into a historical framework. Personally, I prefer Aristotle's discussion of human happiness in the *Nicomachean Ethics*, but I'm an Aristotelian, so never mind. And you should have a look at Solon, too, because Herodotus uses him to express his own views about travel, history, happiness and hubris.'

———

Solon, the great Athenian sage and statesman born in the seventh century BC, has an important walk-on part in the *Histories*. Herodotus uses him as a foil to Croesus. Tell me, the Lydian king asks Solon, who is the happiest man you have ever seen? The question follows a tour of the gold-packed royal treasuries of Sardis. An Athenian called Tellus, Solon answers. What's so good about this nobody, a tetchy Croesus asks? His city was prosperous, he had fine sons, who each gave him grandchildren, was moderately wealthy and died a glorious death in battle for his country, earning the great honour of a public funeral, Solon replies. Okay, says Croesus, getting angrier by the minute, who's second happiest? Two young men of Argos, Solon answers, successful athletes who died a peaceful death in glorious circumstances. Croesus is disgusted. Is my own happiness so contemptible? 'Great wealth can make a man no happier than moderate means, unless he has the luck to continue in prosperity to the end,' Solon answers. Rich men lose their fortune, the poor get lucky. The important things are to avoid trouble and enjoy 'the blessings of a sound body, health, freedom from trouble, fine children and good looks'. If you can have – and keep – all that until you die a peaceful death, only then can you be called happy. Then, the *coup de grâce*: 'Look to the end, no matter what it is you are considering. Often enough God gives man a glimpse of happiness, then utterly ruins him.' With the snubbed ego of the super-rich, Croesus dismisses Solon coldly, 'firmly convinced he was a fool'. And what happens to him? Atys, his only son and heir, is promptly killed in a hunting accident, then he loses his empire to Cyrus. You always pay for your hubris in Herodotus.

———

We have a late lunch in town, hunched over a bottle of retsina and a copy of the introduction to Marianna's 1836 edition of the *Histories*. I'm fast acquiring Patrick Leigh Fermor's passion for this much maligned wine, converted to his conviction that 'one of its secrets is drinking it with unstinted abundance. It seems to have an alliance with the air in the promotion of well-being. Many people think that it bestows the gift of bodily health as well; a belief I accept at once without further scrutiny.' I'm getting through a litre of the stuff a day and have never felt better.

Marianna's great-great-grandfather Andreas Koromilas chose to publish Herodotus as a patriotic inspiration for his embattled country-men, still reeling from the wars of independence. Freed at last from the Ottoman hold in 1829, Greece was still an embryonic state whose borders would continue to evolve over decades of more turmoil. It was only recognised by the Ottomans in the Treaty of Constantinople in 1832, the same year the Great Powers saw fit to install the Bavarian King Otto as the new Greek monarch. You could say Greek confidence and identity needed bolstering. Who better to provide it than Herodotus?

'Why have I chosen Herodotus above any other Greek writer?' asks the translator, A. Radinos. Antigoni reads on:

> Herodotus is the oldest historian. He can show us that Greeks who live in Asia Minor and the Balkans come from the Greek mainland. Greeks will discover through Herodotus that they are not barbarians, they'll learn who they are, where they come from and who their neighbours are.

Greeks need to understand the historical context of their relationship with their neighbours. 'Greece, which is separated from Asia Minor by a narrow sea, today has virtually the same relationship with Asia which it had at the time of Triops, Dorus and later Pericles.' (Triops was the mythical founder of Cnidus. Dorus, son of Hellen, the mythological forefather of the Hellenes or Greeks, was said to be the founder of the Dorian tribe.) For Persia then, in other words, read Turkey in 1836. 'The victories of our ancestors inspire the victories of this war.' The road of history, with a bit of help from Byron, runs straight and true from Thermopylae to Missolonghi.

Radinos was hardly alone in drawing such parallels, of course. In 'The Isles of Greece' (*Don Juan*, canto 3) Byron plays up this romanticised history of ancient Greece:

> The mountains look on Marathon –
> And Marathon looks on the sea;
> And musing there an hour alone,
> I dreamed that Greece might still be free;
> For standing on the Persians' grave,
> I could not deem myself a slave.
>
> A king sat on the rocky brow
> Which looks on sea-born Salamis;
> And ships, by thousands, lay below,
> And men in nations; – all were his!
> He counted them at break of day –
> And when the sun set, where were they?
> ...
>
> Must *we* but weep o'er days more blest?
> Must *we* but blush? – Our fathers bled.
> Earth! render back from out thy breast
> A remnant of our Spartan dead!
> Of the three hundred grant but three,
> To make a new Thermopylae!

Antigoni looks at me. 'I had a student who told me once that the Greeks fought the Turks – not the Persians – at Marathon. I was furious with her, but maybe she wasn't so stupid after all.' She continues: 'Talking about the Turks, I was in Constantinopoli fifteen years ago and this Greek man saw me and asked me where I was staying. When I told him I was living with a Turkish classmate, he went crazy and started saying, do you know how these people live, they're barbarians, they eat with their hands, they don't use knives and forks, they'll abuse you, they'll rape you, they think all foreign women are prostitutes. He kept telling me how much I'd suffer at the hands of the Turks. Of course, I didn't suffer in the slightest. I had one of the best times of my life.'

'If you really want to have a look at Greek–Turkish relations,' says Sofka, 'you should go up to Thrace and visit Xanthi and Komotini. You'll see Turkish Muslims and Greek Christians living side by side, mosques right next to churches.'

We are sitting in Brasserie Valaoritou in the heart of Kolonaki, the chic, coffee-drinking heart of Athens beloved by writers, intellectuals and luxury-goods shoppers with money to burn. Sofka and her husband Vassilis have become my Herodotean travel guides, helping devise an itinerary in Greece that takes in war, religion, history, politics, architecture, the Aegean, places Herodotus wrote about or visited, travel by sea and land, Greek–Turkish relations and pointers towards Patrick Leigh Fermor (who is to travel writers what Delphi was to ancient Greeks). I'm after sex, too, as much as I can get. All in tribute to the sexually curious Herodotus.

One of the most Herodotean tales I've come across in this vein is the story of Dimitra – or Mimi – Papandreou, the onetime air hostess who in the late 1980s caught the eye of the sixty-nine-year-old prime minister Andreas Papandreou. Although he had just recovered from major heart surgery, Papandreou, founder of the Greek socialist party Pasok, suddenly discovered a new zest – or was it lust? – for life and started bringing his blonde mistress to European summits and diplomatic receptions, horrifying many Greeks and prompting the joke that he had discovered a new sexual position: making love with one foot in the grave. After ditching his wife of thirty-seven years, Papandreou married Mimi, who was half his age. She quickly revealed she had no intention of remaining above the political fray and angered Pasok politicians by running the prime minister's office and screening access to her ailing husband, maintaining an entourage that one critic described as consisting of 'wizards, witches, astrologers, priests, confidence tricksters and lesbians' and repeatedly threatening to run for office. She was called a new Eva Perón, a presidential harlot and many things far worse. Pictures and montages of a topless Mimi started appearing in the Greek tabloid press, including one that purported to show her in an intimate pose with another naked woman, one of her holding a penis and another of a naked Mimi in church. Financial and political scandals stalked the Papandreous throughout the 1990s, the most embarrassing of which was a $200 million bank embezzlement of which he was later cleared in dubious circumstances. Andreas died, sick and doubtless exhausted, in 1996. He was seventy-seven.

Herodotus might have considered Mimi, who went on to have a short-lived career as a chat-show hostess, both his saviour and his nemesis.

❦

Sex aside, some of the places, for instance the battle sites of Plataea, Salamis, Mycale and Thermopylae, are straightforward. Delphi, Olympia, Samos and Sparta likewise. Herodotus and I have made the foray to Plataea, beginning with the end, as it were, traipsing across brown corduroy fields, clambering over rocks among shepherds and their flocks on the site of the battle that in 479 put paid to Xerxes' plans to conquer Greece. We have made the obligatory pilgrimage to Thermopylae, headed into the dark-shadowed Asopos Gorge and retraced the secret Anopaia Path across the hills, the route made infamous by the Greek traitor Ephialtes. Herodotus tells us that Ephialtes indicated the route to Xerxes 'in hope of a rich reward' and provides a mine of detail about the topography of Thermopylae, which has enabled historians ever after to gain a clear understanding of how one of the world's most important battles was fought.

We have clambered up the mound – 'the little hill at the entrance to the pass' – where the 300 Spartans made their last stand and saluted the roadside statue of a spear-brandishing Leonidas above the legend

ΜΟΛΩΝ ΛΑΒΕ, MOLON LABE, come and take them. We have paid our respects at the statue of Eros honouring the 700 Thespian dead, who are otherwise airbrushed out of the Thermopylae story, though not as ruthlessly as the 400 Thebans, who don't even get a statue. We have even been for a dip in the sulphurous hot-water springs that give the place its name.

In Athens I've taken Herodotus for a walk up and down the street named after him. He's flattered to find himself in Kolonaki, rubbing shoulders – streetwise – with Plutarch, Pindar, Solon, Cleomenes and Heraclitus, which is no more than he deserves. Herodotus Street is home to Enny di Monaco, one of the most expensive boutiques in Athens, a bank, a maritime corporation, hair salon, gourmet cheese shop, preppy men's outfitters, art gallery, elegant jewellers, an S. T. Dupont outlet, cosmetics shop, furniture store and Italian ice-cream seller. Having come this far, I feel duty-bound to ask Greeks on Herodotus Street what they think of the great man. 'He was a great writer,' says a security guard standing outside Dioryx Maritime Corporation. 'I'm very proud of him. I don't know the details, but he was a fine historian.'

So with Athens nearing its Herodotean end, we're ready for the north. Thrace is about as far away from the capital as you can get in Greece, tucked away like an afterthought in the little-visited north-eastern corner of the country. Xanthi and Komotini are so far east they're not even included on my map. It is a hike, to say the least, but who am I to complain? Herodotus scoured the known world for his stories, sailed to the ends of the earth (almost) to research his work of a lifetime. He wouldn't have let little logistical details like that get in the way. He'd have been booking the next boat, donkey, horse, mule, ox-cart – perhaps the occasional chariot if he was feeling flush – and getting on with it.

So far I have been travelling on the writer's miserly budget, keeping expenses down in the Spartan simplicity of the British School in Athens. Herodotus would have been travelling in greater style, I feel, indulging in more luxury. I owe him some glamour. As Voltaire observed, 'The luxury of Athens formed great men of every description.'

All this is an excuse for breaking the journey north at the heinously expensive Imaret (from the Turkish for 'pilgrims' hostel') in the port town of Kavala, one of the world's most inspired conversions of historical properties in recent years. The former *madrassah* (religious school) complex belonging to Mohammed Ali Pasha, founder of the modern Egyptian state, is more monument and museum than hotel. Built in 1817 by Kavala-born Mohammed Ali, it was once a school, *hammam*, offices, prayer hall and soup-kitchen. Strictly speaking it is a digression, but a journey without digressions is not worth making and few writers have been as digressive as Herodotus.

I arrive late one night beneath a loose black sky lazily folded into the sea. Orion is askew tonight, knocked off balance by his celestial hunting dogs. The town is stacked up like a theatre on the slopes of Mount Simvolon overlooking the port. Battalions of whitewashed houses and trees form a defensive barricade around the shore. The Imaret stretches out in the lower reaches of this theatre like a serene fortress in thrall to the Turkish–Venetian citadel whose crenellated walls graze the skyline far above.

If the Imaret is a museum, its curator is the formidable Anna Missirian, an elegant Egyptophile with deep pockets (the restoration cost 7 million euros) and no time for nonsense. She is a handsome middle-aged woman with the effortlessly bored demeanour of the super-rich. Diamonds the size of pearls only add to her allure. Light sparkles from her at every angle: flashing rocks jostle for space on her fingers, forests of silver chains are draped around her neck, and diamond clusters drip from her ears. She is something of a jewel.

We chat over several glasses of whisky and endless volleys of cigarettes, all the while Missirian keeping a gimlet eye trained on her guests for any signs of indecorum. Tales abound of plutocratic visitors sent packing for failing to show due reverence to her monument. The *madrassah* students' cells have been exquisitely restored into seductively lit rooms of Oriental charm and comfort in courtyards lined with orange trees, stone arches and fountains. It is hard to imagine amid all this refinement, but only a few years ago the Imaret was a rotting hulk on the hillside of Panagia, abandoned by the Egyptian government that owned it.

'The Imaret isn't a hotel,' she says with a hint of warning. 'It's a monument. And everyone who comes here has got to remember that and treat it with respect.' She has no qualms about expelling guests. An upmarket, Greek Basil Fawlty, she once threw out a vastly rich Russian who made repeated complaints about the service and then compounded his errors by opening his door with a determined erection to the fore, much to the shock, if not the awe, of the chambermaid. As if this was not enough, he then threw a plate at the poor woman. He was ejected in half-naked ignominy minutes later (another example of hubris leading to nemesis, you could say).

Missirian, a tobacco-magnate-cum-hotelier of Olympian wealth, is also a devout Herodotean. 'Oh, I loooovve him!' she purrs, ordering another pair of malt whiskies and lighting a cigarette. 'Herodotus is the world's first cosmopolitan.' After three hours on a bus gliding through the dark wilderness of eastern Macedonia and Thrace, rumbling catatonically past neon-lit urban wastelands, the whisky has gone to my head like a tracer-bullet and this bejewelled plutocrat's interest in Herodotus is startling, to say the least. But perhaps it shouldn't be, given her love of Egypt. It was Herodotus, after all, who first unlocked the doors to Greece's antique neighbour.

A waitress brings two whiskies and deposits plates crowded with foie gras on toast, smoked-salmon blinis and dainty club sandwiches. Hurrah for luxury! I have done the Spartan thing in Athens long enough, it is time to wallow in speculative Herodotean splendour. Even the light is extravagant here, with bright chandeliers and candle-light glittering in an array of brilliant crystal and lustrous diamonds. I sit back whisky-dazed and gem-bedazzled listening to Missirian pouring forth on Greek and Turkish identity. Herodotus has set her ablaze.

'I believe in cosmopolitanism!' she declaims grandly. 'I see myself as a descendant of both the Byzantine and Ottoman empires. I see myself as part of a crescent moon arcing from Kavala to Constantinople to Cairo, not from Kavala to Athens. It's ridiculous that Turkey ends and Greece begins at Alexandroupoli. The north is rich in both Byzantine and Ottoman history. Herodotus would have understood all this. The notion of pure Greek blood is rubbish. Think about it. We've had the Crusaders, the Slavs, the Ottomans coming in, of course we're a mixed race. Greeks are completely stupid to think they are related to the ancient Greeks. I'd love to be Pericles' cousin, but it's just not true. Who are the Greeks? Greece never even became a nation until the middle of the nineteenth century. Until then it was just an idea based on culture and ancient history.'

She leans forward conspiratorially. Diamonds twinkle. Her voice lowers to a nicotine-laced whisper. 'People exaggerate the differences between Greeks and Turks. Even Mehmed the Conqueror was quite Greek in culture, you know, but Greeks don't like to admit this.' She sighs at the stupidity of her fellow countrymen, drains her whisky and looks at me sadly. 'He was even fluent in Greek.'

In an effort to build bridges between Arab and Western cultures (an expression which recalls Xerxes building his bridge across the Hellespont not so much to admire Greek culture as to destroy it), Missirian founded the Institute of Mohammed Ali. It is dedicated to researching what she calls 'Eastern traditions', playing host to Egyptian academics and organising cultural events. A celebration of the life of the Greek poet Constantine Cavafy, a native of Alexandria, is planned with the Biblioteca Alexandrina. Greek governments, she says, have mishandled the Turkish-minority issue in Thrace until recently, making the people feel like Turkish rather than Greek Muslims. 'You must talk to the Turkish consulate in Komotini and the Greek consulate in Xanthi about this. Now let's have another whisky. I think you'll have another, won't you?' I will.

She remembers reading Herodotus when she was an eighteen-year-old girl sitting by the Nile, totally absorbed in her surroundings, watching cats, mosquitoes and the palm trees and plants along the riverbanks. 'I thought, my God, Herodotus got it completely right! He was so clever in what he wrote about Egypt, how he described it, so accurate about the nature and wildlife, the people and the places. You know, he appreciated Egyptian culture so much. Since that time I've been more interested in Egypt than anywhere else in the world. Oh, I just loooooove Herodotus!'

I have had my fill of Herodotus for the day, primarily because I have had my fill of fine malt whisky and Virginia tobacco. The elegant bar is swaying before me, in time with Missirian's talismanic diamond earrings and the alternately rising and dipping, dripping cut-glass chandeliers. I seem to have been surveying this scene through the bottom of a crystal tumbler all evening, but it is quickening now. Curtains billow around the windows like phantoms. The Oriental rugs on the wooden floor are taking on a life of their own, rolling up, up and away, borne aloft on a magic-carpet zephyr that picks up my floating body and carries it off into the swimming night. My limbs are alternately weightless skimming across this star-filled sky and drowsily heavy inside the revolving bar. The crackling fire is spitting sparks, Missirian is talking away a dime to the dozen but I can't make any of it out now, she's spinning away into a spiral of Egypt and Turkey, candlelight and Cafavy, golden Greece, Orphean mysteries, Alexandria and diamonds and somewhere out there, lost in this seething mael-strom, Herodotus is telling me it is time to go to bed.

---

What did he get up to in his spare time? Did he have late nights, carous-ing into the early hours with fellow travellers, clinking wine-filled mugs with merchants waiting for the next boat across the turquoise waters? I think he did. He would have been the finest drinking com-panion imaginable. Did he wake up with a thick head from time to time, ruing his overindulgence the night before and swearing he would never touch the damned grape again? How did he treat his hangovers? A spoonful of honey and a bite of lemon? What did he eat for breakfast on the move, how did he live? If only we knew. If only there was a bit more to go on. But history has swallowed up the answers so we can only imagine. The potted biography we can piece together is woefully incomplete. Dionysios of Halicarnassus, Hermogenes of Tarsus, Photius the Patriarch of Constantinople, Diodorus Siculus, Aulus Gellius and the Byzantine lexicon the *Suda*, all are impenetrably silent on the human details of Herodotus' life.

I am wondering about this – Herodotus' hangovers and breakfasts – this morning because my head is throbbing, my brain has turned to glue and I'm transfixed by the sight of a soft-boiled egg sitting in front of me resplendent in a starched linen hat. Fortnum & Mason teas whichever way you look. Hand-Picked First-Flush Darjeeling. The winding blue, green and gold florals of Haviland Impératrice Eugénie china. A cleaner in impeccable period linens and matching bonnet is waxing the floor. A muffled sheen works its way across the surface, sending forth a soothingly sweet, woody perfume that lingers in the air. Outside, gulls float across the windows like bright motes, drifting lazily in and out of the skyline. Some pause to sit – and shit – on the forest of Imaret chimneys sprouting from the many-domed roof shrouded in lead flashing, surveying the scene with glassy eyes. Behind the grey cashmere sea the tip of the harbour mole is just visible as a red-and-white barber-pole. Fishing boats bob in the ruffled harbour and wind whips through palm trees on the corniche. A gleaming white crucifix stands defiantly atop the mountain, divine protection for the cascading town below.

Before heading off to tackle Greek and Turkish officialdom further east, I wander slowly around this Egyptian–Greek mosque–*madrassah*–soup-kitchen–hotel, given to the town of Kavala by Mohammed Ali before Greece even existed. Generations of devoted buttocks have worn smooth grooves into the square stone seats on which the faithful sat and performed their pre-prayer ablutions around a semi-circular congregation of taps. The cavernous, broad-domed edifice which was once the mosque is now a chic library housing Missirian's designer mezzanine office. The chessboard is a clash of civilisations, a religious battlefield on which rival armies of red-crossed Crusaders and tur-baned Saracens – with their discreetly veiled queen – vie for victory. Lozenges in the old mosque's ochre dome proclaim the supremacy of Allah and Mohammed, veneration for the caliphs Amr and Ali. The hammered brass crescent that once adorned the roof lies on the stone floor, displaced by a twinkling icon of the Virgin Mary and Christ sitting triumphantly on an office shelf.

The road east of Kavala is an exercise in desolation this morning. Trembling in the wan winter sunlight, the landscape has had a collective nervous breakdown. Worn out by all these wars and treaties, the ethnic questions and endless disputes over identity and nationality, it collapses into the bleak, mist-mired horizontality of the Low Countries. Gaunt trees shiver in tightly marshalled little copses. Only as we near the town of Xanthi, driving alongside the Nestos river, does the landscape perk up to the point of offering a backdrop of fir-clad mountains to raise the spirits. Mosque minarets and church crosses joust for supremacy – or perhaps they coexist quite happily – in the fringe of villages tumbling down from the valleys towards the local capital.

The director of Xanthi's Ministry of Foreign Affairs bureau is an urbane diplomat wearing a buttoned-up black shirt in fine wool, a blue blazer and grey flannels. Elegant European football manager meets silver-haired professor and citizen of the world. He smiles when he discusses the 'games of identification' played in Greece's north-eastern region. The 'Turkish minority' is no such thing. Instead, he talks breezily of the 'Muslim minority'. The government wants to help them integrate, not assimilate, into Greek society, so that they can learn their own language, practise their own religion and learn enough Greek to circulate in Greek society as citizens with all their rights. The Turks, however, are bent on exporting their 'nation-building tendencies' to Muslim minorities not just in Greece but also in Bulgaria, Romania and Skopje (the Greek government objects to the republic's use of the name Macedonia).

In the past, the Greek government pursued a counterproductive communitarian policy, he argues, keeping the minority out of main-stream society and damaging the economic and cultural development of Thrace. Then, in 1991, Athens suddenly saw the error of its ways and changed tack, reaffirming the principle of *isonomia* – equality before the law (the very word used by Otanes in the *Histories* when urging his fellow Persian conspirators to choose popular govern-ment) – and *isopoliteia*, equality of civil rights.

The Greek and Turkish governments disagree on two specific issues. First, what he calls 'the mufti game'. Greece reserves the right to appoint religious leaders for the Muslim minority. There are two 'official' muftis. However, the minority wants to choose its own clerics, so has elected two other muftis from within 'a very narrow constitu-ency'. Second, minority education. The minority would like to see more minority schools. Athens would like fewer. There are regular squabbles over the curriculum, religious education, textbooks and so on.

The diplomat's eyes twinkle. 'We'll manage with these small games. It's not big stuff. Our partners in the EU understand our problems with

Cyprus, the Aegean and the Greek minority in Constantinople [though he admits no corresponding Turkish minority in Greece], the seizure of Greek lands and properties and so on. But we believe in the future of Greek–Turkish relations. They must relax a bit. They feel offended, not just by Greeks, but by Europe and the West in general.'

On my way out, he stops in front of his bookcase and pulls out a Turkish edition of Herodotus, smoothly telling me what an excellent translation it is. Then, after presenting me with a handsome book on local architecture, he takes out another volume. The cover shows a shattered street scene, shop windows smashed in, bewildered shop-keepers sitting amid piles of rubble and pedestrians gingerly picking their way through the carnage. *Mechanisms of Catastrophe: The Turkish Pogrom of September 6–7, 1955, and the Destruction of the Greek Community in Istanbul.*

Twenty-five miles to the east, the Turkish Consulate-General is a fort-ress of high walls, security fences, closed-circuit television cameras and a heavily armed guard force. I haven't seen so many pistols since I was living in Baghdad. My guidebook says Komotini is a shining example of Greeks and Turks living together. Crescent and cross throng the skyline.

The vice-consul, a serious young man in a black suit, striped tie and rimless specs, seems less sanguine – certainly less relaxed – than his Greek counterpart. He accuses Athens of denying the ethnic identity of the Turkish minority. 'The Greek position is that there is no Turkish minority in Thrace,' he begins. Although this is strictly correct under the provisions of the Treaty of Lausanne in 1923, which among other things governed the exchange of populations between Greece and Turkey and refers to a Muslim – rather than Turkish – minority, Turkey sees no reason why those who consider themselves Turkish should not call themselves a Turkish minority.

I grip the chair leg tightly. This is going to be a long haul, especially with a hangover. I'm already sweating. Perhaps it was a mistake to call on the Greek Ministry of Foreign Affairs and the Turkish Consulate-General on the same morning.

Next, there is an ongoing problem of freedom of association for the Turkish minority. In 1984, the government closed down the Turkish Union of Xanthi and the Turkish Youth Association of Komotini, both established in the 1920s, because it objected to the use of 'Turkish' in the title. Ankara's official policy is that there is only one minority in Thrace and it's Turkish. Athens acknowledges Pomaks and Romanies within the Muslim minority but no Turks.

'So who are the others, then, those who aren't Pomaks or Romanies? This community has lived here for 800 years. They came here in the thirteenth century, before the Ottomans, and lived here under the Ottoman empire, for a long time as a majority. In 1923, around 75 per cent of the population was Turkish, now it's fifty–fifty. They see themselves as different, due to the proximity to Turkey, due to religion and language, and because Greeks and Turks have waged war against each other.'

The list of grievances and points of contention between Athens and Ankara rumbles on. Denial of citizenship, disagreements over muftis and the administration of *waqf* Islamic foundations, the lack of minority schools, arguments over whether they should be called Turkish Minority Schools or Muslim Minority Schools, grumbling compromises to call them Minority Schools. He says it's impossible to elect an independent MP from within the Turkish minority under Greek law. The minority population is too small to meet the 3 per cent national support required for a candidate's election.

Despite all these difficulties, despite the wrangling intransigence between the old adversaries, the vice-consul – like his Greek counterpart – remains optimistic about the future of bilateral relations. Diplomats are professional optimists. Relations are better than they have been in the past. The vice-consul's Greek colleague recently paid a visit to Komotini and though they disagreed on almost everything, they agreed that dialogue was the way forward.

There is something terribly formulaic – occasionally spirit-sapping – about all this officialspeak, but if that's what's required to keep the peace between these historically hostile antagonists, it's a small price to pay. The heartfelt disagreements about muftis and minority schools are profoundly important to the two communities, but they are no more than petty quarrels when you consider the history of these two peoples and nations at war. In Marianna Koromila's dusty edition of the *Histories*, the translator drew a dark parallel between ancient Greece's traumatic relations with Persia and the young nation's hostile relationship with the Ottoman empire. They were 'virtually the same', he argued, writing amid the desperate turbulence of 1836.

And yet we have come a long way from the battlefields of Marathon and Missolonghi. We have, for now at least, said farewell to these deadly confrontations. None of this means that man's boundless capacity for war will not suddenly re-emerge between Greeks and Turks amid the high passes of Thrace or the sun-kissed waters and cerulean skies of the Aegean. For the time being we will leave the Greek and Turkish diplomats in their more or less cordial antagonism and simply observe that peace prevails.

We must leave because Herodotus is calling us several hundred miles away. Something historically irresistible is happening in the Balkans.

# Thessaloniki: History on the Front Line

*Happy is the country which has no history.*

Attributed to Montesquieu

Nenad Sebek is sitting in his office eyrie, high on a hill in the old quarter of Thessaloniki, holding forth on an extraordinary new history. He is director of the Centre for Democracy and Reconciliation in South-east Europe, an organisation with a mission that sounds challenging, to say the least. Perhaps this is why he smokes with such a controlled intensity, lighting cigarettes back to back in neat, practised movements as though only through a constant intake of tobacco can peace and prosperity be brought to this feuding corner of the continent. The ashtray is fighting a desperate battle, over-whelmed by the frontal assault of stubs. His office sits on the first floor of one of the freshly restored old Turkish houses tucked away among the spider-web streets of labyrinthine Ano Polis, the Upper City, separated and protected from the downtown bustle by the massive ramparts erected by Emperor Theodosius in 390. It is smart for an NGO, with high ceilings, wooden flooring and black-and-white portraits of needy people, just the right side of elegant without being over the top. Sebek's style, like that of his office, is NGO chic, a brown suede waistcoat thrown over a checked shirt and a pair of dark jeans. A pair of glasses magnifies an animated pair of almond eyes beneath an ordered nest of dark hair. An atmosphere of brisk sincerity hovers in the room. It is noon and he has a five o'clock shadow.

I have made this pilgrimage, this Herodotean digression, to Thessaloniki to discover how Herodotus' invention – the study of the past – is being used to shape the contours of the future. The ambition of this brave new history in the Balkans is genuinely startling and would appeal to our enlightened Greek. It is to wrest peace and understanding from conflict and antagonism.

On my overnight journey on a rusting hulk of a ferry, I have been dogged by a sense of guilt for having booked a berth in a cabin, shortly after reading the story of an eighty-three-year-old Patrick Leigh Fermor (whom Herodotus and I dearly hope to drop in on at his home in the Peloponnese) taking an overnight boat from Crete to Athens and only paying for a chair on deck, content with Jane Austen and a bottle of red wine for al fresco company. Another voice says, to hell with it, Herodotus travelled like an aristocrat and it's too cold for such heroics.

A journey by sea offers the chance to dwell on our itinerant historian as he pursues his world-changing quest across these waters. I stare down from the deck at a blue sea billowing like a roaring blanket alongside the hull. Three distinct layers of patterns on the water fan out from the ferry: white marble gives way to petticoat frills that widen in turn into placid troughs and gentle valleys. Further off, silver-white sunlight burns off the divide between sun and sky so that gulls swim effortlessly through the waters while above them fishing boats glide gracefully across the heavens.

I wonder how Herodotus dealt with the banality – never mind the romance – of travel. How did he cope with language barriers? Did he ever have financial worries? Was he trading along the way? How did he occupy himself waiting for the next boat, who did he speak to on board? Did he mix with the hoi-polloi or was he secreted away from the illiterate masses in luxurious seclusion? Was he travelling with friends or family or were his the solo footsteps of the pioneer? Did his heart ache, just like ours, during long journeys into strange lands? Had he left a wife and children behind? Herodotean travels oscillate regularly between the sadness and serendipity of solitude.

'Herodotus, hey?' Sebek begins. Lips curl around a cigarette into a smile. 'You know, Atatürk said that history writing is as important as historical events. It probably was in Herodotus' time, too. How he wrote about the Persian Wars, how he described Greece's neighbour and enemy, how he preserved all those important events in the *Histories*. It certainly is today in this region with all these old adversaries sharing borders. Serbia–Croatia, Greece–Turkey, Bosnia–Serbia and so on.'

He talks as fluently and passionately as he smokes, outlining an innovative Balkan history amid room-filling clouds of nicotine. The monologue pours forth. Questions and attempted interruptions are brushed away with the impatient flick of an extended cigarette. Sebek's Joint History Project is intended to combat Balkan nationalism in the region's school history books. It offers an alternative version of the past, a more balanced portrayal, shorn of ethnocentric stereotypes and nationalist ideology, of the seven centuries from the emergence of the Ottoman empire to the cataclysm of the Second World War.

It is history on the front line. Herodotus unbound. Taken out of the classroom and thrown on to the political stage. A story of how history can foment discord and wars, sharpen divisions, demonise neighbours, how it can increase understanding and tolerance, help promote peace and reconciliation. For once, it is history as an active force, with a message and a moral voice. Passionately dispassionate.

Thessaloniki, or Salonica, as the city is known more romantically, is not strictly on our Herodotean itinerary. It was only founded a century after his death, in 315 BC, when the future King Cassander of Macedon named it after his wife the Princess Thessalonica, a half-sister of Alexander the Great. But we wander in his spirit, not just his slipstream. I can't see Herodotus passing on the opportunity to witness history in the making.

The Centre's first step into history was the Joint History Project. Before introducing new textbooks, it kicked off with a study of how the subject was taught. The result was *Clio in the Balkans*, a 550-page whopper, the only comparative study of history teaching in the Balkans. 'Everyone here teaches history from an ethnocentric perspective,' Sebek says. 'We are good, everyone else is shit. We are the victims, all the others are aggressors. *Clio* shows how history has been abused, how it depicts Us versus Them, Our Country Right or Wrong.'

*Clio* is impressively wide-ranging. It surveys Islamic religious education in Bosnia, 'Otherness in the Turkish Historical Discourse', Tyranny and Despotism in Greek Historiography, the presentation of Europe in Former Yugoslav Republic history books, multi-ethnic empires and national rivalry in those of Bulgaria, and so it goes on.

There are painstaking studies of how Greece and Turkey teach the disputed history of Cyprus. Turkish Cypriots wallow in the martyrdom of victim–heroes killed by 'murderous' Greeks. Greek schoolbooks indoctrinate students with the 'Hellenism' of Cyprus, deploring the Turkish 'massacres' of Venetians in Nicosia and Famagusta during the Ottoman conquest of the island in 1570–1 and the more recent desecration of Christian cemeteries by Turkish soldiers. There is an unconsciously Herodotean echo in the slogan used by both sides: 'I won't forget.'

Broadly speaking, according to *Clio*, the rewriting of history in Yugoslavia since 1989 has seen the suppression of those themes and forces that once unified its peoples and a fresh emphasis on those that divide them. Conflicts between them in the present are presented as unchanging throughout the past so that wars and separation are inevitable, what Christina Koulouri, series editor of the new textbooks, calls the 'logic of dissolution'.

The study includes a forensic examination of the Serb vilification of Croats and the Croat denigration of 'greater-Serb hegemonism'. Serbian histories proudly depict the Serbs as the most vigorous fighters of fascism during the Second World War. The Ustasha are 'extreme nationalists, chauvinists and racists'. Half a century later, a Serbian historian lays the blame for the break-up of Yugoslavia squarely at the door of the Vatican and its old bugbear Croatia. Present difficulties are explained through past injustices, lodged deep in the historical memory so that national history becomes no more than a badge of victimhood.

Croatian historians, in turn, sink their knives into the war-ravaged corpse of Serb nationalism, dismissing the first Yugoslavia as an exercise in Croat-crushing and greater-Serb belligerence. Ustasha atrocities pale into insignificance when compared with the vicious brutality of the Serbian Chetniks. Moving into the Nineties, Croatian historians have little doubt who bears responsibility for the wars in Yugoslavia. 'Driven by the hate towards everything Croatian and Catholic, the great-Serb aggressors have tortured, killed, slaughtered and chased Croatians and other non-Serbs,' writes one.

The pages of our muse *Clio* run with crude stereotyping and hatred. In secular Turkey, history books stress the Muslim identity of Turks while presenting Christendom as essentially hostile. The words 'Crusader', 'Christian' and 'European' are used interchangeably throughout. Special opprobrium, of course, is reserved for the Greeks, who are accused of calling their neighbours 'barbarians', just as Herodotus referred to the Persians in the first sentence of the *Histories*, when many among his Greek audiences would have understood the word as meaning genuinely barbarous and barbaric. Coverage of the 1919–22 Greco-Turkish War – known here as the Turkish Liberation War – quickly descends to sarcasm and satire:

> The Greek soldiers showed that they were wonderful runners. Hoping to save their own lives, they ran so fast that even our cavalry could not catch them. A coward is dangerous. While fleeing, the Greek units burned the villages and towns where they passed through. They pierced even defenseless persons with their bayonets. The Greeks, always and everywhere, describe the Turks as Barbarians. When they launched soldiers to Anatolia, they said: 'We are providing civilisation to the Turkish Barbars.' But, when they left our beautiful Anatolia, they spread blood and tears, they left behind them pierced corpses of babies and women, and ruins and ruins . . . This is the Greek conception of humanism and civilisation.

Greek history books emphasise a serene cultural continuity from ancient Greek civilisation to the present day, underlining the nation's ancestry as founder of the civilised West and highlighting its European identity at the expense of the Balkan. They largely exclude any positive Ottoman contribution from the fall of Constantinople in 1453. Byzantine glory is allowed to continue only in the teeth of 'slavery' and repression under the aggressive and uncivilised Turks. Ottoman rule is 'Ottoman tyranny', four centuries of untold suffering under barbarian 'despots', 'tyrants' and 'warlike Turks'.

History here is cultural and intellectual terrain, fought over by rival armies of tweedy professors, education ministries and bureaucrats with the same blinkered tenacity and aggression the armies of these fractious nation-states so recently paraded on the battlefield. History is war, religion and contested identity.

So what to do about this melting pot of antagonistic, nationalist histories stirring up ideological soup for future conflicts? Replacing them isn't an option. It's a political impossibility. 'National history is something people are very touchy about,' Sebek says, chain-smoking away and talking a mile a minute. 'Nationalism and ethnicity remain extremely deeply rooted here.' The lobes of his ears rise and fall like empires. 'If you think France, Britain or America are any different you're wrong. I went through the British education system and it was incredibly Anglocentric.'

Sebek's organisation, in recognition of these sensitivities, offers four new textbooks as an alternative history syllabus, to be used as supplementary texts in the classroom, taught alongside the more traditional, nationalist histories in those countries that wish to participate. To Sebek's surprise, the Serbian government was the first to support the project. Editions have been published in the Serbian, Greek and English languages, to be followed by versions in Albanian, Bosnian, Croatian and Macedonian. Funding has come from the US, Germany and the Stability Pact for South-eastern Europe. The four volumes in the series cover the Ottoman Empire, Nations and States in South-east Europe, the Balkan Wars and the Second World War. They are intended primarily for fifteen- to eighteen-year-old secondary school students.

'When I learnt history at school, I was just taught this is what happened, these are the facts. That was it. In these textbooks we give original sources and provide multiple perspectives. For example, in 1912 the Serbs marched into Kosovo. Was that occupation or liberation? We give both versions. We say, this is what the people wrote at the time. You have the grey matter. Figure it out. We don't give conclusions.'

Once the final text is agreed, nothing can be removed from future editions but an extra paragraph is allowed on a particular subject if it is considered extremely sensitive. It's history as an ongoing dialogue, not a final verdict. Thus in the Serb edition extra material has been added on the controversial Croatian Cardinal Alojsije Stepinac. 'Most Croats consider him a martyr,' says Sebek. 'He was jailed by communists, died in prison and was later beatified by Pope John Paul II. Most Serbs consider him a murderer, Croats think he's a saint. Serbs see him as a war criminal because he did nothing to stop the massacres in the concentration camps. So in the Serb edition there is an extra paragraph which says, okay, these are the Croat sources, these are the Serb sources. Both views are presented.'

In fact, the Second World War proved the most contentious subject for the historians involved in the project. 'That war probably gave us more headaches than anything else because first, it was more recent, and second, the Serb-versus-Croat thing today is basically a continuation of the Second World War. The Serbs teach that in Croatian concentration camps it was official policy to kill a third, convert a third, and expel the rest. The Serbs believe 700,000 were killed in Jasenovac, mostly Serbs. The Croats admit to 30,000. How can you reconcile 700,000 with 30,000? The answer is you can't.'

The volume on the Ottoman Empire proved relatively smooth, something of a surprise given the traditionally controversial, fiercely contested historical ground. 'Turkish history says the Ottoman Empire was incredibly enlightened, a heaven of religious tolerance, a golden age for the Balkans – basically, you lot were lucky to have us. According to Greek history books, it was 5 centuries of rape, slavery and butchery. We've moved away from all that. In our Ottoman Empire workbook, for example, we've got a Turkish historian talking openly about the Armenian massacres.'

Sebek, a microcosm of the Balkans' identity crisis, combines Serbian and Croatian blood with British citizenship. The multicultural spirit is also reflected in the assorted nationalities of his staff, who come from Bosnia, Macedonia, Germany, Greece, Ireland, the US and the UK. He says it was 'a minor miracle' to get the sixty historians from eleven countries to agree on the material for the four history volumes. This in itself is a historical-cum-diplomatic triumph. There is little more contentious in life than having one's history edited and rewritten by scholars from other – historically hostile – countries.

He lights another cigarette, summons his German assistant and asks her to fetch the quartet of books.

———

Herodotus would have a lot to take on board – apart from two-and-a-half millennia of history to catch up on – if he flicked through one of the workbooks. This is an intensely political concept of history. And yet some of its messages might have appealed to the man whose history calls, elegantly and explicitly, for greater understanding between rival nations and cultures.

Its stated aims are to change the teaching of history by rejecting nationalist history, presenting differences and conflicts openly instead of painting 'a false picture of harmony', encouraging children to develop identities beyond 'the boundaries of political geography', stimulating critical thought by presenting different versions and interpretations of the same event, and promoting an ability to evaluate human acts and make moral judgements. It seeks 'to mould responsible citizens with moral values, able to resist any attempt to manipulate them'.

The new, morally charged history can be a lot of fun. Storytelling reigns triumphant. There are Croatian soldiers writing about lice in their underwear, the Greek Nobel laureate Odysseas Elytis describing life on the Albanian front, poems about the ideal qualities of the Ottoman sultan ('Let him give up drinking'), children playing war games, Muslim men divorcing Christian women, Russian propaganda, Greek famines, Turkish earthquakes, Romanian plagues, Bosnian blood-brotherhood, national anthems, newspaper front covers and reports, royal decrees, sporting contests, patriotic flag-waving, suffering animals at war, doctors' battlefield reports, outbreaks of cholera, nursing anecdotes, Red Cross missions, the burning of villages and the flight of refugees, excerpts from memoirs, letters from husbands to wives and from sons to mothers, eyewitness reports, such as Fitzroy Maclean's portrait of Tito, music and dancing, tavern songs, religious rites and regulations, papal correspondence, apprentice contracts, agriculture and spinning mills, charters of the guilds of grocers and soapmakers, the treatment of prisoners, executions, picaresque tales of travelling by camel on the *haj* to Mecca, cartoons, maps, manifestos, posters, searching questions to test the imagination as much as the intellect – the range is extraordinary. In fact, it is positively Herodotean in its freewheeling move beyond the narrowly political and constitutional history first conceived by Thucydides.

Students are left in no doubt about the undesirability of war and the 'universality of human suffering' it entails. Sometimes the human tragedies are so wrenching, the brutality of war so sickening, the misery so pervasive, you feel like slitting your wrists. This is peacenik history for a post-war generation.

Inspiring stories are scattered throughout the text to 'insert a glimpse of optimism' into the darkness of war and illustrate humanity surviving in even the most difficult conditions. We find 'sport as a way of overcoming nationalism', in which Greek Cypriots support a Turkish Cypriot football team on the brink of relegation, a moment of battlefield solidarity between the Ustasha and communist Partisans, the rescue of Jewish Turks by a Turkish diplomat in Marseilles, a touching act of generosity from Romanian soldiers to Russian prisoners of war. In 1913, an observer spots a Serb soldier sharing his meagre rations with Turkish children dying from famine. 'Have you read about any humanitarian acts carried out by the "opposite side" in your textbooks?' the new history book asks. 'Do you believe that such acts of compassion are possible in times of war?' And then, before we get too swept away by these currents of idealism, 'Do you think that this is a real situation or could it be a propaganda story?'

Herodotus would be thrilled to discover there's even space for sex. In the Ottoman Empire volume there's a delicious extract about adultery from the magnificently entitled *Adventures of Baron Wenceslas Wratislaw of Mitrowitz: What He Saw in the Turkish Metropolis, Constantinople, Experienced in His Captivity, and after His Happy Return to His Country, Committed to Writing in the Year of Our Lord 1599*. 'What was the author's attitude towards the adultery?' the book asks the spotty teenagers. The story could have come straight out of the *Histories*.

It is impossible for me to avoid narrating the story of a Turkish lady who had an affair with our janissary Mustafa. She was young and her face was quite pretty. Mustafa invited her for entertainment one afternoon and I supplied him with candies and the best wine . . . That lady had a very old husband, who had little confidence in her. She did not know how otherwise to reach the place of assignation in good time, that is at the agreed moment just before sunset (our sergeant usually went out for his prayers at this time). So she told her husband she was going to the bath. She took also her two maid-servants, who carried her clothes, as usual, in big tubs made of copper covered with carpets, and who were walking just behind her and passing in front of our building. The beautiful women's public bath was not far away, Ruka – the wife of the Turkish Sultan – had the bath built and entry was forbidden to men on penalty of death. The lady, while she was walking and passing by our building, notified the janissary that she would come to the assignation. The distrustful husband was walking just a little behind her and when she entered in the public bath he stayed just opposite and waited for her. But who is able to foil the wile of a woman? She passed by our house in a green dress, but in the public bath she changed into other clothes she had brought with her and, leaving her maid-servants there, she came out and met the janissary wearing a red dress. He welcomed her and greeted her in his apartment, he entertained her excellently and after the dinner, he let her go out again from the back door. She went to the public bath for a second time, washed and went back to her house with her husband. I cannot admire the wile of that woman to the degree it deserves, and many times I and the janissary used to laugh when we recalled it.

It beats the history I learnt at school.

Reactions to this ambitious history project have, predictably, differed wildly. Sebek has received 'tons and tons of compliments'. Universities in America, Germany and Japan are already using the books. 'At the same time we've been crucified.' A flash-of-teeth smile sparkles through the fug. Another cigarette flies into a pair of pursed lips. The most vociferous criticism has come not from Serbia, Croatia or Turkey, he says, but from within Greece. 'The best attack we've had is that we are a "Soros-inspired Anglo-American Zionist conspiracy to reinstate the Ottoman empire in the Balkans."'

Critics never engage directly with the content of the history books, he says, never point out any factual inaccuracies. They rely instead on name-calling, branding the project a 'this or that conspiracy'. 'We knew we'd be a finger in the eye for every ethnocentric historian in the region. We knew we couldn't survive if someone said, look, on page 57 you got this wrong or you made a mistake on page 33 or something. We had to get everything right.' Sebek says it's too early to judge the success of this regional history programme. The new history has to bed in. 'We need to be present in schools for at least ten years to have an effective impact on people's mentality. It's a long-term process.'

Sebek was a journalist for twenty-seven years before he entered the NGO world. Much of his career was with Radio Belgrade and the BBC World Service. As a former war correspondent who covered conflicts all over the world, he says he has witnessed firsthand the dangers of history taught irresponsibly. 'This is where you instil into the young a sense of victim mentality, a feeling that everyone around them is their adversary and that's how it's always been. I've seen the destructive elements of history on the front line. I believe history is one of the fields where if you teach it badly you produce serious damage way ahead in the future. If you tell a ten-year-old his country has always been beaten up by its neighbour throughout its history, and then ten years later it's war, he's wearing uniform and he's got a gun in his hands and his leaders are saying, "They're still slaughtering us," this is what he believes and he goes on the rampage. I've seen it happen.'

Sebek has another target in his sights. Now that there is a new regional history from the Ottoman empire to the Second World War, he wants to take the story forward to cover more recent conflicts. He shakes his head, looking down at an ashtray overflowing from his exertions. 'What's being taught now about the wars of the Nineties is graphic porn,' he says. 'We're the good guys and we're innocent, everyone else are guilty bastards. It's immensely damaging and we've got to do something about it.'

For a moment there is silence. Smoke drifts towards the ceiling. The distant groan of a ship's horn filters up from the port. 'Tudjman, Milosevíc, Izetbegovíc, they all played a part in this. I believe this old style of history teaching – which is nationalistic, hateful and wrong – contributed enormously to the savagery of the wars in the Balkans.'

# 12

# An Exorcism

*Human history becomes more and more a race between education and catastrophe.*

H. G. Wells, *The Outline of History* (1920)

IT WAS THE roaring that drew me nearer. One moment I was sitting peacefully in the golden light of Thessaloniki's Basilica of Aghios Dimitrios, the largest church in Greece, admiring the fading wall paintings, mosaics and carved Byzantine eagles, quietly plotting the next stage on the Herodotus trail, when suddenly a strange rumbling began, low and barely audible at first, then steadily getting louder and more menacing. Some sort of struggle was taking place: a series of blows, slaps, punches, like the sound of pillows being plumped, followed by gasping, tortured screams. An old woman in widow's weeds praying several rows ahead of me looked up, startled, crossed herself quickly and bowed her head again, anxious to escape the evil of whatever was making the noise.

I got up and walked down the nave, unable to suppress my curiosity. This was not the kind of sound you ever heard in a church. There was nothing musical or serene about it, no solemn chant or heart-lifting chorus. It was dark, violent, demented. A woman strode out of the basilica in a hurry, then another man left. The old woman finished her prayers and left, too. Towards the apse three women were grouped in an apprehensive huddle, faces visibly shocked. One, a doll-like beauty with white face, raven hair and fragile features, wore an elegant fur jacket over spray-on tight jeans and teetering high heels, kitted out for the catwalk rather than the church.

Then another rushing roar and I could see it came from a small booth with glass windows, the sort of small shop you find in cathedrals selling ecclesiastical souvenirs and religious paraphernalia. Lines of icons hung inside, facing out, frosted images of dragon-slaying St George, Christ the Life-giver with burnished halo, the Lamentation at the Tomb with a madly wailing Mary Magdalene, hands thrown towards the heavens over a recumbent Jesus. An elderly, cassocked greybeard sat on a chair. Kneeling in front of him was a slumped figure, head buried in the priest's lap so that all you could see was the outline of his back, rocking back and forth uncontrollably. If it didn't sound so evil, you'd think you were watching a priestly blowjob. Every few moments the old man thumped the figure hard on the back.

Then both figures were still. The priest was panting and out of breath. Candlelight glistened in drops of sweat that dripped down his brow like tears. Beside me, the snooping trio of women were murmuring to each other, ashen-faced. A menacing monologue rose from the booth, a babbling stream of anger and hatred. Suddenly, the priest picked up his Bible and started reciting from it, whacking the figure on the back again and again with his free hand as the scriptural torrent and the hellish ranting raged on. The kneeling man groaned in pain every time he was hit. Suddenly he lunged away from the priest, desperately trying to get away, but the old man clung on, shaking, and only then I noticed that the victim was a woman, not a man. It seemed impossible because no woman, surely, could snarl with a voice of such Stygian depth and darkness. The women next to me were frightened. Voices were raised for an instant and then they hurried away on high heels, click-clacking on echoing stone, and were gone. My heart was thumping against my ribs.

Another unearthly growl started up again. The air felt chill around me. The old priest looked tired and haggard. I had a vision of him locked in a monumental battle between good and evil.

A whisper behind me made me jump. 'It's an exorcism,' said the voice. It was a young, French-speaking priest who introduced himself as Father Athanasios. Rarely has the sight of a black cassock and crucifix brought so much relief. Inside the booth, the woman was writhing around in front of the priest, arms flailing and striking his upper body while the flood of venom poured forth. 'She's possessed by demons,' Father Athanasios said. His tone was matter of fact. He could have been telling me she had a cold.

The wild-animal movements, the guttural snarls, the spitting-rage monologue that was like vomiting speech, were disturbing to watch, but it was impossible to turn away. All that was missing were the vapour trails as the woman spoke. I could almost fancy I saw them. The demonic voice was that of the white-eyed girl Regan strapped to her bed in *The Exorcist*.

'What's she saying?' I asked.

'This is not her speaking, of course,' he corrected me. 'This all comes from the Devil. He controls these demons inside her.'

'What's he saying, then?'

There was another blood-curdling yelp. The old priest whacked the prostrate woman, who was sobbing uncontrollably now. The violence was taking its toll on both of them. In an hour or two purple bruises would be spreading like continents across the woman's back. Father Athanasios listened.

'He's saying how terrible Lazarus smelt when he came out of the tomb. He's saying he has taken this woman, that she belongs to him now.' He winced as the stream-of-demon-consciousness sped on. 'He's insulting Jesus Christ and mocking Father Dimitrios and our religion. He says he'll eat Father's heart, that he's a murderer.' He turned away in disgust. 'It's all evil.'

Inside the booth, Father Dimitrios poured a few drops of holy water on to the woman. Immediately, she was in a frenzy again, hissing and growling, as though scorched by the water. In a film steam would have risen from her back. The elderly priest was mumbling prayers, commanding the devil to leave the woman's body, straining to speak over a voice that came straight from hell. Both of them kept at it, one voice frail yet insistent, the other a subterranean baritone. It was the culmination of the duel and it lasted several minutes.

And then there was a final, ejaculatory howl and the woman collapsed silently to the floor. Calm returned to the amber gloom of the basilica. The priest passed a folded white handkerchief across his brow, head still bowed. He had prevailed but he looked shattered. It was the end of the performance.

The woman rose to her feet, looking stunned, exchanged a few words with Father Dimitrios and marched out quickly, handbag swinging. Still shocked, I asked Father Athanasios who the woman was.

'Oh, she's a doctor,' he said blithely. 'She comes in every Monday.'

# 13

# Lunch (and a Good Deal of Retsina) with
# Patrick Leigh Fermor

*I never thought it would come to this, to my speaking on history. But as concessions to one's age go, a lecture on the subject appears inevitable. An invitation to deliver it suggests not so much the value of the speaker's views as his perceptible moribundity. 'He is history,' goes the disparaging remark, referring to a has-been ...*

Joseph Brodsky, *Profile of Clio* (1991)

FROM ONE END of the country to the other. Eleven hundred miles south by train and car. From the sludgy skies and twisting valleys of Thrace to the sky-cracking chiaroscuro of the Taygetus mountains and the limpid seas of the Peloponnese.

A pause on the other end of the line. A lot is hanging on this. Will he or won't he? Has the journey across the length of Greece to meet a Herodotean hero been in vain? I have turned up in the Outer Mani fishing village of Kardamyli where the great man lives, cunningly holed up in the hotel run by a friend of his to give me the best chance of a meeting. All that's needed now is an invitation.

*All*, an inner voice says – what are you talking about? You're trying to doorstep one of the greatest British heroes of the Second World War, one of the finest writers in the English language, an icon of travel writing who is now in his nineties, who's hard at work trying to finish the elusive third volume of what would be among the greatest trilogies in modern literature, a man who doesn't even know you and has already declined an interview, a knight of the realm who has walked across a continent, secluded himself silently with Trappist monks, fallen in love and run away with a princess, fought for his country, joined a Greek cavalry charge and swum the Hellespont – and you say *all*?

Oh, come off it, says the other voice, don't be so bloody feeble. This is a man who kidnapped a German general on Crete in 1944 and then drove through twenty-two checkpoints impersonating him, evaded capture for eighteen days during an island-wide manhunt before spiriting him on to a boat bound for Cairo – having first bonded, in Latin, over a shared passion for Horace's *Odes*. This is no time for reticence. It's all or nothing.

Who'll break the silence first? I have called to announce my arrival in Kardamyli, already mentioned in a blizzard of correspondence and phone calls on my behalf from mutual friends in Athens. The introductions have been made. There's nothing more to be said.

Then, at last, the words I have been longing for.

'Well, why don't you come for lunch?'

Eureka!

———

It is probably stretching it to call him a Herodotus of our times, but the thought has occurred. When you get the chance to meet the man known to all his English friends as Paddy and to Greeks by his *nom de guerre* Mihali, you drop whatever it is you are doing – in Thrace or otherwise – and beat a path to his door. I can dress it up in any number of ways. I can claim to be pursuing him as a war veteran just as Herodotus interviewed veterans of the Persian Wars; or I can be hoping to speak to him as travel writer to travel writer across the generations; perhaps as cross-cultural philhellene. I could call it another Herodotean digression, I suppose. It doesn't matter. I would do battle with the shapely Sirens, tackle the labours of Hercules, run the gauntlet of Scylla and Charybdis, suffer the throat-parching torments of Tantalus and the muscle-ripping agonies of Sisyphus to meet the venerable Sir Patrick Leigh Fermor.

I have been pestering him in letters from England, requesting some time to discuss his life and travels and Herodotus. Back came a card in scratchy spider ink telling me that unfortunately he would be travelling, Herodotus wasn't really his thing and he was sorry he couldn't help. It took me a while to realise it was probably better not to mention Herodotus in initial contacts with people, especially in Greece, where everyone thinks if you're writing about him you must be an academic and possibly, therefore, a bit weird. He scares people off.

The only option was to seek him out in Kardamyli and give no quarter. Direct action. In the finest tradition of Herodotus. If he ever needed to check out a detail, to speak to someone for certain information, he went off and did it.

There is a lovely passage – one of my favourites in the *Histories* – when he is discussing the worship of Hercules and how in his opinion it was the Greeks who took the name from the Egyptians, not the other way round. So what does he do to investigate his theory? Simple. He takes to the seas, travelling across much of the known world with wonderful nonchalance, downplaying the whole thing as though it was nothing more than a jaunt. 'To satisfy my wish to get the best information I possibly could on this subject, I made a voyage to Tyre in Phoenicia, because I had heard that there was a temple there, of great sanctity, dedicated to Heracles.'

What a traveller!

I turn up late, flustered, flushed and sweating horribly. I have been hiking up to the tiny, mountaintop church of Aghia Sophia, high above the prickly Viros gorge, past the mythical graves of the mythical Dioscouri, the twins Castor and Polydeuces, sons of Zeus and Clytemnestra, immortalised in the constellation of Gemini. It's not every day you get to see the tombs of Zeus' children and I have spent too long admiring these shadow-filled hollows cut into the mountain. Then, after rushing up to the wide-skirted summit and rushing back down again, I couldn't find his house and got lost.

The housekeeper waves me down a vaulted stone gallery, cool air ruffling through the arches, an architectural reminder, perhaps, of Byzantium which in a sense has always been Leigh Fermor's true north. It was to historic Constantinople – never Istanbul – that he set out on his serendipitous, marathon walking tour from the Hook of Holland as a thrusting eighteen-year-old, a journey immortalised half a century later in the densely beautiful prose of *A Time of Gifts* and *Between the Woods and the Water*. The world has been awaiting the longed-for third volume ever since.

From Byzantium I step back into England, through the leaves of a stout beech door, into the sort of room to make a writer swoon. Betjeman called it 'one of *the* rooms in the world'. Leigh Fermor once wrote that it passed 'the stern Mitford test' ('all nice rooms are a bit shabby') with flying colours. Whitewashed walls, flagstone floor and panelled wood ceiling frame a space that is both sitting room and library. Bookshelves rise from floor to ceiling. Light streams in from tall windows thrown open towards the sea. In the garden to the north I can pick out a congregation of tufty cypresses, olive trees and rosemary hedges. Inside, piles of books jostle for space with armchairs, cushions, icons, sculptures, lamps, bowls and boxes, maps, Turkish kilims, *flokkati* rugs of shaggy goats' hair, Browning, James Joyce, Madame de Staël, several feet of dictionaries, atlases, Greek–English lexicons, Oxford Companions and Cambridge histories, Harrap and Larousse, a 1984 *Who's Who*, Lemprière, Fowler, Brewer, Liddell and Scott, pictures by the late Greek artist and Leigh Fermor's friend Nico Ghika, three Edward Lear Cretan scenes, goats by John Craxton, Jamaica foliage by Lucian Freud, a Robin Ironside of a statue waking up in a museum. In Leigh Fermor's words, 'Where a man's Eleventh Edition of the *Encyclopaedia Britannica* is, there shall his heart be also.'*

My first sight of him is etched indelibly into my otherwise dreadful memory. An alarmingly handsome figure is sitting in the sun-bleached garden room a step down from the library, clasping a Loeb edition of Herodotus. For a moment, I think the man who stands up to greet me in this literary Elysium must be a house guest since he looks no more than seventy.

'How very nice to see you,' he says. His English is polished gravel, the voice of a more civilised generation.

* For a lovely essay on this room see 'Sash Windows Opening on the Foam' in Patrick Leigh Fermor's *Words of Mercury*. Writing about his groaning bookcases, he observes that 'if one is settling in the wilds, a dozen reference shelves is the minimum; and they must be near the dinner table where arguments spring up which have to be settled then or never'.

There is something poignant about coming face to face with a man of action and literary hero no longer at the height of his powers, surrounded by the history of his travels, a life of writing exquisitely. On these shelves stand the tools of his craft, pored over lovingly and plundered for decades to bring forth books of dreamlike brilliance. Nothing so unusual about meeting a ninety-one-year-old diminished by his years. It is the knowledge of what he once was, a vigorous soldier–scholar who sashayed through life with a *con brio* flourish on the battlefield and in print, that makes the present seem so brutal. He is young and vital for his years, but time is catching up. The great grow small, said Herodotus, and the small grow great.

I begin by calling him Sir Patrick. He insists on Paddy. When I apologise for arriving late, he takes vicarious pleasure in my lung-busting climb. Later, I discover from his old friend the former prime minister Tzannis Tzannetakis, who translated some of his writing into Greek, that when they worked together on the island of Kythera, Leigh Fermor used to go hiking in the mountains for hours every day. Business only began in earnest at 5 p.m. when the Englishman would hit the tobacco and whisky, pushing on through with these bibulous literary adventures until 1 a.m. when Tzannetakis couldn't take another drop (shades of Churchill and Roosevelt).

'You've kept me up till 1.30 in the morning with this,' he says breezily, waving Herodotus in front of me. 'I've been reading about the battle of Marathon.'

I apologise for inflicting the Father of History on him.

'Absolutely not. He's rather engaging. Now what would you like to drink? My sight's not very good so do help yourself.'

We walk over to a table lost beneath a shimmering forest of glass bottles. After his pro-Herodotus opening gambit, I have a spring in my step. This is going to go well. *En route* to the drinks table we pass one of the room's greatest treasures, a circular inlaid marble table made by Freya Stark's *marmorista* in Venice. Only Leigh Fermor could get away with describing it thus: 'Based on a tondo in the chancel of S. Anastasio in Mantua, white flames of Udine stone radiate from the centre of a design of subtle grey carsico and *rosso di Verona*.'

He still has an enviable head of hair and is crisply dressed in blue checked shirt, russet tie, a blue jumper and corduroys. Red socks betray a note of flamboyance. In fact, he looks preposterously well for a man of his vintage. A more debonair specimen of the literary warrior would be difficult to imagine. In an instant I understand something I have had difficulty believing in a eulogising profile of Leigh Fermor in the *New Yorker*: the story of a dinner party in which a woman in her early thirties, dazzled by his dash, made a concerted play for him. He was in his early eighties at the time.

'I've already had a vodka and tonic so I won't have anything,' he says. I pour myself a stiff drink from a very large, obviously much used, green bottle with the handwritten legend 'OUZO'. He draws discreetly alongside and pours himself a second vodka. His constitution is said by friends to be as robust as his wartime record.

The ouzo seeps joyously through my system and I'm desperate for a cigarette. Is it all right to smoke?

'Oh, please do,' he says in magnificent approval. 'I used to smoke a hundred a day.' He excuses himself to hunt down an ashtray.

One question hangs over our meeting which I am keen to dispense with as soon as possible. What news for all the Leigh Fermor devotees awaiting the third volume which would see him reach his beloved Constantinople after all these decades?

'That's the plan, of course,' he says. 'I've been rereading my notes and getting things in order. Clearing the decks. It's all I seem to do these days. But it's all a bit grim. I'm finding writing rather difficult.' He says he has tunnel vision and at the moment is confronting the disconcerting sight of an interviewer with two pairs of eyes and four nostrils. He does not type, has never been very keen on dictating and has no secretary. It is, as they say, in the lap of the gods.

'Charge on,' is the cue for lunch. We leave the library and return to the world of Byzantium, taking our places in the gallery at a table set for two. A limestone arch encircles a sunlit scene of bougainvillaea amid a diaphanous blaze of green foliage. Olives, oaks and fruit trees descend in the distance. Paddy – as he has now become – sits beneath a headless statue of Earth Mother Cybele, dug up near Palestrina. Four well-fed cats hover expectantly ('They do rather well, the beasts') and a squadron of buzzing flies makes merry around us. Centre-stage is a tall carafe of irresistibly chilled white wine. In fact, it's retsina, for which my host apologises when I ask what we are drinking.

'I'm terribly sorry. Dreadfully rude of me. I didn't ask you. I have some proper wine next door.'

Absolutely not. I tell him I can't drink enough of it and have been quaffing my way through Greece in a pine-scented haze of retsina.

He nods in vigorous agreement. 'I've been drinking it for fifty years and it's done me no harm.'

We set to our lunch of Herculean pork chops, luxuriating on a bed of garlic and onions, with spinach, potatoes and tzatziki. The retsina in the carafe descends with the winter sun. We chat about all things great and small, prowling the corridors of a mind which has rejoiced in life, love and learning with the freewheeling passion of the true autodidact. A comment about his time at King's School Canterbury, where his housemaster diagnosed 'a dangerous mixture of sophistication and recklessness', elicits affectionate thoughts of Christopher Marlowe, another King's man who got into high-spirited scrapes. Leigh Fermor's career at the school came to a premature end when he was expelled for fraternising too closely with the town's female population. Nellie, the greengrocer's daughter, was heartbroken.

The kidnapping of General Karl Heinrich Kreipe on Crete on 26 April 1944, when Leigh Fermor was living rough in occupied Crete as a major in the Special Operations Executive, is a *Boy's Own* tale of unimaginable derring-do from an era – virtually gone – where individual valour was still possible on the battlefield. It reminds me curiously of Herodotus, who regularly singles out warriors who have distinguished themselves in battle and, God knows, in those days it was slashing, stinking, brutal hand-to-hand fighting. At Marathon, for example, he mentions a number of men killed 'fighting bravely', including the unfortunate Cynegirus, brother of Aeschylus and son of Euphorion, who had his hand cut off with an axe. At Thermopylae, he praises a number of soldiers, among them the Spartan Dieneces with his famous 'we shall have our battle in the shade' remark.

And the reason Herodotus records these heroic acts, of course, goes right back to his famous opening line, the earliest formulation of history, so that great deeds are neither 'forgotten in time' nor 'without their glory'. The fact that we are even able to discuss Dieneces' battlefield braggadocio 2,500 years later shows how successful he has been. Dieneces' joyful bravery in the face of certain death has not been forgotten. In fact, it is one of several Herodotean vignettes used to memorable effect in the film *300*.

If Herodotus had witnessed the Second World War, he might well have commented on the 'marvel' of the kidnapping of General Kreipe on Crete, a nail-shredding operation fraught with danger. If he had, he would have singled out Leigh Fermor for special notice.

At half-past nine that night, the general's car was driving towards Heraklion. On a quiet bend, two Feldpolizei corporals stepped into the road, waved down the car and asked whether this was General Kreipe's vehicle. It was. Suddenly men sprang from ditches, swarmed all over the car and pulled out the driver after bashing him on the head. The stunned Kreipe was hustled into the back where he was encouraged to keep quiet by three Cretans and a knife at his throat. Leigh Fermor was one of the corporals. Now he took his place suavely in the front, lit a cigarette, swiped Kreipe's hat and promoted himself immediately to the rank of general. The car sped on towards Heraklion which the Anglo-Cretan team of brigands had to pass through to get to the pre-arranged dropping-off point. Before they reached it, however, they had the small matter of those twenty-two separate checkpoints to negotiate. Leigh Fermor spoke only halting German. The slightest mistake could end with a bullet in the head. One by one they bluffed their way through. At one particularly heart-stopping checkpoint it started to look sticky. The car was slowed down until it was almost stationary. Inside the vehicle pistols were cocked in a spirit of do or die. This was General Kreipe's car, they barked imperiously, and the driver put his foot down again. They escaped into the night, feigned a beach getaway to deter pursuit and unloaded their simmering general. The outrageous escapade had been a triumph.

Being a literary fellow, Herodotus would have been unable to resist reporting the now legendary exchange between Leigh Fermor and Kreipe recorded in *A Time of Gifts*. The conversation took place in the hills as German search parties consisting of thousands of soldiers scoured the island in a terrifying manhunt.

> During a lull in the pursuit, we woke up among the rocks just as a brilliant dawn was breaking over the crest of Mount Ida. We had been toiling over it, through snow and then rain, for the last two days. Looking across the valley at this flashing mountain-crest, the general murmured to himself: *Vides ut alte stet nive candidum Soracte* . . . It was one of the ones I knew! I continued from where he had broken off: *nec iam sustineant onus Silvae laborantes, geluque Flumina constiterint acuto*, and so on, through the remaining five stanzas to the end. The general's blue eyes had swivelled away from the mountain-top to mine – and when I'd finished, after a long silence, he said: '*Ach so, Herr Major!*' It was very strange. As though, for a long moment, the war had ceased to exist. We had both drunk at the same fountains long before; and things were different between us for the rest of our time together.

Horace's *Odes* 1.9, an exhortation to pile on the logs, let the wine flow and dance the night away, provided a common cultural reference point amid the tumult of war. Don't worry what tomorrow will bring, it says, just enjoy the moment. Within a couple of weeks of the magical Horace exchange, General Kreipe was herded on to a boat and spirited off to Allied headquarters in Cairo.

Leigh Fermor's awards have flowed ever since. His typically intrepid exploits in the SOE, where he rubbed shoulders with David Stirling, Fitzroy Maclean and Wilfred Thesiger, above all the audacious kidnapping, were recognised with an immediate DSO. An OBE followed. Literary laurels greeted the publication of his first book, *The Traveller's Tree*, in 1950 and the plaudits have never stopped. Cretans adore him to this day. He is an honorary citizen of Heraklion, not to mention Kardamyli and Gytheio. The Greek government made him Commander of the Order of the Phoenix, and in 2004 he was knighted in the UK for services to literature and Anglo-Greek relations. 'The queen touched both shoulders with the sword,' he says. 'I wasn't expecting that. My wife Joan wasn't keen on all these honours and things and I oiled out of it the first time I was asked. Her father, though, was terrifically keen.'

His latest honour comes from the Travellers Club, which presented a specially commissioned bust of Leigh Fermor that now sits in pride of place alongside Sir Wilfred Thesiger, another of the club's favourite sons and fellow soldier–writer. He describes it as 'rather terrifying'.

Ice cream arrives. 'I couldn't resist it,' he says.

I ask him whether he shares the feeling of nostalgia and regret, apparently so pervasive in Greece, at the loss of Constantinople to the Ottomans in 1453. His writing seems to reflect this pain.

'Only in a romantic sense,' he says. 'You can't just forget 2,500 years of history and call it Istanbul. I deplore the Turkish role in Eastern Europe, but of course you can't blame them. It would be like blaming the laws of hydrostatics for flood damage. And I've liked every Turk I've ever met.'

Though he is not a political man, preferring to remain beyond the fray, he is, above all, a European. In the confrontation between East and West there seems little doubt as to where his sympathies might lie. I wonder whether he feels the Western world and its way of life are under threat?

'It does rather feel like that, though I haven't been keeping up on it as much as I should have,' he replies.

We head back to the library for Greek – not Turkish – coffee. At my elbow there is a splendid photograph, taken recently, of Leigh Fermor and Earl Jellicoe, wartime comrade and commander of the Special Boat Service.* Both men wear dark suits, their chests a riotous patchwork of medals. Leigh Fermor's left hand rests jauntily on his hip, his right leans suggestively on a walking stick. Even in his tenth decade, there is an unmistakable poise and defiant swagger.

He picks up Herodotus again and I tell him a Greek academic has advised me to regard him not as a person but as a text.

'Oh dear,' he frowns sympathetically. 'What a terrible way of looking at him. He seems frightfully engaging. I'm enjoying discovering him enormously.'

The text is laid out with Ancient Greek on one page and the English translation on the other. I can't help hoping he is reading the *Histories* in English. Anything else would be too demoralising. He

---

* George Jellicoe, the 2nd Earl Jellicoe, died in February 2007.

looks at me with a twinkle in his eyes. 'You know, if I gave myself a month, I think I could brush up on my Greek and get cracking on this. I'm rather rusty, but I don't think it would be all that difficult. Your chap Herodotus might be just the encouragement I need.'

Ancient Greek and I parted company when I was nine. To hear a man in his early nineties talk about buckling down to his alpha declensions, aorist tenses and passive deponents almost brings me to tears – of elation and despair.

After coffee, we walk through the French windows on to the terrace, a harmonious symphony of olive trees and stone benches set among terracotta tiles and pebble mosaics beneath a cloud-troubled sky. Across the water to the west lies the rump of Messenia and the mountains of Morea. Beneath us is Leigh Fermor's private cove and steps down to the sea. This is the house that Paddy built, with his late wife Joan, in the mid-1960s.

He sits for a few photographs while we swap notes on travel writers young and old. He asks after my travels in Greece and when I say I have just returned from the north, he says, 'I did some wandering around up there when I first came to Greece, when I was twenty.' This is an understatement on a Herodotean scale. The 'wandering' led to *Roumeli*, one of the twentieth century's finest travel books. He admires Bruce Chatwin, who was a frequent visitor to the Mani – and the Leigh Fermors – in the Eighties, and Jan Morris. On the back cover of *Words of Mercury* Morris salutes him as 'the greatest of living travel writers'. Leigh Fermor abhors the travel-writer label, though, regarding it as a lesser literary category. 'It's rather like being called a sports writer,' he grumbles.

I have trespassed on his time long enough. On our way out, he suddenly leads me to another building, half hidden by the olives and cypresses. A fleeting glimpse into his writing room and inner sanctum: papers everywhere, more zigzagging stacks of books, a towering blue-and-white ceramic light from Portugal. His hero Byron stares at us from a plate in the centre of a broad chimneypiece. The door closes and the momentary magic spell is over.

'Do drop in again if you're ever in the area,' he says. Mentally, I start making plans to leave my wife and become his amanuensis. I thank him for the afternoon and wish him luck with Herodotus, in English or in Ancient Greek.

'There's lots of sex in it, you know,' I say by way of encouragement.

'Really?' he says, suddenly galvanised. He chuckles. 'Could you point out the best bits?'

# 14

# 'Fill High the Bowl with Samian Wine!'

*History is not what you thought. It is what you can remember.*
W. C. Sellar and R. J. Yeatman, *1066 and All That* (1930)

A PIECE OF ASH from Captain Vassilis Theodore's cigarette lands on the Cycladic island of Kea. The bridge is dimly lit and thick with smoke. Officers pace up and down, pausing occasionally to consult a chart beneath the blue-green glow of tilted computer screens, before walking off trailing slipstreams of nicotine behind them. They are like white-shirted ghouls of the night looming in and out of the smoke-torn darkness against the steady baritone of the engines. Outside the sea glistens darkly beneath the constellations, an endlessly writhing sheet of liquid metal.

Captain Theodore is outlining our overnight journey to Samos on board the *Express Santorini*. With a Beaufort scale-9 gale roiling the eastern Aegean with winds of over fifty miles an hour, our departure from Athens has been delayed several hours. From the port of Piraeus we will head first south and then, once the mainland is behind us, east to Kea. Poised above the chart like Aeolus, god of wind, he sends the piece of ash tumbling east in the hurricane of his breath. Anticipating the arc of our own crossing, it skims across his charts towards Siros, onwards to Tinos and Mikonos, breaking up and getting smaller with every island hop until I wonder whether it will make the final leg, a long stretch north-east into the fringes of the Dodecanese, past Ikaria and on towards the Turkish coast. In the end, there is no telling. Just as it is closing in on our final destination of Samos, where Herodotus and I will say goodbye on the island of his exile, another pile of ash falls from his cigarette and the eastern Aegean is momentarily obscured beneath a heaving storm.

Herodotus probably enjoyed a number of conversations with the skippers who bore him across the Aegean and Mediterranean on his lifelong travels. We have seen him, for example, noting that a day's sail from the Egyptian coast the water was 'eleven fathoms, muddy bottom'. Ship captains would have been excellent sources of local information and, equally, of tall stories. Both would have appealed to the travel writer and indefatigable raconteur.

Coming from Britain, a country that treasures its seafaring heritage, revelling in the heroics of men like Nelson, Collingwood, Ralegh, Rodney, Drake, Cook, Jellicoe (father of Leigh Fermor's wartime comrade George) and Beatty, I'm also thinking about the Greeks' prowess on the seas, a tradition already well established by Herodotus' time that makes British boasts seem somewhat inflated by comparison. Describing the build-up to the battle of Salamis, Herodotus has Artemisia, Xerxes' only female commander, advise the Persian general Mardonius against taking on the Greeks at sea. 'Spare your ships and do not fight at sea, for the Greeks are as far superior to your men in naval matters as men are to women,' she warns. Xerxes admires the woman's spirit but doesn't listen. His fleet is routed.

In a brief history of Greek shipping, Spyros Polemis, chairman of the International Chamber of Shipping and President of the International Shipping Federation, a man who describes himself as a passionate sailor and yachtsman, writes that 'The Greeks, more than any other people in the world, have remained, during their entire, very long history, mariners without interruption, they have loved the sea, they have thought of it as a beautiful element, and they believed it had godlike powers.'

Seamanship came naturally to the Greeks, he writes, due to several uniquely favourable circumstances. The first was landscape. The relentlessly mountainous terrain has always proved a serious challenge to productive farming, which occurs on only 20 per cent of the Greek landmass, and harvests have generally been poor. The sea was a rational way out, a bridge to new trading opportunities. Greece's geographical location was the second advantage, sitting at the crossroads of the ancient world's shipping lanes. To the south, Egypt and Libya. To the west, Italy, Asia to the east and the Balkans to the north. 'The distances were not great and for thousands of years our seamen were navigating under clear skies, almost always in sight of land.' Third, the vast coastline, with its inlets and natural harbours, wide bays, beaches and innumerable islands, offered the perfect playground for the budding sailor. 'It was natural that such beautiful surroundings would inspire the Greeks and would also instil in them a love for the sea.' The final factor in Polemis' affectionate analysis is the Greek climate, which rarely allowed anything as unpleasant as a hurricane or typhoon to spoil the idyll. His concluding observation on Greek weather would bring tears to the eyes of rain-sodden British sailors shivering uncontrollably in their thermals and waterproofs: 'The temperature was always pleasant, blue skies, clear atmosphere, and the sun almost a permanent source of light. Such an environment does make for a freer spirit, strengthens the imagination and makes people optimistic, liberal and daring. In other words, it created the necessary conditions for the Greeks to become very good shipping men.'

Greek control of the modern world's shipping suggests this preeminence on the high seas is no mere flash in the historical pan. The country has the largest fleet in the world and Greek shipping carries a scarcely credible 95 per cent of the planet's total volume of trade. There's no question about it: the shipping expertise and commercial acumen live on. But, and this is a rather different question, are the Greeks still a nation of sailors?

'I tell you, in summer everyone's a captain,' Theodore says with a conductor's flourish, scattering the ash away with a sideways sweep of his hand, stubbing out his cigarette and lighting another. Samos, perched provocatively close to the Turkish mainland, disappears beneath an ebullient grey smudge. 'The passengers are always questioning the captain's decision, why is he going into the port like this, he's got his line all wrong, he can't be any good. The old people are the worst. They've got a little fishing boat and they think they know everything about the sea. And then in the winter they all disappear below like rats.'

Like many salt-encrusted skippers, Captain Theodore delights in recounting scrapes on the high – or, in fact, generally calm – seas.

These waters see a lot of smuggling and trafficking in speedboats, he says, and more leisurely stowaways on the Patras–Brindisi route. Boats built for ten sink under the weight of 300 desperate dreamers. There's the story of the Italian coastguard whizzing around his ship having a running – or sailing – gun battle with a boat of Albanian smugglers and illegal immigrants. 'What could I do?' he guffaws. His ghoulish officers, sensing a yarn, step out of the shadows to listen. 'We were in the middle of a pitched battle . . .' With his right hand he describes an enormous circle, his cigarette a glowing epicentre representing the *Express Santorini*, to re-enact the high-speed chase around his ship. He mimics a man cradling a gun. 'We just carried on as they raced around us shooting. Both boats had machine guns, can you believe it? Bullets flying everywhere. I didn't care too much about the Albanians, it was my ship I was worried about.' He breaks into laughter, looks up, and the officers scurry back to their monitors like cockroaches darting away at the flick of a light switch.

The seas were no less adventurous in Herodotus' time, with shipwreck a constant danger. Sailing close to land had its navigational advantages, but bore its own risks in the event of a sudden change in the weather. Storms cause havoc throughout the *Histories*, more often than not for the landlubber Persians, mighty warriors on the land, slightly pathetic at sea. The first victim is a section of Darius' fleet which, after sailing from Croton in southern Italy, is quickly wrecked off the Iapygian coast. Later, leaving Acanthus, the Persians are attempting to double Athos but before rounding the promontory, Herodotus writes, 'they were caught by a violent northerly gale, which proved too much for the ships to cope with'. Three hundred ships with over 20,000 men were lost. Many drowned, still others died of hypothermia. And for those shipwrecked mariners left kicking and gasping at the surface, thinking they had survived the worst, the sea had a final, fatal surprise in store. 'The sea in the neighbourhood of Athos is full of monsters,' Herodotus explains, 'so that those of the ships' companies who were not dashed to pieces on the rocks, were seized and devoured.'

Xerxes fares little better at sea. His uncle Artabanus, who has already warned him against invading Greece, tells Xerxes the sea is one of his greatest enemies. There is no harbour large enough to protect the vast Persian fleet in the event of storms. The king is in no mood to listen. His fleet has reached the Magnesian coast between the town of Casthanea and Cape Sepias. The first ships that arrive make fast to the land, those that follow are forced to anchor offshore in lines, eight deep, since there is extremely limited mooring space on the beach. 'At dawn next day the weather, which was clear and calm, suddenly changed, and the fleet was caught in a heavy blow from the east – a "Hellespontian", as the people there call it – which raised a confused sea like a pot on the boil,' Herodotus writes. 'Four hundred ships, at the lowest estimate, are said to have been lost in this disaster, and the loss of life and treasure was beyond reckoning.'

The shipwreck was not all bad news, Herodotus explains in a classic postscript.

> It proved, however, to be a very good thing indeed for a certain Magnesian named Ameinocles . . . for he subsequently picked up a large number of gold and silver drinking-cups which were washed ashore, and found Persian treasure-chests containing more gold, beyond counting. This made him a very rich man, though in other respects he proved less fortunate; for he met with the distressing disaster of having killed his son.

Quite how is never explained.

Perhaps the most famous example of the Persians being over-whelmed by the sea comes, as we have seen, when Xerxes, having succeeded against all the odds in building a bridge across the Hellespont linking Asia to Europe, then watches as a 'storm of great violence' smashes it up. Incandescent with rage, he orders the Hellespont to receive 300 lashes and hurls a symbolic pair of fetters into the water.

We don't know how or when Herodotus got to Samos, but he may well have sailed there into exile from Halicarnassus, some time after falling foul of Lygdamis. Perhaps he was sent creeping up the island-strewn coastline, swinging out south from the peninsula before turning north inside sleek, whale-shaped Kos, then skirting the Dodecanese past Kalimnos, Leros, Lipsoi, Arkoi and Ankathonisi, 'almost always in sight of land' as Polemis observes, before touching down on the southern shore of Samos with a lifetime before him. If he did arrive at the ancient harbour of Samos, now the fishing village and resort of Pythagorio, he would have been able to gaze up at the mighty hilltop fortifications built by the island's sixth-century tyrant Polycrates, neatly zigzagging around the town. They are still there today, splendidly crumbling walls and squat towers watching over a colourful tableau of fishing boats and waterfront restaurants far below. And if this is where he did disembark for his first taste of exile, Herodotus would certainly have drawn up alongside the vast mole, a quarter of a mile long, another survivor of the megalomaniac's monumental building spree.

In later years he may even have made this same journey from Athens, sailing out from Piraeus, the port we have left behind this evening in an unconscious, indirect connection to Herodotus. It was Themistocles, one of Greece's most famous and controversial maritime figures, who fortified Piraeus heavily as part of his policy of Athenian naval expansion. Themistocles, one of Herodotus' contemporaries, is a leading character in the climactic stages of the *Histories*.

Whatever the truth about Herodotus' time in Samos, whether he spent a decade there or never set eyes on the place, we know he's familiar with much of its history as well as its chief monuments because there are numerous references to the island throughout the *Histories*. Here he is on the island's trio of marvels:

I have dwelt longer upon the history of the Samians than I should otherwise have done, because they are responsible for three of the greatest building and engineering feats in the Greek world: the first is a tunnel nearly a mile long, eight feet wide and eight feet high, driven clean through the base of a hill nine hundred feet in height. The whole length of it carries a second cutting thirty feet deep and three broad, along which water from an abundant source is led through pipes into the town. This was the work of a Megarian named Eupalinus, son of Naustrophus. Secondly, there is the artificial harbour enclosed by a breakwater, which runs out into twenty fathoms of water and has a total length of a quarter of a mile; and last, the island has the biggest of all Greek temples known. The first architect of it was Rhoecus, son of Phileus, a Samian. These three works seemed to me sufficiently important to justify a rather full account of the history of the island.

And the passage seems to me sufficiently important to justify a rather full visit. Or, to be more precise, a revisit because I have been to Samos once before, fleetingly, before Herodotus and I were in a committed relationship. I can remember a Captain Iannis Mamuzalos, master of the *Flying Dolphin Samos 4*, discussing ancient navigation techniques, grumbling about the Turks, and telling me proudly that 'sailing is in our blood'; I recall a traipse through the Temple of Hera in warm, streaming winds, a torch-lit scramble into the Eupalinos Tunnel and a skin-chastening snorkelling expedition alongside the Polycrates harbour mole, but the scribbles in my little black Moleskine are all too spare and sparse from this short-lived trip. I have toyed with the idea of ignoring Samos on this Herodotean tour through Greece and making do with the material I've got, but in the end I am returning because otherwise I will be defeated by memory. I am not yet eighty-eight – perhaps I never will be – but I feel like the American writer Martha Gellhorn who cursed her geriatric memory shortly before she died in 1998:

> I have no grasp of time and no control over my memory. I cannot order it to deliver. Unexpectedly, it flings up pictures, disconnected with no before or after. It makes me feel a fool. What is the use in having lived so long, travelled so widely, listened and looked so hard if at the end you could know what you know?

I mention this now because as I sail to Samos in an anonymous black night, slipping through the molten metal waters, I can't help dwelling on the problem of memory, both mine and Herodotus', and wondering how on earth he dealt with it. I am returning to Samos after only three years to refresh my memory. He wouldn't have been able to revisit places at the drop of a hat to check something he wasn't sure about, he didn't have the options we have in our bristling technological arsenal – books, cameras, telephones, digital recording devices, laptops, internet, email and all the rest of it (and how soon these will seem quaintly old-fashioned). Often, he would have had to reconstruct scenes, conversations, encounters, descriptions and arguments from information that presumably he had acquired many years earlier.

Leigh Fermor did much the same in *A Time of Gifts*, published in 1977, more than forty years after his original journey across Europe. It was 'like reconstructing a brontosaur from half an eye socket and a basket full of bones', he wrote of the demands it made on his memory. In some instances, he resorted to creative writing. Not unlike our Greek historian, perhaps.

So was Herodotus noting things down furiously wherever he travelled, with his fifth-century BC equivalent of a Moleskine notebook and pen? Or was he committing prodigious amounts of material to memory? Some combination of the two? However he did it, one can only marvel at the scale of his achievement.

'No one in Samos knows anything about Herodotus. You're wasting your time here.' Dimos, a magnificent Samian version of Asterix's hefty friend Obelix (with ponytail rather than pigtails), downs another shot of *souma*, the island's eye-watering local spirit. He pauses, tweaks his vigorous chestnut moustache thoughtfully and wipes his mouth on his shirtsleeve. 'No one cares about him, either,' he adds, burping disdainfully for good measure.

We are mooning about in a café in the mountaintop village of Manolates, high above the northern coast of Samos, overlooking a valley that during the long, cool nights rings to the rejoicing song of the nightingale. Beneath us, cascading pell-mell down the slopes of Mount Ampelos, are forests, bijoux vineyards and the occasional explosion of a flame-orange tobacco field. Smoke twists into the sky from the homespun *souma* distillery below us. The vines, moist in the morning dew, glisten like jewels. Beyond them is the quiet beach resort of Aghios Konstantinos and then, raising the eye into the sun-steamed haze, nothing but burnt sea for miles and miles. The next piece of land, fifteen miles to the north, is Turkey. Clouds roll past like pearls, chased off by a treacly sun. The crystalline light slows everything down, though this may be the effect of drinking several rounds of *souma* at ten o'clock in the morning.

'All we learn about Herodotus is that he was Father of History,' Dimos goes on. 'That's it. Everyone has to learn ancient history in

Greece but no one pays attention.' Yet Dimos himself, an occasional olive farmer in his thirties, is something of a Herodotean. And he must have paid some attention because he can still remember. 'When I was a small boy my father used to read me passages from the *Histories* as bedtime stories. He always chose the exciting stuff, mostly battles in the Persian Wars. Scenes like the Spartan soldiers oiling their bodies and combing their hair before the battle of Thermopylae, the fighting at Plataea, Salamis, Mycale. I loved it. It was my favourite book. It still is. The thing about Herodotus is that his language is very easy.' So it is. Lucian was one among many classical authors to admire the limpid style. 'Herodotus' prose', Aubrey de Sélincourt remarked more recently, 'has the flexibility, ease and grace of a man superbly talking.'

Dimos needs galvanising. We clink our glasses once more in a final toast to Herodotean adventures on Samos, down another glass of *souma* and head off for the Eupalinos Tunnel, a maudlin Dimos moaning about the lack of women on the island. We motor down the mountain, negotiating a series of hairpin bends through what could almost be a lush rainforest, a vista of soaring pines, dripping vines and river water sloshing across a leaf-stencilled road. After the sun up on the summit, this sudden chill is blissful, the soothing shock of plunging your head into a basin of iced water. The landscape is a surprise.

Samos defies the conventional picture of a Greek island that is all rock, beaches and tourists. How clever of Zeus and Hera, Antony and Cleopatra to seek out such a quiet corner of the Aegean for their romantic trysts, a temperate, mountainous island and a place so fertile, joked the fourth-century BC comic poet Menander, that even the hens gave milk. As Professor Graham Shipley notes in his history of Samos, the ancients admired the island greatly, remarking upon its natural beauty and the bountiful crops that its favourable climate allowed. You get a good sense of how it was regarded by studying the series of names by which Samos was known: Anthemis (flowery one); Melamphyllos (dark-leaved one); Dryoussa (Oak Island); in his *Natural History* Pliny referred to it as Kyparissia (Cypress Island). Then there were Aeschylus and the lyric poet Anacreon, who both wrote of the island's numerous olive trees. Samian olive oil was praised to the skies for being the 'whitest' of them all, a reference to the most coveted first pressing. It was only the irreverent humorist and knockabout sarcastic bugger Apuleius who spoiled the party. 'The soil is not receptive to corn, not worth ploughing, and more fertile for olive-groves,' he jeered. 'It is scratched neither by the vine-dresser nor by the kitchen-gardener,' an entertaining observation that hardly tallies with the verdict of Aethlius of Samos, who remarked on the twice-yearly crops of figs, grapes, apples, pears and roses. As late as 1610, wine growing was noticeable by its absence, according to the English poet and traveller George Sandys, who described Samos as 'fruitfull in all things but vines'.

To this day, Samos is still noted for the excellence of its honey, while oenophiles know that the island's 'vine-dressers' scratch the soil profitably to grow the splendid muscat grapes that go into the gorgeously ambrosial dessert wines that so appealed to Byron. 'Fill high the bowl with Samian wine!' he roared and I have been doing little else since I arrived. As for the name by which we know the island today, the meticulous Professor Shipley goes on, Strabo thought it came from a Phoenician word meaning 'high', a distinct possibility when you discover that between them Mounts Kerkis (4,700 feet) and Karvounis (3,780 feet) account for more than half of the island's surface area.

The mountain-jungle peters out as we descend, eventually giving way to a coast-hugging road, threaded through an outer girdle of rocks, that takes us towards the town of Pythagorio, named after the island's favourite son Pythagoras, the sixth-century BC polymath, philosopher and mathematician. I wonder what he would make of this curious posthumous tribute if he returned today. He is celebrated in cafés, restaurants and bars along the waterfront, on Pythagorean theorem $a^2 + b^2 = c^2$ T-shirts and, more formally, in a handsome sculpture facing the Polycrates harbour mole. Here he stands at the base of a right-angled triangle, opposite a leaning hypotenuse bronze, his right hand stretching up towards the heavens to make his history-changing measurement. His left hand holds a right angle.

Sadly, there is no sign of Herodotus in this pretty little harbour of Bar Iliads and Restaurant Pythagorios because he wasn't a local boy who made good. The Herodotean connections in Samos are monumental. And unlike so many of the other monuments described in the *Histories*, the Tunnel of Eupalinos, which seems to have impressed him the most of the three great Samian engineering feats he describes, has survived in robust health. Being underground and empty, it has been spared both the ravages of the elements and the pillaging of thieves.

It's difficult to get excited about a tunnel. Whichever way you look at it, it's basically just a hole in the ground. As long or as short as you like. Probably damp, possibly dark. The Tunnel of Eupalinos, however, is in a category all of its own. In fact, it's a triumph of engineering which deserves nothing less than amazement and wonder. At the risk of becoming a tunnel bore, let me explain.

Designed to bring water to ancient Samos (today's Pythagorio) from the bubbling Ayades spring north-west of the town on the other side of Mount Kastro, it was built in the sixth century BC by Polycrates, the tyrant ruler of Samos. The tunnel and the aqueduct it contained represented a secure water supply, part of a series of defensive measures taken in the face of a Persian threat emerging from the middle of the century. Polycrates, flexing his muscles in the Aegean and amassing the region's most formidable fleet, had his own expansionist ambitions in these waters. Fortifications at home were the prelude to, and sequel of, conquests abroad.

In its time the tunnel was justly considered the eighth wonder of the world, an elegant demonstration of the sophistication of Greek engineering and the extent of Samian power under Polycrates. Like many autocrats before him and since, Polycrates wanted the project completed yesterday, so it was decided – and this is where the story gets really interesting – to start tunnelling from both sides of the mountain to halve the building time.

This was the most remarkable feature of the tunnel that Herodotus specifically mentioned in his description of Samos. For once the graceful de Sélincourt translation misses a trick because there is no reference to the Greek word αμφίστομον, *amfistomon*, meaning 'having two openings' or 'with a mouth at either end', as the nineteenth-century Rawlinson translation puts it. It sounds a minor omission, but Herodotus admired the Eupalinos Tunnel precisely *because* it was dug from both ends simultaneously. This immediately created two formidable problems. In order to meet in the middle, the two tunnels had to be correctly aligned and at the same elevation.

How did he do it? To this day, we don't know the answer. We know that Greek technology did not extend to magnetic compasses, surveying instruments or topographical maps. And notwithstanding Pythagoras' pioneering efforts, maths did not offer the Greek engineer very much to go on either. The first major compendium of ancient mathematics, Euclid's *Elements*, only hit the bookshops two centuries later.

So two teams of slaves, armed only with picks, hammers and chisels, hacked through 1,133 yards of solid limestone, 590 feet beneath the mountain summit, for somewhere between eight and fifteen years, meeting each other in the middle with only the slightest, most marginal, deviation. Where the two tunnels came together, the northern shaft was just two feet higher than the southern, a discrepancy of less than one-eighth of a per cent of the distance excavated, according to the American mathematician Professor Apostol, who calls it 'an engineering achievement of the first magnitude'.

In fact, the Tunnel of Eupalinos is really two tunnels. One of them, the main shaft, is on the level throughout. The second, much narrower and deeper than the main tunnel which it runs alongside, is the water channel, which drops steadily as it hurries towards the town, further complicating overall construction. At the northern end of the tunnel, the water channel is about ten feet lower than the floor of the tunnel. By the time it reaches the southern end, it is thirty feet beneath it. Barely wide enough for one man to stand in, the water chute is nevertheless meticulously carved, lined at the bottom with clay gutters. Craning your neck over for a peek into the stony depths is enough to give you vertigo and claustrophobia.

How Eupalinos managed to do all this is still a mystery. There are no written records of the construction. It is possible the calculations were based on a series of right-angled traverses around Mount Kastro from one tunnel entrance point to the other, keeping the same elevation throughout. This would have allowed Eupalinos to calculate two lengths of a right-angled triangle, leaving Pythagoras' famous hypotenuse as the necessary line to tunnel. The precise direction in which to dig could then be deduced by laying out two more triangles at the respective entrances and extending the hypotenuse from the rock, as we can see in the diagram. The only problem with this theory is that the technique of using a surveying instrument called a dioptra to measure triangular traverses is credited to Hero of Alexandria, who lived 500 years after the Eupalinos Tunnel was finished. Other possibilities include placing a series of sighting markers over the mountain to calculate the required elevation. The true story may never be known.

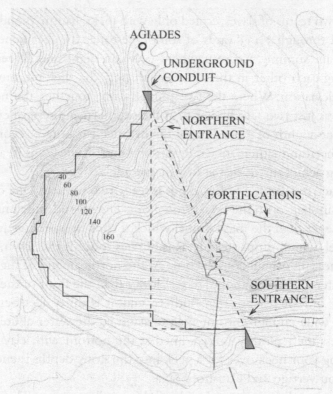

Whichever methods he used, he created a masterpiece. It was the longest tunnel in the world and only the second to be excavated from both ends. The first, the Hezekiah Tunnel of Jerusalem, built in about 700 BC, is thought to have followed an existing water course, thereby avoiding the sort of engineering difficulties facing Eupalinos with his mountain of limestone. We know the tunnel was a success, so much so that it was still being used to bring water into the town until Byzantine times. Some time between then and the nineteenth century it retreated into obscurity – not difficult when you are a tunnel – and then disappeared, more or less, from the sources. French, and German archaeologists dabbled in the nineteenth century and it was left to the Greeks to install lighting and open up a section of the southern half to visitors in the twentieth.

Another difficulty Eupalinos had to contend with, of course, was working for a tyrant. He might have been the finest engineer of Megara, but reputation would have been no protection in the event of a cock-up. Get the project wrong and he was toast. This would have concentrated the mind.

The most pressing difficulty Dimos and I face is locating the thing. We have been hacking around for an age in the long grass looking for the northern entrance, which has a lot of kudos attached to it on the grounds that it is not the southern entrance, a tourist attraction which only allows visitors a hundred yards or so in before a large iron gate prevents further access. The disadvantage of the northern entrance is not so much that it is inaccessible as completely invisible on a vast, tree-studded mountain face submerged in grass, prickly bushes and uprooted pines. After a couple of hours gathering mosquito bites and scratches, the light-headed jollity of the *souma* has been replaced by a temple-throbbing headache. Dimos is fast losing what little faith he had in me and my risible tourist map of the island. As a rule, Greeks do not 'do' travel writing.*

'I mean, why this tunnel is so important?' he asks, slashing at a mosquito. 'It is hole in the ground. Why so exciting?'

I murmur something about exploring connections with Herodotus. He is unconvinced.

'But if you must see it, we can go to main entrance. We don't find nothing with that map.' He is sweating so heavily I can almost see him losing weight in front of me. A melting obelisk.

---

* The most notable exception is Nikos Kazantzakis, the lion of twentieth-century Greek literature. Famous the world over for his novel *Zorba the Greek*, he is also cherished by Greeks for a body of exquisite travel writing. The epitaph on his simple stone tomb in Heraklion harks back to the defiantly Greek spirit that runs through the pages of Herodotus: Δεν ελπίζω τίποτα. Δεν φοβούμαι τίποτα. Είμαι λεύτερος, 'I hope for nothing. I fear nothing. I am free.'

Eventually, we stumble across a stone-walled passage, open to the air but well hidden beneath half-a-dozen fallen pines. It slopes down dramatically to a tiny, arched aperture in the rock. An iron gate that once guarded the entrance has been thrown to one side. The tunnel is as open as you like. My heartbeat quickens. Often enough on the Herodotean trail, I have been staring into the void where once great cities and monuments have risen and fallen. The inevitable disappearance of the architectural evidence beyond a pile of stones that are more or less evocative, depending on your mood, can be a little wearying sometimes. Yet here, for once, the perfectly dark void is something tangible, the strongest Samian link to Herodotus. Without waiting for Dimos, I switch on my torch and plunge in. It is a grand start to the tunnel expedition.

A few seconds in and something soft flutters past my face in a whisper of cool air. The atmosphere does not feel at all Herodotean in the jaunty sense of the word. It's positively scary. Now I can feel something scrabbling around my feet. Then something collides with my hair with a squeak and I bang my head sharply against the wall, which only intensifies the headache. More furry swishing about my ankles.

'Aaaargh! Dimos! Get out!'

I don't even know if Dimos has come into the tunnel yet, and I don't stop to find out, because within seconds of my descent into the tunnel I'm rampaging out again, hands and arms flailing, legs convulsing like a scarecrow on hot coals, shouting maniacally as I try to dislodge a bat from my hair and a rat that has shot up my trouser leg.

Dimos surveys me doubtfully. 'Just little animals,' he says in the same tone I use with my stepdaughter when she is shrieking about spiders in the bathroom. 'What is problem? I think you need more *souma*.'

After this inglorious beginning, our next entrance is more stately, though I am reduced to surreptitiously scuffing my shoes and tapping the walls with my torch to encourage the tunnel's residents to move on ahead of me. Shafts of torchlight struggle through a darkness so complete it is viscous. The narrow beam of naked light seems only to wrap it around us more tightly.

Turn off the torches several hundred yards in and there is no light at the end of the tunnel. The chill and silence are millennial and belong only to the dead. The tunnel could be an ancient tomb complex entered for the first time in centuries; a sense of trespass and danger hangs in the musty air. This is not a place for children or anyone who believes in ghosts. Deeper in still, thickets of stalactites drip-grow from the ceiling.* Tiny globes of suspended mineral water at their tips glitter and glow like diamonds.

And yet, apart from all the bats, rats and spiders, apart from the teeming spirits of the dead, it is wonderfully human and alive. The hand of man is there for all to see. It is evident in the rows of neat brickwork and the carefully set roof, shaped like a tight circumflex accent. You can feel it most poignantly when the tunnel is at its widest and you run your fingers over the chiselled lines of rock, step by tiny, serrated step, along the floor and roof. Each chisel blow lives on in jagged stone and when you stand still for a moment and collect your straying thoughts, you're whisked back more than twenty-five centuries to a scene of dark, choking confusion.

Two men from the digging team of a dozen are working on the face together, a cloth tied round their mouths and noses to protect them from flying shards of rock and the dust that envelops them. The acrid smoke from oil lamps that hangs in the air around the clock only adds to their discomfort. Lungs burn and fingers are raw, hands patterned with scars from several years of tunnelling. Legs and arms are bleeding, sweat and rock-dust mingling in the open wounds. Backs, necks and knees are ruined, forever sore from the hours of unnatural hunching, hauling, stretching, craning, lifting, squatting. How many hours have they spent in this polluted darkness, longing for the touch of sun on their skin and a fresh, pine-perfumed breeze in their faces?

---

* For anyone who loves words there is something etymologically satisfying about seeing a stalactite in Greece. Seeing them in an ancient Greek monument is even better. The word comes from the modern Greek σταλακτίτης, *stalaktitis*, which in turn comes from the French *stalactite*. The French word derives in turn from the Greek *stalaktos*, meaning 'that which drips'. And what about etymology itself? Where else would the word come from, via Latin, but Greek: ετυμολογία, *etymologia*, the branch of linguistics which studies the origin of words, from the ancient Greek *etymos*, meaning true or authentic. A history of words, in other words.

The connection you feel here is nothing to do with kings, battles or empires. It is an atavistic tie that springs up instinctively, without prompting, and binds us to our fellow man across an otherwise unbridgeable divide of so many centuries it barely makes sense. History separates us from these struggling tunnel slaves yet at the same time unites us with them in a narrative that emphasises the human qualities at work. The tunnel is much more than a rat-infested old monument. It represents the unquenchable spirit of human endeavour, man's primordial efforts to master his environment and harness the forces of nature to meet his needs. The signs and signals are everywhere. The tunnel is about back-breaking work to complete the virtually impossible, a vital part of one man's preparations for war. It shows us a touch of vanity, too, perhaps a dash of arrogance, the desire of a ruler to impose himself, on nature, science, his people, the island of Samos itself. Polycrates was a bit of a show-off.

Had the tunnel been perfectly aligned, we would probably marvel even more and applaud Eupalinos' unbridled genius. As it is, a survey of the two shafts shows that about halfway between the northern entrance and the meeting point in the middle, the tunnel starts zigzagging curiously, while the southern route is much straighter. Another mystery presents itself. What was the point of these changes of direction when the calculations must have been made so carefully? Perhaps the northern team was forced to avoid patches of softer rock unsuitable for tunnelling, a little to the left here, then right, left again and so on. Had this been the case, imagine how much the deviations would have thrown Eupalinos' calculations, how much harder the project became. With a cross-section of about six feet by six, he only had to be a couple of yards out, over about 567 yards – giving a margin of error of less than 0.4 per cent – and the tunnels would miss each other completely.

Or maybe, and this is the more humanly irresistible suggestion, the northern team was ordered to switch course like this to maximise the chances of meeting in the middle. The one thing to avoid at all costs was having two parallel shafts that never met, a disaster that would probably have resulted in the swift execution of Eupalinos and his team of engineers and luckless slaves. Assuming the elevation was correct, if one tunnel remained straight the other, if it zigzagged, would eventually meet it, as we can see in the diagram. And there are signs, too, that Eupalinos did something similar with the vertical alignment of the two shafts to minimise the risks of missing each other in the rock. As they approached the anticipated join, the northern team started raising the height of the roof while maintaining a level floor, the southern crew doing exactly the opposite, keeping the roof at its set level and lowering the floor. So the two shafts don't meet in the middle with perfect precision. That would be too obvious. Whatever we might think about the wiggles and the wobbles, Eupalinos has taken another secret to his grave.

NORTHERN ENTRANCE

JUNCTION

SOUTHERN ENTRANCE

Far beneath the summit of Mount Kastro, the slave-diggers can at last hear something faint. The northern tunnel is veering sharply to the left. Tap, tap, tap, Is that the southern crew at last, after all these years? It seems hardly possible. More digging, more chiselling and the noises are getting louder and louder until there is no mistaking it. They start calling out to each other, their greetings muted by the stone that still separates them, each man, desperate to be the first to break through, suddenly throwing himself into the task with furious abandon, faster and faster, splinters of rock flying in the choking gloom until, with a final frenzied blow, the last chunk of limestone between the two crews is sent smashing to the ground in a cloud of rock-dust and the two history-making teams are united. More than

500 feet underground, the narrow chamber they have cut with their callused hands vibrates to the sound of shouting and celebratory cheers, slaps on the back, sweaty hugs and handshakes amid the fearful, noisy, reeking darkness. One of the team rushes back to convey the good news to Eupalinos who, when he hears it, cannot disguise a distinctly relieved smile. Of course, he knew it was going to be all right all along, he says to himself. It had just taken a very long time.

***

'This is enough now,' Dimos says. 'Enough! I don't want any more Herodotus.' There is an edge to his voice. He can go no further. He is firmly wedged between the walls. The tunnel has narrowed and the roof has dropped to the point where all I can see in front of me is a mass of sweating flesh and rock. I can't resist the urge to give him a firm push from behind to try to force him through but the only result is an exasperated gasp and a plaintive fart. He's stuck. The tunnelling expedition has come to a sticky end.

***

Late afternoon a couple of days later. White airplane snags rip across a denim sky. Something is missing. I can feel it. Or rather I can't because it has gone. I've spent an hour or so in the south side of the tunnel, taking pictures for the last time, and instead of going home to my room on the other side of the island, have climbed up the ridge above Pythagorio to clamber among the wind-whipped walls and towers of Polycrates' scattered fortifications. Something has disappeared and I don't know what it is. I pat my pockets one by one and suddenly realise with horror that the one thing I can't possibly afford to lose has gone. My Moleskine notebook, with a month's writing in it. The contents of my pockets spill to the ground. Cigarettes, lighter, handkerchief, sunglasses … No sign of the book. When your memory is as bad as mine, this is a disaster. Cameras, wallet, car keys, all pale into insignificance when compared with that black rectangle. Somewhere in its back sleeve is the little slip of paper containing a potted history of the travel writer's favourite notebook and the horribly appropriate words from Bruce Chatwin to which I have never given much thought: 'Losing my passport was the least of my worries; losing a notebook was a catastrophe.' It is.

The light slips away. The sky that was pink a few moments ago is bruising into night, towards the impenetrable blackness of a Whistler *Nocturne*. There is menace in the wine-dark sea. I must find the book. Hurrying down the mountain, I console myself with the comforting thought that it is almost certainly on the passenger seat of the hire car parked hundreds of feet below outside the Eupalinos Tunnel. No need to panic. But when I get to the car, it isn't there. My stomach feels more twisted by the minute. I can't lose the book. It just can't happen. I am not Herodotus, or Paddy Leigh Fermor. I need those notes. I start up the car and drive into town. A glimmer of relief when I realise I must have left the book on a local supermarket shelf while choosing a bottle of retsina earlier in the day. Thank God. The man in the shop recognises me and smiles. He must have it. But he doesn't. He is gravely sympathetic, says he saw me holding the book when I came in, but is sure I didn't leave it behind. There aren't many options left. If it is on the vast face of the mountain, thick with long grasses, bushes and rocks, it's gone. The last chance is around the statue of Pythagoras on the waterfront, but this is starting to feel desperate and the sky is indigo. A familiar shape sits among the shadows by the philosopher–mathematician's feet. Eureka! I stoop to pick it up with pounding heart. It's an abandoned radio. Until now, I have been convinced I'll find the book, but I'm beginning to feel sick. The Herodotean history I have been compiling has melted into the night.

There's no point going back to the mountain, but what else to do? The sky has merged into the rock and night has arrived. Listlessly, knowing the notebook is gone for ever, I hack around, slipping, tripping, going through the motions, peering into the inky mountainside with the torch's feeble beam. In my mind I go through all the notes and numbers, interviews, thoughts, digressions, meanderings and meetings contained in those pages. It's too much to lose. I can't do all that again. Minutes drag by, then an hour, and another. Time has run out. When should I accept the inevitable and give up? I've cut my wrists on a prickly bush, twisted an ankle hauling myself over a rocky outcrop. I've been zigzagging uselessly across the side of this immense mountain, this giant literary thief, for hours and still it won't give me back my book. I stumble back down in sickly silence. It is time for divine intervention. I close my eyes and pray. God, please return my notebook to me. Give me back Herodotus. A long pause. I will it to happen, envisaging the book sitting on the mountain. I open my eyes. The faltering beam of the torch is pointing straight ahead to a bare block of rock, a fragment of the Polycrates wall. And there, insouciant in the glare, indifferent to the heart-stopping panic it has caused, is my Moleskine. I give thanks to God, to Herodotus for this fancifully Herodotean moment, and to Polycrates for building his wall – and tunnel – where he did.

So who was this mountain-cutting megalomaniac and what was he up to? For the answers to these questions we must turn to Herodotus. 'Polycrates was the first Greek we know of to plan the dominion of the sea,' he tells us, before adding the wonderfully endearing catch-all caveat, 'unless we count Minos of Cnossus and any other who may possibly have ruled the sea at a still earlier date.' This is like saying Herodotus was the first historian we know of, unless you count all those who may have come before him, whose writings were lost in the silence of time. Herodotus' colourful pen-portrait of the tyrant of Samos shows a muscular opportunist at the height of his powers, a power-crazed Pirate of the Aegean.

> Polycrates had seized power in the island, and at the outset had divided his realm into three and gone shares with his brothers, Pantagnotus and Syloson; later, however, he killed the former, banished the latter (the younger of the two) and held the whole island himself. Once master of it, he concluded a pact of friendship with Amasis, king of Egypt, sealing it by a mutual exchange of presents. It was not long before the rapid increase of his power became the talk of Ionia and the rest of Greece. All his campaigns were victorious, his every venture a success. He had a fleet of a hundred penteconters [fifty-oared galleys] and a force of a thousand bowmen. His plundering raids were widespread and indiscriminate – he used to say that a friend would be more grateful if he gave him back what he had taken, than if he had never taken it.

A number of observations:

1. Fratricide has rarely stood in the way of an ambitious man and a throne.
2. Samos was one of Egypt's earliest Greek trading partners. Perhaps it was in this cosmopolitan atmosphere, fostered by open commercial and cultural exchange, that Herodotus, already exposed to different influences in Halicarnassus, first heard tales of the wonders of Egypt, a powerful incentive to travel there himself.
3. Even in the sixth century BC, the Greeks loved a celebrity. Polycrates' brazen conquests were 'the talk of Ionia and the rest of Greece'.
4. His force of 100 fifty-oared galleys and 1,000 archers does not sound huge by today's standards, more bijou island army than embryonic national fleet. Herodotus' numbers are always suspect, but Polycrates obviously had enough men under arms and warships at sea to cause havoc in the Aegean and along the Greek littoral.
5. The expression that someone would be more grateful if given back what had been taken from him than if nothing had been taken in the first place has been around for ever.

Piracy paid, as it always has done, and trade with Egypt flourished during the tyrant's reign, so that Herodotus could observe that 'apart from those of Syracuse [in Sicily], no other tyrant in the Greek world can be compared with Polycrates for magnificence'. A good deal of the revenue flowing into Polycrates' coffers was spent in a frenzy of architectural exhibitionism. It was a good time to be an engineer, architect, surveyor or bricklayer.

Herodotus tells us that the pharaoh Amasis (570–526 BC) demonstrated his goodwill to Greece by sending presents to be dedicated in Greek temples across the archipelago. The temple of Hera in Samos received two statues of Amasis 'which until my own time stood behind the doors in the great temple', a token of the Egyptian's friendship with Polycrates. Part of the exchange between Samos and Egypt, it seems, was sexual, though we know by now that Herodotus was hardly shy about dropping sex in wherever he could.

He writes of a Samian called Xanthus taking the beautiful, wildly glamorous prostitute Rhodopis to Egypt to ply her trade in Naucratis.

She became 'so famous', says Herodotus, 'that every Greek was familiar with her name'. He goes on to rubbish the theories that Rhodopis
ever earned enough money to have a pyramid raised in her honour.
She was good, but she wasn't *that* good.

———

The story of Rhodopis is Egypt's Cinderella. Herodotus says the
Thracian slave girl knew another celebrity among her fellow slaves,
none other than the world's most famous storyteller, 'Aesop the fable-
writer'. The story that has come down to us, perhaps via Aesop, was
first documented by Strabo about 400 years after Herodotus. It mingles
fact with fiction, relating how the bottom-of-the-pile Thracian girl
comes to marry the Egyptian pharaoh Amasis. Kidnapped by pirates
and sold into slavery, she's taken to Egypt where the other servant girls
mock her mercilessly for her pale skin, green eyes and blonde hair. She
is given all the hardest chores. One day her libidinous owner spots her
dancing alone and is so enraptured by her beauty that he gives her
a pair of golden slippers. Amasis, meanwhile, is holding court in
Memphis and invites the local population to attend a festival of
dancing, singing and feasting. The other servant girls get dolled up for
the party but don't allow Rhodopis to join them, giving her a long list
of unpleasant chores to do instead. Sadly, she takes herself off to wash
a bundle of clothes in the Nile and puts her slippers on a rock, only
to see the falcon–god Horus swoop down from the sky, snatch one up
in his beak and fly off. Whose lap should he drop it in but that of
Amasis. The Egyptian king, understanding this is a divine sign, decrees
that every girl in Egypt must try the slipper on. She whom it fits will
be his queen. The nationwide hunt begins. After much searching,
Amasis fails to finds his mate by land so takes to the Nile on his royal
barge, the wind filling the purple silk sails as he continues his romantic quest. Seeing the royal vessel approach, the servant girls rush down
to the landing to try their luck while the ever-modest Rhodopis hides
in the rushes. Amasis spots her and now it's her turn. The other girls
watch aghast as it slips on perfectly. And the charmingly bashful
Rhodopis has the other golden slipper to prove it. Amasis is enchanted,
but the servant girls still haven't given up. Spiteful to the last, they tell

the pharaoh Rhodopis is a slave and not even Egyptian so he can't marry her. On the contrary, he replies, 'She is the most Egyptian of all . . . for her eyes are as green as the Nile, her hair as feathery as papyrus, and her skin the pink of a lotus flower.' And so, we presume, they live happily ever after in one of history's earliest rags-to-riches tales.

Any reckoning of Polycrates' career must take into account the grandeur of his building projects and the security and prosperity they conferred. Before Polycrates, the twin pillars of Samian defence had been its fleet of warships and the straits dividing the island from the mainland. Polycrates added the protective cordon of truly monumental city walls, the size of whose stone blocks still inspires awe today, as does the remarkable preservation of a number of towers high above the town. Wandering around the windswept hills above Pythagorio, you can't fail to be impressed by the robustness and precision of these fortifications and the vigorous sense of power and style they project.

A large (by ancient standards) fleet of pirate warships required a safe harbour. Polycrates built one, grand enough to be singled out for particular notice by Herodotus with a breakwater so long it completely altered the shape of the coastline and, in time, spawned a new name for the town, Tigani, meaning frying-pan, though this is not what comes to mind when you see it on a map.

It is a deep hollow enclosed by seven artificially straight lines and a long seawall, creating a harbour whose distinctive shape sends the imagination whirling off on a mythical tangent. A careless Greek god, speedboating with his cousin Poseidon, has been knocking back jars of sweet Samian wine for a few lazy hours and is becoming more capricious by the minute. He's on holiday for a few days from Thrace where the weather isn't quite as gorgeous – it's grim up north – and the sun and the wine are starting to get to him. Here, give me the wheel, he bellows to Poseidon, draining another jar, barging his host out of the way with a violent guffaw, the wind whistling in his beard. Poseidon, who has been matching him jar for jar, is too drunk to object, thinks the whole thing is a bit of a laugh. In his stupor he forgets to tell his northern visitor, a landlubber if ever there was one, that the waters round here are quite narrow, fails to mention there's this huge breakwater in Polycrates' brand-new harbour, got to be a bit careful as you come round, come to think of it should be somewhere around heeeeEEERE . . . STOPPPPPPP! But it is too late.

There is a terrific smash, a thunderclap from the heavens, and Poseidon's sparkling speedboat, pride of the oceans, a gift from his latest nymph, rams straight into the Polycrates breakwater. With a wrenching roar the great stone edifice is hurled across the water by the force of the impact, the giant blocks of marble submerged beneath the foaming waters that heave and buckle. The boat is crushed in an instant, Poseidon sinks to the sea-floor in a daze as his cousin cartwheels through the heavens and across the harbour, handlebar moustache splayed against his cheeks, before landing with a crash halfway up the mountain in a smoking crater amid a volley of skyward-shooting rocks. Hundreds of feet beneath him, the swirling sea drains away from the base of the breakwater, the stones rise dripping from the foam as they tear across the seafloor behind a tidal wave that rises higher and higher as it sweeps over the harbour, curls and crashes over the far shore, sending a sheet of water ripping up the mountain. Fishermen's homes are flattened, cats and dogs are drowned in the deluge and a pair of teenage lovers heavy petting in one of the fortified towers die in a watery embrace, skulls smashed like coconuts against the walls. And then, when the waves have subsided, the rocks from the crater have fallen back to earth, the last ripples from the sinking boat have finally disappeared and all is quiet, Poseidon's country cousin hauls himself groggily to his feet, stares out at the sunbright waters and scans in vain for his sunken friend of whom there is no trace. No sign, either, of the speedboat. Something odd has happened. The harbour looks very different all of a sudden. He could swear something has changed. He rubs his eyes to make sure, cranes his neck to one side and squints in the blinding fulgor of sunlight. There is no question about it. The frying-pan has disappeared. And there, in its place, is a pair of thunderously large buttocks.

# Wassailing Gods, Pious Priests and Tearful Monks

*[History] hath triumphed over time, which besides it, nothing but eternity*
*hath triumphed over.*

Walter Ralegh, *The History of the World* (1614)

THE STILL SMARTING, *souma*-befuddled Dimos has no interest in joining Round Two of the Polycrates Monuments Mentioned by Herodotus Tour ('And I don't come to the temple either') so I slope off alone to Pythagorio with a snorkel and flippers for company. From the road that snakes across the mountains high above the town, the sea is a sudden flash of mercury and even from here, several miles away, the harbour mole is clearly visible, the modern incarnation of Polycrates' 525-yard breakwater that surged out into twenty fathoms of water. In the nineteenth century the mole was rebuilt using material from the original structure.

Down in the harbour, a scoop of pastels and primaries bright with white houses, a handful of fishermen bob about in tiny boats, mending their nets and calling out greetings to passing friends. A chorus of '*Ti kanis?*', What are you doing?, '*Ti omorfi mera*', What a beautiful day, '*Ola kalla*', Everything's fine, and the day wears on. A platoon of cats languidly prowls the waterfront, noses tilted to the sea. Once in a while a discarded scrap of fish describes a graceful parabola across the azure sky, all languor vanishes in a flash and the morsel lands in a maelstrom of raised hackles, bloodcurdling howls, hisses, flashing claws and fighting fur. Past the strip of afternoon-sleepy bars the old seawall begins its vigorous thrust out into the water towards the Turkish mainland.

It is tempting to see something hugely symbolic about the direction in which it points its defiant finger, straight towards the formidable bulk of Mycale which even in the white glare looms unmistakably before us, rocky reminder of the Greek naval triumph in these waters that brought the cataclysmic Persian invasion to an end in 479 BC. There is a grim resolution, too, in the crisp blue-and-white church that sits in draughty isolation atop the ridge high above me, overlooking the Mycale Straits. At the summit of the bell-tower a crucifix stands watchful guard against the island's eastern neighbour. It's far too laid back to admit it, and few on the island would even think it, but a glance at an atlas confirms the point: Samos is Europe's final frontier, its easternmost redoubt. Across the water lies the old enemy, today the Dar al Islam, the Muslim world, the Persian empire that was.

Had it been built half a century later, you would think that Polycrates' harbour wall, an ostentatiously powerful example of Greek technology and engineering, was deliberately aligned like this to commemorate the victory over the Persians in stone. In fact, the local weather conditions would have been paramount in deciding which line to take out to sea, but the precision of the one-in-the-eye jab at Mycale is uncanny. If, like Jesus, you could walk on the water and wanted to go from Pythagorio to Mycale your route couldn't be simpler: start on Polycrates' break-water and carry on straight. The grey-green Turkish mountain grows higher and higher with every step, dominating the prospect.

Halfway up the breakwater the *Pythagorio* ferry languishes in rusty oblivion, an elderly matron suffering the indignity of an internal examination and refit. Peeping behind its hull, two boys fish on the harbour side. Silvering bait plops into the turquoise. The woolly hat clapped over their ears does not augur well for a snorkelling expedition on a late afternoon in November. At the southern end of the mole, as near to the Turkish coast as it gets, I peel off my clothes reluctantly and plunge in for a bracing inspection of these quasi-Herodotean ruins.

The water is dagger-cold, a stabbing blade that slices your breath away and then punches you in the solar plexus to make sure it hurts. With an involuntary thrashing of legs and arms I am enveloped in a cocoon of phosphorescence, bubbles foaming up like soda from the hyaline depths. Vistas of shattered stone are nothing new on the Herodotus trail but underwater, magnified in their secret desolation, they startle. The building blocks of a pirate kingdom, foundations of an empire that came and went in a flurry of island conquest, are scattered pell-mell across the seabed in a luminous grave. Needles of sunlight illuminate a flotilla of tiny fish darting this way and that, escaping into the shadows beneath my clumsy strokes. I splash around uselessly for a few minutes, lost amid the rubble, and return spluttering to the surface to the general hilarity of the fishermen.

Fishermen and fish feature in one of Herodotus' taller stories about Polycrates. The Egyptian pharaoh Amasis, a superstitious fellow, is troubled by his ally's apparent invincibility and the countless victories he's notching up at sea. He writes the tyrant of Samos a letter expressing his unease. It is another reminder of Herodotus' conviction that human fortune is a distinctly finite commodity. Greatness is fine while it lasts, but the gods can't abide endless success and innumerable victories. Sooner or later, they'll ruin you. So beware.

> Amasis to Polycrates:– It is a pleasure to hear of a friend and ally doing well, but, as I know that the gods are jealous of success, I cannot rejoice at your excessive prosperity . . . Now I suggest that you deal with the danger of your continual success in the following way: think of whatever it is you value most – whatever you would most regret the loss of – and throw it away: throw it right away, so that nobody can ever see it again.

For some reason, Polycrates, instead of telling the pharaoh to mind his own business and get lost or dismissing him privately as a jealous crank, is impressed with the unsolicited advice. He rummages through his bursting treasure chests until he fishes out his most prized possession: a signet ring of emerald set in gold, 'the work of a Samian named Theodorus'.*

---

* There is a ring of truth, so to speak, about this little detail in an otherwise apocryphal tale. Theodorus of Samos was a well-known sculptor and architect living in about 560–520 BC, when the island was a major centre for Greek sculpture. He is mentioned once elsewhere in the *Histories* as the possible sculptor of a silver mixing bowl which could hold over 5,000 gallons of wine for the festival of Theophania at Delphi. The bowl was given to the sanctuary by Croesus of Lydia. Theodorus was one of the pioneers of hollow casting in bronze, what Professor Shipley calls 'the crowning achievement of the Greek sculptor's art', the other being Rhoecus, who may have been his father and is cited by Herodotus as one of the first architects of the Temple of Hera on Samos.

He commands a penteconter to take him out to sea and then, when he is far from shore, whips the ring out and hurls it into the water.

Several days later, a fisherman catches a fish so magnificent he thinks it will make a worthy present for his lord. He presents it to Polycrates, who receives it graciously and invites the fisherman to join him for dinner. Off the fish goes to the royal kitchen, where the cooks slice it open, only to find the signet ring in its belly. Hurrah, they cry, sensing a reward, and hurry off to the king to present it to him. Stunned, Polycrates fires off a letter to Amasis telling him what has happened. Five hundred miles to the south, sitting in his capital of Sais on the western Nile delta, Amasis shakes his head as he reads the letter. He knew there was something fishy about Polycrates, he knew it all along, he says. 'He forthwith sent a messenger to Samos to say that the pact between Polycrates and himself was at an end. This he did in order that when the destined calamity fell upon Polycrates, he might avoid the distress he would have felt, had Polycrates still been his friend.'

The portrait of Polycrates warns us that no good will come of his piratical triumphs. And so Herodotus makes the graceful segue, still pursuing this story, to Sparta's fateful campaign against Samos, its first foray across the Aegean. It is 525 and Polycrates has sneakily thrown his lot in with the Persian king Cambyses, who is in the midst of mounting his expedition against Egypt, now under Amasis' son and short-lived successor Psammetichus III. Polycrates kills two birds with one stone. He secretly sends Cambyses 'a request to apply to Samos for a contingent of troops' and the Persian gladly complies. The Samian contribution is forty triremes, every man among the carefully selected crews suspected by Polycrates of disloyalty. The force is despatched to Cambyses with instructions never to allow them to return to Samos. Later, however, they make their escape, have some inconclusive skirmishes with Polycrates before travelling to the Peloponnese to persuade the Spartans to join them in common cause against the tyrant. Their numbers swell with the addition of the Corinthians.

But for once the legendary martial prowess of the Spartans is held in check. Herodotus describes the pitched fighting with an immediacy and sense of position that is striking to anyone familiar with the local topography. 'In an assault on the defences they fought their way forward to the tower near the sea, on the side of the town where the suburbs are, but Polycrates brought a strong party to meet the threat and drove them off.' The fortifications along the ridge above town held. But then the Spartans broke through 'at the upper tower on the ridge which joins the high ground' and swarmed through into the town. If the Spartans had all fought as valiantly as Archias and Lycopes, says Herodotus, they would have carried the day, but the small force of invaders was cut off and killed.

There is a classic pro-Samos aside from Herodotus here. 'I myself once met at Pitana – his native village [in Sparta] – the grandson of this Archias,' he says, showing off his journalistic skills. 'He told me his father had been called Samius in memory of his grandfather's heroic death in Samos, and his respect for the Samians was due to the fact that they had honoured his grandfather with a public funeral.'

After an unsuccessful siege of forty days, the Spartans return empty-handed to the Peloponnese, and Polycrates lives to fight another day. So what of the tragic inevitability of a great man's ruin? How does his stirring defeat of the invading Spartans square with the Herodotean worldview? The answer is, it doesn't. Not yet. But Herodotus is not finished with Polycrates and nor, it seems, are the vengeful gods. His version of the last chapter of the Polycrates story is as entertaining as – and only marginally more credible than – the ring-in-the-fish tale.

A man called Oroetes, the Persian governor of Sardis, has it in for Polycrates. Determined to crush the Samian tyrant, he sends him a message, the gist of which is this: I know you want to master the whole of Greece. I can help you do it. You haven't got enough money to do it, but I have. Why am I offering to help you? Because I know Cambyses is planning to have me killed. Come and spring me from here and I will reward you with enough money to make Greece yours. If you don't believe how rich I am, send me your most trusted man and I'll open up my coffers to him so you'll know I'm serious. Polycrates, his lust for power unsated, despatches a man called Maeandrius to inspect the loot.

'Oroetes, however, as soon as he knew that someone was actually on the way and must shortly be expected to come and view his treasure, filled eight chests with stones very nearly to the brim, topped them up with a thin layer of gold, fastened them securely and kept them ready for inspection.' It is the stuff of fairytales. Maeandrius, perhaps discouraged from inspecting the chests too closely, doesn't dig a little deeper to see whether all that glitters really is gold. He sends the all-clear to Polycrates, who at once prepares to visit Oroetes in person.

His daughter does her best to dissuade him, but he tells her to shut up, threatening her with the ultimate paternal sanction in sixth-century Greece, to 'delay her marriage for many years' if she doesn't. He should have listened to her, of course. As soon as he lands he is impaled and killed. 'Oroetes had him murdered, and the dead body hung on a cross.' You can almost hear Herodotus sigh as he brings the Polycrates story to a close with a rueful nod to the role of fate, the gods and the vicissitudes of human fortune: 'This, then, was the end of the long-continued prosperity of Polycrates. It was just as Amasis, king of Egypt, had previously foretold'.

Polycrates would have been encouraged to see the Persian Great King Darius avenge his death with the murder of Oroetes, part of an imperial campaign to bump off troublesome nobles. But his perforated body would have squirmed in its grave to see what the Persian monarch did next to his island kingdom.

To find out what happened we must return to the *Histories*. Darius is in bed with his wife Atossa (where else would he be with Herodotus?). The unfortunately named woman is one of history's earliest examples of the ambitious wife. And the sequence is one of the first royal bed scenes in world literature.

'My Lord, with the immense resources at your command, the fact that you are making no further conquests to increase the power of Persia, must mean that you lack ambition,' she purrs. Her hand slides softly down his chest to stiffen his resolve. 'Surely a young man like you, who is master of great wealth, should be seen engaged in some active enterprise, to show the Persians that they have a man to rule them.' Darius groans. He's been preparing to bridge the straits of Bosphorus between Asia and Europe to attack the Scythians, he says with a slightly quavering voice. Atossa disappears beneath the sheets to begin her own active enterprise.

The story – not to mention Atossa's foreplay – gets more gripping. 'Never mind about the Scythians for the moment,' she reproaches her husband. 'They are yours for the asking at any moment you please. Look – what I want you to do is invade Greece.' What strategic objectives lie behind this suggestion? What carefully considered calculations put an invasion of Greece ahead of Scythia? Atossa is admirably clear about it. 'I have heard people talk of the women there, and I should like to have Spartan girls, and girls from Argos and Attica and Corinth, to wait upon me.' These Persian maids are such a bore, darling, she's saying. I need some new help about the palace. Something more exotic.

In fact, there's rather more to Atossa than the conviction that Greek servant girls are the latest must-have accessory. Darius' beautiful wife is motivated less by the need for home help than by an abscess on her bosom. First it was merely embarrassing, now she is 'dangerously ill'. The only man who can treat it is Democedes, Polycrates' doctor of old, a physician of such skill and renown that the Samian poached him from Athens by multiplying his salary twelve times, the sort of thing that keeps Premiership football running two-and-a-half millennia later.

Democedes has told Atossa he'll only cure her if she swears to do him any service he asks, 'adding that he would not ask for anything she could blush to give'. You can picture Herodotus lowering his head as he relates this little caveat, surveying his audience knowingly over his half-moon spectacles, enjoying the innuendo. Atossa agrees. And what is it Democedes wants? Quite simple. He wants to go home. So an invasion of Greece it must be.

Darius, who is not in the most commanding position to argue the point, agrees with his wife. Who wouldn't? Atossa reminds him he has in his court the perfect source of information on Greece. Democedes, she suggests, would make an excellent guide. The guileless Darius says he'll send a reconnaissance mission to Greece and, when he has all the intelligence he needs, he'll launch his war.

And so the Persian fleet sails west. Samos is 'the first place, either inside or outside the Greek world, to fall to Darius', Herodotus remarks. It is Samos in particular, he continues, because a very curious thing happened once in Egypt which bound Darius to the island. Polycrates' exiled brother Syloson was in Egypt during Cambyses' campaign there. Darius, who at this time was a member of Cambyses' guard and not a man of great consequence, caught sight of Syloson's flame-coloured cloak while he was in Memphis, and was suddenly seized with a desire to possess this sartorial treasure. He offered Syloson money for it but the Greek refused and gave it to him for nothing, slightly startled by the request, as you would be.

Spool forward to the death of Cambyses, the revolt against the Magi and now Darius is on the throne. Time to cash in the favour, thinks Syloson, and journeys to the royal capital of Susa to see what he can extract from the king. Darius offers to shower him with gold and silver but no, says Syloson, all he wants is for the Persian king to recover his native Samos for him because it has been seized by one of the family's servants, a man called Maeandrius. Do this, he asks, without killing or enslaving a single man on the island. Darius agrees to the request.

Samos is in turmoil after the murder of Polycrates (it was for several decades). Maeandrius calls a public meeting of all the citizens of Samos and tells them things are going to change. Tyranny and dictatorship are not his style. Though he could be their 'absolute master' if he wanted, instead he's going to give up his power and make everyone 'equal before the law'. He's offering them their liberty, he says grandly and waits for a tumultuous applause. Nothing. No sign of gratitude whatsoever. Only a deafening silence. The Samians are a truculent lot.

> One of his audience, a man of repute named Telesarchus, at once sprang to his feet. 'What?' he cried; 'that's a fine speech to hear from a low-born rogue like you! Far from being fit to govern us, you ought rather to account for the money you have had your hands on.' This was enough to show Maeandrius that, if he surrendered the tyranny, somebody else would be sure to seize it; so he changed his mind and determined to hold on to what he had got.

He withdraws to his citadel, sends for the leading men of the island one by one, under the hilarious pretence of showing them 'his accounts', and claps them in irons. Shortly after this, he falls ill and his ambitious brother Lycaretus decides to have them all put to death as a prelude to taking power. 'So, it seems, the people of Samos did not want liberty,' says Herodotus sharply. The Persian threat is mounting to the east and all the Samians can do is fight among themselves.

Darius' force lands on Samos to restore the exiled Syloson and 'nobody lifted a finger against them'. Maeandrius' 'crazy brother called Charilaus', disgusted by this feeble display, urges resistance to the Persians from his prison cell and offers to lead it in person. Maeandrius agrees, slips quietly off the island and leaves his brother to it. Charilaus and his men slaughter the leading Persians, but the general Otanes, as soon as he learns of the outrage, sends the main force back to the island to regain control. Boiling with rage, he puts out of his mind Darius' command not to kill or capture any Samian and return the island to Syloson intact. Instead, he orders a scorched-earth response. It is a massacre. People are killed indiscriminately, in the citadel, in temples, wherever they hide. And with a last reference to fish, Herodotus brings his story to its dramatic and bloody end: 'As for Samos, the Persians took the entire population like fish in a drag-net, and presented Syloson with an empty island.'

There is a final Herodotean flourish, unexpected even by his standards. 'Some years later, however, Otanes contracted some disease of the genital organs and that, in conjunction with a dream he had, induced him to repopulate the place.' History, conquest and sexually transmitted diseases, warts and all.

———

So Polycrates paid with his life for his addiction to conquest. And the island he had made into a pirate kingdom, feared across the seas, formidably defended, rich in produce, and with some of the most magnificent monuments in Greece, passed easily into the hands of the Persians, who depopulated the place before returning it to his younger brother. The days of unchallenged rape and plunder were over, replaced from about 517 by an altogether less glamorous era of pliant, pro-Persian quiescence.

The Eupalinos Tunnel and the harbour breakwater pay silent tribute to those earlier, halcyon times, but perhaps even more evocative is the Temple of Hera, or Heraion, which rots away in sublime solitude on the coastal plain of Chora. Samos is shaped like a whale, a little like Kos albeit without the svelte good looks of its southern colleague, and the Heraion sits – these days it is difficult to say stands – in the heart of its abdomen, east of either its flipper or paunch, depending on how you see it, on the south-east of the island.

In its time, Polycrates' great religious centrepiece was of an unearthly splendour. Our Samos expert Professor Shipley reminds us how the Samian aristocrats used to frolic winsomely at the festival of Hera with this quotation from the island's epic poet Asios in the fifth or sixth century BC:

> And they, too, when they had combed their flowing locks, used to go to Hera's precinct, all bound in fine robes. Their snow-white tunics used to reach to the floor of the broad earth, with golden brooches shaped like grasshoppers on them. Their tresses waved in the wind like golden bands, and cunningly worked bracelets were about their arms.

The construction of the temple was a powerful sign. It denoted prosperity and prestige, a sort of island one-upmanship, while bestowing Hera's godly favour – or, in Shipley's phrase, 'hegemonic force' – upon Polycrates' relentlessly piratical campaigns. According to Samian tradition, Hera, the cow-eyed sister-wife of Zeus and goddess of marriage, was born here on the banks of the Imbrasos river, beneath a wicker bush. That plant supposedly survived until the time of Pausanias, the Greek travel writer of the second century AD, and was at the heart of this cult of Hera. In 1963, a felled tree trunk was discovered in excavations near the great altar of Rhoecus – our Samian architect – prompting jaw-dropping claims that this was the very bush originally honoured as Hera's birthplace. Legend has it that the goddess's marriage to Zeus also took place here.

So, although the low-lying land was a uniquely unfavourable site, thanks to the river's shifting alluvial deposits, there was no question of building the temple elsewhere. This was where it had to be. A sanctuary to Hera had existed here since at least the second half of the second millennium BC. If Polycrates could run the world's longest tunnel through a mountain, building a super-sized temple (more than 360 feet long by 180 feet wide) on dodgy ground was not going to be beyond him.

Today, the once magnificent edifice has subsided, leaving only a single teetering column as reminder of a more august age. The scale of the temple complex is more impressive in an aerial view. Here what look like a powerful set of perimeter walls but are actually only the remains of the temple foundations convey a sense both of the difficulty of building in this marshy corner of the island and of the sheer size of the sanctuary in its full glory. If these massive walls were only the foundations, you can't help wondering how high it must have soared into the sky. The temple would have been visible for miles at sea, a welcome mark of divine protection for sailors and fishermen, travellers and traders. Quite simply, it was, as Herodotus remarked, 'the biggest of all Greek temples known'.

This afternoon, it crouches beneath mighty Mycale, the mountain's lower flanks invisible in the distorted light so that the triangular, Pythagorean peak seems to float lightly on the sea, a volcanic eruption roaring out of the depths. This is an arid corner of the island a world away from the rainforest, mountaintop Manolates, flanked by a bank of swaying rushes, autumn-tinted trees and smaller, sun-dried, green-flecked hills, dwarfed by Mycale. High on the ridge running above the plain of Chora, eight wind towers roll and revolve in the piercing sky. It is endless work, as thankless as the dozen labours of Hercules that Hera, jealous of the hero who had been born to Zeus after his three-night tryst with lovely Alcmene, did her utmost to make even more ghastly.

Close to, the single standing column, sole survivor of raids, wars, earthquakes, vandalism and time, looks like a clumsy tower of aspirins or recreational drugs erected by some pill-popping obsessive. The third and fourth tablets down from the top have been knocked out of line, as has the eighth, adding to the sense of precariousness. And yet it has stood like this for centuries. For hundreds of years travellers have been painting their Orientalised oils and watercolours, all peach sunsets and red-capped, moustachioed men in voluminous pantaloons, standing next to a lopsided column by the edge of the water.

I am not alone, after all. First of all, there is the insistent chorus of birdsong, a musical accompaniment that has been here far longer than the temple. Then there is the human sound of history in the making, a team of bearded-scruff archaeologists knocking mud off their shovels and banging scrapers together in a tinnient din.

Next to me, posing superbly, a tragic-looking archaeologist with bohemian movie-star glamour is staring into the wind, auburn hair scattering across her face as she rolls herself a cigarette with liquorice papers. I join her on a bench overlooking the rubble-ruin of the Heraion, giant columnar pills strewn pell-mell across the grasses by our pharmaceutically inclined friend. A shattered Monopteros here, a fragment of Hekatompedos there, marble trochilus, Ionic capitals, peripterals and peribolos, pteron, amphiprostyles, stoas . . .

The mayhem of these tumbled stones, bleached marble and soft buff Samian limestone, is less the hallowed site of religious serenity than the aftermath of a particularly wild party of wassailing gods. Something like the morning after the millennium before. Divinely sized debris every which way you look. Piles of Titans' Paracetamols, Dionysian Diazepam, Herculean Ecstasy, Apollonian Alka-Seltzers, heroic-sized Extra Strong Mints for the drug-free gods with a sweet tooth looking for that restorative sugar kick. Poseidon, having recovered from his speedboat accident, has been celebrating the departure of the oikish, provincial cousin who caused it. To the weary irritation of the other gods, with the inevitable exception of Dionysus, who is goading him to drink ever more and faster, he is downing 5,000-gallon mixing bowls of wine and smashing up Hera's temple, uprooting columns and hurling colonnades this way and that in his drunken high spirits. Reeling, weaving, staggering, he teeters and totters across Hera's sanctuary, bellowing, burping and guffawing in drunken confusion before he crashes down with an earth-quaking roar, flattening the great Altar of Rhoecus with his outstretched hands which are punctured at once by a volley of marble splinters. He groans and curses with the pain of a dislocated shoulder, clutching a sprained ankle as he crawls off into his watery home. Far-fetched and fanciful, of course, but there are few things more capricious, wanton or destructive than a Greek god in a fury. Or on a bender. And here, right in front of me, is the proof. Nothing left standing bar the eccentric stash-of-pills column.

Elektra, the archaeologist with a glinting nose-stud, thinks this is all nonsense. She would probably prefer Patrick Leigh Fermor's evocation of a more innocent sort of ecstasy experienced in sites like this. 'A spell of peace lives in the ruins of ancient Greek temples,' he writes in *Mani*. 'As the traveller leans back among the fallen capitals and allows the hours to pass, it empties the mind of troubling thoughts and anxieties and slowly refills it, like a vessel that has been drained and scoured, with a quiet ecstasy.'

She surveys the scene with the tragic seriousness of a compulsive rearranger of fallen stones, seeking order from the chaos of history. It's a mess. 'This is the biggest Ionic temple in Greece and yet the government doesn't even have enough money to excavate it,' she says. 'We archaeologists are very sad about this.' When she was a little child she says she used to feel a sense of awe when she visited an archaeological site. Aged fifteen she watched the third Indiana Jones film and then, in an instant, she knew she would be an archaeologist. 'I always loved history and I like very much to be out, to be able to see, to imagine what these places were like in ancient times,' she says dreamily. 'It is a great thing, no?' Her face is lit with the passion of the impractical romantic. In her widening eyes I can see the reflected white discs of stone, stacked (now that the picture of the godly revels has faded) like mislaid backgammon counters, as she smokes away.

Herodotus leaves us with a last glimpse of the Temple of Hera in Book 4, in an aside about another Samian celebrity, the engineer Mandrocles who built Darius' pontoon bridge across the Bosphorus, opening the way to a Persian attack on the Scythians and an invasion of Europe. The king was so delighted with the result, says Herodotus, that he loaded Mandrocles down with presents. Mandrocles spent some of his reward on commissioning a painting of the bridge-building, with an enthroned Darius surveying his army crossing the water in front of him. He then presented the picture to the temple of Hera, with these words inscribed upon it as a memorial to his achievement:

> Goddess, accept this gift from Mandrocles,
> Who bridged the Bosphorus' fish-haunted seas.

His labour, praised by King Darius, won
Honour for Samos, for himself a crown.

A case of history being written by the winners? Yes, but not entirely.
The inscription does not tell the whole story. Mandrocles evidently
did very nicely for himself out of the Persian campaign. He had a good
war, as they say. Funnily enough, he completely forgot to mention one
thing: Darius' invasion of Scythia was a humiliating failure.

Herodotus' interest in religion in the *Histories* is a constant, as is his
fascination with how two civilisations with different customs – and
religions – came to confront each other in war. Today it is the Greek
Orthodox Church which serves as the bastion of Greek identity and,
in some minds at least, a European bulwark against the encroaches of
Islam from the East. Occasionally you feel that in Samos.

As the writer Takis Michas said back in Athens, religion in Greece
is the cement of identity, the country's social glue. 'It's like we are
Greeks, we are Orthodox. It's not a question of metaphysics or of
finding solutions to life's mysteries. That's not the point of the Greek
Church. Its origins are very different from those of the West. The wars
of independence were also wars against Muslims, so part of the Greek
identity is defined against Muslim domination.'

This Greek concept of a national religion has important consequences for those who do not subscribe to the faith. 'In a certain sense
the minorities are second-class Greeks,' Michas said. 'Jews, Muslims
and Catholics are seen as lacking something because the constitution
says Greece is Greek Orthodox, implying that if you're not there's
something wrong with you. The Orthodox Church is like communism, either you belong or you don't. When you join, you're
joining the Mafia.'

One evening, relaxing after the Herodotean triathlon of tunnel,
temple and breakwater, I drive off into the heart of southern Samos,
right in the middle of the island–whale's flipper–paunch. The monas-

tery of Megali Panaghia, built in the sixteenth century, occupies a special place in Samian hearts as a meeting place of the resistance during the struggle for independence in the early 1820s.

Dimos is unimpressed when I tell him I am off to meet Father Sotirios, chancellor to Bishop Efsevius of Samos. I have been put in touch by the office of Archbishop Christodoulos, the Turks-are-barbarians head of the Greek Orthodox Church. Dimos is quick to squash the name-dropping. 'Pah!' he snorts, downing a *souma*. 'You know what we call Christodoulos? Juntodoulos, after the junta.' Like many younger Greeks, he's no great supporter of the Church. He says it's mired in an idealised view of its own history. 'All these priests are the same, their minds are stuck in Byzantine empire. They want to retake Constantinople, reconquer Asia Minor. They say the Church ended the Turkish occupation. The Church did this, the Church did that, they have nothing to do with Christianity. Nothing! These priests only talk fear, fear of the Turks, fear of NATO, fear of globalisation, fear we lose our Greek Orthodox character, they say the anti-Christ is coming from the Jews. The young do not like this, we are not following them. This is why the churches are empty.'

He pauses. 'They're always calling the Turks barbarians. Now remember Herodotus, what he wrote about the end of the battle of Plataea. One of the Greek soldiers said, let's cut Mardonius' head off, just like the Persians did to Leonidas at Thermopylae. And the Spartans said, no, we're not like the barbarians. The Church is not like that. There is no love thy neighbour. Muslims can't even worship in Athens because there is no mosque. They have to worship underground. And in Juntodoulos' mind, they're all barbarians.'

Dimos' Herodotus reference is spot on, though it is more a critique of the Persians and the Aeginetans than an injunction to love thy neighbour. After the Greek victory at Plataea, Lampon, an Aeginetan, approaches Pausanias, Spartan commander of the Greek forces, and advises him to decapitate Mardonius' corpse and impale it on a pike. This will avenge the Persian dishonour to the body of Pausanias' uncle Leonidas. Pausanias bristles. 'First, you exalt me and my country to the skies by your praise of my success; and then you would bring it all to nothing by advising me to insult a dead body, and by saying that my good name would be increased if I were to do an improper thing fitter for barbarians than Greeks . . .'

Dimos downs another shot of *souma* with majestic disdain – and streaming eyes – and lights a cigarette. 'Talk to Sotirios, you will see I am right. Pah!'

---

Father Sotirios is a magnificently bearded and bespectacled specimen of holiness, tranquillity and charm. He is wrapped in a black, wide-sleeved cassock and the obligatory matching *kalimafhi*, an elongated, pillbox hat. An oversize crucifix dangling from his neck rests halfway up the mountain of his stomach, as though the onward journey to the summit of such a prodigious peak is just too much to tackle. He is a Greek Friar Tuck, exuding the bonhomie of a practised gourmand. This is a man, one suspects, who could eat half a cow, a couple of chickens, a side of ham and still have room for baklava and ice cream, washed down with a bumper of wine and a carafe of sweet Samos muscat to round it off.

He is the same age as me, in his mid-thirties, and is enchanted by my middle name of Salvatore, the Italian equivalent of his priestly title. He is something of a Church historian, too. St Justin, he tells me as soon as we meet, was the second-century philosopher martyred by the Romans. As for the Church in Samos, it dates back to the very earliest times, brought across the water by St John of Patmos, author of the Book of Revelation. The island of Samos has a distinguished Biblical pedigree. It is mentioned in Acts 20:15 in the course of Paul's journey to Ephesus: 'And we sailed thence, and came the next day over against Chios; and the next day we arrived at Samos, and tarried at Trogyllium; and the next day we came to Miletus.' Moving on from Church history, he says Samos was famous in ancient times because of the superb timber its forests produced, perfect material from which to build fleets of triremes.

Of all the 6,000 Greek islands, or at least the 227 inhabited ones, Samos lies closest to the Islamic world that is regarded with such misgiving in certain, especially ecclesiastical, quarters in Greece. I ask Sotirios about the Church's relations with Islam. 'Under the Turkish occupation, we had 400 years of Islam on top of us,' he chuckles. 'Not in Samos, but the rest of Greece. Samos has never had a mosque.' A number of people on the island have already pointed this out to me with pride. Everyone is equal in the eyes of Christ, he hastens to say, then adds a caveat. 'People in Greece who are not Orthodox cannot be Greek in the full sense of the word. We have been united for seventeen centuries since we received the Christian faith. From 1453 to 1821 many gave their lives, just because they were Christian.' He says that when Archbishop Christodoulos used the word 'barbarians' to describe Turks, he did so in good faith. 'This was to protect the people from dangers.'

I ask him what he makes of Olympianism, an increasingly fashionable – if fringe – return to the worship of the twelve gods of ancient Greece. A Greek court has recently given the religion official recognition. The Church has not welcomed this novel example of historical continuity, dismissing its followers as 'miserable resuscitators of a degenerate dead religion who wish to return to the monstrous dark delusions of the past'. You can imagine what fun Herodotus would have had with this. The first morning I met Dimos, he was having a vigorous, *souma*-fuelled argument with the café owner, a noisy Olympian who was taunting him, as a member of the Orthodox Church, for worshipping icons. Father Sotirios shares his Church's contempt for these neo-historical Olympians. 'They don't believe in anything. They just want a free life without any laws. If I believe in a god who has two women, I can have two women. If Ares can kill, so can I. If I believe life consists only of drinking and dancing, I'll believe in Dionysus. This is not religion. If you are interested in real religion, I will show you something very special tonight.'*

He invites me to return to the monastery to attend a very rare sacrament at the heart of Orthodox religion, the initiation of a new monk. Among the small population of the island such events hardly ever happen – the last time was several years ago – which is why Alexis, a new friend on the island, is so eager to accompany me. Alexis is a

---

* Contrast this with Joseph Brodsky's argument that 'one of the saddest things that ever transpired in the course of our civilisation was the confrontation between Greco-Roman polytheism and Christian monotheism, and its known outcome. Neither intellectually nor spiritually was this confrontation really necessary.'

louche, shaven-headed hotelier whose ensemble of jeans, anorak, baseball hat and chewing gum suggest he's not a church-goer in the traditional mould of this evening's congregation: middle-class Samos in its Sunday best. Alexis surveys Father Sotirios carefully. 'He looks like a heavy-metal guy,' he says dispassionately. 'All these guys look the same to me. Lots of fat priests with big beards.'

We move into the golden gloom of the candlelit church. A handful of coloured glass lamps suspended in mid-air glow like fireflies, clusters of orange, pink, green and red illuminating icons of stern-faced saints among the muted frescoes. The vaulted roof is a harmony of russets, forest greens and faded mustards and astronaut-helmet haloes that have long lost their lustre. A pair of ostrich eggs hang from the shimmering brass orbs of the two chandeliers, trailing red velvet tassels beneath them. Above them, regularly spaced among the row of saintly icons, are the twin-headed Byzantine eagles, guardians of this fortress of the faith. Outside the church, there is a rhythmic knocking of wood on stone, steadily getting faster. Inside, a murmuring hush of anticipation amid the perfumed gloaming. This is a religion that communicates powerfully, magnificently, to the senses. The great and good of Samos make their way towards the iconostasis as they arrive, bowing, crossing themselves with a practised flick of the fingers, reverently kissing a pair of icons.

Alexis is attracting disapproving stares. 'I'm the worst person you could be here with,' he says. 'Guess which one's the monk's mother.' He points across to a red-eyed woman snivelling into a handkerchief. The man next to her, smartly uncomfortable in a new suit, looks bereft and bewildered. He is struggling to contain the emotion. 'They've lost their son. He's getting married to the Church and there aren't going to be any grandchildren for Mum and Dad.'

The ceremony begins. Priests come and go, preening ecclesiastical peacocks among the drab, grey-suited, head-scarved pigeons of the bourgeoisie. Rich vestments, embroidered and brocaded, red and gold, sky-blue and silver, purple and gold, green and gold, with the sus-pended orbs of light they are like fireworks fizzing through the night. Some carry three-pronged candles, swishing in fine silks and satins, another, shining in a magenta vestment emblazoned in gold, wafts through the vaulted church swinging a golden incense burner, bells ringing half hidden in his smoky trails. One of the most gorgeously dressed priests, in iridescent aquamarine and gold, strides in with a staff bearing an icon flanked by candles, a cloaked Poseidon bearing his burning trident. All of the costumes are different, each one highly personalised, yet every member of the priestly entourage has one thing in common. They are all extremely well fed.

Bishop Efsevius takes his place on a stately pulpit–throne several steps above the common herd with the dignified sloth of high office. He presides like a pontiff, imperial resignation in every movement, supreme authority in his almond eyes. He has the biggest beard.

One hand rests on a gold-and-silver staff. Around his neck hang two spectacularly ornate, jewel-encrusted medallions, one a crucifix, the other an enamelled portrait of Mary and the infant Jesus. A scrum of supplicants bows before him, priests and deacons jostle to kiss the ring on a wearily extended hand. To others, further afield, Efsevius flashes his fingers in a wizardly, evil-dispelling benediction, thumb touching fourth finger, a gesture reflected across the centuries in the icon of a richly robed crimson Christ hanging above his pulpit. A peal of bells rings out like rain, then a deep drumbeat, while next to us a choir of middle-aged men and one woman begin a dirge-like chant. Lost in this seduction of the senses, I wonder what sort of impression religion made on the ancient Greeks, with their soaring temples alight with fires of sacrificial flesh, splendid priests murmuring mysterious incantations amid the smoke. In both ages, sound and spectacle lifted man from the mortal sphere towards the heavens.

The Greek Church takes pride in this appeal to the senses. There is the story in an old Russian chronicle of Prince Vladimir of Kiev, in search of a religion for himself and his people, sending out envoys in 987 to report to him on the various faiths of his proselytising neighbours. The Muslim Bulgars on the Volga were dismissed as miserable, pork-resistant teetotals, the Jews chided for losing Jerusalem, a sure sign of God's disfavour. In Constantinople, however, his envoys were overwhelmed by a divine liturgy in Aghia Sophia. 'We knew not whether we were in heaven or on earth for on earth there is no such splendour or such beauty, and we are at a loss to describe it,' they are said to have reported. 'We know only that God dwells there among men.' When they reported back to their sovereign, so the story goes, Prince Vladimir opted for the Orthodox Christian faith.

'It reminds me of the Hare Krishnas,' says Alexis.

Bishop Efsevius reads from the Scriptures, a junior priest holding a Bible in front of him though he knows the verses by heart and barely lowers his eyes to the text. One of the more elderly deacons, with flowing Moses beard, brings in a lace-lined basket of five giant bread loaves. Five candelabra are placed on top. His colleague with the incense follows, circling the basket in swirling smoke. Efsevius flicks another wizard finger at Sotirios who rushes off to fetch the loaves, presenting them in a show of priestly deference to the bishop to be kissed. An acolyte arrives at the bishop's feet to present him with a cream silk shawl, then Efsevius rises from his pulpit–throne in all his glory, a priest holding his sparkling train. He addresses the congregation with soothing words. Megali Panaghia, empty for so many years, is now filling up once again. The parents of Konstantinos, soon to be Father Amphilochios, are not losing a son, they are gaining one. It is a great pleasure seeing a young man and talented theologian like Father Amphilochios pledging his life to Christ. It is yet another sign of the Church's solid health.

Childlike Konstantinos appears before him and now the parents are sobbing. A ripple of raised handkerchiefs flutters across the front row. The young man is in tears, too, as he takes off his priestly robes and dons the monk's habit, shedding the skin of one life and taking another for the new. Friends and family swarm about him like moths attracted by the glittering iconostasis and honeyed candlelight. Once again, the air is woven with incense, bright with strutting-peacock priests and vibrating to the celebratory dirge of the choir. My last sight of the Church's latest recruit is a slight young man being tugged and pushed like flotsam, hugged, clasped and kissed, submerged in the bitter–joyous emotion of the moment, face wet with tears amid a swirling mass of well-wishers.

'Like a lamb to the slaughter,' says Alexis.

Teasing out Herodotus' religious views, or at least what we know of them from the *Histories*, is an exercise in literary archaeology. To begin with, we know he was writing at a time when controversy over religion was raging in Greece. The inroads of science and rational examination were advancing, but religious convention was challenged at one's peril. Herodotus would not have had to look far to see the consequences of questioning established religion too closely. His contemporary, the philosopher Anaxagoras, had fallen foul of prevailing Athenian mores by arguing that natural phenomena such as earthquakes, meteors, rainbows and eclipses were the product of scientific processes, as opposed to the result of divine intervention, signals of the gods' displeasure or approval. He considered the sun a piece of molten metal rather than a deity. After three decades in Athens, he was arrested for these dangerous opinions and released only after Pericles' personal intervention. Even that did not stop him being packed off into exile to the Ionian city of Lampsacus (in the eastern Dardanelles in Turkey). Socrates' fall from grace, and his ultimate execution, can also be explained, in part, as a reflection of what James Romm, author of an excellent little volume on Herodotus, calls the 'religious conservatism' of his age.

So what clues does Herodotus leave which can shed some light on his attitude towards religion in this febrile climate? The answer is quite a number, scattered apparently randomly across 600 pages. And as we might expect, the picture that emerges is bright, typically characterful and nuanced. Herodotus, in religion as in politics, was a moderate. Were the gods responsible for shaping the earth or was there a scientific explanation for phenomena such as gorges? Herodotus allows his audience to decide for itself, while dropping hints to indicate where his own sympathies lie.

> The natives of Thessaly have a tradition that the gorge which forms the outlet for the river was made by Poseidon, and the story is a reasonable one; for if one believes that it is Poseidon who shakes the earth and that chasms caused by earthquake are attributable to him, then the mere sight of this place would be enough to make one say that it is Poseidon's handiwork. It certainly appeared to me that the cleft in the mountains had been caused by an earthquake.

As he says, 'if one believes' in earth-shaking Poseidon, then the story is perfectly 'reasonable'. Does he believe it? Diplomatically, he avoids spelling it out, contenting himself with the once again entirely 'reasonable' observation that the landscape does indeed look like it has been formed by some terrific upheaval.

Sometimes, if people get too carried away, he tilts his lance against what he considers extreme gullibility in the field of divine intervention and apparition. For example, he rubbishes those Greeks who fell for 'what seems to me the silliest trick which history has to record', the disguise of a six-foot beauty called Phye as the goddess Athene, part of a hilariously elaborate trick intended to restore Pisistratus, the deposed tyrant of Athens, to power. 'The Greeks have never been simpletons,' Herodotus remarks. 'For centuries past they have been distinguished from other nations by superior wits; and of Greeks the Athenians are allowed to be the most intelligent; yet it was at the Athenians' expense that this ridiculous trick was played.'

The story is too good not to dwell on a little longer. The mightily tall blonde, dressed up in a shimmering suit of armour, was mounted on a chariot. Messengers ran ahead telling the people that the goddess Athene herself was on her way. She was showing Pisistratus a great honour by bringing him home to her Acropolis, and so they should welcome their old ruler back. 'They spread this nonsense all over the town,' Herodotus explains to his audience's amusement, 'and it was not long before rumour reached the outlying villages that Athene was bringing Pisistratus back, and both villagers and townsfolk, convinced that the woman Phye was indeed the goddess, offered her their prayers and received Pisistratus with open arms.' One of the first recorded examples of the talismanic spell a long-legged woman can cast and an indication, if the tale is not as tall as Phye herself, of the religious climate of Athens only a century earlier.

'And now I hope that both gods and heroes will forgive me for saying what I have said on these matters!' he says in typically cheerful style. There is no desire to inflame religious sensibilities, no wish to say something that might get him into trouble with the authorities and jeopardise the lucrative nationwide lecture tour.

Elsewhere, as Romm remarks, Herodotus seems happy to report nameless gods descending on to battlefields, joined sometimes by semi-divine heroes, without blushing. In Herodotus' world, gods pop up in important dreams, too, such as the elusive phantom who urges a sleeping Xerxes not to renege on his decision to invade Greece. He does not challenge the story of the Athenian messenger Pheidippides who claimed to have met the god Pan on a mountaintop *en route* to the Peloponnese, nor does he question the notion of Helen of Sparta transforming an ugly baby into the most beautiful woman in Sparta.

Sometimes he does nail his colours to the mast in the clearest sign of what looks like a traditional, if less and less intellectually fashionable, outlook in fifth-century Athens. He is the avuncular, generous-hearted *Spectator* reader, minus the tweeds, clinging on to an orthodoxy that is slowly slipping away. There are times when he expresses conventional views, for example on gods punishing men for failing to accord them due respect. Thus, when he talks about a Persian army involved in a long siege against the Greek town of Potidaea in Thrace being destroyed by a sudden and entirely unexpected tide, he sees a pattern at work: 'This excessive tide and the consequent disaster to the Persians are put down by the people of Potidaea to the fact that the men who met their deaths were the same ones as had previously desecrated a shrine of Poseidon, and the statue of him which stands just outside the town.' Far-fetched? Ludicrously naive and old-fashioned? Herodotus doesn't think so. 'Personally, I think their explanation is the true one,' he says.

Nor is this the only example of Herodotus seeking a traditional religious explanation for significant, history-changing events. Reporting the battle of Plataea, he expresses his 'wonder' that the Persians hadn't been able to seek sanctuary in the holy precinct of Demeter. Not a single Persian body was found on consecrated ground, he says, though there were a huge number of corpses all around outside. How did this come about? 'My own view is – if one may have views at all about divine matters – that the Goddess herself would not let them in, because they had burnt her sanctuary at Eleusis.' Divine vengeance for a mortal blunder. In the story of what happened to Delphi during Xerxes' invasion, he accepts without question Delphi's miraculous escape. Straight-faced, he reports sixty Greeks and a priest, aided by magically appearing weapons, thunderbolts and conveniently crashing rocks, overcoming the Persian hordes.

Just as Herodotus seems to uphold convention in his stated positions on religion, so he seems equally keen on dreams, seers and oracles. In one instance he is quite straightforward about it. 'Now I cannot deny that there is truth in prophecies, and I have no wish to discredit them when they are expressed in unambiguous language,' he states in the midst of a portrait of the battle of Salamis, citing these verses from the oracle of Bacis foretelling a Greek victory at sea.

When they shall span the sea with ships from Cynosura
To the holy shore of Artemis of the golden sword,
Wild with hope at the ruin of shining Athens,
Then shall bright Justice quench Excess, the child of Pride,
Dreadful and furious, thinking to swallow up all things.
Bronze shall mingle with bronze, and Ares with blood
Incarnadine the sea; and all-seeing Zeus
And gracious Victory shall bring Greece the day of freedom.

Not only that. Herodotus will brook no opposition on this point, he tells his audience with a steely glint in his eyes. When the language of a prophecy is as clear as this, 'I do not venture to say anything against prophecies, nor will I listen to criticism from others.'

Dreams come from the gods and like oracles they may be misinterpreted but cannot be wrong. The Median king Astyages has a dream in which his daughter Mandane passes water in history's greatest feat of urination, a pee of such epic proportions that it inundates the entire continent of Asia, a sign that the girl's child – Cyrus – will one day become its sovereign. Later, when he is king of Persia, Cyrus has a troubling dream of Darius with a pair of wings, one spreading over Europe, the other over Asia. Rightly, he interprets this as a sign of the younger man's preordained rise to power. He seeks to have him executed but dies himself shortly afterwards, campaigning against the Massagetae, clearing the way for Darius to take the Persian throne and fulfil the dream. Fate, the will of the gods, call it what you will, cannot be avoided.

So is Herodotus unable or unwilling to listen to other people's views on religion? Is he so clear in his mind that he will not entertain any 'criticism from others'? From what we already know about him, we would think perhaps not. There is a lovely passage in which Xerxes and his uncle Artabanus, Darius' brother, discuss the significance of a disconcerting dream the king has had warning him not to put off his invasion of Greece. Darius interprets this, as Herodotus would, as a divine sign. The older man has an altogether different explanation, one which most of us would subscribe to today:

> You imagine, my son, that your dream was sent by some god or other; but dreams do not come from God. I, who am older than you by many years, will tell you what these visions are that float before our eyes in sleep: nearly always these drifting phantoms are the shadows of what we have been thinking about during the day; and during the days before your dream we were, you know, very much occupied with this campaign.

Yet Artabanus admits he may be wrong. The two men agree to test the origins of the vision by having Artabanus sleep in the royal bed to see whether he is visited by the same dream. He is, of course, and is terrified by what he sees. A phantom leaps out of the darkness and confirms the warning he gave the Persian king. He is on the point of 'burning out Artabanus' eyes with hot irons' when the courtier jumps up with a shriek and runs off to Xerxes to go through the dream with his master. He has a sudden change of heart (as you might) – what we would call a policy U-turn today – in a vindication of the Herodotean worldview. 'Tell the Persians about the vision which God has sent us; make them prepare for war . . . and, as God is offering you this great opportunity, play your own part to the full in realising it.' Never mind that this dream, divine or otherwise, is luring Xerxes to defeat. Herodotus' gods are perfectly content to drive a man to his destruction. We go back once again to the gospel of Solon: 'Often enough God gives man a glimpse of happiness, and then utterly ruins him.'

The Artabanus and Xerxes dream sequence is a little like removing the back of a finely crafted Swiss timepiece to study its complicated movement. In it we see the workings of Herodotus' mind, how he posits two alternatives, assesses their merits and then reaches his – admittedly predetermined – conclusion. The process is completely modern, the underlying belief quaintly antiquated, an excellent illustration of how easily Herodotus encompasses both ages.

Religion and religious traditions are not to be sneered at in Herodotus. They're too important to be mocked. As Romm writes,

'One finds no trace in the Histories of the scoffing sophistication of Aristophanes' Socrates – so much more in tune with our own, postmodern sensibilities . . .' Those who would mock another man's faith will, in Herodotus' world, pay dearly. Cambyses is punished for his arrogance in mocking Egyptian religion. His unholy behaviour brings about the devastating defeat of his campaign. The army he sends to destroy sacred Siwa is, as we have seen, swallowed up for ever in the burning sands of the Sahara, a fitting end to its impious mission. When Cambyses dies, after gangrene has set in from an accidental, self-inflicted wound to his thigh, it is no coincidence that the fatal injury is 'just in the spot where he had previously struck Apis the sacred Egyptian bull'. Herodotus' verdict is quite clear: the overweening Persian has met his just deserts. From a religious sneer to an agonising death is but a small step.

---

The journey with Herodotus is drawing to a close.

Father Sotirios presents me with a sprig of basil on my last night in Samos. It is a Greek tradition to give basil to departing travellers, he says. 'There is a very beautiful Christian story about basil. In 327, St Helena, the mother of Emperor Constantine, travelled from Rome to Jerusalem to look for the Holy Cross. Of course, they didn't know where to dig to find it – Jerusalem was full of ruins – and so they could not find anything for a long time. Then they were drawn by the perfume of basil in the air to a small hill and suddenly they discovered many basil plants. And this was where the cross of Christ was buried. So God revealed the site of the crucifixion to St Helena through basil. This is a true story. You will find it in Eusebius of Caesarea's writings.'

'All myths have a nucleus of truth,' says Alexis.

Father Sotirios glares at him. 'This is not a myth,' he replies sternly. 'This is Church history.'

We are sitting in a waterfront restaurant in the squintingly bright harbour of Samos town with Professor Giorgos Angelinaras, a philologist friend of Father Sotirios whom he wants me to meet to talk about Herodotus. Angelinaras is more of a Thucydides man. He is a pleasant, buttoned-up member of the Samos bourgeoisie, a quietly religious chorister and Byzantine specialist. For someone like this,

Herodotus is bound to be a bit too exuberant, fun, flash and, in the final analysis, fanciful. Thucydides is the honest grafter some people will always prefer over the stylist showman. In cricketing terms, it's methodical Boycott versus cavalier Gower, the one all dour application and sleep-inducing rigour, the other a joyful expression of easy grace. The first you can always rely on, the other, for all the sublime beauty of his craft, can be maddeningly erratic: one day an exquisite century of flashing finesse, the next a cheap dismissal wafting lazily to third slip.

But there is a ray of Herodotean light amid the professor's gloom. It turns out that even this sceptic has been smitten by the mellifluous prose of the *Histories*. 'I found him fascinating because he offered this great panorama of civilisation and information about everything under the sun. It was as though you could go travelling with him. This was at a time when we had no television, no comics, nothing like that. We all liked him because of his many strange stories, for example, the way he writes about Egyptians, all their mannerisms and customs, their religion and history, everything about them. I suppose the attraction was that it wasn't a straightforward history.'

Alexis is sitting next to Father Sotirios. The gum-chewing arch-secularist has suddenly discovered an interest in the Orthodox Church. 'I used to want to be a priest,' he says. 'I'll ask Sotirios about it. Maybe it's not too late.'

I almost collapse with laughter. Divorce, drinking, getting high on Samos' finest grass, not to mention his laid-back interest in New Age spirituality and a tireless dedication to the island's nightlife, do not suggest a putative priest.

'Sotirios is a very good contact to have,' he says conspiratorially, telling me the story of how, after a Samian was arrested recently for possession of drugs, a priest intervened on his behalf and, *Kyrie eleison*, the lad was released.

The two unlikely companions, brought together by a random Herodotean connection, chat away. Alas, it's not possible for Alexis to become a priest. He is married to a woman who is not Orthodox, so there go the beard, the splendid vestments and the ecclesiastical jewellery. The good news is that he can become a monk if he likes, although this will require his wife's written approval. He looks crestfallen. The dream is fading almost as quickly as it appeared. The monastic life is too austere for this irrepressible hedonist.

Outside, the *Penelope* ferry slides into the harbour, cleaving the reflected constellations in the oil-black water. Passengers prepare to leave on this brief skip across the sea. The stars and planets overhead speak of grander journeys, future history-making voyages of discovery where new frontiers will be crossed to reach new worlds millions of miles from this quiet corner of the Aegean. We will continue exploring, guided on these epic quests for knowledge – though few will know it – by the smiling spirit of Herodotus.

Professor Angelinaras bows a dignified farewell and I leave Alexis deep in conversation with Father Sotirios, who asks for Christ's protection for my journey home and repeats his invitation to join him on his annual pilgrimage to Mount Athos.

# Bibliography

Ali, Tariq, *Bush in Babylon: The Recolonisation of Iraq*, Verso, London, 2003

Anderson, Brian and Eileen, *Landscapes of Samos*, Sunflower Books, London, 1989

Anderson, Jon Lee, *The Fall of Baghdad*, Abacus, London, 2006

Andrewes, A., *The Greek Tyrants*, Hutchinson, London, 1956

Apostol, Tom, 'The Tunnel of Samos', *Engineering & Science* No. 1, 2004

Bakker, Egbert J., de Jong, Irene J. F., and van Wees, Hans (eds), *Brill's Companion to Herodotus*, E. J. Brill, Leiden and Boston, 2002

Beck, Sara, and Downing, Malcolm (eds), *The Battle for Iraq*, BBC, London, 2003

Bichler, Reinhold, *Herodots Welt*, Akademie Verlag, Berlin, 2000

Blottière, Alain, *Siwa: The Oasis*, Harpocrates, Alexandria, 2000

Boedeker, Deborah (ed.), 'Herodotus and the Invention of History', *Arethusa* 20, 1987

Bonnard André, *Greek Civilization from the Antigone to Socrates*, George Allen, London, 1959

Briant, Pierre, *Histoire de l'empire Perse: De Cyrus à Alexandre*, Fayard, Paris, 1996

Brodsky, Joseph, 'Profile of Clio', in *On Grief and Reason: Essays*, Hamish Hamilton, London, 1995

Burckhardt, Jacob, *The Greeks and Greek Civilization*, HarperCollins, London, 1998

Burn, A.R., *Persia and the Greeks*, Duckworth, London, 1984

Burrow, John, *A History of Histories: Epics, Chronicles, Romances and*

*Inquiries from Herodotus and Thucydides to the Twentieth Century*, Allen Lane, London, 2007

Bury, J. B., *The Ancient Greek Historians*, Dover, New York, 1958 [repr. of 1909 original]

Carr, E. H., *What Is History?*, Penguin, London, 1987

Cartledge, Paul, *The Greeks: A Portrait of Self and Others*, Oxford University Press, Oxford, new edn, with Afterword by R. Evans, Palgrave, 2001. 2nd edn 2002

——, *Thermopylae: The Battle That Changed the World*, Macmillan, London, 2006

——, *The Spartans: An Epic History*, Pan, London, 2003

——, 'Sparta and Samos: A Special Relationship?', *Classical Quarterly* 32, 1982

Chandrasekaran, Rajiv, *Imperial Life in the Emerald City: Inside Baghdad's Green Zone*, Bloomsbury, London, 2007

Cole, Erma Louise, *The Samos of Herodotus*, Tuttle, Morehouse & Taylor, New Haven, Connecticut, 1912

Cook, J. M., *The Greeks in Ionia and the East*, Thames & Hudson, London, 1962

——, *The Persian Empire*, J. M. Dent, London, 1983

Davies, Vivian, and Friedman, Renée, *Egypt*, British Museum, London, 1998

Dewald, Carolyn, and Marincola, John (eds), *The Cambridge Companion to Herodotus*, Cambridge University Press, Cambridge, 2006

——, 'A Selective Introduction to Herodotean Studies', *Arethusa* 20, 1987

Elton, G. R., *The Practice of History*, Flamingo, London, 1984

Evans, J. A. S., 'Father of History or Father of Lies?', *Classical Journal* Vol. 64, No. 1, 1968

——, *Herodotus, Explorer of the Past: Three Essays*, Princeton University Press, Princeton, 1991

Evans, Richard, *In Defence of History*, Granta, London, 2000

Fagan, Brian, *From Stonehenge to Samarkand: An Anthology of Archaeological Travel Writing*, Oxford University Press, Oxford, 2006

Fehling, Detlev, *Herodotus and His 'Sources'*, trans. J. G. Howie, Cairns, Leeds, 1989

Fisher, Nick, and van Wees, Hans (eds), *Archaic Greece: New Approaches and New Evidence*, Duckworth, London, 1998

Flory, Stewart, *The Archaic Smile of Herodotus*, Wayne State University Press, Detroit 1987

——, 'Who Read Herodotus' Histories?', *American Journal of Philology* 101, 1980

Fornara, Charles, *Herodotus: An Interpretative Essay*, Oxford University Press, Oxford, 1971

——, *The Nature of History in Ancient Greece and Rome*, University of California Press, Berkeley and London, 1983

Gellhorn, Martha, 'Memory', in Ian Hamilton (ed.), *The Penguin Book of Twentieth-Century Essays*, Penguin, London, 1999

Gould, John, *Herodotus*, Weidenfeld & Nicolson, London, 1989

——, 'Herodotus and Religion', in S. Hornblower (ed.), *Greek Historiography*, Oxford University Press, Oxford, 1994

Graves Robert, *The Greek Myths*, 2 vols, Folio Society, London, 2000

Green, Peter, *The Greco-Persian Wars*, University of California Press, Berkeley and Los Angeles, 1996

Harrison, Thomas, *Divinity and History: The Religion of Herodotus*, Oxford University Press, Oxford, 2002

——, 'Herodotus and The English Patient', *Classics Ireland* 5, 1988

Hart, John, *Herodotus and Greek History*, Croom Helm, London, 1982

Hartog, François, *The Mirror of Herodotus: The Representation of the Other in the Writing of History*, trans. Janet Lloyd, University of California Press, California and London, 1988

Herodotus, *The Histories*, trans. A. de Sélincourt, ed. with notes and introduction by John Marincola, Penguin, London, 2003

——, *The Histories*, trans. R. Waterfield, ed. with notes and introduction by Carolyn Dewald, Oxford University Press, Oxford, 1998

——, *The Histories*, trans. G. Rawlinson, ed. with notes and introduction by Rosalind Thomas, Everyman's Library, London, 1997

——, *The History of Herodotus*, trans. George Rawlinson, Dent, London, 1936

Holland, Tom, *Persian Fire: First World Empire and the Battle for the West*, Doubleday, New York, 2005

Hornblower, S., *Mausolus*, Clarendon Press, Oxford, 1982

How, W. W., and Wells, J., *A Commentary on Herodotus*, 2 vols, Clarendon Press, Oxford, 1912

Howell, Georgina, *Daughter of the Desert: The Remarkable Life of Gertrude Bell*, Macmillan, London, 2006

Immerwahr, H., 'Historical Action in Herodotus', *Transactions and Proceedings of the American Philological Association* 85, 1954

Kapuściński, Ryszard, *Travels with Herodotus*, Allen Lane, London, 2007

Karabell, Zachary, *Parting the Desert: The Creation of the Suez Canal*, John Murray, London, 2003

Kelly, Saul, *The Hunt for Zerzura: The Lost Oasis and the Desert War*, John Murray, London, 2002

Kenrick, J., *The Egypt of Herodotus*, B. Fellowes, London, 1841

Koromila, Marianna, *The Greeks and the Black Sea: From the Bronze Age to the Early 20th Century*, Panorama Cultural Society, Athens, 2002

Koulouri, Christina (ed.), *Clio in the Balkans: The Politics of History Education*, Center for Democracy, Reconciliation in South-east Europe (CDRSEE), Thessaloniki, 2002

——, (ed.), *Teaching Modern South-east European History*, Workbooks 1–4, CDRSEE, Thessaloniki, 2005

Kuhrt, Amélie, *The Ancient Near East c. 3000–330 BC*, 2 vols, Routledge, London and New York, 1995

Lane, William Horsburg, *Babylonian Problems*, John Murray, London, 1923

Lang, Mabel, *Herodotean Narrative and Discourse*, Harvard University Press, Cambridge, Massachusetts, 1984

Lateiner, D., *The Historical Method of Herodotus*, University of Toronto Press, Toronto, 1989

Lattimore, R., 'The Wise Advisor in Herodotus', *Classical Philology* 34, 1939

Layard, Austen Henry, *Discoveries in the Ruins of Nineveh and Babylon*, John Murray, London, 1853

Leigh Fermor, Patrick, *Mani: Travels in the Southern Peloponnese*, John Murray, London, 2004 (originally 1958)

——, *Roumeli: Travels in Northern Greece*, John Murray, London, 1966

Lister, R. P., *The Travels of Herodotus*, Gordon & Cremonesi, London, 1979

Lloyd, Alan B., *Herodotus: Book II. Introduction (I) and Commentary (II, III)*, 3 vols, E. J. Brill, Leiden, 1975–88

Luraghi, Nino (ed.), *The Historian's Craft in the Age of Herodotus*, Oxford University Press, Oxford, 2001

MacGinnis, John, 'Herodotus' Description of Babylon', *Bulletin of the Institute of Classical Studies* 33, 1986

McNeal, R. A., 'The Brides of Babylon: Herodotus 1.196', *Historia* 37, 1988

Mahdy, Christine al, *The Pyramid Builder*, Headline, London, 2003

Malim, Fathi, *Oasis Siwa from the Inside: Traditions, Customs and Magic*, Al Katan, Egypt, 2001

Manley, Deborah, and Abdel-Hakim, Sahar (eds), *Travelling through Egypt from 450 BC to the Twentieth Century*, American University in Cairo Press, Cairo, 2004

Marincola, John, *Authority and Tradition in Ancient Historiography*, Cambridge University Press, Cambridge, 1997

——, *Greek Historians*, Oxford University Press, Oxford, 2001

Marett, R. R., 'Herodotus and Anthropology', in *Anthropology and the Classics*, Clarendon Press, Oxford, 1908

Mitchell, B. M., 'Herodotus and Samos', *Journal of Hellenic Studies*, 95, 1975

Momigliano, Arnaldo, 'The Place of Herodotus in the History of Historiography', *Historia* 43, 1958

——, *Studies in Historiography*, Harper & Row, New York, 1966

Murray, Oswyn, 'Herodotus & Hellenistic Culture', *Classical Quarterly* 22, 1972

Myres, John L., *Herodotus: Father of History*, Clarendon Press, Oxford, 1953

Newton, C. T., *A History of Discoveries at Halicarnassus, Cnidus and Branchidae*, Day & Son, London, 1862

——, *Travels and Discoveries in the Levant*, London, 1865

Nightingale, Florence, *Letters from Egypt: A Journey on the Nile 1849–1850*, Parkway, London, 1987

Oates, Joan, *Babylon*, Folio Society, London, 2005

Ondaatje, Michael, *The English Patient*, Vintage, New York, 1993

Oppenheim, A. L., *The Interpretation of Dreams in the Ancient Near East*, Transactions of the American Philosophical Society, Philadelphia, 1956

Plutarch, *The Malice of Herodotus*, trans. with an introduction and commentary by Anthony Bowen, Aris & Phillips, Warminster, 1992

Powell, J. E., *A Lexicon to Herodotus*, Georg Olms Verlagsbuchhandlung, Hildesheim, 1960

Pritchett, W. K., *The Liar School of Herodotus*, J. C. Gieben, Amsterdam, 1993

——, 'Some Recent Critiques on the Veracity of Herodotus', in *Studies in Ancient Greek Topography IV*, Berkeley and Los Angeles, California, 1982

Raaflaub, Kurt, 'Herodotus, Political Thought and the Meaning of History', *Arethusa* 20, 1987

Redfield, James, 'Herodotus the Tourist', *Classical Philology* 80, 1985

Rennell, James, *The Geographical System of Herodotus*, 2 vols, London, 1800, 1830

Rihll, T. E., and Tucker, J. V., 'Greek Engineering: The Case of Eupalinos' Tunnel', in Anton Powell (ed.), *The Greek World*, Routledge, London, 1997

Rijksbaron, Albert, *Temporal and Causal Conjunctions in Ancient Greek, with Special Reference to the Use of epei and os in Herodotus*, Hakkert, Amsterdam, 1976

Rodenbeck, Max, *Cairo: The City Victorious*, American University in Cairo Press, Cairo, 2005

Romm, James, *Herodotus*, Yale University Press, New Haven and London, 1998

Roux, Georges, *Ancient Iraq*, Penguin, London, 1980

Saggs, H. W. F., *The Greatness That Was Babylon*, Sidgwick & Jackson, London, 1988

Sandys, George, *A Relation of a Journey begun An: Dom: 1610*, Barrett, London, 1615

Sattin, Anthony, *The Pharaoh's Shadow: Travels in Ancient and Modern Egypt*, Indigo, London, 2000 de Selincourt, Aubrey, *The World of Herodotus*, Secker & Warburg, London, 1962

Shipley, Graham, *A History of Samos 800–188 BC*, Clarendon, Oxford, 1987

Starkey, Paul, and Starkey, Janet (eds), *Travellers in Egypt*, I. B. Tauris, London and New York, 2001

Steele, James, *Turkey: A Traveller's Historical and Architectural Guide*, Scorpion Publishing, Buckhurst Hill, 1990

Stern, Fritz (ed.), *The Varieties of History: From Voltaire to the Present*, Macmillan, London, 1970

Stobart, J. C., *The Glory That Was Greece*, Sidgwick & Jackson, London, 1978

Strassler, Robert (ed.), *The Landmark Herodotus: The Histories*, Pantheon Books, New York, 2007

Tannahill, Reay, *Sex in History*, Cardinal, London, 1989

Thomas, Rosalind, *Herodotus in Context: Ethnography, Science and the Art of Persuasion*, Cambridge University Press, Cambridge, 2000

Tyldesley, Joyce, *Pyramids: The Real Story Behind Egypt's Most Ancient Monuments*, Viking, London, 2003

Waters, K. H., *Herodotus the Historian: His Problems, Methods and Originality*, Croom Helm, London, 1985

——, *Herodotus on Tyrants and Despots: A Study in Objectivity*, Franz Steiner Verlag, Wiesbaden, 1971

Waywell, G. B., *The Free-Standing Sculptures of the Mausoleum at Halicarnassus in the British Museum*, British Museum Publications, London, 1978

Winstone, H. V. F., *Gertrude Bell*, Barzan, London, 2004

Zinovieff, Sofka, *Eurydice Street: A Place in Athens*, Granta, London, 2005

# Index

Aaronovitch, David, 103
Achaemenid collections in Musée
   Achéménide, 204–205
Acropolis, 17, 209
Acropolis (Athens), 206
Adultery in Ottoman empire, 255–256
*Advancement of Learning, The* (Bacon),
   50
Aegean Sea, 226, 275–276, 277
Aeschylus, 13–14, 282
Aesop, 296–297
Aethlius of Samos, 283
Afghanistan, 105
Ağan, Mazlum, 54
Agasicles, 32
Aghia Sophia (Church of Holy Wisdom),
   222–223, 264, 317
Agriculture in Egypt, 158
*Ahram, Al* (newspaper), 182–183
Ain Gubah, Siwa, Egypt, 173–175
Al Azhar, 137, 138
Alamein Memorial, 165–166
Alamein War Cemetery, El, 164–166
Alexander the Great, 120, 123, 175–176,
   198
Alexandria, Egypt, 184
Alexis (friend on Samos), 315–318,
   324–326
Ali, Mohammed, 169
"Allah Had No Son" (Christians in
   Baghdad), 91–92
Almásy, Count László de, 22, 168, 178
Alpözen, Oğuz, 40–41, 54
Amasis, pharaoh of Egypt, 294, 295,
   296–297

Ameinocles, 278
American Enterprise Institute, 77
Ammon, oracle and temple, 167, 169,
   174, 175–176
Ammonians, 167–168
Amphilochios, Father, 318
Anacreon, 282
Anaxagoras, 318
Ancient Greece, 183, 207, 234, 239–240,
   311
Ancient Greece and Ancient Iran
   conference (Athens), 197–200,
   201–205
*Ancient Halicarnassus Bodrum* (film), 64
Angelinaras, Giorgos, 324–326
Anis, Mouneer, 138
Ano Polis, Greece, 247
Anopaea Path, 16–17
Antigoni (friend in Athens), 229–232,
   233–235
Apuleius, 283
Archaeological Museum (Athens),
   215–217
Archaeologists, 53, 121, 311
Archaeologists, nautical, 42–45, 50–51,
   52–53
Archias, 303
*Architectura, De* (Vitruvius), 56, 59–60
Architectural legacy of Nebuchadnezzar,
   113–114
Arion (lyre-player and singer), 9
Aristagoras, 209–210
Aristotle, 13, 232
Artabanus (Herodotus' wise man),
   72–73, 322–323

Artaphernes (Persian military
  commander), 11, 13
Artemis, Temple of (Ephesus), 58
Artemisia (Persian commander), 18, 32,
  275
Artemisia, queen of Caria, 57, 62
Artemisium, Battle of, 17
Asia Minor, Western, Greece and (map),
  xvi
Asia Minor and Greece, 233–234
Assyrians, 44, 103
Astyages, Median king, 322
Aswany, Alaa al, 148
Athene, goddess, 320
Athene, priestess of, 32
Athenians, in Battle of Marathon, 12–14
Athens, Greece
  Ancient Greece and Ancient Iran
    conference, 197–200, 201–205
  Archaeological Museum, 215–217
  birth of Greek democracy, 207–208
  and golden age of Greece, 19–20
  November 17th marches, 215,
    217–219
  Parthenon, 206–207
  priests in, 219–223
  strolling through, 206
  war with Sparta, 208–209
  Xerxes' destruction of, 17
Athens Polytechnic, 214–215, 217–219
Atossa, wife of Darius, 304–305
Augustine, 119

Babylon
  author's attraction to, 87–88
  Biblical references, 69
  destruction of, during Iraq war,
    107–108, 121–122, 133
  Esagila, temple of Marduk, 122–123
  Hanging Gardens, 127–128
  Herodotus on, 101, 112, 128–129
  Jewish captives in, 131–132
  Lion of Babylon, 126–127
  Processional Way, 121–122

returning to Iraqis, 109, 130–131
  Saddam's "restorations," 123–126
  See also Iraq
Babylonians, 7, 8, 111–112, 116–119
Bacis, oracle of, 322
Bacon, Francis, 50
Baghdad, Iraq
  arriving at Baghdad International
    Airport, 78–81
  Assassin's Gate suicide bombing, 80–81
  history of, 86
  International Zone, 82–91
  National Museum, 101–104,
    105–108, 109–110
  Neighborhood Advisory Councils, 97
  Red Zone, 89
  Route Irish, 81–82
  soldiers' driving style in, 82, 109
  See also Babylon; Iraq war
Bahaa (driver in Siwa), 171
Balkan nationalism, alternative version
  of, 252–256
Basil, Christian story about, 324
Basilica of Aghios Dimitrios
  (Thessaloniki, Greece), 258–261
Bass, George, 42, 43–44, 46, 48, 51–54
Bell, Gertrude, 104, 105–107, 123
Bestiality, 126–127, 160, 171
Between the Woods and the Water (Leigh
  Fermor), 265
Bible, 69, 112–113, 114, 116, 131–132,
  156, 314
Bitumen (mortar), 125
Black magic in Siwa, Egypt, 172–173, 177
Blade Runner (Scott), 25
Blair, Tony, 75
Blottière, Alain, 174
Bodrum, Turkey
  aristocratic elite, 35
  Çanan's guidance in, 35–36
  Castle museum, 38–41
  growth of, 55
  Halikarnas disco, 64, 65–66
  Herodotus in, 64–65, 87

Herodotus junction, 40–41
Mausoleum of Mausolos, 39–40,
    56–62, 63–64
Museum of Underwater Archaeology,
    42, 45
restoration of, 55–56
tourist business, 33–34, 56
and *Uluburun,* 42–45, 48–50, 52–53
waterfront, 34, 37, 55
*See also* Halicarnassus
Bodrum gulets, 37
"Bodrum Wants its Mausoleum Back"
    *(Turkish Daily News),* 64
Boeotians, 209
"Books" found on *Uluburun,* 45, 53
Breakwater at Polycrates' harbor,
    296–298
Briant, Pierre, 203–205
Britain, speculation on invasion by
    Turkey, 227
British, 75, 98, 100, 105. *See also* Iraq war
British Museum, 58, 61–62, 64, 204–205
Brodsky, Joseph, 75, 315
Bronze Age, 42–45, 48–50, 53
Buddhas of Bamiyan, 105
Burleigh, Michael, 76
Bush, George W.
    advisors of, 74, 100
    and anti-war advice, 77
    Iraq war as personal conflict, 71
    lack of humility, 78
    Mission Accomplished speech, 71–72,
        80
    Muslims' fear of attack on Islam, 99
    using Thucydides to justify Iraq war,
        230
    writing history, 76–77, 100
Byron, Lord, 234
Byzantine empire, 223, 239–240

Cairo, Egypt, 141, 179–185, 186–189
Çakir, Mehmed, 42, 49
Callimachus (War Archon), 12–13
Cambridge University, 137–139

Cambyses, Great King of Persia
    Egyptian campaign, 93–95, 139,
        166–168
    lost army of, 168
    overview, 4–5, 71
    and Polycrates, 302–303
    price for arrogance, 324
Canaanites, 44, 45
Çanan (historian in Bodrum), 35–36,
    40–41, 62–64
Candaules, king of Lydia, 178
Cannadine, David, 100
Canning, Sir Stratford, 59
*Cape Gelidonya* (shipwreck), 48, 52, 53
Carian civilisation, 36–37, 62–64, 225
Carr, E. H., 2–3, 21, 22
Cartledge, Paul, 224
Cassander, king of Macedon, 249
Castle of St. Peter (Bodrum, Turkey), 34,
    38–41
Cats, self-immolating, 160
Cavafy, Constantine, 240
Chalcidians, 209
Champollion, Jean-François, 193
Charilaus, 307
Cheney, Dick, 74, 100
Cheops, pharaoh of Egypt, 181–182
Children in Egypt brought up in silence,
    142–143
Christianity, 89–92, 219–223, 317–318,
    324. *See also* Greek Orthodox
    Church
Christodoulos, Archbishop, 220, 313
Church of Holy Wisdom (Aghia
    Sophia), 222–223, 264, 317
Cicero, 3
Cinderella story, 295–297
Cithaeron, Mount, 18, 201–202
*Civitate Dei, De* (Augustine), 119
Cleisthenes, 207–208
Cleomenes, king of Sparta, 208–209
Cleopatra's Spring (Siwa, Egypt), 173–175
*Clio in the Balkans* (Joint History
    Project), 249–252

*Coming Up for Air* (Orwell), 55
Communication, feasibility of, 199–200
Constantinople/Istanbul, Turkey, 222, 271
Constitutional Debate *(Histories)*,
    211–213
Copper ingots from Bronze Age, 42–43,
    44
Corinthians, 209, 302–303
Croatians, 250–251, 253
Crocodiles and Egyptian plovers, 159,
    162
Croesus, king of Lydia, 5, 6, 108–109,
    232–233
Culture and customs
    belief in one's own as best, 24,
        95–100, 252
    defiling at your peril, 97
    of Egypt, 160–161
    Gomaa's tolerance, 138–139
    Herodotean focus on, 9, 21, 41–42
    Herodotean tolerance, 5, 65, 81, 93,
        145, 160–161, 249
    historical inquiries into, 21–22
    introversion of Greek academe,
        198–199
    Joint History Project vs. ethnocentric
        history lessons, 249–256
    Pindar on, 96
    recognition of Byzantine and
        Ottoman history, 239–240
    of suicide bombers, 80–81
    *See also* Sex and sexuality
Curtis, John, 133
Cypriots, 44, 45, 250, 255
Cyprus, 250
Cyrus, king of Lydia
    in Babylon, 120–121, 127, 132
    and Croesus, 108–109
    dream about Darius taking power,
        322
    exploits of, 12, 120–121
    Musée Achéménide presentation on,
        204
    and River Gyndes, 120

Däniken, Erich von, 180
Dar al Ifta (House of Fatwa), 187
Darbandi, Mohammed Reza, 198
Dardanelles (Hellespont), 14–15, 77, 278
Darius, king of Persia
    Atossa's convincing request, 304–305
    conquests of, 5
    demonstration of cultural
        conditioning, 95–96
    Ionian revolt against, 210
    loss of ships at sea, 277
    plan for destruction of Athens, 11–12
    and Syloson, 306, 307
    war with Scythians, 72–73
Darius, son of Hystaspes, 212–214
Datis (Persian military commander), 11,
    13
Davies, Norman, 76
Deghedy, Inas al, 190–192
Deif, Assem, 182–184
Delphi, Greece, 230–231, 301, 321
Demaratus, king of Sparta, 209
Demeter, holy sanctuary of, 321
Democedes, 305
Democracy, 71–72, 77–78, 97–98,
    207–213. *See also* Greek democracy
*Demos* (the people), 208
Diakos, Athanasios, 220
*Diary of a Teenage Girl* (film), 191–192
Dieneces, 15–16
Dimos (guide on Samos), 281–282,
    287–292, 313–314
Diodorus the Sicilian, 127
Dionysius, 3
Diptychs found on *Uluburun,* 45, 53
Divine ancestry, 146–147, 175–176
Divine intervention, 294, 296–297,
    319–320
Divine retribution, 10, 202, 321
Dolatowska, Agnieszka, 119–126
Dorian tribe, 36–37
Duff Gordon, Lady, 158

East, 34–35, 137–139

*See also* West vs. the East; *specific eastern countries*

Efsevius, Bishop, 317–318

Egypt
  agriculture, 158
  British intervention and occupation, 75
  Cambyses military campaign against, 166–168
  Carians in, 37
  contrasts and contradictions, 55
  Herodotus in, 150–151, 159–161
  Labyrinth at Hawara, 151
  mathematics in, 183–184
  Missirian's interest in, 240
  mummification process, 151–154, 193–194
  pharaohs of, 146–149, 154–155, 181–182, 294, 295, 296–297
  religion in, 189–190, 192
  and Samos, 294, 295
  sights and splendor of, 139–140, 141, 142
  tomb of Sennefer, mayor of Thebes, 149–150
  traveling in, 139–141, 184–185
  women in, 186–188, 190–192
  *See also* Cairo, Egypt; Nile River; *specific Egyptian cities*

Egyptians, 44

Elektra (archaeologist on Samos), 310–311

*Elements* (Euclid of Alexandria), 183, 285

Elton, Geoffrey, 2–3

*English Patient, The* (film), 22, 178

*English Patient, The* (Ondaatje), 22, 168

Ephialtes (traitor), 16

Esagila, temple of Marduk (Babylon), 122–123

Etemenaki, Babylon, 114

Ethiopia, 167

Etruscans, 24

EU (European Union), 201, 220, 226–227, 243–244

Euclid of Alexandria, 183, 285

Eupalinos Tunnel (Samos, Greece)
  author's adventure, 287–290, 292
  building of, 283–287, 290–292

Euphrates River (Babylonia), 120–121

European Union (EU), 201, 220, 226–227, 243–244

Evans, Richard, 76, 206, 224

Exorcism, 258–261

*Express Santorini* (vessel), 274–275, 276–277

Fadel (man in Baghdad Dining Facility), 91–92, 97–99

Fakhry, Ahmed, 173

Farouk, King of Egypt, 177

Fatwas, 138

Festival of Theophania (Delphi, Greece), 301

Fishawy, Ahmed al, 186–188

Five pillars of Islam, 192

Fleischer, Ari, 99

*Flying Dolphin Samos 4* (vessel), 280

Flying serpents, 6

"Free Besieged" (Solomos), 214

Al Futuh, Abd al Monem Abu, 190

Gailani, Lamia al, 125–126

Galal (guide in Egypt), 144–145

Gellhorn, Martha, 280

George, Donny, 101–104, 105, 124

German archaeologists in Babylon, 121

German memorial to soldiers killed in Iraq, 83

Gibbon, Edward, 76

Gindanes tribe, 34

*Glory That Was Greece, The* (Stobart), 20

Gold-digging ants, 6

Golden age of Greece, 19–20

Gomaa, Sheikh Ali, 137–139, 187

Gonville and Caius College (Cambridge, England), 2

Great Pyramid of Giza, 181–184

Greco–Turkish War (1919–22), 251

Greece
 Ancient Greece, 183, 207, 234, 239–240, 311
 and Asia Minor, 233–234
 culture of, 19–20
 drinking wine in, 233
 introversion of academe, 198–199
 military training, 227
 prowess on the seas, 275–276
 student strikes and uprisings, 214–215, 217–219
 and US relations, 215, 226
 See also specific Greek cities
Greece and Western Asia Minor (map), xvi
Greek democracy
 and Battle of Marathon, 13
 birth of, in Athens, 207–208
 Herodotus as recorder of, 24
 Herodotus on, 209–210
 Orthodox Church in constitution, 312
 Parthenon as symbol of, 207
 as political expedient, 208
 religion and, 221–223
Greek islands, 34, 226, 274, 278, 314. See also Samos, Greece
Greek Orthodox Church
 appeal to the senses, 316–318
 history of, 219–223
 importance of, 226, 312
 and Islam, 314–315
 Megali Panaghia monastery on Samos, 312–313, 314–318
 youth of Greece versus, 313
Greeks, The (Cartledge), 224
Greek–Turkish relations
 and Aghia Sophia, 222–223, 317
 Greek national religion and, 312
 and Istanbul/Constantinople, 222, 271
 and Muslim minority in Thrace, 243–244
 public animosity, 220, 222, 225–227
 schooling in, 230
 Turks and Persians compared, 234–235

Green Zone. See International Zone
Guardian (newspaper), 74–76, 103, 133
Gyges, king of Lydia, 178

Halicarnassus, 31–32, 34–35, 36, 48, 54–56, 57. See also Bodrum, Turkey
Halikarnas disco (Bodrum, Turkey), 64, 65–66
Halliburton, 88
Hameed, Abdul Aziz, 103
Hammurabi, king of Babylon, 111–112
Hanging Gardens (Babylon), 127–128
Happiness, Solon on, 232–233
Harbor mole (breakwater) of Polycrates, 242, 279, 283, 296–298, 299–301
Haroeris (solar god of war), 162
Hatzopoulos, Miltiades, 199–200
Hawass, Zahi, 151–152, 155
Healthcare in Babylonia, 116
Hecataeus of Miletus, 146–147
Hegel, 19
Hellenism of Cyprus, 250
Hellespont (Dardanelles), 14–15, 77, 278
Hera, temple of, 280, 307–311
Heracles/Hercules, 48, 264
Hermotimus (eunuch), 9–10
Hero of Alexandria, 286
Herodotean studies, 205–206
Herodotus
 beliefs of, 202–203
 biographical information, 33, 36, 41–42
 bust of, in Bodrum, Turkey, 38–39, 40
 critics of, 3–4, 10, 26, 62–63
 digressions celebrating life, 6–8
 in exile, 278–279
 focus of, 20, 37–38, 201
 Greek professors' support for, 198–199, 200–201
 Ikram's description of, 192–193
 memory skills, 280–281
 moral and spiritual message, 5, 71
 personality, 7–9, 23, 38, 51, 182, 229
 prophetic writing, 5–6

religious views, 318–324
style, 3, 10–11, 200
travel writing, 7–10, 69–71, 325
See also *Histories* (Herodotus)
"Herodotus' Description of Babylon"
(MacGinnis), 119, 128–129
Herodotus Street, Athens, 237
Hezekiah Tunnel (Jerusalem), 286
*Hijab* veil in Egypt, 189–190
Hinnawy, Hind al, 186–188
Hippias, 208
Historians, 3–4, 10, 26, 62–63, 74–76
Historical advisors for world leaders, 100
*Histories* (Herodotus)
joys of reading, 22–25
Leigh Fermor's edition, 271–272
as oral presentation, 70
pocket-book edition, 228
History
human fascination with, 21, 25, 56
as inquiry vs. reports, 1, 5–10
non-Herodotean interpretations of,
21, 22
as vital force, 99–100, 252–256
History and Policy initiative (British),
100
*History of Discoveries at Halicarnassus,
Cnidus and Brachidae* (Newton), 59
Hogarth, David, 105
Holland, Tom, 17
Homer, 10, 45, 53, 231–232
Homer, archaeological interpretations
of, 53
Homosexuality, 36, 169–171, 170, 173
Hoplites (Greek infantrymen), 12–13,
16, 18, 219
Horace, 263, 270
Horoscopes, birth of, 160
Horus, son of Osiris, 147
Hospitality *(philoxenia)*, 224–225
Hot Gates (Thermopylae pass), 15, 16
Hubris-leads-to-nemesis argument,
71–72, 76, 100, 232–233, 239
Humvee, unarmoured, 130

Hussein, Saddam, 77–78, 103, 123–126
Hymen repair operations, 188

Ignatieff, Michael, 76
*Ijtihad* (interpretation), 192
Ikram, Salima, 192–194
*Iliad* (Homer), 10, 45
Imaret (pilgrims' hostel), Kavala, 237–242
Immigration into Greece, 226
Immortal forces, 16
Imperialism of US in Iraq, 97–98
*In Defence of History* (Evans), 206, 224
India, 8
Institute of Mohammed Ali, 240
Institute of Nautical Archaeology (INA),
42, 43–45, 51, 52
International Zone (Baghdad)
checkpoint into, 82–86
dining in, 88–91
Ionian revolt against Darius, 210
Iran, 197–200
Iraq, 78, 86, 97, 115–116. *See also*
Babylon; Baghdad, Iraq
Iraq war
acronyms for, 79–80
Herodotus possible response to, 97,
100–101
historians' anti-war opinions, 75–76, 78
looting, 108, 121–122, 126, 133
Peloponnesian War compared to,
71–72
*Stars and Stripes* news stories, 83–85
*See also* Bush, George W.; United
States Marines in Iraq
Is (Babylon), 125
Isagoras, 208
Ishtar (Babylonian goddess), 118, 119
Ishtar Gate (Babylon), 119–120, 121
Islam, 169, 189–190, 192, 314–315. *See
also* Muslims
*Islamic Invasion* (Morey), 92
"Isles of Greece, The" (Byron), 234
*Isonomia* (equality before the law, 243
*Isonomia* (popular government), 211–212

*Isopoliteia* (equality of civil rights), 243
Istanbul/Constantinople, Turkey, 222, 271

Japanese attempt to construct a pyramid, 183
Jellicoe, Earl George, 271
Jerusalem, 114, 115
Jewelry found on *Uluburun,* 44
Jinn spirits, 172–173, 177
John of Patmos, Saint, 314
Joint History Project
  four new textbooks written by, 252–256
  global reception of, 256–257
  overview, 249
  Sebek interview, 247, 249–250, 252–253, 256–257
  study of how Balkan history is taught, 249–252

Kabul Museum (Afghanistan), 105
Kapuściński, Ryszard, 230
Karageorghis, Vassos, 198–199, 200–201
Karatzaferis, Giorgios, 225
Kardamyli, Greece, 262, 264, 272. *See also* Leigh Fermor, Sir Patrick
Karkaletsis, Stavros, 225–227
Karnak Temple (Luxor, Egypt), 145–146
*Karshif* (soil with salt rocks, Siwa), 172, 175
Kassites, 44
Kavala, Greece, 237–242
Kazantzakis, Nikos, 287
Kea island (Cycladic, Greece), 274
Kellogg Brown and Root (KBR), 88–89
Kennedy, Paul, 75–76, 78
Kilane, Sheikh Fathi, 176–178
Kom Ombo, Egypt, 159, 162
Komotini, Greece, 244–246
Koromila, Marianna, 227–229
Koromilas, Andreas, 228–229, 233
Kos (Greek island), 34, 278
Koulouri, Christina, 250
*Kouroi* statues of naked youths, 215–216

Kreipe, Karl Heinrich, 268–270
*Kroke dilos* (pebble lizard), 161–162

Labyrinth at Hawara, 151
Lacedaemonians, 159
*Laconic Apophthegms* (Plutarch), 200
*Lagbi* (fermented juice), 170
Lampon (Aeginetan), 313
Late Bronze Age, 42–45, 48–50, 53
Leigh Fermor, Sir Patrick "Paddy"
  author's lunch with, 266–273
  *Between the Woods and the Water,* 265
  biographical information, 262–263, 264–266
  books by, 265, 269–270, 272, 281, 311
  *Mani,* 311
  on retsina, 233
  *Roumeli,* 272
  *Time of Gifts, A,* 265, 269–270, 281
  *Traveller's Tree,* 270
  *Words of Mercury,* 265
Leonidas, king of Sparta, 15–17, 199, 210, 236–237
Libya, 34, 167, 174, 175–176
Lion of Babylon, 126–127
Longinus, 3
Looting after US invasion of Iraq, 108, 121–122, 126, 133
Lucian, 3
Luis (US security contractor Marine in Iraq), 102, 104, 110
Luxor (Thebes), Egypt, 143, 145–146, 151–152, 154, 158–163
Lydia, 5–8, 24, 108–109, 178, 232–233. *See also* Cyrus, king of Lydia
Lygdamis, the tyrant of Halicarnassus, 33

MacGinnis, John "Herodotus' Description of Babylon," 119, 128–129
*Madrassah* (religious school) complex, 238
Maeandrius, 303–304, 306–307
Magic in Siwa, Egypt, 172–173, 177
Magnesian coast, 278

*Malice of Herodotus, The* (Plutarch), 3–4
Malim, Fathi, 170–173, 177
Mamuzalos, Iannis, 280
Mandrocles, 311–312
*Mani* (Leigh Fermor), 311
Manolates, Samos, 281–282
Marathon, 11
Marathon, Battle of (490 BC), 11, 12–14
Mardonius, 18, 201–203
Marriage by auction in Babylon, 129–130
Masistes, 32
Masistius, 18, 201–203
Massagetae (Caspian Sea region), 8
Mathematics, 182–184
Mause, Lloyd de, 170
Mausoleum of Mausolos (Bodrum, Turkey), 39–40, 56–62, 63–64
Mausolos, King of Caria, 56, 57
McKendrick, Neil, 2
Mecca, leaflet on pilgrimage to, 89–91
*Mechanisms of Catastrophe* (Vryonis), 244
Medes forces (Persian), 16
Mediterranean trade routes in Late Bronze Age, 45, 53
Megabyzus, 212, 213
Megali Panaghia monastery on Samos, 312–313, 314–318
Mehmed II, sultan of Turkey, 223
Mehmed the Conqueror, 240
Memphis, Egypt, 143–144
Meryt, "Chantress of Amun," 150
Mesopotamia, 27
Michas, Takis, 312
Middle East and North Africa (map), xvii
*Mihrabs* (internal niche in mosques), 104
Military junta of Papadopoulos, 214–215
Militiades, 12–13
Mill, John Stuart, 14, 204
Min (fertility god), 144–145
Min/Menes, king of Egypt, 143–144
Minos of Crete, 36
Missirian, Anna, 238–241
Mitropoli (Athens), 221
Mohammed Ali Pasha, 238

Moleskine notebook, search for, 292–294
*Molon labe* ("come and take them"), 15, 199–200, 236–237
Momigliano, Arnaldo, 211
Monarchy, 211–213
Montaigne, Michel de, 17
Montesquieu, 204
Morey, Robert, 92
Mortar (bitumen), 125
Mortuary Temple (Luxor, Egypt), 146
Mummification process, 151–154, 193–194
Musée Achéménide (virtual museum), 204–205
Museum of Mummification (Luxor, Egypt), 151–152, 154
Museum of Underwater Archaeology (Bodrum, Turkey), 42, 45
Muslim Brotherhood, 189, 190
Muslims
    and Bush's use of the term "crusade," 99
    civil conflict, 100–101
    false religiosity in Egypt, 186–189
    fear of living near non-Muslim ruins, 144
    as minority in Thrace, 243–246
    as part of Greek identity, 312
    pilgrimage to Mecca, 89–90
    religious tolerance of, 137–139
    stereotyping of, 92
Mycale, battle of, 19
Mycale mountain, 309
Mycale Straits, 300
Mycenaeans, 42, 44, 53
Myndos Gate (Bodrum, Turkey), 55

Nabonidus, king of Babylon, 115
Nabopolossar, king of Babylon, 114
Najaf, Iraq, 106
Nalban, Hadji, 60–61
Napoleon and Talleyrand, 74
Nasamones tribe (Libya), 34
*National Geographic,* 46, 48, 51

National Hellenic Research Foundation (NHRF), 197

National Museum of Iraq, 101–104, 105–108, 109–110

Nationalism in the Balkans, alternative version of, 252–256

Natron for mummification process, 153–154

Nautical archaeology, 42–45, 50–51, 52–53

Nebuchadnezzar II, king of Babylon, 112–115, 123, 124–125, 127

"Nebuchadnezzar Imperial Complex" of Saddam, 124–125

Nefertiti's gold scarab, 44, 50

Neighborhood (UK spelling again) Advisory Council (NAC), 97

*New York Times* (newspaper), 76

Newton, Sir Charles, 39–40, 56–57, 59–62

Newton, Sir Isaac, 180

*Nicomachean Ethics* (Aristotle), 232

Nietzsche, 24

Nile River
above Luxor and Aswan, 158–163
Biblical references, 156
dams on the, 156–158
Herodotus' interest in, 51, 139–140
the source of, 156
yearly flooding, 155–156

*Niqab* veil in Egypt, 189–190

Nooteboom, Cees, 74

North Africa and the Middle East (map), xvii

Nubians, 44

*Oasis Siwa from the Inside* (Malim), 170–171, 172, 177

*Odes* (Horace), 263, 270

*Odyssey* (Homer), 53, 231–232

Oebares, 213–214

Office of Private Sector Development (Iraq), 98

Oligarchy, 211–212

Olympianism, 315

Ondaatje, Michael, 22, 168

Oracle of Ammon in Libya (Siwa, Egypt), 167, 174, 175–176

Oracle of Bacis, 322

Oroetes, Persian governor of Sardis, 303–304

Orthodox Byzantine empire, 223

Orwell, George, 8–9, 55

Otanes, 211–212, 213, 307

Otto, king of Greece, 233

Ottoman empire
conquest of Cyprus, 250
and Greek battle for independence, 220, 233
in Greek history books, 251
Greek relations with Persia and, 246
as integral part of Greek history, 239–240
Joint History Project volume on, 253, 255–256
Treaty of Constantinople, 233
Turkish minority in Thrace leftover from, 245

Oum al Dounia. *See* Egypt

Panionius and Hermotimus, 9–10

Papadopoulos, George, 214–215

Papandreou, Andreas, 235–236

Papandreou, Dimitra "Mimi," 235–236

Parnassus, 231

Parthenon (Athens), 206–207

Pasha, Mohammed Ali, 238

Patizeithes, king of Persia, 211

Pausanias of Sparta, 313–314

Pebble lizard *(kroke dilos)*, 161–162

*Pedzos logos* (language that walks on foot, prose), 10

Peloponnese, 302–303. *See also* Sparta

Peloponnesian War (431–404 BC), 5–6, 35, 71–72

*Penelope* ferry, 326

Pergamon Museum (Berlin, Germany), 121

Persian empire
coups and counter-coups in 521 BC, 211
incompetence at sea, 275, 277–278
punishment for desecrating shrine of Poseidon, 321
and Samos, Greece, 306–307
as terrorizers of the world, 12, 14, 71
Western judgements of, 203–204
Persian Wars (499–448 BC)
Artabanus advises Xerxes against, 73–74
Battle of Marathon, 11, 12–14
Battle of Mycale, 19
Battle of Plataea, 11, 18–19, 201–203, 313, 321
Battle of Thermopylae, 15–17, 199, 200, 236–237
death of Masistius, 202–203
democracy and, 209–210
destruction of Athens, 209
overview, 4–5, 19–20, 34–35
Thebans in, 16–17, 18, 202, 237
Thespians in, 16–17, 237
Petrie, Flinders, 183
Phallic festival in Egypt, 160
Phanes, 32
Pharaohs of Egypt, 146–149, 154–155, 181–182, 294, 295, 296–297
Pheidippides, 13, 321
Philoxenia (hospitality), 224–225
Phrygians, 143
Phye (disguised as Athene), 320
"Pilgrimage, The" (Christians in Baghdad), 89–91
Pindar, 96
Pisistratus, 8, 207–208, 320
Plataea, Battle of (479 BC), 11, 18–19, 201–203, 313, 321
Pliny the Elder, 57–58
Plutarch, 3–4, 193, 200
"Poet, The" (Malim), 171
Polemis, Spyros, 275
Polish soldiers in Iraq, 107–108, 121–122

Political concept of history, 254–256
Political theory, 211–213
Politics and religion in Greece, 221–223, 225–227
Polycrates, tyrant of Samos, 294–295, 301–304, 306. See also Samos
Popular Orthodox Ralley (LAOS) party, 225–227
Poseidon, 297–298, 310, 319, 321
Potidaea (Thrace, Greece), 321
Powell, Colin, 74
Practice of History, The (Elton), 2–3
Prexaspes, 94
Priests
in Athens, 219–223
Herodotus' consultations with, 47–48, 142–143, 154, 219–220
politically-involved Magi in Persia, 211
Processional Way (Babylon), 121–122
"Profile of Clio, A" (Brodsky), 75
Prophecies, Herodotus on, 322
Prose, Herodotus as first writer of, 10
Psammetichus, king of Egypt, 37, 142, 302
Ptolemy V, king, 193
Pyramids of Giza, 179–185
Pythagoras, 283
Pythagorio, Greece, 283, 297
Pythagorio ferry, 300

Al Qaeda, 92–93, 96

Rageh, Sheikh Omar, 176–178
Ramesseum (Luxor, Egypt), 146
Ramses II, 144, 147
Ramses IV, tomb of, 148–149
Rawlinson, George, 8
Red Zone. See Iraq
Redcliffe, Lord Stratford de, 59
Refaat (guide in Egypt), 155
Religion and politics in Greece, 221–223, 315. See also Greek Orthodox Church

Religious intolerance, 89–92, 93–95, 103. *See also* Greek–Turkish relations

Religious school *(madrassah)* complex, 238

Religious tolerance, 103, 137–139

Religious views of Herodotus, 318–324

Renan, Ernest, 76

Retsina, 233, 268

Rhodes, Grand Master of, 39

Rhodopis (Thracian slave), 295–297

River Gyndes (Babylonia), 120

Robinson, James Harvey, 21

Romm, James, 318, 320–321, 323–324

Rosetta Stone (Champollion, trans.), 193

*Roumeli* (Leigh Fermor), 272

Route Irish (Baghdad, Iraq), 78–79, 81–82

Rumsfeld, Donald, 74, 100

Saddam, 77–78, 103, 123–126

Salamis, 17, 322

Samarra, Iraq, 83

Samians, 279

Samos, Greece
    Darius' conquering of, 305–306, 307
    Eupalinos Tunnel, 283–292
    as Europe's easternmost redoubt, 300
    harbour mole, 242, 279, 283, 296–298, 299–301
    Heraion, 307–311
    Maeandrius, tyrant of, 306–307
    Manolates, 281–282
    Megali Panaghia monestary, 312–313, 314–318
    overview, 278–279, 282–283
    Polycrates, tyrant of, 294–295, 301–304, 306
    traveling to, 274–275, 276–277

Sandys, George, 283

Sardis, 105, 108–109

*Satrap* (Persian governor), 199

Schama, Simon, 75

Scott, Ridley, 25

Scythians (Black Sea region), 8, 9, 72–73

Sebek, Nenad, 247, 249–250, 252–253, 256–257. *See also* Joint History Project

*Secrets from the Past* (Hawass), 155

See of Babylon, 103

Sélincourt, Aubrey de, 282

Sennefer, mayor of Thebes, 149–150

Serbians, 250–251, 253

Seven Wonders of the ancient world, 57, 180

Sex and sexuality
    anal sex, 8
    in Babylon, 115, 116–119, 123, 129–130
    bestiality, 126–127, 160, 171
    in Egypt, 144–145, 159–160, 186–188, 190–192
    Herodotus' fascination with, 33–34
    practices of different cultures, 7–8
    and Samian/Egyptian trade, 295–296

Shali, Egypt, 172

Sharm el Sheikh, Egypt, 177–178

Shinar (Sumer), 116

Shipley, Graham, 282, 283, 308

Shipwrecks, 42–45, 47–50, 52–53

Simonides, 216

Siwa, Egypt
    homosexuality in, 169–171, 173
    interview with Sheikhs Kilane and Rageh, 176–178
    magic in, 172–173, 177
    Malim, Fathi, 170–173, 177
    Oracle of Ammon, 167, 174, 175–176
    spring at, 173–175
    traveling to, 164, 167–168, 175
    women in, 171

Smerdis, king of Persia, 211

Smyth, Charles Piazzi, 180

Sobek (god of fertility), 162

Socrates, 318, 324

Solomos, Dionysios, 214

Solon (Herodotus' wise man), 5, 108, 232–233, 323

Sophocles, 4

Sotirios, Father, 313, 314–316, 324–326
Souma (alcoholic spirits on Samos), 281
Sparta, 15–17, 199, 208–210, 236–237,
302–303
Spartans, 313–314
St. George's Church (Baghdad, Iraq), 103
St. Helena, mother of Constantine, 324
Stalactites in Eupalinos Tunnel, 289
Stars and Stripes (newspaper), 83–85
Stepinac, Cardinal Alojsije, 253
Stobart, J. C., 20
Strabo, 112, 127–128, 296–297
Student strikes and uprisings in Greece,
214–215, 217–219
Suda (Byzantine lexicon), 33
Syloson, 306

Talat Abdul Aziz, Mohammed, 157–158
Taliban, 105
Talleyrand-Périgord, Charles-Maurice
de, 74
Tarfottet (women's shrouds), 171
Television in Siwa, Egypt, 177–178
Temple of Athena Parthenos (the
Parthenon), 206–207
Temple of Athene Pronaea, 231
Terrorism as passing crisis, 138–139
Terrorists as criminals, not Muslims,
137–138
Texas A&M University, 52, 53
Thebans in Persian Wars, 16–17, 18, 202,
237
Thebes (Luxor), Egypt, 143, 145–146,
151–152, 154, 158–163
Themistocles, 17, 18, 279
Theodore, Vassilis, 274–275, 276–277
Theodorus of Samos, 301
Theophania, festival of (Delphi, Greece),
301
Thermopylae, Battle of (480 BC), 15–17,
199, 200, 236–237
Thersander, 202
Thespians in Persian Wars, 16–17, 237
Thessalonians, 318

Thessaloniki, Greece, 248. See also Joint
History Project
Thomas, Kristin Scott, 178
Thrace, Greece, 235, 237
300 (film), 200, 210
Thucydides, 3, 21, 193, 230, 324–325
Tigris River (Iraq), 86
Time of Gifts, A (Leigh Fermor), 265,
269–270, 281
Timotheos, Father, 221
Toghrajerdi, Seyed Taha Hashemi, 198
Tolerance, 5, 103, 137–139
Tower of Babel (Babylon), 101, 121–124
Trade, multinational, 45, 52–53, 276, 295
Travel writing of Herodotus, 7–10,
69–71, 325
Travel writing of Kazantzakis, 287
Travellers Club, 270–271
Traveller's Tree, The (Leigh Fermor), 270
Travels with Herodotus ( Kapuściński),
230
Treaty of Constantinople (1832), 234
Treaty of Lausanne (1923), 244
Turanli, Tufan, 46–47
Turkey, 64, 245. See also Greek–Turkish
relations; Muslims
Turkish Consulate-General (Komotini,
Greece), 244–246
Turkish Daily News, 64
Turkish Liberation War (1919–22), 251
Turkish-minority issues in Thrace, 240,
243–246
Tyre, Egypt, 114, 115
Tzannetakis, Tzannis, 266

Uluburun (Late Bronze Age sea vessel),
42–45, 48–50, 52–53
United States, 76–77, 215, 226. See also
Bush, George W.
United States Marines in Iraq
in Babylon, 127, 130–131
at checkpoints, 85–86
constructing military base at Babylon,
107

United States Marines in Iraq *(continued)*
  looting by, 133
  trip from BIAP to International
    Zone, 79–83
*Urfi* marriage, 186
USS *Abraham Lincoln,* 71–72, 80
Ustasha, 250–251

Victim mentality, 99, 249–250, 257
Villepin, Dominique de, 77
Vitruvius, 56, 59–60
Vladimir, prince of Kiev, 317–318

Wadi Natrun, Egypt, 164
War
  morally-charged history teaching
    futility of, 255
  as result of ignoring warnings, 72–77
  soldiers' destruction of conquered
    lands, 107–108, 109, 121–122, 133
  *See also specific wars*
War on terrorism, 99
*Washington Post,* 78
Well of Jupiter (Siwa, Egypt), 173–175
West, 11, 19, 34–35
West vs. the East
  American soldiers on suicide bombers,
    80–81
  Catholicism vs. Orthodoxy, 223
  Christian leaflets ridiculing Muslim
    beliefs, 89–92
  cultural differences, 65
  longevity of dispute, 34–35
  Peloponnesian War, 5–6, 35, 71–72
  and source of mathematics, 183–184
  *See also* Greek–Turkish relations; Iraq
    war; Persian wars
*What is History?* (Carr), 2–3, 21, 22

*Why I Write* (Orwell), 8–9
Women's Rights and Equality
  Consultants (Iraq), 98
Women's rights in Egypt, 187–188
*Words of Mercury* (Leigh Fermor), 265
World War II, 253
Writing boards found on *Uluburun,* 45,
    53

Xanthi, Greece, 242–244
Xanthus (Samian pimp), 295–296
Xenagoras, 32
Xerxes, Great King of Persia
  advice against war with Greece,
    73–74, 275
  and Artabanus' dream interpretation,
    322–323
  assassination of, 19
  and Battle of Thermopylae, 15–17,
    199, 200, 236–237
  Delphi withstands invasion of, 231,
    321
  destruction of Athens, 17
  fury with Hellespont, 77, 278
  loss of ships at sea, 277–278
  plan for destruction of Greece, 14–15
  at Salamis, 18

Yacoubian Building, The (Aswany), 148
Yugoslavia, 250–251

*Zabiba* (calluses from prayer), 189
*Zaggalah* (club-bearers), 169–170, 177
Zarqawi, Abu Musab al, 92
Zhou Enlai, 100
Ziggurat (heaven-grazing temple tower),
    101
Zinovieff, Vassilis and Sofka, 225, 235

CPSIA information can be obtained
at www.ICGtesting.com
Printed in the USA
LVHW091910080123
736725LV00002B/85